PHILIP LONGWORTH

The Cossacks

CONSTABLE

LONDON

First published 1969
by Constable & Company Ltd
10 Orange Street, London WC2

© by Philip Longworth 1969

SBN 09 455850 7

Printed by C. Tinling & Co. Ltd, Prescot, Lancs.

Contents

Illustrations

A*

Acknowledgments

I am indebted to all who have helped in the preparation of this book, and in particular to Mr. Nicholas Vassilieff for his advice and constructive criticism throughout; to Mrs. Eileen Crouch and Mrs. Dorothy Thompson for their speed and efficiency in producing the typescript; to Miss Audrey Frew for her skill in drawing the maps (and interpreting some very rough diagrams); to Mr. F. T. Dunn for compiling the index; and to the following institutions for permission to reproduce illustrations: The British Museum; Novosti Press Agency, APN (pages 277, 308 top, 309, 340 bottom, 341 bottom); Illustrated London News & Sketch Ltd (pages 244 bottom, 245 left, 308 bottom); Radio Times Hulton Picture Library (page 340); Pier Arrigo Carnier, *L'Armata Cosacca in Italia, 1944–45*, published in Milan 1965 (page 341).

Lastly, but by no means least, I am grateful to my publishers, Constable & Co., for their unfailing patience and encouragement.

P.L.

Introduction: Legend and significance

The legend is romantic and spectacular. Mention the word Cossack and any of a number of vivid images is called to mind —a fur-capped horseman, sabre flashing, galloping across the empty steppe; bacchanalian dancers in gaudy eastern costume swirling and leaping to the strum of balalaikas; dark riders with leaded whips slashing into a crowd of demonstrators on the streets of a Russian city.

The romance of legend usually dissolves away at the first contact with the facts. But the touch of reality is not always so destructive. Sometimes it happens that history, so far from reducing a legend, can actually enhance it, produce a story no less exciting, and rounder, more fascinating than the myth. So it may be with the Cossacks—and through the ages they have accreted an extraordinarily thick layer of myth.

Popular conceptions about them owe as much to the

prejudices of time, place and political attitude as to reality. For centuries past the Cossack has been a symbol of terror to Westerners, the object of their fears about the peril from the East; he has been presented as the tool of Tsarist oppression and as the gaunt successor of Genghis Khan and Tamerlane. To the Russians on the other hand, he has cut a dashing figure.

The Cossack used to sing of himself as a free, daring, audacious young fellow, and the refrain was taken up all over Russia. There he was recognised as the personification of courage, audacity—and debauch—and came to fill the niches occupied by Robin Hood, Raleigh and Richard the Lionheart in the pantheon of English schoolboy heroes. He was the chivalrous knight, the noble savage, the pioneer adventurer, the freedom-fighter.

For generations he was the peasant's hero and the poet's inspiration, sung by Pushkin and Yevtushenko, idealised by Tolstoi. Cossacks inspired the work of the great Ukrainian poet Shevchenko, provided the subject of Sholokhov's epic, themes for Mussorgski and Shostakovich and images for popular painters like Repin.

Yet the pictures we have of them do not all coincide. The sympathetic descriptions in Gogol's *Taras Bulba*, for instance, of gallant warriors and earthy libertines, men with a healthy contempt for the false trappings of civilisation who give account to no man, contrast with those of the Polish novelist Sienkiewicz for whom the swarming Cossacks are cruel, self-indulgent, ignorant and vicious—disgusting villains who deserve to die like dogs. Cossacks were lauded as the champions of freedom by progressive thinkers like Radishchev and Herzen and yet reviled by revolutionaries of the later nineteenth century as the hangmen of the Tsars.

Whatever the variations sung upon the Cossack theme its power is undeniable. But the importance of the Cossacks does not lie merely in the fact that they inspired a literature, contributed to the Russian national mythology, and provided a convenient peg on which foreigners and politicians could hang their prejudices. They played several crucial roles in history.

They were the path-finders who 300 years ago pushed across the expanses of unknown Siberia to reach the shores of the Pacific; they provided a vital bulwark of Christendom's defence against Islam; they led almost every important rebellion against the Russian state from 1600 to 1800. Famous as cavalrymen, they were also the pirates of Russia's southern seas; hated instruments of Tsarist tyranny they were once the champions of the down-trodden serfs; infamous slaughterers and rapists they were also quiet fishermen and trappers, the farmers and herdsmen of the rolling Russian prairies.

The Cossacks were not a tribe, they formed no distinctive ethnic group and they were never a nation. Though various of their communities enjoyed periods of complete independence, these were brief and precarious. But though they were pre-dominantly Russian in origin, the Cossacks had a markedly different style of living from the Muscovite. The Muscovite originated in the forest and his life was dictated by the forest. The Cossack, by contrast, was the child of the open steppe. At one with the Russian ethnically, environmentally he was divided from him. The division produced significant con-sequences for both of them.

If the Russians built up an autocratic state to secure them from invasion and to preserve internal order, the Cossack, born of disorder and reared in the dangerous borderland between the Russians of the northern forests and the destructive Tatars of the southern steppes, had the self-reliant man's contempt for security. By presenting the image of an open society to Russian peasants cowed beneath oppressive institutions, by encouraging the downtrodden to fight or flee from authority, the Cossacks came to threaten the foundations of the feudal state, lighting fires of revolt which, on occasion, threatened to engulf all Russia of the forest zone. The stresses between the forces of anarchy represented by the free Cossacks and the forces of despotism represented by the state produced a tension which exercised a profound effect on Russia's development.

For a time the state had to tolerate the Cossacks as the guardians of its frontier against other enemies. But at last, after a long struggle, Cossack independence was crushed and the free Cossacks themselves became not only the subjects of the auto-cratic state but ultimately one of its chief supports. The emotional ideas of social justice which they had promoted among the Russian people were eventually replaced by the intellectual

3

programme of Bolshevism, and it is ironic that by 1917 the nature of their society and of their hopes had changed so much that most Cossacks could not accept the social transformation to which, centuries before, their ancestors had aspired. When Russia was feudal the Cossacks attacked it in the cause of the poor, when Russia turned to the cause of the poor the Cossacks stood by the old regime. In so often standing out against the flow of the times the Cossacks sing a descant to the theme of Russian history.

The Cossack was a product of the frontier and he exhibited its traits. There are striking parallels between him and the American frontiersman; indeed both of them sprang from similar roots. The venturers who sought fortune, freedom from poverty or from religious and political oppression in seventeenth-century western Europe fled to the Americas. Those of eastern Europe fled to the borderland of Tatary to become Cossacks. Nor do the similarities end there. If the American frontier encouraged democracy, so did the Russian. If the American frontiersman disliked taxation and the restraints of law and order, so did the Cossack.

One might even construct a rough model of the early Cossack frontier on the lines of the 'wild West' of popular mythology, with the Cossack representing the American pioneer, the Tatar the Red Indian, and with the Russian army playing the part of the U.S. cavalry. Examination of the institutions of more developed Cossack communities reveals the village ataman in the role of sheriff, and the Cossack elder representing the judge. We find Cossack cattle-rustlers, Cossack ranch-owners feuding with Cossack farmers, and Cossack posses chasing Cossack 'badmen'. High-spirited, coarse-humoured and frequently drunk, brigand, hunter and brawler, this wild dog of the prairies was in many ways closer to the popular idea of the cowboy than was the cowboy himself.

American historians have defined certain characteristics in the American way of life which, they claim, were originally induced by the life on the frontier. Most of these American traits—the 'rugged individualism', the free spending, the worship of democracy, the indifference to intellectual and aesthetic values, the 'restless energy', the versatility, the earthy practicality

4

which the Americans have been said to possess 'to a degree unknown among Englishmen and other Europeans'[1]—were shared by the Cossack in his hey-day.

There were also differences between the American and the Russian experiences of course. While pioneer values influenced the character of the American state, for instance, the Russian autocracy eventually harnessed the Cossacks and succeeded in channelling their energies to its own military and imperial purposes. But it is a curious exoneration of Turner's 'escape' theory[2] that as the Russian state began to seal off the escape routes to the frontier the Russian's initiative to self-salvation burst out in repeated revolution that was often Cossack led. Though the leak which eventually sank the Tsarist state was not sprung in the Cossack lands it was created among a people whose most dynamic representatives would once have fled to the frontier and who now found these frontiers unattainable.

The frontier bred vices as well as virtues. In the Russian south and east as in the American west, life was rough, tough and tended to be short. If the ideal Cossack of earlier times held his own life cheap, he held those of others even cheaper. The law of the sabre or of the gun spelt death to the weak or unresourceful who got in the strong man's way. The violence displayed by the Cossack was in the first place a consequence of the dangerous environment in which he lived, but as the frontier receded it became more and more a reaction to oppression and a function of economic need. In so far as his violence took the particular forms of piracy and robbery—a manifestation of the freedom and initiative that marked the frontiersman—his motivations were probably much the same as those of Black Bart, the famous stage-coach robber of the 'wild West'. Black Bart explained himself succinctly in a few lines of doggerel left behind after one of his exploits:

> 'I've labored long and hard for bread
> For honor and for riches
> But on my corns too long you've trod
> You fine-haired sons of Bitches'.

A Cossack pirate of the Volga or a Cossack *gaidamak*, a member

5

of one of the gangs which pillaged their way about the Ukraine in the eighteenth century, might have said as much, could he have written.

The frontiers had run out for Black Bart. He was desperate:

> 'Let come what will I'll try it on
> My condition can't be worse. . . .'[3]

Cossack rebels often felt themselves to be in much the same position, as might many a negro rioter in Chicago or Detroit. Sholokhov's twentieth-century Cossack hero Georgi Melekhov found no road to take except as a bandit and a fugitive; the Cossack Pugachev, hounded by authority and finding no escape to a quiet, safe future, was driven to raise a hopeless rebellion against the Empress Catherine. The difference between small-scale banditry and full-scale revolt may only be one of degree. Both are forms of social protest of which there is no lack of example in the Western world. On the bandit scale the Cossack brigand has his equivalents in the Argentinian *gaucho*, in Giuliano of Sicily,[4] even in gangsters like Dillinger. And, like the Cossack Stenka Razin or Dick Turpin, the highwayman, they all enjoyed a sometimes considerable degree of popularity among ordinary people who saw them as kicking against authority, against a social system which they, too, resented.

The Cossack as revolutionary is also a universal figure. Germany had its equivalent peasant Wars, France its jacquerie and South America its peon movements. Rome produced a Spartacus, England a Wat Tyler and Russia a Pugachev.[5] Mao Tse-tung, Ho Chi Minh and Fidel Castro are the more successful spiritual descendants of Bulavin, Bolotnikov and Pugachev; the doomed and dashing Stenka Razin was the Che Guevara of his time.

The Cossack is worth examining, then, not only for his own sake, nor even for the light his story throws on the development of Russia, but because he represents a number of universal experiences, because his story is so often relevant to contemporary situations.

Unfortunately for the historian, though the Cossacks preserved their traditions in fable, song and ballad, they were no chroniclers. In fact until the eighteenth century they mostly avoided keeping records which they associated with bureaucracy and authoritarian control. For the most part, then, their story has to be pieced together from the writings of outsiders—from Russian and Polish scribes, from reports of governors and officials and from the memoirs of Western travellers to the Cossack lands. Since the Cossacks stood very much on the fringe of their experience and interests the obstacles in the way of accurate reconstruction are never likely to be satisfactorily overcome by the use of conventional historical tools alone. Anthropologist and archaeologist, etymologist and geographer also have parts to play.

Nevertheless the historical literature which has built up around them is already considerable, though the pictures they present are predictably diverse. Russian writers fall into three broad categories reflecting both historiographical fashions and political views. Of the first, Rigelman and Skalkovski draw an imaginatively romantic portrait of the early Cossacks as the Christian knights of the border while Bronevski and Abaza sing a rousing march to the theme of the Cossack's glory as servant to the Tsar. The second school represented by Shcherbina, Evarnitski and Svatikov lay stress on the democratic, egalitarian tradition in Cossackdom—a reflection of the liberal and republican aspirations in Russia just before the Revolution. The Ukrainian school might also be included with this group. Influenced by German historians of the early nineteenth century, its members propagated the idea of Ukrainian nationalism, presenting Khmelnitski as a national and not merely as a Cossack hero. The leading proponent of this school was Hrushevski and some of his more extreme successors are still to be found among Ukrainians in exile. Nationalist thinking also had an influence on some Russian Cossack exiles, producing at least one attempt to find an historical basis for the existence of a Don Cossack state, 'Cossackia'.

Finally, there are the Soviet historians who emphasise the Cossacks' social and economic history and their role as leaders of the peasant revolt. In the last few years, especially, they have produced a number of scholarly and important works on the subject. Their rigorous class analysis has illuminated many a

7

dark problem, though too narrow and exclusive a use of Marxist historical tools has occasionally obscured the force of other factors. To take two random examples of detail. Golobutski, historian of the Zaporozhian and Kuban Cossacks, seeing discrepancies in wealth as the sole cause of behaviour, concludes that richer men who sheltered destitute runaways in the eighteenth century were only concerned to obtain cheap labour. Yet the Cossack tradition of asylum and the sheer force of human sympathy could also play a part. If White propagandists in the Civil War could persuade Cossacks to act against their own class interests by fighting the Reds, it is conceivable that a richer Cossack of the eighteenth century, indoctrinated in Cossack traditions, should occasionally ignore his immediate financial interests in omitting to grind the face of a poorer comrade. There were certainly instances of his risking his life to save a runaway from his pursuers. Again, in discussing the Don Cossacks of the seventeenth century Soviet historians like Stepanov explain the difference between the pro-Muscovite Cossacks of the south and the anti-Muscovite of the north solely in terms of the fact that the southerners were richer. The economic factor was undeniably important but there was also a not insignificant strategic factor. The Cossacks of the lower Don were still in danger from Tatar raiders to a degree which precluded a break with Muscovy and the loss of its military aid, whereas the northerners were relatively safe from the Tatars and, in greater proximity to Muscovy, had more immediate cause to fear the latter's threat to their freedom.

Despite the number of specialised and regional works on the subject, general histories of the Cossacks are rare. The reasons are obvious. With a history covering some 500 years, involving a dozen communities scattered over 5,000 miles and a multiplicity of themes, the Cossacks present the writer with considerable problems of presentation.

This book represents an attempt, within the necessarily restricted confines of a single volume, to present a general conspectus of Cossack history from the fifteenth to twentieth centuries. Chapter 1 outlines the complex origins of the Cossacks and describes their roles as border guards and robbers, the nature of the societies they developed and the ways of life they led. Thereafter the general narrative has been interrupted in order to provide a more detailed account of certain Cossack experiences as exemplified by historical figures of more than usual interest and importance. In all, four chapters are devoted to individual Cossack heroes. The four are Yermak (Chapter 2), Bogdan Khmelnitski (Chapter 4), Stenka Razin (Chapter 5) and Pugachev (Chapter 7).

Yermak, 'conqueror of Siberia', is the obvious example of the Cossack pioneer venturer and this chapter also takes account of his seventeenth century successors up to the time when the Cossack Dezhnev discovered the north-east passage into the Pacific. Bogdan was champion of Cossack independence, the hope of all Ukrainians who aspired to Cossack status. Razin, the most famous of all the Cossack brigands, led Don Cossacks on the rampage into Persia and then towards the heart of Muscovy. Pugachev, the most celebrated leader of a peasant revolt, raised the Cossacks of the Urals and almost toppled Catherine the Great from her imperial throne. They are all representative men of more than specialised or local interest, but they are also fascinatingly diverse in character and personality. Though Yermak's is still a distant figure it exudes a primeval strength and ruthlessness. Bogdan, the foxy politician and jealous, middle-aged lover, is a corpulent, wise and melancholic hero. The slim and dashing Razin, by contrast, is the gayest of all the Cossacks, while Pugachev, the people's avenger, is a driven man caught up in the tragedy of events he cannot control, and in the end betrayed.

These four 'close-ups' are set in a more formal historical narrative which is chronological in so far as the geographical spread of the subject allows. Chapter 3 deals with the Cossacks' struggles with the Turks and Tatars, their ambivalent relationships with Muscovy and Poland, their contributions to these countries' 'Times of Troubles', and the beginnings of the process by which they were eventually taken over by them. In taking the story from the death of Razin in 1672 to 1814, Chapters 6 and 8 elaborate themes of revolt, military service, and of agrarian and social change, while Chapter 9 describes the Cossacks' ideological enslavement by the state, their life as soldiers and colonisers and the economic development of their territory in the nineteenth century. Chapter 10 observes the Cossacks in the First World War, the revolutions of 1917 and the civil war that followed, and the concluding chapter deals with the Cossacks at home and in exile since 1920.

Though these chapters are on a broader scale and chiefly concerned with political, economic, social and strategic transformation, flesh and blood figures, heroes and villains, still play their parts in them—from the galley-slave Bolotnikov to the gallant Count Platov who rode into Paris at the head of his Cossacks in 1814; from the Princes Dologoruki who mounted punitive campaigns against the Don Cossacks in the seventeenth and eighteenth centuries to Kaganovich who supervised the terrible enforcement of collectivisation on the Kuban in the 1930s; from the little band of stormy-headed Cossacks who conducted an epic defence of Azov against the might of the Turkish Army in 1641 to the 'Red' Cossacks who rode their horses in against the advancing German tanks in 1941; and from the curious Mazepa who rebelled against Peter the Great to the no less intriguing Ataman Krasnov who in the evening of his life found himself heading a Cossack 'state' in the Italian Alps under the protection of the Third Reich.

'The Kozacks, or, if you please Cossacques—
(I don't much pique myself upon orthography,
So that I do not grossly err in facts . . .)'

—Byron, *Don Juan*, Canto LXXIV

1 The birth of Cossackdom

The destroyers had come from the east. Led by the Mongol Baty
Khan, flat-faced, small-eyed invaders clad in hides and iron
descended on the prosperous Dnieper valley like a cloud of
locusts and left it desolate behind them. Towns were sacked,
churches ruined, houses razed, and great piles were made of the
countless dead. The survivors were scattered. An age of darkness
descended on the Russians.

In the year 1240 the Russians had been struck a blow more
shattering and traumatic than that the English had suffered in
1066. The proud city of Kiev, centre of a once flourishing
Christian society and capital of a state which had had ties with
Alfred's England and the glittering Byzantium of the Emperors,
had fallen to a horde of Tatar horsemen. It was almost utterly
destroyed.

The Tatars swept on westwards. Then, checked in central

11

Europe, they turned back. Their Mongol leaders established a centre at Sarai on the Volga river and proceeded to rule their newly conquered empire, the empire of the Golden Horde. It included the steppe-lands from the Oxus in the east to Galicia in the west, and to the north a few disrupted Russian principalities, successors to the Kievan state.

The conquerors were people of the open prairie, strange to the claustrophobic forests where the remaining Russians lived, and they ruled them at a distance. They appointed Russian princelings as vassals to collect their tribute for them and, when this failed to arrive on time or the amount seemed insufficient they raided the offenders and took hostages to ensure their good behaviour. The Tatars controlled the Russians' foreign relations and cut off their contact with the western world. Otherwise they left them alone. In the long terms the effect of the Tatars on Russian life was to be reflected more in national fears than in institutions. But they influenced their military organisation, gave them the term for money, and the word 'Cossack'.

The first Russian Cossacks appeared some 200 years after the fall of Kiev in the perilous no-man's-land between the forests of the north and the rolling plains of Tatary. The circumstance of their appearance is shrouded in mist, surrounded by complexity, but the Cossacks were evidently sons of mother Russia, sired as it were, by the Tatars of the steppe.[1]

The Grand Dukes of Muscovy had slowly emerged as the chief tribute-collectors for the Horde. Using this position to dominate the other princes, they gradually united the Russian people of the forest zone and built up their combined strength to a point where they refused payment to their overlords and resisted attempts to extract it by force. The battles with the Golden Horde were long and fierce, but, attacked by enemies from Central Asia as well as by the Russians, the Mongol Empire began to disintegrate. In its place a number of smaller Tatar khanates were set up—in Kazan, Astrakhan, Siberia and the Crimea. The Russians of the forests were at last free of foreign rule. But they were still plagued by Tatar raiders.

Year after year the Asiatics would teem out to plunder the lands of Muscovy, Lithuania and Poland. They went heavily armed with iron darts, two-edged swords, long bows and quivers full of arrows. Each man took two or three re-mounts to increase their range and speed, and baskets in which to bear off captive children. To deceive the opposition they would approach overland, by moonlight, in groups spaced a mile or more apart, lighting no fire and avoiding the main river crossings. But once into the target zone the groups would coalesce, and then move on like a whirlwind, detaching raiding parties thousands strong to turn the countryside around it into wasteland. They slaughtered, burned, drove off cattle and carried away crops. But their chief prize was captives whom they 'grievously oppressed . . . with hunger and nakednesse', beating the men till they desired 'rather . . . to dye than to live'.[2] An influential prisoner might be ransomed, the rest were dragged away to be sold in the bazaars of the Crimea, where good prices were paid for slaves—sturdy boys to be trained for the crack Turkish janissary corps, strong men to serve a lifetime chained to the oar of a Mediterranean galley, young women to reinforce some Levantine harem.[3]

A chain of forts was constructed along the border and armies levied every spring to repel the invaders, but the Russian farmer as far north as Moscow itself still lived in fear. Mobilisation was too slow, the organisation unwieldy, the tactics too static to respond effectively to the unpredictable, elusive Tatars. The raiders would attack any force sent against them suddenly, out of the sun. A shower of arrows would be loosed at it, and, before it had a chance to recover, the Tatars would be speeding away again by a different route. Guards were needed who could provide an early-warning system of the enemy's approach; warriors were needed who understood the raiders' tactics well enough to intercept them with success.

The demand seems to have been met first by Tatar renegades. For besides the organised armies of raiders there were groups of 'free warriors'—Tatars who mounted private expeditions without permission of their chiefs. These were the pirates of the steppe who saw any vulnerable border village, merchant's caravan or lonely wayfarer as their prize. The Genoese and Greeks, who had trading stations on the Black Sea, had known them since the fourteenth century. They were called 'Cossacks'.[4]

In 1443 just such a band of 'free warriors' had stormed into the lands of Ryazan on a routine kidnapping expedition. But evidently they came to terms with the local Grand Duke for they spent the winter on his lands, and when a crowd of tribesmen invaded Ryazan early in the following year, these Tatars, now called 'Ryazan Cossacks', fought side by side with the Russians at 'a great and very fierce battle at the River Lystan' and helped to drive the intruders off.[5] Tatar Cossacks fought for the Lithuanians in 1445 and, seven years later, Khan Kasimov led his free warriors into the Muscovite service as mercenaries. Henceforth the references to Cossacks multiply.

They were used as border guards and as guides to help emissaries and merchants cross the steppes in safety. An Italian ambassador on his way to Persia in 1474 reported that the Grand Duke of Muscovy had a Tatar in his service who commanded 'five hundred horsemen to guard the frontiers of his territory from the incursions of the Tartars'[6] and in 1502 ten Cossacks of Ryazan, 'men who are acquainted with the Don' were required by Ivan III to accompany the Turkish ambassador across the steppe from Moscow.[7]

The references to these early Cossacks are scattered and imprecise which makes their origins and fates difficult to trace with any certainty. But, like the *ordynskiye* Cossacks who attacked the Crimean Tatars in the Dnieper area and the *meshcherskiye* Cossacks who helped to guard the eastern sector of the fortified line towards the end of the fifteenth century, most of them were probably renegade Tatars or tribesmen of non-Tatar origin. The first Russian Cossack leader was probably Ivan Runo, mentioned as commanding a group of Cossack warriors in 1468, and by the middle of the sixteenth century the Tatar and tribal Cossacks were fast becoming outnumbered by the Slavs who joined their ranks, and the original Cossacks of alien stock were themselves becoming Russianised.

As the watch-posts of Muscovy moved south and more territory was brought under its control, more Cossacks were recruited to guard the line and settle the border country. By the 1570s the Tsar had established a line of seventy-three fortified watch-posts along the frontier,[8] each manned by about ten men who took turn to scan the steppe from watch-towers and to patrol the areas in between. These were mostly recruited from among the wandering Cossacks of the frontier who were urged to settle down under state control as border guards and tillers of the land. Along with Muscovite soldiers and minor gentry, the government granted them land and hunting and fishing rights on an individual basis or else paid them for their services in money or in grain. And like the soldiers and the minor gentry they gradually became a class with a fixed status, known as *gorodovyye kazaki*—'town' or service Cossacks.[9] But besides these hired Cossacks there were others who admitted no lord over them—the free Cossacks, the Russian equivalent to the free warrior Cossacks of the Tatars.

By 1474 free Cossacks of both Slav and Tatar origin were operating beyond the frontier watch-posts, in the no-man's-land of the steppes. Tatar Cossacks roaming the country between the Volga and the Don were 'accounted valiant, as they plunder both Circassians and Russians'[10] and Genoese traders knew of 'robbers and Cossacks' of Moscow[11] who were just as indiscrimate in selecting their prey. Beyond the reach of all authority, Tatar or Russian, these wild marauders threatened any intruder into the rolling prairie and helped to earn it the name of 'the wild country' (*dikoye pole*). 'Only occasionally Cossacks cut across it, seeking, as is their way, someone to swallow up. . . . For they live by plunder, are subject to no man and run across the broad and empty steppes in bands of three, six, ten, twenty, sixty and more men.'[12]

These free Cossacks became a nuisance to the Muscovites and Lithuanians in the north as well as the Tatar Khans in the south, but the Tsars came to recognise them as potentially a friendly element in the wild country of his vulnerable southern border, and began to encourage them to send contingents to serve as scouts and cavalrymen with their armies. In 1570 Ivan the Terrible issued a general appeal to Cossack leaders operating on the Don to provide him with military aid and, next year, when the Crimean Tatars penetrated deep into Muscovy to sack Moscow itself, he granted a charter to a Cossack chief called Nikita Mamin, promising to pay all Cossacks who would follow Mamin's instructions. This step encouraged Cossacks along the river to combine under a common leader. But they would not always conform to Moscow's line, and their continuing raids

The wild country ~ Cossackdom c. 1500–1700

Yaroslav

Nizhni Novgorod

COW

Ryazan

Kasimov

M O S C O V Y

Kazan

Oka

Penza

Syzran

Samara

Tambov

Volga

Voronezh

Saratov

Yaitsk

Yozhsk

aine

e

Don

Khoper

Medveditsa

Yaik (Ural)

Bakhmut

Country

Donets

Miuss

Aidar

Don

The Wild Country

Razdorskaya
Cherkassk
Aksaishaya

Tsaritsyn (Volgograd)

Volga

Azov

Astrakhan

Kuban

Nogai
Steppe

Terek

Kabard

Caspian Sea

Caucasus Mtns

Georgia

Trebizond

0   50   100   150   200 Miles

AUDREY FREW

against the Tatars even when the Tsar wanted peace with the Khan and with the Khan's new overlord, the Sultan, proved a considerable diplomatic embarrassment.

Both Tatars and Turks had come to regard all Cossacks as the Tsar's responsibility. But he had firm control only over the 'town' or service Cossacks, who operated under Muscovite officers and were administered by the army department (*Streletski Prikaz*) or by the department of frontier defence (*Razryadny Prikaz*). Relations with the free Cossacks became the province of the *Posolski Prikaz*, the Muscovite Foreign Office[13]—an arrangement which implied their autonomous status. The Tsar developed an ambivalent attitude towards these free Cossacks. He denied responsibility for them, but he was ready enough to employ them as mercenaries in his army. He condemned their raids on Tatar caravans and their clashes with the Turks, but he would take no punitive action against them. Indeed, once, when he was being pressed by the Nogai Khan to destroy the Cossacks on the Yaik river, he suggested that those of them now serving him at Astrakhan should pretend not to be Yaik Cossacks at all.[14]

Only when the free Cossacks preyed on Muscovite shipping plying up and down the Volga was the Tsar moved to send soldiers out to catch the robbers and string them up, and even then, Muscovite officials tried to distinguish between the pirates and the 'faithful' Cossacks from the wild country who served with the Tsar's armies on campaign. The Tsar asked the 'faithful' to act against the 'robbers', but no sharp distinction existed in reality. Supposedly 'faithful' Cossacks also turned to piracy and Cossack robbers enrolled for service on campaign.

The composition of these free Cossacks had gradually been changing as more Russians came south across the frontier. In 1538, in reply to a Nogai complaint, the Tsar had blamed unruly Tatar Cossacks from 'Kazan, Azov, the Crimea and elsewhere... and also our Cossacks from our borders who mingle with them'. Forty years later, in response to another protest from the Crimean Khan, Tsar Ivan IV, in blaming the free Cossacks, described them as 'runaways from our state and from the Lithuanian lands'. This time, however, he did give an assurance that his frontier guards had been instructed 'not to let anyone through to the Don and to allow in no Cossack from the Don on pain of death'.[15] But the runaways still came to swell the ranks of the free Cossacks in 'the wild country'.

There were potent reasons for these flights across the border. The runaways were fleeing from taxation and famine, debt and punishment. A sixteenth-century English visitor described Muscovy as giving its 'Nobility a kind of unjust . . . libertie to command and exact upon the commons and baser sort of people',[16] and many peasants in Polish territory of the time 'had not enough to satisfy their most essential needs'.[17] As time went on, the motives grew still stronger.

By the end of the sixteenth century Muscovy was turning the screw down on its peasants. In 1581 they were denied the right to leave their villages. The law was to be effective only for a five-year period in order to stop population movements at the time of census, but it was renewed in 1590 and again in 1595, and two years later every peasant who had moved since the census year of 1592 was ordered back to his original home. The people were being tied firmly to their landlords. Muscovy began to vie with Poland in the rigour with which it treated its peasant population. As the gentry and boyars took over most of the common lands, as feudal dues and quit-rents rose and tax collection became more efficient, as peasants were sometimes called upon to work up to five days a week on their lords' land to the detriment of their own, and lost the right ever to leave their masters, the call of 'the wild country' seemed ever more alluring and the trickle of runaways became a stream.

Once in 'the wild country' a man owed no allegiance and was beyond reach of any law. And so they came—the town pauper to make his fortune, the convict to escape his prison, the soldier to practise his military calling to his own advantage. The dispossessed landowner came, the runaway serf, the religious dissenter, the political refugee.

They came primarily to hunt, to trap and to fish. The takings could be rich. Animals and birds seemed to have lost all fear of human beings in the wild country. Geese and herons, storks and swans flew over the estuaries, and there were pheasants, partridges and the rare ortolan on which to feed. Wild boar, deer and antelope beckoned the hunter, there were foxes and beavers to trap and skin, honeycombs to find and the pools and rivers ran thick with fish. But the wild country was no Eden. Whip-snakes lay concealed among the wormwood and vipers hid in the tall feather grass. The buzzard and the hooded vulture hovered lazily overhead, waiting for their carrion, and the mysterious burial mounds that rose up unexpectedly from the featureless plains, marking the sites of unremembered battles, warned of the sudden dangers of the steppe. The intrepid spirits who first crossed the frontiers of Muscovy and Lithuania into the wild country were few and vulnerable. A man alone could not expect to survive in it for long and so they gathered together in gangs for self-protection.

Picture one such Cossack at the turn of the century—a man of about twenty-five with grey eyes, straggly beard and long mustachios. He wears a ring in his left ear and bears the rough-neck's scars—most of his top front teeth are missing, and half the little finger of his left hand has been shot away. He was born a peasant but cannot remember his parents, having followed one Cossack leader or another on the prairie since his boyhood.[18] It was men such as this who formed the Cossack robber gangs of the sixteenth century.

Clashing and mingling with the Tatars of the wild country these Russian frontiersmen learned Tatar ways. They began to use Tatar words like 'ataman' (chief), 'esaul' (lieutenant), 'yassak' (tribute) and 'yassyr' (captives) and gang leaders adopted the Tatar horse-tail standard as the symbol of their authority.[19] They learned to catch and break in the wild horses that galloped the steppe, Tatar-style with nooses hung on the end of the long poles. They learned the Tatars' skills at arms, their tactics, their field-craft and their cunning, and they turned these skills to profit, selling their services as guards to passing merchants, or simply robbing them.

Cossacking was a seasonal occupation. A roofless winter under the howling snow storms offered a bleak prospect even for these tough men, and so each autumn they returned to the border towns to sell their catches and replenish their supplies. Some of the proceeds would be spent on a few days of wild release after the hard, lonely months on the prairie and then, if funds were

Russian captives led away by Tatars

Cossacks fishing in the Yaik river, *from a Nineteenth Century painting*

short, they would go north to find jobs to keep them through the winter and to buy the powder, lead, clothing and the other things they needed for the next season. But their winter refuges were soon closed to them.

The Polish and Lithuanian authorities were tightening their grip over the Ukrainian frontier towns to the south which were centres for the seasonal Cossacks, and when the Tsar, at first to allay the Turks and Tatars and then, more seriously, to sever contact between the increasingly restive Muscovite peasantry and the free Cossacks of the frontier, began to close his borders against them the possibility of seasonal cossacking gradually came to an end. A man might still sneak back across the border but the chances of his being brought to book by the authorities were much increased. And so the frontiersman came to be faced with the choice of settling under the rule of law, perhaps at risk of being made a serf, or of pushing out farther into the wild country and building some permanent sort of life for himself there. Many, especially men with family ties, decided to settle down on the frontier, becoming border guards and farmers under the Muscovite Tsar or the Polish King, or enlisting in the private Cossack armies raised by Lithuanian marcher lords like Dashkovits and Vishnevetski. Others, chiefly the bachelors, went off to build their lives in the wilderness.

During the second half of the sixteenth century Cossacks formed several independent communities in the wild country. Their earlier summer habitations had been rough and temporary —earth shelters dug into the ground or into the side of one of the gullies which scarred the prairie. Now they began to build more comfortable structures that would serve them the whole year round, using saplings, branches and any other readily available materials and roofing them with hides like the nomads' tents. They built communal barracks or grouped their dwellings together in fortified villages, and, since the enemy generally avoided water, they tried to find sites on river islands or on a high eastern bank with a wide view over the other shore. They would fortify their settlements as best they could against marauding Tatars, surrounding them with deep ditches and double fences of wattle filled with earth, and, when timber

B

was available, with wooden palisades reinforced with bastions.

Since the expanding feudal states from which they were escaping were to the north and west of the steppe-lands, the direction that Cossack settlement took was south and east. The earliest and most famous of them were founded on the lower stretches of the Dnieper and Don rivers.

South of its thirteen treacherous cataracts the river Dnieper became a tortuous maze as it wound between its islands and its banks. Prince Dmitri Vishnevetski, the Tatar-fighter who held the towns of Cherkassk and Kaniev in feudal duty to the Polish king, had built a fort on one of the islands with the help of his mercenary Cossacks in about 1550. He soon abandoned it, however, and the Tatars had come and demolished it. But free Cossacks, appreciating the strategic value of the position—for it was difficult to reach from the north and was an excellent watch-post from which to observe Tatar movements to the east —built a camp on or near the site. It was called the Zaporozhian Sech or 'the clearing beyond the rapids'.[20] With thick forest covering part of the area and with the approaches hidden among the sedge and reeds it was an ideal hide-out, a perfect nest for would-be robbers, a stronghold easy to hold against attack. Even so, the Sech was subsequently moved several times for reasons of convenience or security.

The first Cossack settlers on the Don were probably the *sevryuki* mentioned in connection with the plundering of a Tatar caravan in 1549.[21] By that date they had built three or four fortified villages, called *stanitsy*, along the river, well beyond the Muscovite border, and by 1570 there were six such little Cossack communities united under a single ataman based at Aksaiskaya. This centre was presumably too close to the Tatars at Azov for safety because it was soon moved forty miles upstream to another site and, like the Sech, it was subsequently to be moved again.

Soon other Cossack communities were founded still farther to the east. But if the Cossack pirates, so active on the Volga river in the later sixteenth century, built any village there it did not survive long, for Ivan the Terrible's victories over the Tatars at Kazan and Astrakhan in the 1570s had brought Muscovite soldiers to the Volga and made it unsafe for robber Cossack settlement. Most of the Volga Cossacks wintered on the Don, moved south to the Caucasus mountains, settling beside the river Terek,[22] or else went east to the Yaik. Cossack communities were founded on both these rivers by 1600.

The wild country was no place for family life and the first Cossacks brought no women with them, but they soon began to feel their deprivation and, whenever opportunity offered, promptly remedied their lack by stealing slant-eyed girls from their Tatar neighbours in much the same way as the early Romans raped the Sabine women. An apocryphal story relates how a gang of Don Cossacks made a long voyage to the Yaik river, where they chanced across a little group of Tatars whom they killed and a solitary Tatar girl whom they carried off in triumph to their ataman.[23] Captive women were taken as communal house-slaves as well as concubines but they were still scarce and in 1605, according to tradition, Yaik Cossacks mounted a full-scale woman-catching raid over the desert steppe to the city of Khiva. The Khan and his army were away at the time and the delighted Cossacks carried off many a struggling woman as well as much booty. Unfortunately for them the Khan caught up with them on their way back and no more than four of them ever reached home again. But by no means all such expeditions were unsuccessful.

As Cossack settlement grew in size and security immigrants from Russia began to bring their wives and the sexes gradually began to reach a state of balance, but for centuries to come the closer propinquity of many Cossack groups to native tribespeople than to Russia led them to adopt alien women just as they adopted alien customs. Cossacks of the upper Terek were intermarrying with neighbouring peoples in the eighteenth century. Cossacks of the Yaik and Orenburg often took Nogai women to wife and the Cossacks of Kamchatka 'abducted the natives' and shared the women out among themselves as concubines, though usually they married them after they had borne children. As late as the twentieth century the generally darker appearance and smaller stature of the Cossacks on the southern Don, contrasting with the taller and fairer appearance of their comrades up-river, indicated a greater rate of intermarriage by their forefathers with Tatar and Turkish women.

23

It is impossible to estimate the size of the early Cossack settlements with any accuracy. The population must have fluctuated widely as a result of casualty rates in the fighting against the Tatars and of the irregular rate of immigration by new runaways from Muscovy and Poland. The permanent members of the Zaporozhian Sech, the only exclusively male Cossack establishment, were probably less than 3,000 until the seventeenth century though many more might join them from the Ukraine if a profitable raid was in the offing.[24] Elsewhere, natural increase was negligible at least until the seventeenth century, but the pattern altered with the gradual growth of family life. In 1614 there were probably about 6,500 Cossack warriors of the Don and in the course of the next fifty years they had grown to abou 10,000, living in over fifty villages beside the river.[25] They were a small group still, and the Yaik and Terek communities were even smaller. But by 1776 there were reckoned to be 60,000 Don Cossacks fit to bear arms, 10,000 on the Yaik and nearly 3,000 on the Terek. Counting women and children these three communities probably boasted a total population by then in excess of 300,000[26] out of a total Russian population of twenty-two millions.

The early Cossack settlers lived chiefly by fishing and by fighting. Farming was incompatible with life in the wild country. A man might labour to clear a patch of ground, plough, sow and reap, and then see the fruit of all his labour burned or carried off by Tatars, Kalmyks or other nomad raiders. But even when this danger passed Cossacks remained loath to set hand to plough. Farming was associated with slavery in their minds. The free settlers knew that where Cossacks had turned farmer, as many had done in the Ukraine, they had soon fallen under the control of lords. Many of them were descended from runaway peasants and a constant influx of newcomers reminded them of the tyranny of being tied to the land. Hungry immigrants to the Don in the seventeenth century were eventually forced to turn farmer as the only alternative to starvation but even then the weight of established Cossack opinion was against them and the Don leaders ordered that anyone 'who begins to plough and sow' should be 'beaten to death'. Those who wanted to plough, they said, should 'go back to . . . where they came from' for such menial and unwarlike practices would 'bring inglory and dis-honour on . . . the atamans and Cossacks' of the whole Don community.[27] Only towards the end of the seventeenth century did agriculture become accepted as a respectable Cossack occupation on the Don and it played no significant part in the lives of the Yaik Cossacks until the eighteenth century.[28] Arable farming was generally the last occupation in which Cossacks engaged.

Stock-raising, though it was not so frowned upon, was little developed at first because of the danger of raids. If a horse were needed it was easier to steal one from the nomad than to breed it. But horse-breeding became important in the eighteenth century especially on the Don, and the Yaik and Zaporozhian Cossacks also began to raise considerable flocks of sheep on the riverside pastures at about the same time.

It was fish that was the Cossacks' staple food and a principal source of their income in the earlier years of their existence. They might eat meat occasionally, and rye bread when there was grain to make it, but almost always there was fish, fish in bountiful variety, fresh and cured. As late as the nineteenth century the Kuban Cossacks seemed to subsist largely on dried or salted fish and fishing was still the main industry of the Yaik Cossacks as late as the 1760s.[29] It was important, on the Don as well, where if the winter ice on the river was too thick one year, as it was in 1640–41, and the catch poor, many Cossacks would starve.[30]

The rivers were almost virgin to the early Cossack fishermen. Even the Terek, where Chechen and Kumyk tribesmen had fished before, yielded giant herrings, carp, barbel, salmon and sturgeon in plenty. Three kinds of sturgeon, sterlet, carp and an abundance of many other kinds of fish lurked in the rivers and lakes of the Don and giant sturgeon thirty feet long and weighing as much as four hundredweight were lifted from the Yaik. Fish-ermen may be prone to exaggeration but we are assured by a British Ambassador of the seventeenth century that Zaporozhi-an Cossacks fishing the Dnieper caught beluga 'three fathoms long, one of which can hardly be carried by thirty men'.[31]

Fishing gradually took on the characteristics of an organised industry, especially on the Yaik where a special ataman supervised three great fishing expeditions every year. In January and February he would lead out a caravan of sledges bearing Cossacks well-muffed against the cold. Every day he would mark out stretches of the river each to be fished by a team of four or five men who would set to work cutting holes in the ice and proceed to haul their immense prizes, struggling, on to the bank. In the spring the ataman of fishing supervised a three-month expedition. This time the Cossacks went out in boats spearing the sturgeon and catching sterlet, sheat-fish, carp, pike, perch, bream, chub, and other fish in great nets. The catches were far greater than the Yaik Cossacks could consume and during the summer, they set out with carts to distant lakes to fetch in the huge supplies of salt necessary to preserve the surplus. Finally, in autumn, there was an open season lasting from three to six weeks, during which the Cossacks went out in pairs of boats using seines up to a thousand feet long.[32]

The fish the Cossack caught was in great demand in the outside world, especially in Muscovy. Another English traveller sang the praises of the Beluga sturgeon. It was 'whiter than veal', he wrote, 'and more delicious than marrow . . . one of the greatest Dainties that comes out of the watry [sic] Elements, especially his belly, which surpasses the marrow of oxen'.[33] At the conclusion of each season, merchants would come from afar to buy fish and caviar to sell in the markets of central Russia.

The Cossack had to trade. He might have a surplus of fish, fur, hides, honey and wax, he might even brew his own mead and vodka, but he lacked the grain, cloth and nails and the lead, grease, powder and weapons that were necessary for his survival. Even when Cossacks built up permanent communities they were never economically self-sufficient. When the Russian and Polish border towns on which they were dependent were closed to them, Cossacks would sometimes take their goods to Turkish towns like Azov, there to exchange them for grain, cloth and tradesmen's products. More often traders came to them. Visiting Russian, Greek, Armenian and Persian merchants soon became familiar figures in Cossack settlements and sometimes they became a permanent feature in the life of a Cossack community. A suburb grew up outside the Zaporozhian Sech where merchants vended meat, salt and other foods and tailors, bootmakers, bakers and brewers plied their trades. As the number of runaways to Cossack lands increased, communities sometimes acquired their own tradesmen—coopers, blacksmiths, gunsmiths and carpenters, even hatmakers and silversmiths, and Cossack women helped the primitive economy by spinning and weaving or growing fruit and vegetables in front of their huts. But in most communities non-Cossacks had to meet the needs which Cossacks could not or would not provide for themselves.

If fish provided one marketable surplus which Cossacks could trade with outsiders, the other chief sources of income for the early Cossacks were buccaneering and mercenary service. They had learned the techniques of plundering and kidnapping from the Tatars and, in time, graduated from preying merely upon stray travellers crossing the wild country or merchants passing along its rivers to seeking revenue from the Turks and the Tatars. It could be very profitable. The Turks would pay as much as 30,000 pieces of gold in ransom for a kidnapped Pasha and a slave market grew up on the Don which had a turnover of up to 2,000 people a year, fetching between twenty and forty rubles a head. So, as they grew in numbers and experience, Cossacks mounted buccaneering expeditions on the high seas. For the Zaporozhians in particular this became a speciality. They became the terror of merchantmen, even the great Turkish galleys which oared their way across the Black Sea went in fear of them, and by 1600 no town or village on that coast as far as Constantinople itself could feel secure against their sudden raids.

The boats the Zaporozhian pirates used were hardly more than river craft, built up with planks or carved from the trunk of a single tree. Sixty feet long, about twelve in beam and draught, they sat very low in the water and had to be buoyed up with bundles of reeds to enable them to cope with the sea waves. Sail was used but only in fair weather. Usually they were propelled by oars—twenty or thirty to each boat, two men to an oar—with great steering paddles at prow and stern. Such a vessel could be built by sixty Cossacks in as little as a fortnight. They called them *chaiki*, or seagulls.

However small and rough in construction, they were swift enough to reach the coast of Anatolia, 350 miles from the mouth of the Dnieper river in less than two days, and they had important advantages over the much larger ships that sailed the Black Sea. They were more manoeuvrable and easier to turn about than the Turkish galleys and with their small draught they could enter waters too shallow for their lumbering adversaries. The Cossack mariners took full advantage of this.

A hundred or more of these boats would move out from the Sech on a major expedition, crowded with men and crammed with supplies. They carried barrels of biscuit and boiled millet, dried fish and water, but 'no *Aqua-vitae* nor other Strong-waters, for although they be as subject to drunkenness as any other Northern Nation, yet they are wonderfully sober in War'[34] and a Cossack who broke this rule ran the danger of being thrown overboard by his comrades. They were well armed with pistols, muskets and sabres and each boat carried an armament of faulcenots. But their chief weapons were secrecy and surprise. Their chief ally was the dark.

The fleet would paddle silently down river and emerge through the reeds of the estuary into the Black Sea at night, generally when the moon was in its last quarter. Having sighted a vulnerable target the Cossacks would shadow it under cover of night, or from the edge of the horizon by day, and attack out of the sun at dawn or dusk. If the prey, after all, proved too strong for them, they would break off and retreat beyond reach into shallow waters or up some convenient creek, and once laden with booty, they would return to the Sech as swiftly and secretly as they had come.

Throughout the seventeenth century the Zaporozhian pirates, often accompanied by Don Cossacks, were the bane of the ships and coastal towns of Turkey and her vassals. The raids assumed a scale and a regularity that almost amounted to war, though their primary object was economic profit rather than political advantage. By 1600 their frequent success and the disruption it brought in train had become a major concern not only to the Turks, but to the Polish kings who were held responsible for them and who wanted good relations with the Porte. In 1604 the Zaporozhians attacked distant Trebizond and Sinope. Two years later they descended on Kilia and virtually destroyed the important Black Sea port of Varna. In desperation the Turks

За свое͛го ГЕТМА̀нства вда̀ въ Ту́рцѣ мѣ́сто КАФУ:
Ажъ и са́мъ Цѣ́сар Ту́рскїй бы́лъ в вели́ко̑ страху̀:
Бо му̀ Чотырна́дцать тѝ ся ачъ та́мъ лю́дꙋ збѝлъ,
КАТА́РГИ е҆дины̀ пали́лъ, дру́гїи потопѝлъ.
Мно́гꙑ тогды̀ з̑ нєво́лѣ Хртїа́нъ свободѝлъ,
За што̑ го̀ Бг҃ъ з̑ во́нствомъ его̀ бл҃гословѝлъ.

Бо за на́йбо́лшꙋ́ю пѣ́хꙋ собѣ̀ нагоро́дꙋ
Почита́єтъ Ры́цѣръ кгды́ кого̀ на Свобо́дꙋ
Вы́зволитъ: за што̀ грѣ́хꙋ́въ собѣ̀ ѿпꙋщѐнє
Ѡдѐржитъ: А по̑ Сме́рти в Нб҃ѣ въмѣщенє
До́знавалъ нѐ поедина̀ кро̑ть Ту́ринъ пога́нинъ
Его̀ мѣ́нѕтва. и̑ прꙋ́дковенный Тата́ринъ.

The Cossacks raid Keffa

threw a great chain across the mouth of the Dnieper to keep them in, but the Cossacks still came through. When necessary they took a circuitous route along the river Savim and carried their boats overland to the river Miuss and sailed down it into the Don and out to sea. The Turks seemed quite unable to deter them. In 1609 it was the turn of three citadels along the Danube to be sacked, and four years later Zaporozhian pirates joined by Cossacks of other communities mounted two heavy attacks on the Crimea, whose Khan was vassal to the Turks.

The sea-going Cossacks sometimes paid a heavy price for their prizes. In 1614, 2,000 of them returning from Sinope where they had burned the arsenal, were themselves surprised and many of them were killed or carried away in chains to Constantinople for execution. Their comrades were not deterred, however. The next year 4,000 of them set sail in eighty 'seagulls' on a yet more daring expedition, to fire the port of Constantinople itself. A Turkish flotilla caught up with them in 1616 after they had managed to burn the Crimean slave-trading emporium of Keffa but the Cossacks fought back fiercely and forced the Turks to turn for home with the loss of several ships. The Grand Vizier was executed for his failure to maintain adequate defences and a special conference was held by the Porte in May 1618 to find an effective antidote to the Cossacks. But in vain. The raids went on in an ever mounting scale. In 1633, 6,000 Cossacks visited the suburbs of Constantinople again and the following year Don and Zaporozhian Cossacks sailed out on 150 boats and despite a fleet of 500 Turkish galleys harboured there and a garrison of 10,000 men, succeeded in burning installations at the Bosphorus.[35] That year the cost was heavy. More than 100 'seagulls' were lost, over 2,000 Cossacks killed and nearly a thousand fell into Turkish hands. It did not seem to matter. Their established hatred for the Turk and Tatar and, above all, their need for booty overcame all deterrents and by 1630 the Sultan, the most powerful ruler in the world, was reduced to begging the Poles to destroy them.

The quality of these Cossacks had come to be well appreciated by the mighty Turks. The seventeenth-century Turkish chronicler, Najim, wrote: 'it can be stated with confidence that one cannot find bolder men on earth who care less about life and . . .

fear death less. Men experienced in marine affairs say that . . . their skill and daring in sea battles [makes them] more terrible than any [other] enemy'.[36]

The fighting qualities of the Cossacks were as high on land as they were on sea. They had to be. Tatars and Turks presented an unremitting threat even to their larger settlements and as late as 1643 several Don Cossack villages were burnt to the ground and hundreds of their inhabitants killed or taken prisoner. A constant watch had to be kept. Scouts peered out from watchposts in the steppe ready to light warning beacons at the first sight of an approaching enemy and gallop back to seek shelter behind the palisades and ditches of their village. Women and boys had to be prepared to fight together with the menfolk in defence of their homes.

A Cossack stood in constant readiness for action and always went about armed. He was trained to fight almost as soon as he could walk. A Cossack boy soon learned to ride at a gallop, swim his horse across the rivers and stalk game with bow and arrow. An eighteenth-century observer of the Yaik Cossacks observed that 'from their earliest youth they were . . . accustomed to all kinds of difficult equipment, using firearms and lances and shooting well from long bows'.[37] Cossacks were skilled in the use of musket, pistol, sabre, lance, pike and even artillery. Armour they rarely wore, the Cossack having more of an attacking than a defensive spirit, and, trained in the Tatar school of warfare, they aimed to go out to crush the enemy rather than fighting it out at home. The foundation of their method was surprise. For surprise they depended on mobility, and their means of mobility by land was the horse.

The servant was well suited to the master. To western eyes the unshod horse of the steppe looked completely wild but it was tough and could live rough like its rider. Small, light and fiery, it had stamina, a strong back and would eat almost anything. It could survive a bleak winter on the shelterless steppe finding its own meagre sustenance under the snows and yet when necessary it could carry its rider fifty miles a day for two weeks at a stretch. 'Neat, excellent, stomackfull [sic], swift and indifferent good and commodious to undergoe great labours'[38] was how one contemporary traveller saw them.

31

The Cossacks were superb and daring horsemen, rivalling the Mongols in their devotion to the art. Only the Zaporozhians were regarded as better fighters on foot than mounted, and best of all as marines. Yet even they were almost as active by land as by sea, keeping up constant pressure against the Crimean Tatars and teeming into Moldavia and the Polish lands on frequent forays.

Cossacks evolved special formations and tactics to suit the conditions in which they had to fight. They would march out on campaign in a column flanked by their baggage carts and artillery which moved in parallel file—a formation which was designed to give quick, all-round protection on the open steppe against sudden attack by a greater force of Tatars. On meeting the enemy, the two files would swing in towards one another forming a point while the wagons at the rear were closed up to complete a triangle. Cossacks would rush to chain the carts together and, if there was time, overturn them and dig them in. In a matter of minutes they could produce a system of all-round defence, called the *tabor*, quicker to form than a square or circle, but similar in style to the wagon corral of the American West, and designed to meet much the same sort of situation, for Tatar horsemen favoured much the same tactics as the North American Indians. They rarely approached within close range of this obstacle, however, but would ride in great circles around it letting fly clouds of arrows in hope of wearing the Cossacks down to a point at which they could overrun them with a final devastating charge. For their part the Cossacks used their best marksmen to pick off as many Tatars as possible, while the poorer shots supplied them with a steady supply of loaded flint-locks. Once they judged that the enemy had passed the peak of his keenness for a fight, or if they ran out of ammunition, they would charge out on sorties brandishing pikes and sabres. A thousand Zaporozhians in *tabor* formation could hold as many as six times that number of Tatar horsemen at bay and provide a formidable obstacle even to troops trained in western methods.

The favourite Cossack cavalry formation was the *lava*—an inward curving rank preferably long enough to extend beyond the enemy's flanks. As many as three of these lines would charge against the enemy in quick succession, veering swiftly away from strong points and pouring through any weak point in the enemy line like water out of a leaking cistern. Cossacks became famous for their ambushes, the tumult and impetuosity of their onslaughts in flank or rear, and for their command of the more treacherous arts of warfare. Though on the whole they preferred hot-blooded attack to passive defence, when occasion demanded they could show sufficient patience to withstand even an extended siege.

The Cossacks' experience as warriors both on land and water made them much sought after as paid fighters. Their skill at fortification and mobile defence, their courage, resource and ability cheerfully to withstand privation became proverbial, and from the earliest times of their settled existence they were in demand to fight other people's battles. Magnates and marcher barons, princes and kings, all employed them as mercenaries.

The Poles always engaged them as individuals, never recognising a Cossack community as a whole, and preferred to register them for permanent services as a means of absorbing them into the general fabric of the state. There was a bill of enrolment of Ukrainian Cossacks in military service as early as 1524 and in 1572 King Stephen Bathory raised a whole regiment of them issuing each man with a length of cloth and fourteen zlotys a year in pay. From time to time when major military commitments were in view, the Poles also raised some Cossacks on a temporary basis. In 1574, for example, they engaged a number for a campaign into Moldavia and in 1578–9 more were enrolled for war with Russia, each man receiving fifteen florins and cloth for two coats. As the Crown was able to afford to pay more, more Cossacks were registered in the permanent service of the Polish kings and they came to be organised along the lines of the emergent western European armies. By 1625, there were 6,000 'Polish' registered Cossacks, organised on an area basis into six regiments of 1,000 men, each commanded by a colonel and subdivided into hundreds under centurions.

Registration was not merely a means of raising troops; it was a method by which the Polish kings, by nominating the officers of the force and by offering the leading spirits all sorts of rewards of lands, status and special privileges, could tame the

33

unruly mass of Cossackdom in the Ukraine. The 6,000 registered Cossacks accounted only for about a tenth of all the Cossacks fit for service and the gradual erosion of the freedoms of the remainder—or those of them who did not flee to join their rumbustious comrades on the Zaporozhian Sech—soon created a hotbed of revolt in the Ukraine.*

Muscovy, too, employed its 'town' Cossacks on an individual basis, but it also hired troops from among the free Cossacks. In 1552 a number of them—some, no doubt, the same 'robber Cossacks' who were such an embarrassment to Muscovy in her peace-time relations with Tatary—had helped Ivan the Terrible capture Kazan. They served the Tsar at Astrakhan and in the Livonian campaign of 1579, and Muscovy also engaged Ukrainian Cossacks, 500 of whom fought for her against the Polish King at Pskov in 1581.

The Muscovite government would negotiate terms of service collectively through the Cossack atamans, dealing with them much as an industrialist might treat with trade union leaders. In return for their services, the Cossack communities would be rewarded with saltpetre and lead, money, grain, vodka and other supplies. Several such deals were registered with the Don and Yaik Cossacks between 1571 and 1600, and the engagement of Cossacks by the Tsars for specific campaigns soon became an annual feature, providing several of the free communities with a regular source of income. But there was no registration such as the Poles had introduced with their Cossacks in the Ukraine. The Muscovite ambassador who visited the Don Cossacks on his way to Constantinople in 1592 asked, rather than commanded, them to live in peace with the Turkish garrison at Azov, and when the Tsar tried to have his own man, Peter Khrushchev, put in command of their military contingent, the Cossacks retorted: 'We've served the Tsar before but we've never had any commanders but our own. We'll be happy to serve under our own commanders, but not under Peter'.[39]

Muscovy was to gain a virtual monopoly of the mercenary services of the more easterly Cossack communities, but Cossacks from the western settlements were employed by various embattled states. They assessed themselves as 'daring fellows', as

* See Chapter 3.

'knights' and 'eagles', and their reputation as warriors soon extended beyond Poland, Muscovy and Turkey. By 1594 the Vatican had heard that the Cossacks 'move about like eagles—flying first in one direction and then the other' and both Pope Clement and the Emperor Rudolph II, hard-pressed by the rampaging Turks, sent ambassadors to persuade the Zaporozhians to invade Moldavia, inviting them to join together with Transylvania, Wallachia, Poland and Muscovy in a common Christian alliance against the Turks.[40] On this occasion the Zaporozhians turned down the invitation, pleading that Tatar raids had left them with only 400 horses for 3,000 men, and that in any case they were doing enough against the Turks as it was. Perhaps the rewards offered were not high enough, we cannot tell. At any rate they continued their profitable raids on the Crimea and on Turkish possessions on the Black Sea and in 1621 the Polish successes in the Khotin campaign were largely due to the Cossacks in their service—a fact which the enemy appreciated, if not the employer since, that year, the Turks put a price of fifty ducats on every Cossack head. Their reputation soon spread north to Sweden where King Gustav Adolf once referred to them as 'noble knights and warriors, masters of the Dnieper and the Black Sea', and before 1625 they were known in England as 'a kind of men which follow forreigne Warres and prey.'[41]

Sometimes they fought far afield. Two thousand Ukrainian Cossacks, sent by King Wladyslaw, served under Condé against the Spaniards at Dunkirk and in 1683 the Papal Nuncio in Cracow reported the arrival of many Cossacks in the Polish service on their way to Vienna to help relieve the city from Turkish siege, adding that they were 'reckoned to be the best infantry which one can send against the Turks'.[42]

The almost ceaseless warfare between the Cossacks and the Muslim Turks and Tatars gave rise to comparisons between them and the idealised religious orders of chivalry of the medieval west. The bachelor society of the Sech was described as a monkish military community[43] and its Cossacks likened to the Knights of Malta, since 'their principal duty . . . is the conduct of continuous war against the infidels'.[44] But the analogies are hardly apt. Cossacks would fight anyone. Profit came first. If most of

35

their fighting was directed against the Muslims, this was because the Tatars constituted the greatest threat to their safety and because Turkish towns and Turkish shipping offered the prospect of easy plunder. Their loyalty was not exclusive. They would ally themselves with the infidel against the Poles and join the Catholic Poles against the Orthodox Russians, their co-religionists, whenever it suited their interests to do so. As Slavs, they were bound to feel closer to their northern neighbours than to the southerners with different tongues and alien customs, but religious enthusiasm seems to have played little part in the lives of the early Cossacks. There were no priests on the Sech for a long time and contemporaries stressed their contempt for the clergy and reported that Cossacks lived 'in sin without marriage'.[45] The chief Don settlement of Cherkassk had no church until 1660 and even then marriage ceremonies were usually characterised more by pagan custom than by religious prescription. Cossacks as a whole and the Zaporozhians in particular were never abstemious by choice, indeed they were drunken and riotous whenever funds and opportunity offered.

Only in one respect is the comparison between the Cossacks and the idealised description of religious crusading orders valid. Their communities were primarily military communities. They came to be known as 'armies' or 'hosts' (*voiska*). Even so the peculiar political forms that distinguished Cossack associations stemmed as much from the ways in which a small gang naturally manages its own affairs as from the primary need for specifically military organisation. The methods by which Cossacks regulated their communal life were developed from the primitive democratic assembly of the early bands of seasonal Cossacks. When 'Cossackers' returned to the border towns after a season in the wild country they would 'camp down . . . about the towns . . . varying the monotony by holding . . . assemblies where discussion frequently concludes in bloody fighting'.[46] This was democracy in action, and both the democracy and the riotous action became a feature of the assemblies of the permanent Cossack communities.

On the Don, the Yaik and the Terek the assembly was called the 'circle' (*krug*), among the Zaporozhians it came to be known as the *Rada*. Every male Cossack had the right to attend it, take part in its debates and in the annual election of their leaders which took place there. Besides the great assembly meetings were held to regulate the affairs of the smaller social units—the village (*stanitsa*) or, on the Sech, the barrack (*kuren*).

The assembly was the paramount authority. It decided the division of the community's income, plunder and mercenary pay and of hunting, fishing and pasturing rights, much as the small cossacking co-operative (*artel*) divided the collective catch among its members at the season's end. It dealt with ambassadors, sent out its own embassies and decided questions of war and peace. Conclusions were not reached by voting in any formal sense but, as in the pre-revolutionary Russian village council, the sense of the meeting was conveyed by general tumult by the relative volume of the jeers or acclamations. This was the general will at work, or the law of who shouts loudest. It was effective enough in its way but the assembly met only at the beginning of the year or extraordinarily in an emergency. At other times the ataman, as executive, decided matters. He had, however, to answer for his actions at election time.

Then he would stand in bare-headed expectation under the horse-tail banner, which was the symbol of the ataman's authority, encircled by the assembly. If he lost the election, he put his cap on and returned to the ranks. A newly elected ataman—like Caesar—was expected to refuse the appointment at least twice, before allowing himself to be dragged, struggling, to the centre of the ring by Cossack elders who would spatter him with mud as a lesson in humility.

This show of reluctance on the part of a newly elected Cossack chief has its parallels in other societies. The Speaker of the House of Commons is expected to display a similar reluctance to hold representative office, but whereas in medieval England Mr. Speaker was frightened of what the King might do to him, the ataman had excellent reason to fear his own electorate. He might not merely be deposed if he displeased them, he might be beaten to death, as was the Yaik ataman, Ivan Belusov, towards the end of the seventeenth century, when he returned from negotiations in Moscow having accepted orders which the Cossacks did not like.

The ataman was responsible for order and justice but the laws of the Cossack communities were never codified or even written down. The rules were as vague and traditional as the punishments were primitive and harsh. A Zaporozhian thief who gave no restitution within three days might merely be beaten with rods by the man he had wronged, but elsewhere a pilferer could earn himself a slit nose, a severed ear or even death by hanging. A favourite method of execution, often reserved especially for traitors, was to bundle the condemned man into a sack, weighted down with stones or sand, and so toss him into the river. On the Sech, a murderer would be tied to the corpse of his victim and buried alive with him. The ataman's authority in crime and punishment as in other matters depended largely on his popularity and, not infrequently, his physical strength. The 'law' was often enforced by the lynch-mob. Only in war did the Cossacks tend to be orderly and obedient. Here an ataman's authority was complete and he was able to enforce even the death penalty at his own discretion. 'We turn our heads', the Don Cossacks used to say, 'where the ataman turns his eyes.'[47]

As the communities grew and their affairs became more complex, other executive offices were created. The primitive unstable society with a single, undifferentiated, leader, gradually became transformed into a more complicated structure whose affairs were discharged by a number of differentiated office-holders. The ataman of the Host acquired a lieutenant (*esaul*) who assisted with military administration and was responsible for order, and a secretary (*pisar* or *dyak*) who dealt with correspondence and records and ultimately with routine relations with the outside world. There were also elders or judges who constituted the ataman's inner council, and lesser functionaries like the centurion (*sotnik*) who commanded a hundred men in war and the interpreter (*tolmach*). Zaporozhians, more influenced by Polish military organisation which had been imposed on the registered Cossacks of the neighbouring Ukraine, also appointed commanders of artillery and ordnance (*pushkar* and *obozny*) as well as officials responsible for river crossings, taxes, trade, weights and measures. Cossacks were also appointed from time to time as commodores of boats or, on a community or village level, as atamans in charge of the communal autumn mowing or of salt-gathering and fishing expeditions.

As the government of each community became more sophisticated, Cossack institutions tended to become more orderly and to be surrounded by more formality. Atamans often acquired a regalia of maces and seals in addition to the traditional horse-tail standard, and the general assembly accrued a certain amount of pomp. Kettle-drums were beaten, cannon fired and banners and horse-tail standards held aloft. Among the Yaik Cossacks in the eighteenth century, two *esauls* mounted on richly caparisoned horses and preceded by drummers would announce the calling of an assembly, riding round the Cossacks' dwellings, warning everyone to sober up in time for it. The next morning bells would ring out in final summons and at the appointed hour the ataman would emerge from his office by the square, on which the assembly took place, accompanied by the officials and elders of the host. The two esauls would then march forward, place their caps and batons on the ground as a sign of submission, bow to the ataman and elders, and then, taking up their batons, stride away again down the square calling out loudly to the assembled crowd for silence. The ataman would then propose his policies and seek the Cossacks' approval for them. The esauls would move off again, like tellers, gauging the mood of the meeting, calculating it rather by the cheers and rumbles rather than by votes, and then return to the ataman and announce simply: 'agreed' or 'not agreed'.

Gradually Cossack atamans did not merely outline problems to the assembly, recommend courses of action and, having done so, leave the issues open to debate; they came to rule the assembly more and more. An ataman made his decisions in consultation with an inner cabinet of elders and only consulted the rank and file afterwards[48] in circumstances that enabled them merely to say 'yes' or 'no' to questions which were often framed in such a way as to produce the answer he required. Assemblies were called more rarely and distance made it impossible for every Cossack to attend them when they were held. And even so the gathering had become too large for every opinion to be heard. Decision-making came to be vested effectively in the few rather than the many; a sort of oligarchy

39

came to replace the original democracy of Cossackdom.

It was an inevitable consequence of the increasing size of the communities both in area and population. It was also a result of the increasing complexity of affairs, of the emergence of issues which demanded answers more subtle than the general enthusiasm of the assembly could be expected to provide and which created a need for written communication which was beyond the scope of the illiterate Cossack masses. And so the Cossack who could read and write—and he also tended to come from the more prosperous section of the community—came to play an increasingly powerful role, and office-holders came to be less susceptible to control by the community at large.

By the end of the seventeenth century Ivan Kuklya, the ataman of the small Terek community, remarked that the elders of the much larger Don community had become 'lords and governors'. But they experienced a good deal of sometimes violent opposition from ordinary Cossacks nevertheless. A village ataman who fell foul of the Don leaders fled to the Terek threatening to return to the Don and 'cut off the heads of the elders of the Host, tie them up by their beards and hang them across anchors'[49] for abusing their privileges, and sometimes such promises were kept. Until the nineteenth century the ataman and the elite might meet a sudden end if they crossed the multitude, and the assembly could still exercise its veto.

If politically the early Cossacks were democrats, economically and socially they were communists. Plunder and loot was divided equally; meadows and forests, hunting and fishing rights were held in common or apportioned according to need.[50] The sense of brotherhood was overwhelming. Their primitive economy and the absence of significant property differentiations among them admitted no idea of class differences among Cossacks at first. When in 1592 a Muscovite ambassador visited the Don bringing gifts of cloth for the Cossacks and asked that it be allocated according to class or seniority, 'distributing the good stuff to the best' and the coarser cloth to the lesser men, the Cossacks replied that there were 'no great men among them. All were equal', and they insisted on dividing the goods equally among themselves.[51] Again in 1638, when they were invited to send an embassy of their 'best' people to Moscow, they replied that 'they had no best people', that all were 'all equal to one another' and that the ambassadors must be elected by the host.[52]

But the economic equality of Cossackdom, like its political equality, was gradually whittled away as their numbers increased and their economy developed; and as some Cossacks became richer than others social distinctions became clearly apparent.

Racial and ethnic differences counted much less. Until the eighteenth century the growth of the communities depended on immigration rather than on natural increase, and Cossacks tended to welcome any friendly able-bodied foreigner in order to maintain their strength. Once the initial Tatar element had been absorbed, the Russian element predominated, but Poles, Wallachians, Germans and Spaniards found their way to the Sech, and the Zaporozhians would even accept a renegade Jew and value him as a fellow warrior, depsite their virulent anti-semitism. The Yaik Cossacks accepted Kalmyk prisoners in their ranks provided they first became baptised as a proof of their changed loyalty, and by 1725 the Yaik community included men of Polish, Bashkir, Tatar, Kalmyk, Swedish, German, Mordvin and Turkish origin as well as runaways from the Ukraine and Russia and Cossacks originally from the Don. Elsewhere Georgians and Greeks, Finns and Frenchmen made appearances, and the continuing contacts of the Don Cossacks with Turks, Kalmyks and Crimean and Nogai Tatars resulted in frequent sixteenth- and seventeenth-century references to 'newly baptised' non-Slav Cossacks in their ranks.

Candidates had to be tough. There was no room for weaklings among the Cossacks, and often a new entrant had to show what stuff he was made of before he was accepted. A seventeenth-century traveller reported that 'a true *Zaporouski* Cossack' had first to negotiate the dangerous passage over the Dnieper cataracts and 'to have been in a Summers Expedition against the *Turks*'.[53] But no one enquired about a man's previous career. If he was fit and a nominal Christian, the Sech or the *stanitsa* was his sanctuary and the new entrant could spit upon his past.

But by the eighteenth century, when recruits were less needed, entry became more difficult even for Slavs. The lands were beginning to crowd up and Cossacks were thinking more about their pockets. A runaway might work as long as seven years among the Don Cossacks without being accepted as one of their number. They did not want to divide their resources—in particular the subsidies they were receiving from the State—too widely.

By the mid-seventeenth century distinctions had grown between Cossacks, generally those of longer standing, who owned homes and farms (*domovityye* or *dyuzhiye kazaki*)—the 'respectable men' who formed a privileged elite and from whose ranks the atamans and elders were mostly chosen—and the poorer men, generally the late arrivers—the poor bachelors, the naked proletariat, the common people (*seroma, golytba, chern*). On the Don the richer, house-holding Cossacks tended to be concentrated along the lower stretches of the river, while most of the paupers thronged the middle reaches. The distinctions drawn in the records between the 'lower' and the 'upper' Don Cossacks, then, not only indicated the particular part of the territory in which they lived, but implied a variation in social and economic status. The fabric of the equal society began to break down in other communities too, and even Gogol's hero Taras Bulba, though in nostalgic mood he might feel a momentary contempt for his wealth, is an undeniably rich Cossack with a disproportionate influence in the group.

It was still possible for a recent runaway to become a Cossack and for a poor Cossack, given the requisite degree of industry, acumen and luck, to join the ranks of his wealthier, 'respectable' fellows, even to be elected to office; but the prospect became ever more remote. Life in Cossack societies began to run along grooves which diverged on class lines.

Nevertheless, the inequalities between rich and poor, the powerful and the weak, never approached the proportions it did in the Russia of the Tsars, and life on the frontier precluded the introduction of the stricter Muscovite social customs. The position of Cossack women, for instance, was much freer than in Russia where a seventeenth-century English observer remarked that 'the women have great respect . . . for their Husbands for which reason they are exceedingly retired and appear very seldom in publique'.[54] A Cossack woman had to share the hardships, and often the dangers, of her man. In the eighteenth century Yaik Cossack women, dressed in men's clothes, fought alongside their husbands against government soldiers. But they shared in their pleasures too. If by the early nineteenth century the Don Cossacks tended to get drunk at home rather than in public, 'the fair sex made no scruple to partake in these Bacchanalian orgies',[55] and on the Yaik Cossack women were observed to be particularly disposed to 'dandyish displays and love'[56], and even to drunkenness. Manners were generally free and Cossack society tended to tolerate a high degree of sexual licence. Cossack womanhood became famous for their freedom, their independence and their pride, and the young, romantic Tolstoi, when he visited the Terek in the 1850s, was captivated as much by the girls as by anything else he saw in that fascinating land. They seemed so much more natural, and freer, than girls in central Russia.

Life on the border influenced Cossack customs, and contact with the border peoples influenced their dress, an amalgam of the Russian and the tribal, an obvious outward sign of their double cultural heritage. Red shirts and the high-crowned caps trimmed with fur which the Muscovite soldiers used to wear, were common among the Ural Cossacks though like the others they were strongly influenced by the loose, baggy style of the Tatars. Sartorially, the most dashing foreign influences were to be seen among Cossacks of the Caucasus. On the Terek they borrowed the fashions of the Kabardins and Georgians—the *cherkesska*—an open coat sewn with galloons—wooden cartridge pockets worked in bone or silver, worn slant-wise on the chest, a black sheepskin, and the *burka*, an immense cape which almost enveloped man and horse and did duty as a bed roll too.

On the other hand the giant beards which the Terek and the Yaik Cossacks wore were influenced by the great influx into their territory of religious refugees from Russia. The Zaporozhians, by contrast, wore immense mustachios but almost shaved their heads, gathering such hair as remained into a top-knot. The gay clothing in which they were generally portrayed was also a product of oriental influence—colourful baggy trousers with broad golden galloons, belted by silken cummerbunds; bright satin caftans, tall grey hats of the finest sheepskin or turbans resplendent with ostrich feathers and jewelled aigrets; flying cloaks and highly decorated red or yellow boots of the finest morocco.

But the richness and elegance which typified later Cossack dress was not a mark of the earlier or the poorer settlers in the wild country. They had to wear the skins and hides of such animals as they could kill, patch up their worn-out rags or go about half naked. The term the Zaporozhians used for mounting a raid was to go and 'find a coat for one's back' which emphasised their dependence on piracy even to clothe themselves. But a successful expedition, especially against the Turks, not only transformed their appearance; it allowed celebrations on a titanic scale.

Those who survived such an expedition for plunder would celebrate as long as a week, cavorting about in their new finery, scrabbling over rolls of Persian cloth and Turkish damask, rich silks, fine carpets, sequins of Araby and cloth of gold. Some they would sell to visiting traders and for the rest they bustled about like so many squirrels in search of hiding places. That done, they began a long carouse of celebration. A French traveller among the Ukrainian Cossacks, many of whom often joined the Zaporozhians in their exploits, commented that there was 'nobody among them, of what age, sex or condition soever, that does not strive to outdo another in drinking and carousing . . . and no Christians trouble themselves less for t'morrow than they do'.[57] A Zaporozhian danced and drank until he fell, and when he recovered, began all over again. Life was usually short. It had to be lived for the moment and its infrequent opportunities for pleasurable debauch enjoyed to the full when they afforded.

Besides drinking, dancing and song were among the Cossacks' major amusements. Their dancing was highly athletic. Influenced by other border cultures it could be complex as well as spectacular, providing opportunities for the show of licentious humour as well as prowess. They leapt and somersaulted, crouched and kicked with wild abandon and incredible skill to the accompaniment of eight-stringed lutes and a sort of bagpipe. And they sang songs—epics of past heroes and ballads plaintive and melodious, with choruses that thundered up to climaxes of ecstatic sonority.

Cossack communities had different customs and practices of

their own stemming from their different environments and cultural contacts, but the uniting factors were stronger than the divisive ones. In spite of the space which distanced them one from another the free Cossack communities were substantially similar in organisation, spirit and idea. Cossack settlements everywhere were founded in similar circumstances and their inhabitants enjoyed similar status. They shared the same function as border warriors and similar political institutions. They all supported themselves by much the same means and developed socially and economically along much the same lines. But above all they themselves were conscious of their common interests.

Communications between the various groups were frequent from the beginning. The Don Cossack Host was in repeated and friendly correspondence with the Yaik, Terek and Zaporozhian communities and with the Cossacks on the Volga. Men of one community lived for years or settled permanently in the other. One elder from the Sech indicated in about 1625 that he stayed eighteen years on the Don and that 1,000 other Zaporozhians were there too.[58] On the other hand, Cossacks from the Don and Volga fought alongside Ukrainian Cossacks under Sagaidachny at Khotin, and when Ukrainian lords threatened them, the Zaporozhians had the 'help of their brothers, the Don Cossacks'. Nor was the aid one-sided. There was a vibrant sense of honour among these Cossack thieves. Early in 1632 the Don Cossacks declared that they had made 'an arrangement with the Zaporozhians' by which 'the Zaporozhian Cherkessy' would come 'to the Don to help us Cossacks, and for us Don Cossacks to help the Zaporozhian Cherkessy'.[59] The agreement was honoured in blood. Zaporozhians came in their thousands to assist the Don Cossacks in their great struggle against the Turks at Azov and die upon its walls.*

Cossacks from as far afield as Zaporozhiye, the Don and the Yaik would join together whenever some profitable expedition offered. The Zaporozhian and Don Cossacks made over twenty joint sea raids of considerable scale on the Crimea and against the Turks. Razin's revolt, though originating on the Don, aspired to the creation of a 'great host of the Don, the Yaik and

* See Chapter 3.

45

Zaporozhiye'.[60] The Cossack communities never succeeded in achieving political unity but their fellow-feeling spread beyond the confines of community. A sense of common identity was widespread among Cossacks of all the hosts.

'There lived the Cossacks as free men,
All the Don and the Terek and the Yaik Cossacks,
And their ataman was Yermak, son of Timofei . . .'

—Cossack song

2 Yermak and the conquest of Siberia

Most of the early Cossacks who roamed the wild country were
swallowed by obscurity. But Russians still remember Yermak as
a venturer as remarkable as Magellan, a conquistador as fearsome as Cortez, for it was Yermak who led the first successful
expedition into mysterious Siberia and inspired the Russians to
push their frontiers out 4,000 miles to the east, to the shores of
the Pacific.

Tall and broad-shouldered, so legend has it, with a flattish
face topped by a black thatch of hair and edged by a thick black
beard, Yermak seems the personification of the Cossack pioneer.
Born in about 1540, he came of Cossack stock. His grandfather
was reputedly Afanasy Alenin, a destitute migrant from the city
of Suzdal who fled to the forests of the upper Volga to live by
cossacking. His son, Timofei, became a bandit too, and his son,
Vasili, dutifully followed in the family tradition assuming the
pseudonym Yermak.[1]

47

No man was likely to survive long as a Cossack without considerable resilience and an ever-open eye for hidden danger, but Yermak had other ~~qualities~~ as well—great strength, tactical sense, an air of authority and personal magnetism—qualities that brought him to the head of a gang of Cossack freebooters. Along with other bands of 'robber Cossacks' plying their lawless trades along the river Volga, Yermak's men held up caravans, plundered merchant shipping and skirmished with the Tatars. Like them, they moved from one area to another with the seasons, seeking a living for themselves and their comrades: mercenary one season, highwaymen the next, now enrolled in the Muscovite services, now escaping Muscovite soldiers sent out to punish them for their 'lawlessness'.

When Ivan the Terrible advanced down the Volga into Tatar country in the 1570s and pushed through to Astrakhan and the Caspian Sea, Yermak may have fought for him, as did several other Cossack leaders. But the Tsar's advance brought Muscovite soldiers to enforce the Tsar's authority along the Volga, and freebooters like Yermak began to feel the squeeze. The days were gone when convoys sailing up the river towards Moscow laden with goods from Persia, the Caucasus and central Asia could be plundered almost with impunity. The Tsar was determined to protect the Volga traffic, to rid the area of those 'thieving Cossacks'. Though some lingered on in the nearby forests waiting to ambush some straggling vessel, most of the Cossack pirates began to take to other trades. Some joined the Muscovite frontier defence service; others turned to barge-hauling, or joined the Cossack communities settled on the Don, the Terek and the Yaik rivers. Yermak himself went north, to Perm, where he entered the service of a powerful family of businessmen, the Stroganovs.

The considerable fortunes of the Stroganovs had been built on trade rather than on force of arms, and in particular, upon salt and furs. Central Muscovy lacked salt and the Stroganovs had supplied it; furs were the staple of Muscovy's foreign trade, and only the Stroganovs could provide them on the scale required. Their enterprise had expanded both in volume and diversity, until they commanded a vast commercial empire, the largest in Russia. In 1558 Tsar Ivan had granted them a twenty-year licence free of tax and duty to exploit the Perm area, where Stroganov prospectors had found salt. They were also entitled to farm the virgin lands, build settlements, and to raise a private army to protect them. Within a few years they obtained another concession extending their interests farther to the east. But the lands were exposed to raids by tribesmen and the Stroganovs were merchants and industrialists, not men of war, their employees, whom they settled there, were tradesmen and farmers, not soldiers, and before long aggressive bands of Cheremis and Tatars from the east were so disrupting their activities that the Stroganovs began to look about for means of protecting their interests. In 1572 the Tsar had suggested that they engage some 'volunteer Cossacks under a good leader' to stiffen their defences. This they did and about three years later the Stroganovs sent men out to find Yermak and his comrades and persuade them to accompany them 'up the river Kama . . . and daunt their . . . enemies, who threaten their new settlements with destruction'.[2]

Yermak accepted the invitation, and for two years and two months he and his men helped to guard this eastern frontier. But defensive means alone could not secure the Stroganovs' lands; they had to be able to carry out reprisals, take the war into enemy territory. They had already complained to the Tsar that Tatars, Cheremis, Ostyak and Vogul tribesmen subject to the Khan of Siberia were attacking their people and carrying women and children away prisoner. 'Without your permission', they wrote, 'we dare not send our hired Cossacks to chase after the Tatars. Allow us', they pleaded, 'to give pursuit . . and also to build forts in Siberia' to keep them under control.[3]

In making this request the Stroganovs also had an eye to the riches that lay still farther east. They suspected there were copper, zinc, lead and tin deposits there. There was certainly good arable land, forests rich in fur and timber and rich pastures by the Tobol river where the Tatars grazed their cattle. They petitioned the Tsar for another concession, and they got it. Ivan's charter of 1575 allowed the Stroganovs to wage war on the troublesome eastern tribes and on Kuchum, Khan of the Siberian Tatars, who stood behind them. If they defeated him, the Stroganovs had the Tsar's permission to take

The conquest of Siberia

Routes of exploration ➤➤➤➤ Peking ●
100 200 300 400 500 Miles

over his lands and to exploit them tax-free for twenty years.[4]

The Siberian lands were not the Tsar's to give, but if the Stroganovs failed he would lose nothing, and if they succeeded the resultant increase in the provision of furs and minerals would stimulate an expansion of trade, especially with England which would enable Muscovy to buy more of the modern armaments and the military and technological expertise which Ivan so much wanted.

And Ivan wanted to settle with Khan Kuchum. In 1556, Yediger, Kuchum's predecessor, had agreed to pay the Tsar an annual tribute in furs. Then Kuchum, son of the Emir of Bukhara, had invaded Siberia and turned Yediger out. Ivan considered the usurper bound by the previous arrangement. At first Kuchum, who was afraid Yediger's relatives might stage a come-back and was anxious to avoid fighting them and the Tsar at the same time, had agreed to pay. But in time, as he consolidated his hold over the Siberian Tatars and succeeded in exacting tribute from the Voguls and Ostyaks as well, he felt more secure, began to default in his payments, and by 1571 was even claiming to treat with Ivan on equal terms. In 1573 men of a raiding party into the Stroganov country, led by his nephew Mahmetkul, killed one of Ivan's emissaries and the Tsar's slender resources of patience ran out. But a thousand miles away and with other more pressing troubles to attend to, Ivan could not retaliate himself. So now he encouraged the Stroganovs to attack Kuchum on his behalf.

Soon afterwards, Yakob and Grigori Stroganov died and their successors, Semeon and Maxim, seem to have reversed their parents' policy and paid off Yermak, the man who would have led the expedition against Kuchum. But they soon had second thoughts, and by 1577 they were once more building up their private army. Meanwhile Yermak had probably become a robber Cossack again. If so, times would have been hard for him. This was the year of the *streltsy*, the men of Ivan's new standing army with their tall halberds and long, clumsy arquebuses, who came down the Volga to clear out the pirates once and for all, and hanging most of the Cossacks who fell into their hands. It was easy for the Stroganovs to find recruits. But, according to the legend, they seemed particularly anxious to get Yermak

A Cossack assembly on the Sech, *after an Eighteenth Century drawing*

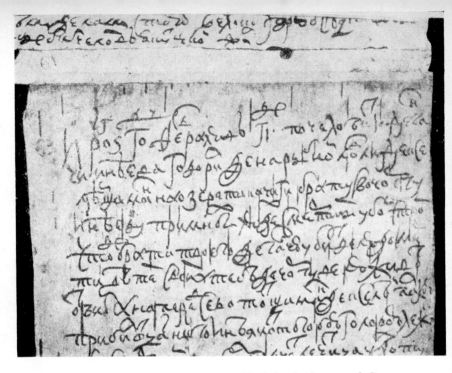

A Siberian Cossack's report on Birch bark, *Seventeenth Century*

The punishment of Volga pirates

back, sending out messengers bearing gifts to persuade him and his colleagues 'to give up an occupation unworthy of Christian knights, to cease to be robbers, and become warriors for the White Tsar, to seek glorious danger and come to terms with God and Russia'.[5]

Many of the Cossacks who now returned with Yermak to the land of Perm now led a settled life with families or captured concubines. But set to work strengthening the new fort of Orel and other defences against the tribesmen, they were not allowed to become soft, and soon Yermak led them out on a retaliatory raid to the very edge of Siberia. The chroniclers assert that besides Cossacks he took scribes, musicians and drummers with him on this expedition, as well as three priests, and an elderly monk. This was probably imaginative clerical embellishment, for there was no room for passengers on perilous ventures of this kind. What is certain is that Yermak forged his unruly crew into a unity. Soon they were all 'thinking thoughts as one'[6]—a unanimity achieved by the simple and effective process of eliminating dissenters. 'Anyone who thought of deserting . . . was . . . bundled into a sack [with a bag of] sand . . . tied to his chest and . . . [thrown] into the water. In this way', writes the chronicler, 'the bonds uniting Yermak's men were strengthened'.[7] More than twenty Cossacks were tipped into the river Sylva to drown and few of the survivors dared argue with Yermak after that.

This expedition was merely a preliminary to a full-scale advance into Siberia. The Stroganovs had already lost six of the twenty years' concession the Tsar had granted them there, and they had become impatient to proceed. And so, in the autumn of 1581[8] a miniature army gathered on the banks of the river Kama and prepared to launch themselves across the Urals, into the mysterious realm of Khan Kuchum.

Yermak had collected 540 'outstanding warriors' together, all well armed with arquebuses, pikes, swords and daggers. Yermak held the overall command. Under him there were five other fierce and experienced atamans, men with ringing names and infamous reputations—Ivan Koltso, who had pillaged Saraichik, capital of the Nogai Khan, and Bogdan Bryazga, Matvei Meshcheryak, Nikitin Pan and Yakov Mikhailov, highwaymen responsible for the recent attack on a Persian ambassador bound for Moscow.[9] All were fugitives from the Tsar's vengeance, ruthless desperadoes and leaders of desperate men.

The Stroganovs supplied the expedition. Each shallow-draughted river boat was loaded with 100 lbs. of rye flour, 70 lbs. of both buckwheat and of roasted oats, and 36 lbs. of biscuit and of salt. There were bags of powder and of shot, and, if the chroniclers are to be believed, butter and half a salt pig for each man, as well as three cannon and 'banners and icons'.[10] The Cossacks set out to the sound of martial trumpets and the beat of drums, with Yermak's personal standards, portraying Saints Michael and Dmitri, fluttering at their head. The pious chroniclers would also have us believe that they left 'singing ... hymns to ... the Trinity, to God in his glory ... the most immaculate mother of God ... to all the heavenly powers and to the holy saints'.[11] But if they sang songs it is likely they were bawdy ones, that they thought of blood and gold rather than of heavenly salvation.

They moved out of the Kama, up the river Chusovaya and soon the lands of Perm were far behind them. Straining at the oars, they passed on upstream, between steeply curving banks and precipices of stone, and turning into the river Serebryanka, continued upwards, further into the Urals. The going was tough. When the waters ran too shallow to keep their boats afloat, they had to dam the river with sails; when rocks and cataracts blocked their way, they had to haul the boats across them. On and up the Cossacks struggled, farther away from familiar country, into 'a world unknown, uninhabited and cold'.[12]

From the distant plains the Urals mountains seemed to touch the sky. Their tops lay 'invisible in clouds' and when the wind tore these away, they seemed to stretch endlessly 'from sea to sea'.[13] It was wild, deserted territory, trodden by few men. Two hundred years before, traders from Novgorod had crossed them and in the fifteenth century soldiers from Novgorod had campaigned against the Ugrians who lived east of the Urals. Russians had heard of the sable-rich forests that lay across the mountains and of the lands of Mangazeya farther to the north, home of the Nentsy, who were reputed to eat their dead and serve up children for the delectation of their guests. Muscovy had traded with the east, across Siberia. But Russians had never settled beyond the Urals and none had trodden the southerly path Yermak was now taking.[14]

At the head-waters of the Serebryanka, the Cossacks abandoned their boats and trekked on eastwards to the river Tagil where they camped for a time, built new boats and set off again, this time downstream. Henceforth progress was faster. At the mouth of the Tagil the fleet swung into the river Tura. They were in Siberia at last, nearing the lands subject to Khan Kuchum.

Yermak's army was small, but Kuchum's realm was sparsely populated. There was a ruling class of semi-nomadic Tatars and the primitive Ostyaks, Voguls and Mordvins paid them tribute. But as the Cossacks travelled on, the Voguls under their chief, Yepancha, lay in waiting for them.

Suddenly a cloud of arrows flew out from the bank towards the unsuspecting venturers. A few Cossacks slumped over their oars; the rest began to bustle. Atamans shrieked orders; the boats parted and re-formed; men grabbed for their weapons. The fight was on.

The ensuing battle was soon over, the Voguls fleeing at the miraculous noise and flashing of the Cossacks' guns. Yermak advanced to take Yepancha's settlement of Chingi-tura, near the site of modern Tyumen, and there he and his men made themselves as comfortable as they could for winter. From Chingi-tura he sent out scouts, some of whom returned with one of Kuchum's tax-collectors. Yermak returned the prisoner with presents and the assurance that he had come in peace. But the now blind Khan, ruminating in his capital of Sibir some 200 miles to the east by marshy bank of the sluggish river Irtysh, was not convinced. He had already heard of the arrival of winged boats bearing 'invincible warriors' from the west with their 'fiery unseen arrows' and 'death-bearing thunder that flies through armour'.[15] The pagan Siberians believed in these tales of the supernatural, and the Muslim Kuchum had himself been disturbed of late by eerie talk of a huge, hairy, white wolf and a little black dog who met every day at noon at the point where the Irtysh river meets the Tobol and fought each other. Day

55

after day they struggled for supremacy . . . and in the end, it was the little dog that won. Kuchum had called in his sooth-sayers. They had told him that the wolf represented Kuchum, the Khan, and the dog a Russian chieftain who would one day rob him of his kingdom.[16] That Russian had now arrived in the person of Yermak and Kuchum was troubled. But he was not enough of a fatalist to surrender without a fight. He summoned his warriors by means of 'golden arrows' and sent them out under his nephew, Mahmetkul, to deal with the intruding strangers.

The snows of winter had melted away, and the first signs came of the approaching heat of summer. By the time the ice broke on the river Tura, Yermak and his men had repaired their boats. Now they resumed their course. For several weeks their advance was virtually uncontested. But, at a point where the river narrowed between steep banks, the Cossacks ran into another ambush.

Mahmetkul had thrown a barrage across the river and hidden warriors among the birch-woods, ready to pounce on the Cossacks when they fouled it. Only the first boat ran into the barrier at night, and under cover of darkness Yermak could answer ruse with ruse. He drew his men back quickly, quietly disembarked them and set them to work cutting down branches, and dressing them in clothes. The scarecrows were assembled in the boats, then rowed on down again towards the barrage by skeleton crews, while the remaining Cossacks crept round, half-naked, to take the Tatars from the rear.

They attacked at dawn, and once more the flash and thunder of the Russians' guns proved too much for the innocent Siberians. They quit the field, leaving many dead behind them, and Yermak went on to the mouth of the river Tavda, where his men rested and he pondered his next move. Despite his victories he must be cautious. Supplies and ammunition were running low. Several Cossacks had been lost in battle and more through sickness. The rest had come far; they were tired after the long winter. And the opposition was growing more determined. Scouts saw a huge crowd of Kuchum's men arrayed at the mouth of the Tobol. Yermak decided to fall back.

But to retreat along the route they had come by would take

too long and the Cossacks could not survive another winter in the Urals. So Yermak sent men out to find a quicker route back into Russia. They reached the source of the river Pelym, then turned back to report. There was no quick route home. Yermak had passed the point of no return. Rather than die of exposure, the Cossacks decided to storm the Tatar capital, Sibir, and shelter there. Cold and hunger rather than honour and glory drove them on along the road of conquest.

Yermak's conquest of Siberia, *from the Remezov manuscript*

It was late autumn when the 400 battle-fit Cossacks approached the confluence of the Tobol and the Irtysh rivers where a Tatar host of 2,000 warriors stood ready for the vital confrontation. Kuchum's hordes rushed forward on horse and foot, and the blind Khan himself, who had had himself carried out on a litter, listened for the shouts of victory. For days, say the chroniclers, the battle raged. The contorted figures of the slain carpeted the damp earth between the rivers. The Cossacks, isolated and ravenous, were near exhaustion. But they had no escape except in victory, and Kuchum's army had a weakness. He and his Tatars were themselves alien to most of his tribal warriors, and in the last resort they would not sacrifice themselves for foreign masters.

These tribal levies were the first to crack. The Ostyaks fled, leaving their leader, Karacha, in Cossack hands, and on the second night the Voguls slipped quietly out of the Tatar camp. Soon only a hard core of Tatars remained, clustering round the blind Kuchum. While imams and mullahs invoked Muhammed's aid, they fought on with desperation. Then Mahmetkul was wounded, and as their general was carried to safety across the river, Kuchum's men saw a vision, high above the clouds—of a 'great king' with 'many armed warriors flying on wings and bearing his throne upon their shoulders'. Their hands trembled, their bow-strings snapped, and they too fled,[17] taking the Khan with them.

The Cossacks buried 107 of their comrades, then most of them slumped to the ground, exhausted. But the atamans were soon roaring again, and the weary Cossacks were forced on once more—on past the meadows and salt-marshes of the sinuous river Irtysh, towards the tall wooden ramparts of Sibir. They were in no condition to fight, but when they reached the Tatar capital they found it was deserted.

Sibir was less a city than a village—a cluster of wood and daub houses within wooden palisades. If reports of the 'abandoned riches',[18] of furs and carpets, gold and silver and precious stones and pearls to be found there were exaggerated, it at least afforded shelter and the Cossacks were soon to profit from their very presence there. Many of the tribesmen, impressed by their victories, decided it would be discreet to pay tribute to the

Cossacks rather than to Kuchum. Soon an Ostyak chieftain arrived bearing gifts of furs and others followed bringing valuable presents and supplies—inducements for the Cossacks to leave them in peace. But Kuchum, though he dared not attack Sibir, was not reconciled to the loss of his kingdom. His warriors kept up a constant watch waiting to pounce on small groups of Cossacks who ventured outside the palisades. And wherever Cossacks went, pale, flat, spying faces would flash out momentarily from behind the trees. 'No Cossack, no bird could fly past' Kuchum's watchmen without being seen,[19] and his watchmen were everywhere.

Yermak knew that the respite was only temporary. Though he had shelter and food now, he was desperately short of men and ammunition. He must send to the Stroganovs for help. The bold Ivan Koltso was chosen to undertake the perilous journey west and winter had already set in when he led a party of Cossacks out of Sibir on skis and narrow sledges. They went by the 'wolf road' along the frozen river Tavda and across the mountains towards the lands of Perm.

Koltso had hardly set out when Maxim Stroganov received an angry letter from the Tsar. The Voguls had been raiding the Russian frontierlands again and as complaints of their depredations reached Moscow, Ivan suddenly turned on the Stroganovs and accused them of provoking their neighbours, succouring Cossack outlaws and of sending them on an adventurous excursion. The Stroganovs were quick to heed the Tsar's warning, and when Koltso and his comrades arrived weary in Perm, they were given an unexpectedly cool reception. The embarrassed Stroganovs hastily sent them on their way towards a confrontation with the grim Tsar in Moscow.

As he prostrated himself before Ivan, Koltso no doubt expected a speedy journey to the gallows. But as he told his story his men were hacking open the bales they had brought with them. More than five thousand pelts—fine sable, bear, beaver, and skins of the rare black fox—tumbled out on to the palace floors, and the Tsar's narrow eyes widened. This was riches indeed. And Koltso's tale showed Kuchum, the feared Siberian wolf, to be no more than a vulnerable border princeling. Now he saw his chance to make good his claim as titular 'Lord of

Siberia'. The threatening Ivan, terror of the Cossack bandits, suddenly became the gracious, all-forgiving Tsar.

Koltso was given an immediate pardon and sent back to Sibir with a kind message, rolls of cloth for the Cossacks and for Yermak himself a silver goblet, a fur cloak and two immense suits of armour of incredible workmanship, embossed with the imperial double-headed eagle. Still more valuable for the Cossacks beleaguered in Sibir were the powder and lead which the Tsar ordered to be sent, and the fighting men who were to follow Koltso back into Siberia.[20]

Meanwhile Yermak and the remaining Cossacks had spent a cheerless winter, venturing outside Sibir only to fish, hunt, and to collect tribute from the natives. They went out in strength not daring to relax their vigilance, but once a fishing party twenty strong had been attacked by Tatars in the night and only a single Cossack had escaped to bring the news back to Sibir. Next day, the severed heads of his nineteen comrades had been left outside the citadel walls.

Within the palisades, the Cossacks were physically safe but the strain of waiting for uncertain rescue, the frugal diet and the wearing game of cat and mouse punctuated by the disappearance of some comrade, proved too much for some members of the shrinking band. Would-be deserters were given short shrift—bundled into a sack and tossed into the river—though Yermak also used other means to raise morale, answering Tatar raids with punitive expeditions in which Cossacks slaughtered many Tatars and tribesmen thought to be sympathetic to Kuchum.

These shows of force brought the submission of more chieftains who agreed to pay Yermak a rake-off in furs. The payment of *yassak*, or tribute, was a Mongol-Tatar institution, which the native tribesmen had long understood. They knew the methods of defining the amount to be paid, that payment would be extracted by force when necessary, that hostages must be surrendered as guarantees, and that, in return, if they behaved themselves, they would be protected from rival collectors such as Kuchum. In essence the tribute system was a protection racket. Yermak's rule of Siberia, as Kuchum's before his, was not very dissimilar from Al Capone's rule of the Chicago underworld.

But as the tribute payments mounted up in the huts of Sibir, ammunition and resilience were running low. Mahmetkul had recovered from his wounds, and the elusive, dangerous Kuchum had not capitulated. Then Yermak got news that Mahmetkul and some Tatar warriors had made camp two days' journey away. The prize was tempting and the ataman decided to risk a sortie for it. Sixty Cossacks were sent out and they succeeded in capturing the Tatar prince. Now Yermak had a hostage and word soon reached Kuchum that if Cossack foragers should be attacked again, Mahmetkul would die. As it happened, the Khan was now threatened from the south as well—by the advance of an army of Kazakhs led by Seidak, kinsman of his defeated rival Yediger. For the moment the pressure on the Cossacks was relieved.

The prospect was further brightened by the return of Ivan Koltso, laden with food, ammunition, gifts and the Tsar's 'joyful and commendatory letters' to Yermak and [his] ... brotherhood;[21] and by the news of the impending arrival of reinforcements. The Cossacks gave vent to their relief by dancing on the river bank till sunrise—much to the astonishment of some watching natives. But Yermak was already planning an expansion of his activities. Almost at once he sent Ataman Bogdan Bryazga and fifty men out along the Irtysh to collect tribute, and he himself led two more similar expeditions.

An apocryphal story describes Yermak's use of his own cunning and the superstitions of the local folk to compensate for lack of numbers. An Ostyak fort was offering strong resistance. Yermak infiltrated an elderly tribesman, whose family was held hostage in Sibir, into the fort as a spy. The tribesman duly reported by means of an arrow shot into the Cossack camp that the fort, commanded by a chief called Demyan, was strongly garrisoned and that its will to resist was founded chiefly on the presence of an idol called Parun. The spy managed to remove it, and at midnight when the Ostyaks came to worship and found it gone, they broke out in such wailings of despair that the Cossacks were able to scale the palisades virtually unopposed.

Demyan and his people were made to swear allegiance to Yermak, but some time later the local wizard found the idol and, representing its return as a miracle, had Demyan

imprisoned for heresy and demanded that the Ostyaks send for
Kuchum. When he heard of the coup, Yermak set out to regain
control, not by force, but like some practical Elijah, by means of
a trial of miracles with this priest of Baal. The wizard claimed it
was Parun that had inspired the revolt and to prove its supernatural powers, ripped his stomach open with a knife. Parun's
magic seemed strong indeed, for, when smeared with grass,
the wound immediately healed up. But Yermak, victor as he
claimed of forty battles without sustaining hurt, possessed an
even stronger, if less subtle, brand of magic. He had a great fire
lit, and tossed the idol into it. Then, as the flames leapt higher
still he hurled the wizard, screaming, after it. Demyan's people
offered no more resistance.

That summer, the Cossacks discovered new territories of
woodland, lakes and marshes. They explored the country east
along the Irtysh as far as the river Ishim, sailed up the river
Tavda and pushed out northwards along the slow-flowing river
Ob. Soon Yermak's power stretched 250 miles north of Sibir
and more and more settlements were made to pay him tribute.
But the Siberian lands rolled on without end and Yermak's
band was growing ever smaller. Even victories brought their
casualties and sickness and accidents were taking a toll.

The arrival of soldiers under Prince Bolkhovski in the autumn,
so far from strengthening the Cossacks, imposed a further burden
on them. The exhausted newcomers had suffered so much from
hunger on the long journey that they had been reduced to
eating their stricken comrades. They brought some gunpowder
but nothing else, except disease. Many died that winter,
Bolkhovski himself among them, and though the situation
became easier with the spring, the outlook for the survivors was
still grim.

Sensing their weakness, the Siberian chieftains began to
plot rebellion. Their ringleader, Karacha, sent word to Yermak
protesting his loyalty and asking for help against Khan Kuchum,
who was attacking him, he claimed. Yermak sent Koltso and
forty Cossacks to his aid, and Karacha received them well. But
as they slept he had their throats cut. This was the signal for a
general rising and soon Karacha had assembled enough tribesmen to lay siege to Sibir. The Cossacks fought back hard.

Matvei Meshcheryak delivered a successful raid on Karacha's camp and two of Karacha's own sons were among those slain. Although reinforcements arrived to swell the tribal force, Karacha was driven away at last, leaving 'numerous corpses' behind him.[22] But it was a Pyrrhic victory. The bold Yakov Mikhailov had been killed, Ivan Koltso and Nikitin Pan were also dead. The 350 remaining government troops were almost useless and only 150 of the original 540 Cossacks were still alive. Yermak's fortunes had reached a new nadir.

Mahmetkul had been sent to Moscow and Kuchum was no longer held in check by consideration of his safety. The Khan had long been planning his revenge, and now he set a plan in motion to obtain it. Yermak had been trying to revive the Siberian trading routes to the east and south. The Khan knew this and used the knowledge to bait the trap, spreading a rumour that a caravan from Bukhara had reached the Irtysh river. As soon as he heard this Yermak took fifty Cossacks and hastened upstream to protect the merchants. Finding nothing, he decided to wait until it arrived, and set up camp on an island in the river.

It was early August but a storm blew up that night. Strong winds lashed up the river waters, the rain came down in sheets, and stabs of lightning briefly lit up the darkly-shrouded river bank. Legend has it that on that terrifying night Yermak had a strange, ill-boding dream. A great fire seemed to be raging in the distance and the river began to turn a bloody red. Yermak's limbs stiffened; he could not move. Only his eyes were drawn to the angry waters. Tatars were crawling out of it—men of terrible aspect, bloody with wounds. He tried desperately to move, but the nightmare's grip was too strong. The spectres came on, inexorably, towards him, and behind them the bloody river clotted to a standstill. Yermak felt himself grasped by iron hands and bound tight against a tree. His shirt was ripped off, eerie figures crowded in upon him. Then suddenly, and mercifully, the apparitions dissolved away.[23]

If dream he did, it was prophetic. Kuchum and his men had been shadowing Yermak, and now had him surrounded. Some intrepid Tatars had even penetrated the sleeping camp unseen and had returned with guns to prove the Cossacks' unpreparedness. The time had come, so Kuchum judged, to strike.

Tatars swarmed across the river, knives in teeth, and crept on to the island. Some Cossacks were slaughtered as they slept, others cut down in confused semi-consciousness. Roused by their groans, Yermak tried to organise resistance, then, realising that this was hopeless, turned desperately to save himself, cutting his way through a mass of Tatars towards a boat that might carry him to safety. Grunting, the metal-clad warrior lumbered on, sword and knife in either fist. Sharp blows rained down on him from all sides, but could not pierce his armour. Then an arrow struck him in the eye. Yermak stumbled, then went on again. Tatars fell with terrible screeches under his feet. Others of them, seeing him vulnerable at last, swarmed round him like a cloud of hornets. Yet somehow the ataman tore a way through them and reached the shore at last.

The effort was for nothing; there was no boat there. In a final bid for life the stricken Yermak flung himself into the Irtysh and tried to swim away. But the Tsar's heavy armour merely carried his protesting body down and down, till it disappeared beneath the lapping waters.

The morale of the Cossacks and soldiers in Sibir collapsed when they heard of Yermak's death. They set out for home, and soon Kuchum's son, Alei, returned to take possession of Sibir. It seemed that all the blood had been shed in vain.

But Yermak's ghost was shortly to recover all his conquests. The Cossack had become a legend, the symbol of the new power bearing in on the Siberians from the west. For years afterwards the natives told with bated breath of how, some time after Yermak's death, a Tatar lad fishing in the Irtysh spied a glinting object waving with the motion of the stream, and, looking closer, discerned a human leg. It was Yermak's corpse. Dragging it out onto the bank, the Tatar and his friends found that the body was uncorrupted. As they stared, blood began to trickle from its nose and mouth. Fearing their old enemy might still be alive, Kuchum's men came and fired many arrows into it. But fresh blood gushed out from each new wound. They left the body out unguarded, hoping that the carrion eaters would destroy it, but they refused to touch it. So they buried the corpse and tried to forget the place where it was hidden. In vain. One night every week a strange blue flame would flicker over the spot. The Cossack's magic was still strong.

And his miraculous power lived on in fact as well as legend, for Yermak had damaged the Siberian Khanate beyond repair and inspired the Tsar with a determination to build an empire in the east. As the remnant of Yermak's force had come homewards from Sibir, they met a hundred soldiers with cannon on their way to reinforce them. Hearing of Yermak's death, they prudently decided to spend the winter out of range of Sibir. But the wheels of conquest had already been set in motion. In 1586, 300 more soldiers joined them, and together they had resumed the advance. That year, on the river Tura, they built the first Russian strongpoint in Siberia, later to become the city of Tyumen. In 1587 a further 500 men arrived and near the old Tatar capital of Sibir they founded the city of Tobolsk. Within two years of Yermak's death the Tsar's men crushed all the remaining opposition and established their rule over western Siberia.

Kuchum fled with his family to the steppe but continued to fight a futile rear-guard action until in 1598 his wives, his sons, most of his retainers, and his remaining treasure fell into Russian hands. The emissaries of Tsar Boris Godunov found Kuchum in the desert surrounded by no more than a handful of followers and a pile of corpses. They offered clemency if he would submit, told him that his family was being treated well. But the blind old man refused. He would not submit 'in happier days, when I was rich and strong,' he said, 'shall I go now to find a disgraceful death?' Poor now, and alone, he spent his days grieving for his favourite son. 'With him I should have been content to live on without kingdom or fortune, without my wives or any other children.'[24] Obstinate and without hope, he wandered on until he met his death at the hands of the Nogais with whom he sought refuge.

By then his old rival, Seidak, was dead too. Defeated by Russian soldiers, he had been enticed to a feast by his conquerors, and there murdered. In the battle that brought Seidak down Matvei Meshcheryak, the last of Yermak's atamans, had been killed. All the chief characters in the story were now dead; only the power of the Tsar remained.

The motive for Russia's move to dominate the east was the

same as that which began the westward push in America—the quest for furs.[25] Furs provided a rich source of income and a powerful stimulus to foreign trade. A sable rich in hair and colour was a present fit for a king and the Tsar presented 400,000 such skins to the Holy Roman Emperor in 1595. Demand was growing, and the immense quantities required could not be supplied from the central Russian forests alone. Siberia promised to be a great new reserve—hence the state's determination to take over Yermak's protection system. The dividends were huge and immediate. By 1600 about a million skins were being sent to Moscow every year—black fox, snow-fox, ermine, beaver, selected squirrel skins, and, above all, the prized sable pelt, the 'Golden Fleece'.[26] They were obtained as tribute from the tribesmen or bought from skilled hunters who sought them out with dogs and were 'dextrous in shooting them in the nose' to save the fur from being marked.[27]

The first Russians who collected these furs on behalf of the Tsar were soldiers and Yermak's surviving Cossacks. But their numbers were soon swelled by Cossacks from the Don and Zaporozhiye, and runaways from central Russia. Murderers were reprieved if they joined the search for new lands and tribute in the east; escaped serfs were often recognised as free men there. And a peasant could become a Cossack in Siberia. In 1630, some 300 vagrant hunters were enrolled by a local governor as 'foot Cossacks' to garrison the new town of Yeniseisk.[28]

A Cossack might support himself by trapping or robbing for furs; or he might become a garrison soldier or tribute collector in the government service. Service Cossacks were paid in money and kind. Sometimes they were given land rights and usually they were exempt from taxes. But the rewards varied considerably from time to time. The governor of Tobolsk gave 'the foot Cossack Ivan Sevrugin' and the forty free Cossacks he had recruited to garrison a fort far out in the wilderness two years' supply of grain and other help in lieu of pay.[29] The Cossacks who formed the first garrison on Kamchatka, on the other hand, received both food and money in return for their duties.

Cossacks were often appointed government agents (*prikazehiki*) to collect tribute on behalf of the Tsar, and like other tax-collectors usually managed to collect more for themselves than for their master. And a Cossack who earned the gratitude of the state might even be raised to the rank of *boyarski syn*, the rough equivalent of an English esquire. But now that the Tsar's governors ruled in Siberia with Muscovite soldiers to back up their authority, the conditions did not exist for the development of a free Cossack society.

Temporary winter camps soon became settlements, the settlements grew into towns as more Russians came east, and the towns were dominated by the Tsar. This spurred individual Cossacks on to play the major role in exploring the vast Siberian expanses and subjugating their people, for there were always men prepared to prospect further as the authority of governors threatened to overtake them. Russia's expansion from the Urals to Alaska is studded with the achievements of such men, drawn beyond the edge of law and order by the prospects of personal freedom and of wealth. Yet, like Yermak, they were to become the unwitting tentacles of the Russian imperial octopus.

The directions the explorers took were still dictated by the river routes. Even in winter the river was their road, as on snow-shoes and on sleds drawn by great teams of dogs they slid along the twisting ribbons of ice into the unknown. The pace was fast. Within a few years of Yermak's death Cossacks had explored the south along the Ob to the edge of Central Asia, and 1,500 miles to the north, they had reached the mouth of the Yenisei and the Arctic sea. As settlements and administrative centres rose up in their wake, Cossack venturers pressed on further. From the upper Yenisei they sailed east and south along the Angara river, and by 1646 a Cossack ataman had sailed round the mysterious, fathomless Lake Baikal.

Having explored the majestic rivers Ob and Yenisei, which cross Siberia south to north, and sailed along their tributaries, they found another, still farther to the east—the Lena which rises near Lake Baikal and falls at last into the Arctic. From here they pushed on, ever eastwards up the Aldan river. But then their way was blocked by mountain ranges towering 10,000 feet up. Henceforth, while some sought a way across by land to the eastern edge of Asia, others risked their lives in boats among the ice-floes of the East Siberian Sea. The Siberian Cossacks, men of the rivers, had become trackers and men of the sea.

The boats of the early Cossacks of the rivers were flat-bottomed, held together by mortice joints or wooden nails and at most thirty foot long. Their ropes were made of leather thongs, the anchors were large stones and the vessels were propelled by oars and by rough sails made of skins. They could hold ten men each and cover some twenty miles a day at most.[30] Yet Cossacks sailed the bleak and dangerous Arctic and into the stormy Pacific in boats not much bigger. Sixty feet long, a dozen in beam, and displacing little more than thirty tons, they could only sail before the wind and a Westerner admitted that a Dutch or English sailor 'would scarcely have dared to entrust his life to such a flimsy craft on a sea that is never free from ice'.[31]

But in 1633 a Cossack called Ivan Perfilev led a party of 'free traders and Cossacks' out of the river Lena into the northern sea in boats such as this, and made a safe landfall, founding 'a new place . . . on the Yana river'. In 1638 another Cossack, Ivan Rebrov, followed this route and probed still further east to find the Indigyrka river,[32] and four years later yet another intrepid Cossack sailed out of the Indigyrka into Arctic and founded Nizhnekolymsk on the Kolyma river, nearly a thousand miles from the mouth of the Lena. And while Cossacks had been edging their way along the northern coastline, others had been pressing eastwards overland. The Cossack Ivan Moskvitin taking a southerly route had found the Amur river and so reached the Sea of Okhotsk.

Barely fifty years after Yermak entered Siberia, at a time when the American colonists still lived east of the Appalachians, Cossacks had penetrated 4,000 miles to the Pacific and a Cossack was said to have visited Japan. Soon even Kamchatka in the far north-east was settled and Russians began to ponder the mysteries of a new frontier across the sea, 'the great land' of 'the unknown people'—Alaska in North America.[33]

Cossacks exploring the vast tracks of the interior trekked as far as 800 miles from their outpost settlements, journeying across the taiga, through forests of aspens, poplars, firs and birches, where reindeer, lemmings and ptarmigan lurked and temperatures fell to minus thirty degrees centigrade. Many set out on such journeys never to return. And the tundra to the north was even less hospitable—a flat, treeless land where the brief summer brought out swarms of giant midges and made treacherous bogs out of the frozen ground. Here Cossacks were lucky to find a few berries, mushrooms or some tree-bark on which to feed, and caught there in winter, when everything froze in temperatures of minus fifty degrees, they spent months swaddled in layers of fur, ice-bound in log cabins.

Frost-bite and snow-blindness were among the lesser hazards and the rough winter shelters they built for themselves were prisons of isolation amid the raging snow-storms and the almost endless night. For months there was nothing to do but keep the fire burning, sing, and re-tell stories told a hundred times before, though a literate Cossack might amuse himself by painstakingly inscribing reports addressed to the nearest governor on scraps of birchbark. A Cossack was fortunate to return whole to a tribute-collection post, though even these hardly constituted civilisation—merely a few rough cabins, surrounded by a stockade thrown up against hostile tribesmen. Comfort there never was, and the risks of starvation and of the sudden arrow of the native were ever present.

The Siberian outback was an environment that bred particular sins and virtues. It demanded courage and resource; it also brought out savagery. The greed of the Cossack pathfinder could lead to unscrupulous extortion, his fear to cruelty, his lust to rape, his hunger to cannibalism. A Cossack would spill blood for an ounce of gold, a few sable pelts, or a native woman. It was a country that made men beasts as well as heroes.

Peter Beketov, a Cossack in government service, exemplified both traits. Going into central Siberia in 1628 to collect tribute from the tribesmen, he braved the uncharted lands, found the source of the river Lena, and built a post which was later to become the city of Yakutsk. He shed his blood for the Tsar, and, in his own words, 'suffered hunger and every sort of hardship, and defiled my spirit, and ate . . . roots . . . fir bark and all kinds of filth, and many times had scurvy'.[34] Beketov collected tribute for the Tsar; he also kidnapped natives to sell as slaves for his own profit.

Hardship can brutalise, as it did the first Russians to reach the Chinese border. In 1643, 112 Cossacks, fifteen soldiers and two clerks led by Vasili Poyarkov had set out from Yakutsk in search of silver. Sailing up the river Aldan, they crossed the Yablonnoi mountains and reached the river Seya. Then the snows set in. They built camp and settled in, trapped there by the winter. But they had not brought food enough to last them through and one by one they began to die. With the scent of death hanging heavy in the claustrophobic atmosphere, the morale of the survivors crumbled right away. They began to eat their own dead and soon they were killing one another for food.

Spring came and the remnant went on to the Amur, the 'Black Dragon River' as the Chinese called it, and sailed on down to its mouth. They found no silver, but plenty of corn and unfriendly natives, including the fabled Dauri. In terror lest they be overwhelmed at last, the Cossacks slaughtered them without pity, took many hostages and stole their belongings. The thirty or so men who struggled back, exhausted, to Yakutsk in 1646 came laden with furs and leading a long rope line of hostages. Poyarkov's reward was arrest and dispatch to Moscow for judgement on his cruelties. A distant government could reap the rewards and yet condemn the means their agents used to gain them.

The Dauris were to learn more of Cossack savagery. In 1650 138 Cossacks led by a private entrepreneur, Yerofei Khabarov set out from Yakutsk with horses and cannon bound for Dauri country. Khabarov knew they paid tribute to the Emperor of China but followed a strategy of terror nevertheless. He robbed the Dauris, kidnapped and slaughtered them in a series of vicious strikes. After one action in which he and his Cossacks had struck down defenceless women and children Khabarov composed a song of victory: 'With God's help . . . we burned them, we knocked them on the head . . . and counting big and little we killed six hundred and sixty-one.'[35] When the inhabitants of one occupied village fled from the conquistadors, Khabarov waited to burn some of his hostages alive before giving chase. Like other European empire builders, these men did not attempt to distinguish between 'innocent' and 'guilty', but slaughtered any being who happened to stray across their path. For the Dauri, the word 'Cossack' came to be equated with torturer, murderer, destroyer and rapist and news of their rampages eventually reached the Manchu Emperor, who sent out a task force to protect the tribesmen. But the Chinese were no match for the ruthless Khabarov. He defeated them, capturing much of their equipment, several silken banners and 830 horses. Having earned a reputation as a second Yermak, his excesses were overlooked. He was raised to the rank of squire and given some villages. His place on the Chinese frontier was taken by a Russian official.

These easy successes went to the heads of the Russians. Some years later when a mandarin came to Nerchinsk to protest about the Cossacks' depredations along the Amur, the governor responded by sending an illiterate Cossack called Milovanov to Peking to demand that the Emperor submit and pay tribute to the Tsar. Milovanov had sense enough to ignore his instructions, and returned with such fascinating news of the Chinese that he was sent post-haste to Moscow where an appreciative Tsar promoted him to the status of squire. Milovanov had avoided a dangerous confrontation with the might of China, and encouraged the government to settle the question of its new border by peaceful means. In 1685 the Tsar's ambassador and an escort of 1,400 Cossacks set out to conclude a Russo-Chinese treaty. But Cossack behaviour along the border had already helped to establish the Chinese opinion of Europeans as despicable barbarians.

Nor was the north-east devoid of its Khabarov. His spiritual successor there was the Cossack Atlasov, tribute collector of Anadyr. Many of the native hunters, reindeer herders and coastal fishermen committed suicide rather than face death or subjection at his hands when he was exploiting the Kamchatka peninsula in 1697. But from the government's point of view he achieved results. In 1701 he carried more than 3,000 sable skins to Moscow and was rewarded with 100 silver rubles, a quantity of cloth and a stipend of ten rubles a year. But even Cossacks in government employ could find it difficult to suppress the old cossacking spirit. On his way back, Atlasov met a Russian merchant and promptly relieved him of his valuable load of Chinese tea, silks and spices. Atlasov was arrested and imprisoned. But the state could not long afford to dispense with

71

a man of his unscrupulous qualities and by 1704 he was not only at liberty again but entrusted with two government cannon and a number of Cossacks and sent out to exploit Kamchatka. He was to prove even more efficient at collecting tribute on his own behalf than on behalf of the state and within five months he had accumulated a considerable private fortune. But this was achieved only by ignoring instructions not to ill-treat those natives who paid tribute. He plundered one tribe and then massacred men of another on the pretext of protecting the first from them. Not even his own Cossacks were safe from him and several of them disappeared in very suspicious circumstances. At last Atlasov's own Cossacks rose up against him, and though he escaped them on this occasion, he was eventually to meet his death at Cossack hands.

Cossacks who rebelled against the hard grip of such chiefs were hanged, or flogged and sent in small vessels and canoes to the Kurile Islands north of Japan to collect tribute there—and they brought bloodshed to the Kuriles. The ruthless colonial exploitation carried out by men like Atlasov turned all eastern Siberia into a holocaust of violence which burned for over a hundred years. The eskimo-like walrus hunters of the north-east coast, the tribes inland and to the south trod the war-path of revenge, killing and mutilating every Russian they could find, burning down the Cossacks' huts, carrying off their women and their children. Troubles were quelled only to break out again. In 1727 a new Cossack strong man, Shestakov, set out to subdue Kamchatka. He seemed successful enough but three years later as he approached a tribal settlement, an arrow struck him in the neck. His reindeer bolted, carrying his sleigh into the camp. He did not emerge from it alive.

The opposition was founded less on resentment of exploitation and Russian dominance than on the methods of collection and the behaviour of the Cossacks. A rebellious native chief offered to collect the taxes on the Tsar's behalf himself, but insisted that his people wanted 'no Cossacks among them'. He was arrested, and Cossacks slaughtered those of his comrades who held out. Tribesmen killed their wives and children rather than let them fall into Cossack hands. A government inquiry laid the causes for the rebellion at the Cossacks' door. A handful were executed, the rest 'forbidden to demand old debts, which they pretend were due from the natives'.[36] But Cossack passions and the government's ambivelance secured a continuation of the troubles, and the tribes were only fully subdued towards the end of the eighteenth century.

But besides these bestial and rapacious traits, Cossacks could display some nobler aspects. Evil characters like Atlasov had brave and comparatively honest counterparts in men like Semen Dezhnev. In 1648 he had set out from the Kolyma estuary with ninety men and six boats into the northern seas. He sailed on eastwards, round the coast until he came at last to the river Anadyr. Unknowingly, he had passed through the straits separating Asia from America—eighty years before Bering and 130 before Captain Cook. It was a momentous discovery, but in human terms the achievement was still greater. Dezhnev's real troubles only started after he had passed the straits. He tells his own story briefly and without heroics. 'When we had passed the mouth of the Anadyr, by the will of God, the sea broke all our boats to pieces'. Many of his people were drowned, 'others were killed by the natives . . . and others again died of hunger. In all sixty-four people lost their lives'. There was no alternative but to go on. With his twenty-four remaining comrades he set out for the river Anadyr 'on sleds and snow-shoes, suffering cold, hunger and want of . . . necessities'. He reached the Anadyr with only twelve men and they near starvation. 'Not wishing to die of hunger', they fought the local tribes, but, unlike some others, refrained from attacking 'those who pay tribute'.[37]

Dezhnev established a fortified post on the Anadyr and stayed there for several years hunting walrus and collecting tribute to bring home with him. But robbed of much of his collection on the way he returned with only '234 sables . . . and about 573 lbs. of Walrus tusks'. The authorities were impressed neither by his discoveries nor their awful cost. Years later Dezhnev applied to the Tsar for recompense. He had set out, he wrote 'on your Majesty's service to those new rivers on my own money . . . and received no salary . . . from you . . . either in cash, grain or salt between 1642 and 1661'. Upon this he received his pay in salt but the grain and cash were still withheld. 'I have risked my life', he pleaded, 'suffered great wounds and shed my blood, suffered

73

cold and great hunger and starved.' He had been robbed by buccaneers and incurred heavy debts. All he wanted for his risks and sufferings was his arrears of pay 'lest I, your humble servant, be tortured . . . in shackling debts and be unable to continue serving your Majesty, and finally perish'.[38]

What the answer was we do not know and the stories of other Cossack venturers will never be told—of men whose only reward for a years-long venture into the unknown was an armful of pelts and a few walrus tusks; of men who failed to return at all. At the end of the eighteenth century, members of a Russian expedition landing in Alaska were mystified by people they found living on its shores. They were distinguished from the Americans by their long beards, prayed from books, bowed before icons and appeared to speak and write in Russian. Were these descendants of some party of Cossacks who left a Siberian settlement in the seventeenth century never to be heard of again?

A few undisciplined Cossacks threw a girdle across the widest continent and with incredible swiftness. It was an amazing achievement. Siberia's native population, though small, scattered and armed only with spears, bows and arrows, was formidable opposition for the tiny groups of poorly equipped invaders, just as Kuchum's Tatars had been for Yermak's force. And the pioneers had to withstand an incredibly harsh climate and terrible isolation to accomplish what they did.

In human terms the cost was high. Yet the Cossacks were no worse than their Western counterparts—slave-traders like Hawkins, or the pitiless Belgians of King Leopold's Congo. And their ruthless qualities were evident in their behaviour to one another, as well as to the natives. Few of his successors possessed Yermak's talents for imposing group order. The comradeship of travellers often failed. Cossacks stole from Cossack, and would slaughter his ataman or murder a comrade to protect some discovery. And there was often vicious rivalry between one exploring party and another. For a long time the government was too weak to keep order among the Siberian Cossacks and since the state could not protect him, a Cossack had to rely on himself for his security. The law of the Cossack venturer became the law of the jungle. The situation goes far to explain the dark image of the Siberian Cossack as the ignoble savage.

Yet despite their viciousness they bear comparison with the Pilgrim Fathers in that they, too, were seeking a new world where they would be personally free, even though free to pursue rather different ends. The Russian government in consolidating its hold over the new territories had spurred the lawless Cossack element ever onwards. Cossacks did not cross Siberia in order to test their wills and their durability against odds. They went for pay, to gather booty, to escape authority. Lacking any historic sense, and deprived of the opportunity to build their own independent community there, they did not think in terms of a collective past and collective future, only of their individual needs—the search for a livelihood, freedom from the interference of other men.

For decades after Yermak's death runaways and individual Cossacks could still find freedom by running farther and farther into the virgin lands. But the days of opportunity were limited. The state was never far behind and in the end it was inescapable. Soon the Cossack had nowhere at all to fly to. If he wanted liberty he had to stand and fight the state.

'Cossacks who gave account to no one . . .
whose number nobody knew'.

—Gogol, *Taras Bulba*

3 The Cossacks and the State

While Cossack pathfinders were blazing trails of exploration
towards the Pacific, relations between the Cossacks of the
southern borderlands and the states of Muscovy and Poland had
undergone great change. While Yermak was in Siberia and in the
years following his death, the grip of Muscovite lords over their
peasants was immeasurably tightened. Then, in 1598, the man
behind this peasant legislation, Tsar Ivan's chief minister, Boris
Godunov, became Tsar himself upon the death of the infant
Dmitri, last of the Muscovite royal line. It was a time of social
upheaval and of famine. Many landlords were unable or unwilling to feed their peasants, and yet these peasants were no
longer allowed to move to other lords who might provide for
them. Boyars began to sack their retainers and, inevitably,
crowds of destitutes took to the roads looking for subsistence.
Many turned to brigandage, and many sought refuge with the
Cossacks of the frontier.

In an attempt to control the situation, Tsar Boris temporarily waived the ban on peasant movement and tried to seal off the borders completely. Cossacks were forbidden to enter Russia, even to trade or to visit their relatives, for fear they might influence the bands of wanderers, incite them to disorder or to leave the country with them. Such announcements had been made before, chiefly to calm the Sultan and the Khans, but this time the rule was rigorously enforced. Intruders who were caught were imprisoned or hanged, and the Cossacks' sense of grievance swelled to a crescendo. They were not people to take such treatment lying down. Yet their complaints were trivial besides those of the mass of starving, homeless peasants. Famine, epidemic, and fiery discontent were sweeping all of Russia and Boris's repressive legislation only exacerbated the situation. The nation's mood was explosive and in 1604 the match was applied. All Russia entered a period of unprecedented anarchy and tribulation which histories in English characterise with gross understatement as 'The Time of Troubles'. And the Cossacks contributed largely to the chaos that ensued.

Rumours spread that Boris murdered little Dmitri, the rightful heir to the throne, that God was punishing the people on account of their 'bad' Tsar. When a man announced himself to be that same Dmitri, thousands of malcontents flocked to join him. Sponsored by the Lithuanian magnate Adam Vishnevetski, and helped by the Zaporozhian Cossacks with whom he had lived, the Pretender marched towards Moscow, calling on the 'free Christian knights', the Cossacks of the Don, to turn 'the evildoer off . . . [the] throne'.[1] In September, Boris sent his man Khrushchev to rally the Don Cossacks to his side but they trussed Khrushchev up and hauled him off to the Pretender's camp.

There were 3,000 Don and several thousand Zaporozhian Cossacks in Dmitri's army. The forces under Muscovite command, including service Cossacks, outnumbered it, and the Pretender was defeated. But he escaped to build up a new army. Four thousand Don Cossacks joined him and in February 1605 they broke through across the snows to relieve the key fortress of Kromy 200 miles south of Moscow.[2] Two months later Tsar Boris died; his son was murdered and in July the

Pretender Dmitri entered Moscow to be crowned as Tsar. But the Terek Cossacks from the far south were soon on the march to Astrakhan, one of their 'young comrades' posing as a spurious 'Tsarevich Peter'; and many Yaik Cossacks from the eastern frontier joined them as they moved on towards Moscow.

In May 1606, 2,000 Polish noblemen rode into Russia's capital escorting Marina Mniczech, who was to be Dmitri's bride. To the people of Moscow it looked like a foreign occupation. They rioted. The boyars conspired to kill Dmitri, Marina was interned, and her Polish friends sent packing. Prince Basil Shuiski, the crafty boyar leader, took an uneasy seat upon the throne. But that autumn another great revolt swept up from the Ukraine.

Its leader was Ivan Bolotnikov. Born a serf, he had fled to the steppe as a boy to become a Cossack. Captured by Tatars he had spent several years chained to the oar of a Turkish galley, but was freed and found his way home from Venice. Now his followers took up the cries for the 'Tsarevich Peter'. Bolotnikov promised to distribute the property of lords and rich men among the poor—and their wives and daughters too. The policy was hugely popular. The Don Cossacks sent a large contingent to join him, many turbulent Zaporozhians also came, and, as they marched north, the Cossack idea captured the people's imagination. Serfs and peasants turned Cossack by their thousands, threw over their landlords and chose their own atamans. The tide swept on almost to Moscow. But the main rebel army was beaten back to Tula, then starved out of it, and Bolotnikov himself was chased to a death by drowning.[3] The 'Tsarevich Peter' and the remains of his force from the Terek plundered their way back down the Volga, turned west towards the Don and the Ukraine, and then dispersed. The storms began to die down—then flared up again.

Tsar Basil Shuiski had turned out to be another Boris, and his desperate attempt to stem the tide of anarchy by re-establishing an iron rule proved no more successful. By the summer of 1608 a second 'Dmitri' was advancing towards Moscow with Polish support and a variegated army of Tatars, Zaporozhians, Don Cossacks under Ataman Zarutski and even Muscovite serving Cossacks. The rebels made camp just outside Moscow where they were joined by Marina, who 'recognised' the new 'Dmitri' as her husband. While the two armies faced each other deadlocked, all vestige of order in the country disappeared. The property of the church, the boyars and the merchants was plundered by robber gangs; expectation of life became totally uncertain. Then foreign vultures came to prey on stricken Russia.

In September 1609 Sigismund King of Poland invaded, and Shuiski called upon the aid of the Swedes, who occupied Novgorod. The second 'Dmitri' was sent flying to Kaluga but the boyars threw in their hands with Poles and deposed Shuiski. In 1610 the Poles occupied Moscow itself.

The boyars agreed to accept Sigismund's son as Tsar if he would convert to Orthodoxy. The people preferred Dmitri, but in December 'Dmitri' was killed in a local fracas. A tragic situation deteriorated into farce. Marina took the Don ataman, Ivan Zarutski, as her lover, and persuaded him to proclaim her year-old son by 'Dmitri', Tsar. Then the Polish King decided to be Tsar himself and when the boyars protested, their spokesmen, including Philaret, Patriarch of Moscow, were arrested and hauled off to Poland.

In 1611, an uneasy alliance was formed between service Cossacks, Don Cossacks under Zarutski, and the Russian gentry militia under Governor Lyapunov. But Lyapunov wanted the restoration of the old order, the return of fugitive peasants to their masters. The Don Cossacks promptly slaughtered him and moved out together with Zarutski and Marina. At last a new, a patriotic, coalition was formed to save Russia from Polish Catholic rule. It was led by Prince Pozharski and a butcher called Minin. Fifteen hundred Don Cossacks under Atamans Mezhakov and Epifanets joined the new army at Yaroslav and in August 1612 they attacked Moscow. With the Poles in the Kremlin were 8,000 Cossacks from the Ukraine and Zaporozhiye. Those with Russian army, servicemen and free, swelled to 8,500. So Cossack fought Cossack to decide who should sit on Russia's throne.

In October the Poles were driven out of Moscow, and at the general assembly called there early in 1613 it was a Don Cossack, Ataman Mezhakov, who cast the first vote to elect a new Tsar, the sixteen-year-old Michael Romanov, son of the Patriarch Philaret. The Poles were still in Smolensk, the Swedes in Novgorod and besieging Pskov, and Cossack king-breakers were still on the prowl. Zarutski and Marina tried to build a Cossack federation in Astrakhan which they hoped would carry them to Moscow, but in 1614 they were captured.

The troubles were almost over, but the trauma was to remain. The sense of backwardness by comparison with foreigners increased; the Russians' fear of foreign intervention became obsessional. The new royal house of Romanov set out to enforce national unity, completing a monolithic autocracy, and a centrality which is characteristic of the Russian state even today. Ever since, Russian governments have demanded a cohesion which is absolute; vicious strikes against nascent opposition movements have been the order of the day. They have not waited for trouble; they have anticipated it, acted pre-emptively like Stalin with his purges. Any group or individual suspected of fomenting anarchy and separatism, anyone thought to be uttering criticism, has been regarded as a potential wrecker, as a traitor.

Cossacks had fought against Tsar Michael as well as for him. But though the Muscovite authorities developed a concern to gain control over the Cossacks, this was a long-term objective. There was no immediate clash with them. For the moment the state and the free Cossack communities needed one another. Muscovy was militarily weak; the border defence system had collapsed. Between 1607 and 1617 tens of thousands of captives had been carried off by Tatar raiders. And the Cossacks of the Don felt themselves extremely vulnerable. With many of their comrades still wandering about Russia, they were down to 1,888 men and they were short of horses, armaments and food. So, when Tsar Michael offered them powder shot, grain, spirits and other presents if they would serve him, they were anxious enough to comply. Next year the arrangement was cemented, the Tsar sending them pay, and a royal banner as symbol of his protection. From September 1615 he even allowed them to trade duty-free with Russian towns. But he was trying to buy their loyalty along with their service, and he took good care to point out how much better he was treating

80

them than Tsar Boris had done. Under Boris, he reminded them, they had been forbidden to travel to Moscow or 'to enter the border towns, to visit your birthplaces or to buy and sell'. Those found had been imprisoned or even executed.[4] Michael, by contrast, was flattering them by calling them 'knights of the glorious Don' and was granting them many favours as 'protectors of the Russian land.'

He had extended the offer to other Cossack communities as well. But the borderlands which the Cossacks inhabited were still wild country and the Tsar had difficulty in tracing all their atamans. So he asked the Don Cossacks to deliver his message 'to the great and glorious . . . Volga and Terek and Yaik hosts and to . . . the atamans and Cossacks of all the rivers'. The messages told of what 'the Autocrat, the lord Tsar and Grand Duke Michael Fedorovich of all the Russias' had done for the Don Cossacks, and promised to reward the Cossacks of other settlements in like manner, offering them 'much money, pay and cloth and saltpetre and supplies' in return for their good behaviour and true service. The Tsar had written to them 'many times' before, so the message ran, 'but without an answer'.[5] This time, however, at least some of the messages got through. The Yaik Cossacks were glad enough to accept the offer, and in 1620 the Zaporozhians had actually approached Moscow, offering their services 'as they served great Russian Tsars in the past'.[6]

The course of the relationship did not run smooth. By 1620 the Don Cossacks had regained sufficient strength and confidence to mount raids and pirate expeditions into the Black Sea, and two years later a Turkish ambassador on his way from Moscow actually saw Cossacks unloading booty they had taken from Turkish ships. The result was a flurry of exchanges between Moscow, Constantinople and the Don. The Tsar privately reproached the Cossacks, but told the Turks that the Zaporozhians must be responsible. The Turks would not believe this. They knew well enough that the Zaporozhians and the Don Cossacks were as thick as thieves usually are, that raiders were setting out from the Don as well as from the Dnieper, and so they retaliated against the Cossacks through their Tatar feudatories. In June 1623 the Don Ataman complained that

81

Nogais and Crimean Tatars from Azov had killed many Cossacks and had driven away many of their horses and cattle.[7] In 1625, 2,000 Don Cossacks avenged themselves, destroying Turkish fortifications at the mouth of the river and burning down Tatar villages near Azov. This time relations between Muscovy and the Don were broken off.

They were resumed again a year or two later. But the Cossacks were so preoccupied with their private war against Azov that when the Tsar called for a contingent to help in the Polish war, they refused, pleading poverty and exhaustion. In 1629 the Patriarch Philaret, the Tsar's father, threatened to excommunicate them for disobeying the Tsar's order by raiding the Crimea and Turkey, and next year the Tsar sent an emissary to the Don with a strong escort to demand their obedience. The Cossacks killed him. Once again relations were broken.

But the Tsar was in no position yet to take too hostile a line. Muscovy's military power was still comparatively weak and Cossacks were needed desperately to augment it in its struggle against Poland. So in 1632 the Tsar swallowed his pride and sent Prince Dashkov to the Don to ask for men to fight at Smolensk,[8] offering pay and other rewards if they would swear loyalty to the crown. Several hundreds were ready to go, but they valued their independence too highly to take the hook together with the bait. They recounted all their past services, from the time Ataman Susar Fedorov fought for Ivan the Terrible at Kazan, to prove that they had never sworn allegiance before. They would serve now, they said, but not on account of any oath,[8] only for pay and for booty. The Yaik Cossacks were also persuaded to serve at Smolensk and were given a banner and other rewards by a grateful Tsar, though only a year before he had ordered merchants to be arrested for selling lead and other supplies to the 'robber' Cossacks of the Yaik.

The war with Poland was also the Tatars' opportunity. With the bulk of the Russian forces concentrated in the west the southern border was left virtually uncovered, and between 1632 and 1634 the Tatars managed to carry away over 10,000 Russians captive. As a result the Tsar became more complaisant in his attitude towards Cossack raids on Tatary. In 1634 Don Cossacks killed many Nogais and took 400 of their young girls prisoner, as well as 6,000 sheep, 5,000 horses and 100 camels. This time they were praised for their efforts, though still exhorted to avoid the Crimea and the Turkish citadels at Azov and Keffa.

As a resurgent Muscovy built up a new defensive line south of the old one, it began to suffer far less from Tatar raids. But the Cossacks' fears were more immediate than the Tsar's, and they were mesmerised by the Turkish fort of Azov at the mouth of the Don.[9] It presented a threat to their prosperity and a challenge to their existence. Cossacks sang of themselves as being fed by the wild beasts of the steppe, the birds of the air and the fish in their rivers. But these were insufficient, even when supplemented by the Tsar's pay. And so 'the dark blue sea finds us', they sang. 'Beyond the sea we find gold and silver, and carry off... beautiful wives for ourselves.'[10] Only to reach the sea these days they had to pass the grim Turkish fortifications at Azov—three citadels, one within the other, with eleven corner bastions armed with many guns. Its walls, twenty feet high and fourteen feet thick, were guarded by 4,000 janissaries, and the whole was surrounded by a ditch twenty-five feet deep. In the shadow of Azov lay Nogai settlements, behind it, the might of the Sultan.

It was a formidable proposition for a mere 5,000 Cossacks of the five settlements along the lower Don, but they were acquiring new strength from an influx of migrants, especially from the Ukraine, many of whom were able fighting men. Early in 1637 the Turks were embroiled in a war with Persia, and the Crimean Tatars were marching against Moldavia. With their enemies preoccupied the time was ripe, the Cossack leaders thought, to destroy Azov. To do this they needed help, and help soon came. The Zaporozhians sent 4,000 warriors to their aid, and a delegation, which had gone to Moscow in January to complain to Foreign Office officials of their serious lack of ammunition, returned with a promise of a ton and a half of sulphur and other military supplies besides grain, cloth and money. And so the Don Cossacks' assembly which met in April 1637 decided that Azov had corked them up too long, that they had stood enough of Turks and Tatars who 'insulted our true orthodox Christian faith... and sold our fathers, brothers and sisters across the sea in servitude'. They voted to 'take the town and destroy the Muslim faith'.[11]

83

They elected a campaign ataman, who straightway took out a scouting party in search of 'tongues'—prisoners who could give information about the fortifications and the garrison at Azov. Then the whole Cossack army moved downstream and on 21st April 1637 it arrived outside the citadel. They tried to take the place by storm and failed with heavy losses. So they turned to other methods.

They cut deep ditches all around Azov, threw up walls of earth and thrust out saps towards the Turkish ramparts. A force of Tatars and Circassians riding to the relief of Azov was thrown back, a Turkish ambassador passing on his way to Moscow intercepted and killed, but the Cossacks could make no impression on the towering fortress. The Turks in Azov stood on the walls and laughed at the puny efforts of the ant-like besiegers scurrying below. They laughed too soon. The Cossacks were gaining strength and experience all the time. A hundred large boats brought several thousand men from the upper Don to reinforce them, and the promised consignment arrived from Moscow.

At last, after nine weeks' trumpeting around the citadel, the Cossacks had enough gunpowder to lay a huge charge to undermine its walls. Early on the rainy morning of 18th June a mighty explosion shook the ground for miles around. As the smoke cleared away the Don Cossacks could be seen rushing through a jagged breach torn in the ramparts; on the far side a cloud of Zaporozhians ran forward with long ladders with which to scale the walls. For three days a desperate struggle went on inside Azov. The surviving Turks were thrown back into the keep, but at last they, too, succumbed. Azov had fallen. The Cossacks had their outlet to the sea.

Only 4,400 Cossacks survived the operation. They scrimmaged around among the ruins, searching for booty and divided it up, sparing a share, too, for the relatives of those who died. Many of them then departed but others arrived, and by November there were still as many as 4,000 Cossacks at Azov and as the weeks went by the place took on something of its former bustling atmosphere as a trading centre. Persian, Greek and even Turkish merchants arrived, Russians selling arms did particularly good business, and, as news of the victory

Zaporozhian Cossacks at play

Cossack women helping their menfolk at the siege of Azov

spread, tradesmen, serving people, peasants and freemen flocked south from Muscovy bringing their modest contributions. Some carried a little grain or leather to barter, others came to sell their services as oarsmen or their labour as masons to repair the shattered fortifications.

Azov became the centre of the Don Cossacks, but they were uncertain if they could keep it long. For the moment the Sultan was embroiled in wars with Persia and with Venice, but sooner or later he would send more force against them than they could withstand by themselves. So in July they had sent to Moscow asking for the Tsar's active help in holding the place. He was not unsympathetic, and his people were fired with admiration for the Cossack David's exploit against the Turk Goliath. But Muscovy could not afford to provoke the mighty Turks. When the Sultan protested, the Tsar dissembled, said Azov had been taken without his permission, that the Cossacks were 'a free people'. He admonished them for taking Azov and for killing the Turkish ambassador, though this was something of a diplomatic façade, since he did nothing to make the Cossacks leave, and continued to send them pay and supplies and to allow merchants to cross the border and trade with them.

All through 1638 and 1639 people poured into Azov, until its population swelled to as many as 10,000. It seemed they would be needed for the Turks made peace with Venice and with Persia and began to fit out a great expedition to recapture Azov. But in March 1640, before it was ready to sail, the Sultan died and the customary struggle between the candidates for the succession dictated a postponement.

Meanwhile the Tsar had been generous with his aid. Besides 6,000 rubles he had sent over 65,000 bushels of flour, 25,000 of biscuit and 10,000 of groats from the granaries of Moscow, 200 barrels of liquor from Voronezh, and five tons of sulphur, three of lead, 350 iron cannon balls and a hundredweight and a half of slow-match from the new arms factory at Tula.[12] But the military supplies were only barely adequate; the food quite insufficient. The Cossacks were soon complaining they had 'nothing to eat or wear', that 'everyone has been suffering from nakedness, from bare feet and from hunger'. Many began to leave Azov in search of sustenance, and by the beginning of

1641 only 1,000 men remained. When he had been fighting the Turks, the Shah of Persia had promised to send men to help the Cossacks. He would not do so now, and rather than let the Turks re-take it, the Cossacks thought of offering Azov to the Tsar. 'And now, Lord', ran their appeal, 'we have no means of holding your imperial domain the citadel of Azov . . . And we humbly beseech you' to take 'the town of Azov'.[13]

There would be no immediate response, but meanwhile, full of hope, they rejected an offer from the Crimean Khan to surrender his Cossack prisoners and pay a sizeable reward for the surrender of the citadel. As news spread that the Turkish expedition would soon set sail, their Cossack comrades rallied to them. Reinforcements including 1,000 Zaporozhians arrived, and soon five or six thousand pairs of willing hands were toiling hard to strengthen the defences, filling sandbags and checking the 200 obsolescent cannon.

Early in June 1641 seventy galleys and nearly a hundred smaller ships bore in towards Azov. The fleet carried the army of Sultan Ibrahim I, a force, which the Cossacks, with heroic exaggeration, estimated at over 250,000 men. Most probably it was no larger than 30,000; but still enough to outnumber the Cossacks six to one.

The Turks pitched their spacious tents all round the citadel, trained 129 huge siege guns on it and called on the Cossacks to surrender. They refused. So, to the blaring of horns, men of the crack janissary corps, backed by Tatars and Moldavians, advanced towards the walls. Several times they rushed forward only to be thrown back. The Cossacks had drawn first blood. But this was merely the beginning of a month's long struggle. Turkish bombardments were soon doing serious damage to the fortifications, and to the Cossacks behind them. As balls weighing half a hundredweight crashed down among them, the Cossacks began to dig. Slowly, laboriously, they threw up earthen ramparts behind the shattered walls; they scratched fox-holes into the ground and hid in them like mice, seeking shelter from the cannon shots. But, industrious as moles, they tunnelled outwards too, burrowing out a network of trenches and saps, and crawled forward along them to lay charges under the enemy's positions, then scurried back again to wait for the explosions.

And while the battle raged on underground the Cossacks made sudden sorties on the surface, raided Turkish ammunition dumps to replenish their supplies and sent fire-ships scudding in against the Turkish fleet. But the pressure against them was unremitting. They suffered four full-scale storms and many lesser attacks, and soon the 800 Cossack women in Azov were fighting alongside their surviving menfolk in the places of the fallen.

Casualties were extremely heavy on both sides, but the Cossacks could afford them less. By the end of September only 3,000 Cossacks remained alive. They were ragged, hungry and utterly exhausted, and most of them were wounded too.[14] Unable to hold out any longer they drew up plans for a suicidal breakout. But as the day for their departure dawned, they noticed considerable activity in the enemy camp. The guns were being dragged away; the tents were being dismantled. The Turks were pulling out before them.

It had been an epic siege, but the cost was heavy. The Cossacks lacked the men, material and money to rebuild the ruins, and as long as they stayed they would be a prey to Tatar raiders. And so, in October 1641, Ataman Vasiliev and his delegation presented their final appeal in Moscow. 'We took it with our blood', he told the Tsar. Now he should accept the town from the Cossacks 'in heredity'.[15] The Tsar was tempted, sent inspectors to Azov and convened a great Assembly. But the estimated cost was far too high. Ten thousand soldiers would be needed to hold the citadel. It would put an extra burden of 200,000 rubles a year on the exchequer. And it would bring war with Turkey, for reports from Constantinople indicated that the Sultan was still determined to re-take the place. So it was that towards the end of April 1642 the Tsar enjoined the Cossacks to 'abandon' Azov, 'and return to their old settlements'[16] on pain of incurring his 'royal anger'. With members of their delegation held as hostages in Moscow to ensure their compliance, the Cossacks destroyed what remained of the fortifications, and reluctantly departed. The Turks soon took their place. The sacrifice had been for nothing; Azov would be rebuilt, the Cossacks cut off from the sea again.

The exhausted Don Cossacks were now becoming a prey to the Tatars and the wrinkle-eyed, ear-ringed Nogais on whom they themselves had used to prey. In April 1642 Tatar raiders burned down the Cossack settlement of Manych and hustled its inhabitants away into captivity. In June, the Don capital, Razdorskaya, was besieged, and in the winter of 1645–6 their new capital, Cherkassk. Other Cossack villages were destroyed, their defenders slaughtered, their families, horses and cattle driven away. And as the Turks and Tatars took their revenge, the battered Cossacks of the Don were driven closer into the arms of Muscovy.

They appealed desperately for help, and Muscovy gladly responded, sending them money and supplies, turning a blind eye to runaways bound for the Don and even raising recruits to help defend them. By May 1646, 3,205 men had arrived and with their help the Cossacks got past Azov to the sea, boarded several Turkish ships, conducted a retaliatory campaign under a Muscovite commander against the Crimean Tatars, and so beat up the Nogais that the raids momentarily ceased. But many of the newcomers soon left[17] and in 1647 Cherkassk lay under siege again. The Cossacks asked for soldiers to protect them, and next year the government sent Andrei Lazarev with a thousand troops to their aid. But Lazarev tried to act the governor over them, began to order them about, and to look for unofficial runaways among them. The Cossacks' reaction was measured. They intercepted money and supplies destined for Lazarev and his men,[18] and shared it out among themselves.

The Don Cossacks' period of absolute independence was already drawing to a close. In 1632 when their representatives had been forced to swear loyalty to the Tsar, the full assembly had repudiated that promise. But by the middle of the seventeenth century the Cossacks were heavily dependent on Muscovy economically, and they knew it. The barges carrying the Tsar's pay down to them each year were met with an increasing degree of ceremony. And the authorities began to exploit their reliance on it. The process of breaking in the border Cossacks, of forcing them to obey the Tsar's demands, had already begun. But a land-locked Muscovy, threatened as it was by stronger powers to the north, west and south, could not yet afford to antagonise them to a point at which they might seek alliance with the Tsar's enemies or be goaded into confrontation with the state. As yet they were treated benignly, as little allies. But the government was paying the Cossack pipers, and it would soon demand to call the tune.

Big brother seemed friendly enough, but his beady eye was calculating their weaknesses. The Tsar's envoys sent to the Don in 1646 were instructed to behave respectfully towards the Cossacks, but to act as spies—to report on their numbers and their fortifications, count their guns, equipment and ammunition stores, estimate how much grain they imported from the Ukraine, and their plans in general.[19] In the light of this information, their annual pay was soon cut by half. In 1648 Ataman Yakovlev complained that the grain sent was enough for only 1,000 men, and that the money allowed established Cossacks a measly ruble and a half and newcomers nothing at all.[20] Increases were deliberately kept lagging behind the new growth of the Don community, so that as more runaways arrived, tensions were set off within the community that Moscow could exacerbate and exploit to further her own ends.

Despite the wide expanses that separated them, the various Cossack communities were subject to much the same conditions, difficulties and pressures, and the pattern which emerged in the relationship between Muscovy and the Don was repeated elsewhere. The Yaik Cossacks living in the low-lying plain east of the Volga, 500 miles to the north-east of the Don, had been persuaded to serve with the Muscovite army at Smolensk, but while the young men were away, the Kalmyks had laid siege to their chief settlement. Somehow it had held out until their return, but the continued pressure of aggressive tribesmen forced the community into reliance on Muscovy just as the Don Cossacks had been, and from 1646 a contingent of soldiers was actually stationed on their lands. They, too, were economically dependent on Muscovy as well. They had to get salt, essential to preserve their fish, from pans deep in tribal areas or else from Muscovy where the government controlled the sale. Samara and Syzran, the nearest markets for their surplus catch on which their economy depended, might at any time be closed to them, and though the Tsar exempted them from double trading duty he might always cancel that concession. The Tsar paid them for the warriors they sent to serve him, but again, not generously, and by 1700 the pay was sufficient for less than a fifth of the 2,000 Cossacks of the Yaik community.[21]

The Cossacks who had settled by the gushing river Terek in the far south under the shadow of the towering mountains of the Caucasus, were paid on an individual scale—at first a ruble and a quota of flour for the atamans, and half a ruble and a rather smaller share of flour for ordinary Cossacks, double on campaign. Though they learned from friendly tribesmen how to grow maize and cultivate vines and silk worms, the Terek Cossacks managed to eke out only a very primitive existence, suffered much from fevers, and with the adoption of Islam by their nearest neighbours, lost ever more of their numbers from raiding parties. They were reinforced, largely by Muscovite soldiers and their families and by foreign prisoners of war sent out by the government, and though these newcomers were successfully absorbed into the community, the dependence of the Terek Cossacks on Muscovite goodwill was to become just as marked as those of the Don and of the Yaik.[22] Only an influx of renegade elements from the Don and the great distance which separated them from Moscow, helped them to preserve an essential independence longer than most other Cossack communities.

But the more easterly communities were only gradually falling into dependence on the state; Cossacks in the west were already dominated by it. The Cossacks of the Ukraine had developed differently from the rest. They had multiplied much faster here than to the east across the steppes, many had taken to the plough, and they had become subject to Polish interference, for as sectors of 'the wild country' had promised to change into an agrarian borderland, expansionist Lithuanians and Poles from the north and west had shown themselves anxious to bring the Ukraine within the ambit of organised government. This process was now almost complete, but in reacting against it, the Cossacks plunged the Ukraine into anarchy and brought troubles to the Polish state which, if less serious than they had wrought in Muscovy during the Times of Troubles, helped permanently to sap its strength.

The tensions in the Ukraine had been mounting for over 150 years, ever since nobles and gentlemen from Poland and Lithuania had first moved in. In 1569 Lithuania and Poland had united and the Ukraine had become formally a part of Poland, the most feudalised state in eastern Europe. And the intruding Polish gentry were Catholics, not Orthodox like the Cossacks. Products and proponents of an alien culture and an alien system, which they had gradually forced on the Ukraine, they had become the more hated and despised by the rough Cossacks living there as they had grown richer, more arrogant, and more effete.

The Polish kings had hired some Cossacks as militiamen, paying them in money and in cloth and granting them tax immunities. In time, only these of all the Cossacks who had settled down to farm the empty steppe were recognised as free from the authority of, and feudal obligation to, the Polish-Lithuanian landlords. Their names were inscribed in a register, and it was reckoned that this minority of 'registered' Cossacks, at least, would have an interest in supporting the system, and help to tame their less privileged comrades.[23]

Yet despite economic concessions, and the grant of a special regalia, the kings were not entirely successful in forging the registered Cossacks into a separate caste imbued with a loyalist spirit. The regalia was alien, so was the title 'Hetman' accorded to their commander, whereas strong ties of blood and fellow-feeling linked them with Cossacks excluded from the register and with the fiercely independent Zaporozhian Cossacks still safe from state interference in the 'wild country' to the south. Much to the Poles' annoyance they would frequently pocket their pay and promptly go off to join the Zaporozhians on some profitable expedition.

As for the unregistered Cossack majority, the Poles refused to recognise that they had any rights at all. As early as 1582 the Cossacks had complained that the governors were 'inventing' duties, extorting taxes from them, confiscating their property when they died, and throwing them into gaol without just cause.[24] When their pleas were ignored they had resorted to other ways to rectify their grievances, and in 1591, with Zaporozhian support, Christopher Kosynski had raised a rebellion. His followers, it was said, had been possessed by extraordinary 'stubbornness and self-will', taking no heed of God, the King, nor of 'the most frightful consequences' to themselves.[25] They had

91

been defeated nevertheless, but before long riots and revolts were sparking off in the Ukraine like reports from a Chinese cracker. In 1595 Cossacks went ravaging into the western Ukraine, others, including a number of registered Cossacks, careered north into White Russia, and the peasants joined in *en masse* in a desperate attempt to free themselves from their lords. 'The whole Ukraine', complained Hetman Zholkewski, had 'gone Cossack.'[26]

But these risings failed and many Cossacks and Ukrainian peasants fled to the Sech and to the Don. Those who remained hoped for security as free farmers, but in vain. The very presence of free Cossacks in the Ukraine was an incitement to the tied peasants the Polish gentry had imported into the country. The Poles would tolerate a few Cossacks raised to the status of Polish gentlefolk, and more were necessary to man the frontier defences, but the majority, they insisted, must be down-graded to the rank of peasants and serfs. In 1596 the Poles, declaring them to be traitors, began to take over their lands.

Some registered Cossacks, exempt from these expropriations, and attracted to the richness and sophistications of the Polish gentry's way of life, began to identify their interests more closely with the Polish oligarchs than with the Cossack brotherhood. Their old loyalties might have receded altogether had it not been that the Poles tried to force their Catholicism on the predominantly Orthodox Ukraine.

The Jesuits had started work there in the 1570s and by 1596 the Orthodox Metropolitan of Kiev had been persuaded to submit to the Pope, though retaining Orthodox rituals in his diocese. The ecumenism of this Uniat church was not popular with most Ukrainians. Catholicism was the religion of the foreign oppressor, and as pressure on them increased, their loyalty to the Orthodox creed and their contempt for the Uniates had become ever fiercer.

Yet after the disturbances of the 1590s there was no major confrontation between Pole and Cossack for several years. The Poles needed more Cossacks to fight the Sultan and the Tsar; the Cossacks had needed the pay this service offered. But the reckoning was only postponed. Cossacks returned from the wars less than ever inclined to subject themselves to the rule of lords.

Moreover the Poles could not always afford to pay the extra Cossacks they hired, and some who were dismissed without pay in 1613 promptly raided royal estates to take their due.

Meanwhile the restrictions on Cossack freedom had been mounting. It had been decreed that the entire population should be subject to the jurisdiction of the local gentry or the bailiffs of the royal estates. In 1609 government agents had reported that Cossacks were ignoring these instructions. They were satisfied with their own system of government, would defer only to 'their own ataman courts'. So the Poles had abolished them and the Cossacks had been bound 'to subject themselves to the authorities of the places where they live',[27] where necessary by means of force.

And the Cossacks had other enemies besides the Poles. In 1616 predatory Tatars of the Crimea swept right through the Ukraine and into Podolia, and carried a host of captives away with them. Many a Ukrainian Cossack straightway joined the Zaporozhians in a retaliatory raid on the Crimea to liberate these prisoners. This prompted a Turkish protest to the Poles, who responded by warning the registered Cossacks not to attack the Tatars. They also forbade them to accept recruits without government permission. The registered Cossacks had to be kept under their control, and yet it was to the man who had led the raid on the Crimea that the Poles turned when they themselves were threatened.

Sagaidachny had been Ataman of the Zaporozhians. Now he was appointed Hetman of the registered Cossacks. In 1619 he negotiated the increase of the register to 3,000 while conceding that registered Cossacks should only be allowed to live on crown estates. As a result many Cossacks were evicted by private landlords. Outraged Cossacks elected a rival hetman and threatened to tear the country apart again in civil war, but common cause against the Turks dispelled the threat. In 1620 the Poles asked Sagaidachny to raise 20,000 Cossacks for the defence of the realm and with the climate changed he was able to procure concessions. An Orthodox hierarchy was re-established under the Patriarch of Jerusalem, and one major Cossack grievance was, at least temporarily, allayed.

The Cossacks gave good service in the war. Sagaidachny won a great victory at Khotin in 1621 and the Turks were forced to

D*

make peace. But the Cossacks did not profit from it. While at Khotin they had asked the King to register every Cossack who had served in the war and to allow them to live on private as well as royal estates. But for the victory they might have had their way, but, like the councillors of Hamelin, anxious to be rid of the Pied Piper once he had cleared their town of rats, the Poles were concerned only to discharge the Cossacks at minimum cost once the danger was over.

The Cossacks returned disconsolately to homes they thought their own. Many of them, especially in the south-eastern Ukraine, continued to avoid paying rent on land they or their forefathers had got by squatter rights, at a time when it was part of the 'wild country'. Others still lived in shanty suburbs of the towns, refusing to pay dues. In 1622 there were over a thousand 'disobedient' Cossack households in the Cherkassk area alone, and since Cossacks themselves drew up the lists there were always more Cossacks registered than the number the King specified. By 1622 even the Poles reckoned they would be fortunate in effectively limiting the register to 5,000.

The concession was too small. In 1625 the Cossacks rose again, but the Poles managed to find a leading Cossack, Mikhail Doroshenko, who was prepared to compromise. The Poles regained control upon promising to register 6,000 men, though only the 'best', most reliable elements. The new deal satisfied no one. The Polish gentry in the Ukraine felt unsafe, the Cossacks still felt threatened. Both sides resorted to myth calling up inaccurate visions of an ideal past to support their arguments. The 'illegal' Cossacks insisted on their 'ancient privileges', while a Pole writing in 1625 bemoaned the changes in their ways. Once, he claimed, the Cossacks had been 'unacquainted with plenty and intemperence'; but now the ranks of those 'old and worthy warriors' were swelled by a 'crowd of unwarlike rustics' given to 'quarrels and mobbing. . . . Prudence has been replaced by plunder, discipline by unrestrained tumult, subjection to authority by wilfulness'.[28]

Storm after storm broke out. In 1630 some 10,000 Cossacks burst out of the Sech and into the Ukraine, where, joined by many registered Cossacks, they defeated an army of 12,000 Poles. But the movement collapsed when the Poles promised to increase the register to 8,000. Two years later Cossacks refused to fight the Russians. After some trouble the Poles got them to march but next year they killed their unpopular commander and marched back home again. The Poles were forced to call a truce with the Russians, and once again restored order by a judicious increase of the register.

The Poles had long considered the Zaporozhians to lie at the root of their troubles with the Ukrainian Cossacks. They were the guardians of the Cossacks' liberty and an attraction to all the oppressed in the Polish empire. The tide of runaways to the Sech was growing and the registered Cossacks stationed on the border could not be relied on to cut the traffic. So the Poles built the fort of Kodak above the rapids, and garrisoned it with mercenary dragoons. The Zaporozhians pulled it down. The Poles immediately rebuilt it.

The affair highlighted the growing tensions. The fifty-year tax exemptions, which had encouraged some Cossacks to settle down and serve the Polish order, were running out. Cossacks now had to prove title to the land they farmed, which few could do, or else fall under the gentry's private rule. Discriminatory laws were not only proliferating, they were being enforced. Cossacks were even forbidden to make or brew liquor. Yet the law did not protect them: a gentleman, it was said, could kill a Cossack and go unpunished. Many registered Cossacks, seeing nothing but slavery ahead of them, were leaving for the Sech; a large section in the Polish Sejm, or parliament, was demanding the liquidation of the register, an end to the recognised Cossack caste. Both sides began to smell blood.

At the last moment the King was persuaded not to abolish the register, though only in return for ensuring that it did not exceed the number officially laid down. But in May 1637 the Poles announced a 'purge'—and sparked off another conflagration.

Backed by both Zaporozhians and registered Cossacks of the Ukraine, a Cossack called Pavlyuk was declared Hetman and led a new outburst of terror in which Cossack loyalist officers were killed, estates sacked, and Cossack forms of government introduced. But Polish troops crushed the rising and carried Pavlyuk off to Warsaw to be beheaded.

A new register was drawn up and each man made to swear

loyalty. This was done very hurriedly for in February 1638 5,000 Cossacks had gathered on the Sech under a new leader, Ostryanitsa, and they were soon on the march. The Poles drove them out across the Russian border but then had to cope with yet another rebel force under a new leader, Dmitri Guna.[29] Guna, too, was beaten, but the Poles had had enough of Cossack lawlessness. This time even the privileged registered Cossacks were made to suffer.

Though as many as 60,000 men claimed Cossack status the register was limited to 6,000; all officers were to be appointed by the government, not elected as before; travel to or from the Sech was banned on pain of death. The pace of enserfment was quickened, oppression of the Orthodox Church increased. The Ukraine was fast becoming a police state founded solely on the interests of the Polish gentry.

The Cossacks bowed sullenly under the whips of their alien masters. According to the Ukrainian chronicler called 'the Eye-Witness', they were being reduced to a condition 'no better than that of slaves', grooming the squires' horses, filling their store-houses, tending their dogs. In war their status was no higher. Often deprived of their pay and plunder, their bravery earned credit only for their commanders and if one were missing it was said he had deserted. They were subjected to 'barbaric punishments for the least offence. Even children have been killed and many a time our . . . women and daughters have been subjected to abuse. . . . It would be bad enough if it was only the squire who robbed [us], but . . . some wretched Jew will also enrich himself [at our expense] . . . invent various taxes . . . [for Orthodox] weddings, impose a duty for christening children, collect a levy for milling grain. . . . They force us to join the Uniates . . . sell up the church plate' and drive the Orthodox priests away.[30]

'The Eye-Witness' wrote with the bias of a Russian Orthodox monk, but his feelings were shared by the mass of Ukrainians. For nine long years they suffered this regime without open protest. And yet when at last they made their greatest bid for freedom, they were led not by some poor Cossack excluded from the register, nor by some fiery Zaporozhian, but by a member of the Cossack 'gentry'.

'. . . faced with threatening neighbours and
constant danger, he . . . got used to looking
them straight in the eye, forgetting that
such a thing as fear existed . . .'

—Gogol, *Taras Bulba*

4 Bogdan Khmelnitski and a Cossack struggle for independence

The appearance of the Ukraine in the autumn of 1647 (see pp.
16-17) belied the mood of its inhabitants. The countryside around
Kiev seemed quiet, idyllic. The gently undulating prairie was
speckled with daub and wattle cottages gleaming white under
the gold of their straw-thatched roofs. There were neat hamlets,
picturesque towns, and, occasionally, the crenellated walls of a
fortress thrust upwards from the ground. The forms of men and
women could be seen gathering in a generous harvest. Heavy
wagons groaned their way to market, and sometimes a carriage,
with a gentleman inside, would overtake them, sending up puffs
of dust as it rocked its way over the rutted tracks. Farther south,
towards the marshes and islands of the Dnieper estuary and the
hidden camp of the Zaporozhian Cossacks, the fields merged
into the rippling grey of the untouched steppe. The whole aspect
seemed peaceful, languorous—matching the serenity of the

endless, rolling countryside. Only the peace was superficial.

For the Polish gentleman nodding in his carriage, this was indeed a golden age; but the hearts of the Cossacks and the peasants about him were corroded with hate. Only the power of their Polish governors kept them subdued and a Cossack was about to prove that this power too was superficial. In doing so he set loose a stream of violence as destructive as any Europe was to know in that century of wars.

He was born in 1595, son of a registered Cossack called Mikhail Khmelnitski and christened Bogdan—the gift of God. By local standards the father was a rich man, a 'respectable' Cossack in Polish eyes, whose loyalty had been rewarded with the status of squire and recognition as owner of a small estate. Like Taras Bulba's sons Bogdan received a good education—at Kiev, and at the Jesuit College at Lvov—so that, unlike most Cossack boys, he learned Latin and Polish, and classical legends as well as Cossack tales. But he also learned how to ride a horse and use a musket and a sabre, and like many another fit young Cossack bachelor he spent some time as an apprentice warrior with the Zaporozhians on the Sech. So Bogdan was a product of two cultures: he was a Cossack, but something of a Polish gentleman as well. Either strain might have become dominant.

He had some military adventures early in life and was taken prisoner by the Turks, spending two years in captivity before being ransomed in 1622. But henceforth, despite the discontent and the periodic anti-Polish outbursts going on around him, the general current of Bogdan's life ran smooth. He was a 'respectable', a relatively secure Cossack, and he tried to concentrate on his private affairs with some success. He married Anna Somkova, a Cossack girl, fathered five children by her, and reached the high office of Secretary of the registered Cossacks, which brought him local influence and a useful salary. He had an estate; he was prospering; he wanted peace. But it was difficult to retire from the world in such unstable times.

There were few Cossacks who had not been implicated in the anti-Polish rising of 1637, and though Bogdan seemed to have been less involved than most, he was demoted from Secretary of the Host to centurion of the Chigirin regiment of registered

Cossacks. Nevertheless he retained his estate and, like any Polish gentleman, engaged a Jew to open a liquor shop to swell his income.[1] One of the tiny group who formed the fortunate but diminishing tip of the Cossack iceberg, he counted his blessings. Yet he was daily made aware of the plight of the Cossack mass, and he, too, was to feel the Polish yoke. It was to change him.

The first stage of his metamorphosis began one day in 1646 when Czaplinski, the deputy crown bailiff of Chigirin, seized his best horse for alleged tax arrears. Soon afterwards, Koniec-polski, the bailiff, challenged Bogdan's right to own an estate, and demanded proof of his entitlement. This was not unusual in itself. Other registered Cossacks had had similar experiences. But personal motives as well as general policy entered into this case. His wife had died, and Bogdan had no taste for widower-hood. He had position, prosperity, and a flowing moustache which added much to his attractions. In a word he was eligible. Yet he did not marry. Instead he brought a girl called Helen to live with him at Subbotov. Her origins are as mysterious as her hold over men, but whatever her other qualities might have been, fidelity was not one of them, and among those who considered they had a prior claim on Helen's affections was the same Czaplinski who was pressurising Bogdan.

Next spring, while Bogdan was away trying to establish his rights to the estate, horsemen galloped down the road from Chigirin to Subbotov. Led by the jealous Czaplinski, they burst into Bogdan's homestead and set fire to the mill and to the granary. When Ostap, Bogdan's ten-year old son, protested, they beat the child to death. Leaving a guard upon the house, Czaplinski rode off, carrying Helen away with him.

At one stroke Bogdan, at the age of fifty-two, was reduced from wealth to ruin, deprived of a son and of his mistress. He applied for redress, but the authorities seemed indifferent. Czaplinski admitted that his man had beaten Bogdan's son but denied that the child had died as a result. He admitted abducting Helen but alleged that Bogdan had kept her at Subbotov against her will. It was a Pole's word against a Cossack's and Bogdan could get no satisfaction. And yet Czaplinski was not content: he wanted Bogdan out of the way and sent assassins after him. Warned by his friends, Bogdan managed to elude them, but now he was a fugitive, a middle-aged wanderer, who wore a coat of chain mail against the killer's knife.

The embittered Cossack plotted his revenge. Unable to obtain it by recourse to law, he thought of force, and since his fellow Cossacks constituted the only available force, he set out to exploit their discontent. Henceforth, his grievance as an individual merged with those of his people. 'I have decided to take revenge upon the Polish gentry', he told some registered Cossack friends, 'not only because of the offence done to me personally', but because of the campaign against the Russian Orthodox religion and 'the outrages inflicted on the people.' His motives were mixed. The mourning father, the ambitious soldier, the jealous lover and the politician fired with the vision of liberating his people from a foreign yoke were all inextricably intertwined. But the call was clear and confident. 'As an individual I am powerless', he said, 'but you, my brothers will help me.'[2]

In fact they were reluctant to help at first because, as they claimed, of their oaths of loyalty—and also because they were not inclined to risk losing such favours as they still enjoyed by joining a rebellion which offered doubtful prospects of success. But Bogdan brandished a document before them which would allow them to claim that by fighting the Polish lords they would be serving the King's interests. The document, purportedly issued by the King, promised to restore Cossack privileges, increase the register to 12,000 and to withdraw Polish troops from the south-east Ukraine if the Cossacks would attack the Crimean Tatars. It had been issued in Warsaw, Bogdan told them, in 1646, when the two *esauls* of the registered Cossacks, Ivan Barabash and Ilya Karaimovich, had met the King. He himself had been present, and could assure them of the King's wish to draw the Cossacks into a great Christian alliance directed against the Muslim world. Only the Sejm had been opposed to the plan and since the King could not act in opposition to them he had given Barabash, the *esaul*, a copy of the agreement, which was to come into effect at some unspecified date. How had he obtained the document, then, if Barabash had sworn to keep it secret? Bogdan explained how he had got Barabash dead drunk over dinner one night and sent an agent off to hoodwink his wife into handing it over. It was a tall story, but as Bogdan spoke, he began to take on credence as leader of a hopeful cause, and by the time he had finished many Cossacks wanted to believe him.

Genuine or fake the document was political dynamite. The Poles knew it. They were already hot on Bogdan's trail and soon caught up with him. He was sent to Chigirin under arrest, but old friends there helped him to escape. Together with his son Timofei he fled to the Sech.

He arrived one night in December to a rather cool reception. With a Polish garrison nearby at Kodak the Zaporozhians were cautious nowadays. Besides they remembered his previous loyalty to the Poles. Bogdan eventually convinced them of his change of heart, but as they explained, they lacked sufficient resources to launch a rebellion by themselves. They had tried too many times before and failed. So Bogdan sent messengers to raise the Don Cossacks and went in person to the Crimea to seek the support of the Tatar Khan, Islam Girei III. Here he turned the document to advantage in a completely different way. The King, he explained, intended to invade the Crimea with Cossack help. The Tatars would be well advised to strike first with the Cossacks on his side.

The Khan was doubtful. Even supposing the document to be genuine, his master, the Turkish Sultan, would have to be convinced. Meanwhile he had instructions to keep the peace with Poland. On the other hand, mused the Khan, the Crimea was hard hit by famine, and plundering the Polish *pans*' estates would bring relief to his people. But how could he do this and avoid the Sultan's anger? Then he thought of one of his feudatories Tugai Bey of Perekop. Tugai was powerful, a potential rival. If Tugai were sent to help the Cossacks and things went badly, he could be disowned and so discredited. If things went well, he, the Khan, could arrive in person, and claim all the credit. Either way he could not lose. The Khan roused himself, and sent word to Tugai Bey to ride with 4,000 men to Bogdan's aid.

Meanwhile emissaries disguised as monks were flitting secretly across the Ukraine with Bogdan's call to arms. 'You, whose fathers recognised no laws, who never subjected themselves to kings, be slaves no longer . . .'.³ In village after village Cossacks responded, heading for the Sech singly or in small groups, avoiding the patrols of Polish horsemen. But the fort of Kodak, above the rapids, barred their way. So, towards the end of January Bogdan led the Zaporozhians out to attack it. Thirty dragoons of the garrison were killed, the rest put to flight and most of the registered Cossacks there came over to him. With Kodak neutralised the Cossacks swarmed south. By the beginning of March some 5,000 had gathered on the Sech. Still Bogdan waited. Yet more were on the way.

Then, one evening in mid-April 1648, the cannon of the Sech roared out to signal muster. That night and the next morning motley crowds of Cossacks streamed into the central square responding to the call—so many that they overflowed the meeting ground, and the concourse had to be transferred to a great meadow outside the Sech. The somewhat paunchy figure of Bogdan Khmelnitski, accompanied by the Ataman of the Sech, emerged into the centre of the throng. The crowd fell silent as he began to speak.

He told of his sufferings—the murder of his son, the rape of Helen, the confiscation of his property. He described his escape from Czaplinski's assassins. This was the way the Poles rewarded a Cossack for his services! They were anxious enough for them to fight their battles, he roared, but in peace they treated them worse than dogs. It might be the Ukrainian Cossacks who were suffering now, but the Zaporozhians would also feel the Polish whip, if they did not move now.

The crowd was with him. A voice proposed Bogdan as Hetman and a great shout of approval went up. The Ataman of the Zaporozhians sent for the horse-tail banner and the drums of war, the cannon roared again and frenzied Cossacks hurled up their caps and fired their guns into the air.

Soon a swarm of men and horses was moving northwards out of the Sech, clusters of flags and horse-tail banners bobbing above the swell, and a huge red banner, sewn with the image of an archangel, fluttering at their head. There were 8,000 Cossacks on horse and foot, four guns, and, in the rear, Tugai Bey's 4,000 swarthy Tatars.

The Poles knew they were coming. The Crown Hetman,

Potocki, had sent his son Stephan south towards them with an army of levies, regular troops and white-coated registered Cossacks. In numbers the forces were roughly equal; in artillery the Poles had the advantage. But young Potocki divided his army, sending his Cossacks on by water and taking the rest with him by land. And Bogdan had a secret weapon. His agents had been at work among the registered Cossacks. The two *esauls* were unshakeably loyal, but several colonels were already subverted, and preparing to desert. When they met Bogdan's army near Zheltyye Vody, half-way between Kodak and Chigirin, they flung their banners in the river and led their men over to the other side. Barabash, a handful of loyalists, and some German mercenaries were killed or put to flight.

Young Potocki's 6,000 remaining troops were now heavily outnumbered, but, too proud to retreat, he drew his men up in a square, and waited. One morning early in May the Cossacks crossed the stream which separated them from the Polish square and in their customary triangular formation crept towards it spitting fire. The battle went hard until midday, when some unenthusiastic Ukrainian peasants, pressed into Polish service, deserted, and young Potocki withdrew the remains of his army behind the cover of some earth-works.

It was a strong position, but Bogdan showed himself to be no mean general. The Tatars whom he sent to the Polish rear refused to attack until they could see which side fortune favoured, but by the following morning there could be no doubt. With the Cossacks swarming forward, and the Polish baggage train exposed, Tugai Bey brought his Tatars in to seal off the Poles' only road of escape. Potocki's situation was hopeless. Bogdan called on him to surrender but Tugai Bey pressed on with his attack. Tatar arrows whipped into the crowded mass of Poles. One struck the young Potocki, and the wound proved mortal. The firing ceased at last.

His father, stationed with 8,000 men a hundred miles away, could scarcely believe the news. He retreated, but at a lumbering pace, and ten days after his son's defeat, Bogdan overtook him near Korsun. The Tatars galloped straightway into the attack, and the Cossacks, sabres flashing, followed in behind them. The Poles began frantically to dig themselves in, held out till nightfall, and then withdrew again through the cover of a nearby forest. But Bogdan was determined they should not escape. While his main force struck out after them, he took his fastest horsemen galloping round to head them off. Sent stumbling back into a muddy ravine, the Poles were trapped. Two thousand cavalrymen made a desperate bid to break out. Only half of them succeeded; the rest were cut down. The peasant levies had already deserted; now the remaining Polish regulars laid down their arms.[4]

Potocki and some eighty other lords fell into Bogdan's hands together with thousands of horses, wagonloads of supplies, and forty-one invaluable guns. The Tatars were rewarded with the noblemen, who would fetch a rich ransom, and every Cossack received a handsome share of loot. That night the camp went wild with celebration. Barrels of wine were torn open, singing and shouting rent the air as men pranced and tripped, to the accelerating thrum of balalaikas, over the stripped bodies of the Polish dead.

The victory at Korsun let loose all the avenging Furies. Serfs in the Ukraine would no longer obey their masters; estates as far north as White Russia were sacked and burned. Peasants from Galicia and central Poland rampaged their way east to join the Cossack army. Recruits poured in from the Don,[5] Moldavia and Wallachia—gypsies and vagabonds, peasants and Cossacks, the last well armed, the rest with forks, flails, scythes, even the jawbones of animals fixed to staves.

As the rabble fanned out over the Ukraine, the long pent-up hatreds, social, ethnic, and religious, overflowed. The have-nots revenged themselves on the haves, slaughtering anyone dressed in Polish style, lynching Catholics, stringing up gentlemen with the heads of their wives and children hung round their necks. Men were flayed or burned alive, children slit open, women disembowelled and sewn up again with cats inside them.

The Jews were a major target, and sometimes Polish gentlemen hastened to betray their Jews to save themselves. At Tulchin the insurgents were prepared to spare the Poles for ransom, 'but we'll not pardon the Jews', they said. 'They are our sworn enemies. They insulted our religion ... we have vowed to destroy all their tribe.' Men, women and children were promptly handed over. The Cossacks 'knocked nails into them, burnt them, hacked off their limbs'.[6] Only Jews who would apostasise were spared, and few were ready to betray their faith. Cossacks burst into synagogues, wrenched out the sacred Scrolls of the Law, and, frenzied with vodka, shoved Jews down upon them and cut them to pieces. Thousands of children were thrown into wells which the Cossacks then filled in with earth.

The Jews of Kiev were more fortunate. They fell into Tatar hands, were transported to Turkey, and eventually ransomed by their co-religionists. But tens of thousands were slaughtered in the weeks which followed Korsun and it was the Jews who suffered most. Many more were massacred as the war progressed, or died of the plague that followed it.

The terror produced a counter terror. Prince Jeremy Vishnevetski, a Lithuanian magnate and convert to Catholicism, thundered south with a crowd of dispossessed gentry and their retainers to the rescue of their hard-pressed co-religionists. They battled into Volhynia and Podolia 8,000 strong, like old crusaders with the name of Jesus on their lips and the blood of children on their swords. When he recaptured Nemirov, whose people had fraternised with the insurgents, Vishnevetski had them tortured in such ways 'that they really feel they're dying'.[7] But militarily his progress was slowed down by the Cossack colonel Krivonos, or 'crooked-nose', his equal in brutality.

Though he had Krivonos chained to a gun for a few days as a punishment, Bogdan seemed little concerned about the massacres. He had other preoccupations. Immediately after Korsun he had gone to Chigirin. There he had found Helen, and this time he married her. Bogdan had what he wanted but this was no time for him to retire from the political scene. The Poles had been defeated, but they would not sue for peace. They had been thrown out of the Ukraine before, only to return. So Bogdan offered to settle with them. His terms were moderate in the circumstances—distribution of the Cossacks' back pay, freedom for the Orthodox Church in the Ukraine, relief from taxation and ill-treatment, confirmation of Cossack privileges set out in the secret charter, the document which had played so vital a part in launching the revolt.

He even reaffirmed his loyalty to the crown, though the

protestation sounded empty for the King had died shortly before the battle of Korsun. The Polish monarchy was elective, not hereditary, and a successor had not yet been chosen. For the time being, therefore, power rested with the Sejm, and the Sejm was implacably hostile to Bogdan and the Cossack cause. But Bogdan was not counting on an agreement, and he made good use of the temporary lull, calling on the Don Cossacks for more help, sounding out the Tsar in hope of support, and solidifying his alliance with the Crimean Tatars. That August a new military oligarchy gained power in Turkey. They relaxed the reins on the Crimean Khan and encouraged the Cossacks. But no Tatars had yet arrived when, late in the summer of 1648, Bogdan heard that the Poles were gathering a great army together and headed west from Chigirin.

The Polish force, 40,000 strong, was commanded by a triumvirate of princes—Zaslavski, Koniecpolski and Nicolai Ostrorog. Immensely rich and cultivated men, they were militarily incompetent and neither they nor their underlings would sacrifice one tittle of their accustomed luxuries on campaign. Vast trains of gilded carriages bore them into the Ukraine. The gentlemen in armour who formed the famous Polish heavy cavalry would jog along proudly for a mile or two, then stop for the next banquet. Discipline was lax, and the Dutch, German and Hungarian mercenaries were soon sneering at their disdainful, cavalier commanders. By the time this rabble of aristocrats reached the Pilyavka river and camped confidently on marshy ground it was almost mid-September. Bogdan was nearly upon them.

Thanks to their foreign mercenaries, the Poles withstood the first Cossack onslaughts. For two days the battle raged, the Cossacks being driven back time and again with heavy losses. Then, on the second night the Poles heard a great commotion in the Cossack lines and prisoners reported the arrival of a huge Tatar army led by the Khan. In fact they numbered only 4,000, but Bogdan made them seem more numerous, sending them in next day with a crowd of Cossacks dressed as Tatars and shouting 'Allah'. The Poles massed to meet the attack, a feigned retreat drew two Polish regiments into ambush; then Krivonos tore in against them from the rear.

That night Zaslavski decided he had had enough, and led the chastened Poles away towards Lvov, leaving nearly 100 guns, 120,000 carts and plunder worth ten million zloty behind. When Bogdan advanced through the morning mist he found the Polish camp deserted. He pressed on to Konstantinov, and then to the citadel of Zbarazh. It was deserted, and, deprived of living victims, the Cossacks took their vengeance on the dead, defiling Catholic churches, digging up the corpses of Polish gentlemen and flinging them to the dogs.

Bogdan now had to decide whether to advance on Warsaw, and belie his claim of fighting for Cossack rights alone, and not against the Polish state, or to mark time and allow the Poles to regather their strength. A meeting of Cossack chiefs decided to go as far as Lvov. Here they met resistance, though the inhabitants were soon persuaded to buy them off at the modest cost of 200,000 zloty. Rebel forces also surrounded the citadel of Zamostye, but their offensive spirit was on the wane. Cossacks and peasants, willing enough to fight near home, lost much of their offensive spirit when they were away too long. Now it was autumn, time for the harvest, and many of them began to take the road back to their farms. The campaign was petering out in a series of aimless, inconclusive skirmishes.

Bogdan was content to hold his own and wait for a new King to be elected,[8] who, so he hoped, would be able to make concessions and reach an honourable compromise. In November 1648, the Sejm chose the late King's brother to succeed him and as a sign of good will Bogdan raised the siege of Zamostye—though not before he had wrung a payment from its burghers—and withdrew to await consideration of his proposals. These were not extreme. He did not demand Ukrainian independence, only an increase in the register, a broadening of Cossack rights, the establishment of Orthodoxy—in short, a degree of Cossack home rule. The King soon agreed to most of the demands in principle and promised to send out commissioners to negotiate the details.

Bogdan rode east across the snows, as contemporary accounts have it, resplendent in cloth of gold and mounted on a white charger, and entered Kiev just before Christmas to a tumultuous and triumphant welcome. Bells clashed, guns thundered and the people cheered. Priests and burghers came in procession to greet him; scholars and poets declaimed their eulogies of the man who, in the evening of his life, had suddenly risen through tribulation to the state of hero.

Bogdan spent the holiday in domestic comfort, but with a troubled mind. He was drinking very heavily and suffering severe bouts of melancholy. Responsibility was weighing heavily upon him; the future seemed uncertain. The King's commissioners would soon arrive and he must make a settlement with them that would last. He could not afford to satisfy all his followers. Many Cossacks so far excluded from the register must now be included in it of course, but he knew there must be limits to his demands, and he was not anxious that the Ukrainian peasants, who had contributed so much to his success, should gain much from the rebellion apart from religious freedom. Bogdan would not have their status changed. After all, he was a landlord himself; he even had his Jew. The social structure of the Ukraine had become far more complex than that of the Sech or of the Cossack settlements on the Don, the Terek and the Yaik in the underpopulated borderlands to the east. There were too many conflicting interests for a reversion to the democratic communism of the ideal age of Cossackdom to be thinkable.

Anyway, he was not in a position to demand too much. Poland had been defeated, but she could always rely on powerful Catholic neighbours like Austria if pushed too far. The Ukraine, on the other hand, lacked reliable allies and her economy could not withstand a permanent state of war. Bogdan was trying to set the diplomatic scene to his advantage. The Tsar was sympathetic, sent him gifts of sable, offered supplies of grain and salt but no military alliance. Moldavia and Transylvania, his neighbours to the south-west, also sent envoys, but they were countries of little power or consequence. Turkey was strong and disposed to an agreement with him, but Bogdan dared not allow his relations with the Sultan to alienate the Tsar.

By the time the Polish commissioners arrived at Pereyaslav in February 1649 after a long journey through a hostile countryside Bogdan could count on considerable outside sympathy, but not on sufficient military support. At noon the next day he faced the commissioners in public on the little square of the town.

It was obviously a home match. The roofs of the surrounding

houses were black with sympathetic onlookers, as he stood, handsomely dressed, at the head of his senior officers. The crowd stirred as Adam Kisel led the Polish delegation forward. He brought gifts—a royal charter confirming Bogdan as Hetman, a sapphire-encrusted sceptre, a red banner emblazoned with a white eagle. But feelings were running too high to allow the Polish representatives an easy hearing. Almost at once Kisel was interrupted by an angry Cossack colonel and Bogdan had to roar for silence. Beginning again, Kisel announced that the King 'forgave' the Cossacks for their rebellion; and would grant freedom for the Orthodox religion in the Ukraine, a register expanded to 20,000 and the return of Cossack prisoners. But Bogdan must lead an attack against the Turks and Tatars.

However reasonable Bogdan might privately consider these proposals, the mass of his supporters expected much more. Pressed by his extremist followers, he issued a whole stream of new demands in the days that followed. He was in no position, he explained, to make a private deal. A full Cossack assembly must confirm any terms agreed between them, and it would insist that the Uniat and Catholic Churches in the Ukraine be closed, that a recognised border be traced between the Ukraine and Poland, that the Cossack hetman should decide on the number of Cossacks to be registered, and that the Poles never again give Prince Vishnevetski a command. When the Commissioners protested, Bogdan's demands grew greater and his temper worse. He brought up personal as well as public issues; insisted that his old rival Czaplinski be handed over to him for punishment.

The subtle fox had become a lion. The Poles reported that Bogdan 'flew into rages, shouted with such fury, that we, listening, were turned to wood'.[9] All Kisel's moderation, and he was an Orthodox Christian himself, was of no avail. At last they agreed to extend the truce until May while Bogdan's latest demands were considered in Warsaw.

The truce was never properly observed. Bands of Cossacks and of Polish gentry continued to terrorise the land. As expected, the Sejm rejected the Cossack terms outright and put a price of 10,000 zlotys on Bogdan's head. The time for talk had passed. Sending some Cossacks to hold back troops advancing south

from Lithuania, Bogdan marched west, making a direct bid for
the support of the poor by addressing a proclamation to 'the
common people' first and only then to the Cossacks. The appeal
raised about 20,000 recruits. And the Crimean Khan came to his
support bringing a host of Tatar warriors—Nogais from the
steppes of Astrakhan wearing sheepskins and huge fur hats,
swarthy sharp-shooters from the southern Crimea clad in
brightly coloured blouses, quivers bristling with arrows slung
across their backs. Men said that Bogdan's army was the biggest
that had trod this ground since the time of the Huns and
Tamerlane.[10]

Against it came a Polish army about 10,000 strong under
Prince Jeremy Vishnevetski. The two sides clashed at Zbarazh
towards the end of March. After some heavy fighting Bogdan
forced the Poles back into Zbarazh and then laid siege to them.
They were still there in August, hanging on grimly, even though
they were reduced to feeding on 'the Flesh of Dogs and Horses'.[11]
Then news came that the King was bringing another army to
their relief.

Bogdan already knew this. Cossack women, infiltrating deep
into enemy territory, and runaway serfs had brought reports of
Polish movements weeks before. Bogdan knew that the King
had gathered some 20,000 men by now, that the advance was
inexorable, that his own avowals of loyalty must be broken;
that he must fight the King.

Leaving the infantry behind at Zbarazh, Bogdan and the
Khan moved out with their attendant hordes of mounted men,
and swiftly covered the seventy miles which separated them
from the unsuspecting King. The Poles were bogged down in the
mud, crossing a river near Zborow, when the attack came, and
by nightfall, his position hopeless, the King sent a letter to the
Khan promising a large and lasting tribute if he would desert
the Cossacks. Next day the Cossacks, some thought, were almost
ready to deliver a final blow without the Tatars' aid, when cries
of 'truce' sounded down the ranks. Bogdan had called a halt.

He claimed later that only his loyalty to the King had stopped
his pressing home the last attack. This was a politic lie. The
Khan's changed attitude, bought by Polish gold, was probably
the real persuader. But it was hardly a betrayal. The Khan

took care to put the Cossacks' case before the King and insisted that he grant them amnesty. Bogdan may have had little choice but to accede to a settlement, but the terms he obtained were good.

The treaty of Zborow, concluded a few days after the battle, allowed a register of 40,000. The eastern Ukrainian provinces of Kiev, Bratslav and Chernigov were to form a distinctively Cossack area from which Jesuits, Jews, Polish soldiers, and Catholic landowners were to be barred. The King's governors would remain but only deal with external relations and non-Cossack affairs. The Orthodox Metropolitan of Kiev was given a seat in the Sejm and, not least, Cossacks were allowed to distil spirits and wine duty-free. Bogdan fell on his knees before the King to ask for pardon, which was granted just as formally, and he was confirmed in office as Hetman, responsible only to the King.

The armies dispersed—the Tatars plundering their way back to the Crimea, the defenders of Zbarazh arriving to a hero's welcome in Warsaw, Bogdan to create a new order in the Ukraine.

He organised the Cossacks on a regional basis into sixteen regiments varying considerably in size. Each was commanded by a colonel and divided into sub-regional 'hundreds', also with considerable variations both in number and in complement.[12] Civil and military administration were to a large extent co-terminous. Though the burgher courts continued to function Cossacks also sat on them,[13] and though the towns retained their own administrations they became subject to the Cossack government in practice.

Bogdan's military headquarters at Chigirin became the centre, too, of civil government. The old Cossack staff titles were retained, but in practice the *obozny*, commander of artillery and ordnance, acted as chief of staff, the Secretary of the Host became a sort of Secretary of State, and the general *esaul* a chief of police. Legal and constitutional forms remained much as before, but the pattern of power had changed. On every level the machinery for running an army was geared to administering a state within a state. It was a system that bears comparison with the early Prussian civil service, and with the rule of Cromwell's major-generals in contemporary England. But, influenced by Polish forms, it differed markedly from the governmental systems of other Cossack communities, including the Sech.

Bogdan always treated the Zaporozhian ataman with respect, and made a practice of consulting him, but the Sech remained outside the system. Whereas the Zaporozhians maintained their democracy, Bogdan arrogated most powers to himself, insisting on the right to cancel the elections of all officers as the old-style hetmans had done. Like a head of state, he minted coins bearing his own name, and like any military dictator he kept a personal bodyguard. Though formally subject to the decisions of a general assembly, he rarely called one. But autocrat though he was, his powers were limited—and, in a sense, created—by the fragility of the political situation. He had to satisfy the restless mass beneath him, and yet avoid another clash with Poland which might bring ruin on the order he had created.

A registration of 40,000 Cossacks still failed to accommodate up to ten times that number who now claimed the status.[14] Bogdan was forced to dissemble. He registered 50,000 and ascribed another 20,000 to a private army raised by his son Timofei. A master politician, he kept two lists: one for submission to Warsaw, the other, much larger, for internal purposes.

Even so, most peasants had to be content with the freedom to follow the Orthodox religion—and outside the three Cossack provinces they had not even that satisfaction. It was a sour experience to return to landlords' rule again even if their masters were not Catholics. Feeling themselves betrayed, many fled to virgin lands east of the Dnieper populating what came to be known as the *Slobodskaya Ukraine*. And many serfs who remained, having once tasted freedom, now refused to accept the old system again. They had the sympathy of some of the Cossack colonels, one of whom, Nechai, Colonel of Bratslav, actually led a riot against the local magnate Koretski, and earned Bogdan's displeasure. That winter there were many peasant disturbances in the Ukraine. Bogdan set out to suppress them and this did not endear him to the peasantry. In March 1650 runaways to Zaporozhiye chose themselves a new hetman to rival Bogdan. The movement was stamped on, its leader executed, but Bogdan felt it necessary to make some concessions to the lower orders.

He was reconciled to Colonel Nechai and closed his eyes to some anti-Polish disturbances which forced Kisel, among other landlords, to flee the Ukraine.

But Bogdan dared go no further without inviting another war with Poland. Even if the Ukraine could defend itself alone in the short term, another war would bring ruin to the countryside and threaten economic chaos and collapse. Powerful allies were no easier to find than they had been. He pressed the Tsar for a firm alliance without success. The Turks offered him 'an everlasting peace', allowing the Cossacks free navigation of the Black Sea and the Aegean, and free trade with the Turkish Empire, but the terms were exclusively commercial. Venice offered an alliance, but it was directed against the Turks not Poland.[15]

So Bogdan set about forming a confederacy of little powers with Moldavia, Wallachia and Transylvania. His plan was a curious mixture of political strategy and dynastic ambition, and included a marriage between his son, Timosh, and Roxanda, daughter of Lupul, Lord of Moldavia. But before anything came of it, Polish troops clattered into the Ukraine yet again.

Aware that Bogdan was conducting talks with foreign states in contravention of the Treaty of Zborow, they had begun secret preparations several months before, proceeding carefully at first for lack of funds. But there was no lack of unemployed mercenaries to be hired at reasonable prices now the Thirty Years' War was over and by the beginning of 1650 the Poles had raised a considerable force of professionals. They struck in February and drew first blood, surprising the Bratslav regiment at Krasny while the Cossacks, celebrating a holiday, were mostly drunk. They were soon overwhelmed and their colonel, Nechai, hero of the Podolian peasants, was among those killed.

Colonel Bogun halted the Poles at Vinnitsa and another Cossack force went north to guard against an invasion from Lithuania, gaining time for Bogdan to rally the people for war. But this time the forces were slow to gather. The people were tired, afflicted by famine and depressed at Nechai's death. And now, Bogdan himself was struck down by a personal disaster.

A barrel of money had been missed from his chancery. Bogdan delegated his son, Timosh, to investigate the loss. Suspicion fell on one of Bogdan's favourites, and under torture

113

the man confessed not only to stealing the gold, but to committing adultery with Helen, Bogdan's wife. It was further alleged that Helen planned to poison her husband. In a daze, Bogdan agreed to her execution. Timosh made all the arrangements. The lovers were stripped, lashed together and so hanged above the city gates.

Always disposed to melancholy, Bogdan sought oblivion in drink. Overwhelmed by domestic tragedy, the great leader, the consummate politician, forgot the public crisis and sat irritable and unapproachable in his rooms. His aides could rouse him from his torpor to intermittent bouts of action only with the greatest difficulty and sometimes not at all. It was May, and the King was already on his way to take command of the main Polish army, before Bogdan moved. He headed for Zbarazh, there to await the arrival of the Khan, who had set out reluctantly at the insistence of the Turks. The battle took place in June at a place called Berestechko.

Bogdan's army was smaller than the enemy's, and most of it no better than a rabble. But it was made up of passionate men, Ukrainians fighting for their homes, their rights, their freedom, and fired by a religious spirit of crusaders. The Cossacks, followed by the Tatars, swept into attack 'like thunder clouds blown by a storm'.[16] They were thrown back with heavy casualties. Tugai Bey of Perekop, whom the Khan had sent to help in 1648, was among those killed. That evening the Khan warned Bogdan that if there were no victory the following day, he would probably withdraw.

Next morning the field was obscured by mists wafting up from the surrounding marshes. The Cossacks had corralled their wagons into a *tabor*; the Tatars were drawn up in a semi-circle to their left. Bogdan, temporarily emergent from his alcoholic fog, rode round the ranks, bearing an orb and a sword blessed in Jerusalem, to encourage the men.

This time, it was the Poles who attacked, and about three in the afternoon they succeeded in making a small breach in the *tabor*. They were soon driven out again, but the Khan had seen the incident, and promptly turned his horse away. His *beys* and *mursas* followed, and soon the entire Tatar contingent was sweeping away from the battlefield.

Bogdan himself immediately set off after the Khan, leaving command to a Colonel Dzhedzhaliya. As the rains poured down on the bloody field of Berestechko, the toll of dead mounted and doom loomed large for the heavily outnumbered Cossacks. They fought on, hoping for Bogdan's imminent return, shortened the perimeter, scarred the ground with trenches, made brave sorties. But the red pennants of the enemy crowded ever closer round them; a torrent of missiles tore into their ranks; the ground trembled constantly beneath their feet.

Still Bogdan did not return. It is not clear why. Either he was kept prisoner by the Khan, or else he was persisting in his efforts to bring the Tatars back, realising that if he failed the battle was lost anyway. In any case the Khan, chewing his sunflower seeds and spitting the husks out periodically upon the floor, remained impervious to Bogdan's fretting. This was the Cossack's problem, not his.

Morale in the Cossack camp began to fall. At night extra guards had to be posted to check the increasing flow of deserters. Dissensions arose among the colonels, and at last Dzhedzhaliya asked for an armistice. The Poles insisted that Bogdan and all the senior officers surrender and submit to the Sejm's decision on their future and that of the Ukraine. The rebels, especially the peasants, declared they would rather die than accept such terms, and after a stormy assembly Dzhedzhaliya was replaced by the more popular and dashing Colonel Bogun.

The Cossacks prepared to fight on, slaughtered their prisoners, passed on encouraging rumours of Bogdan's imminent return, sang lusty choruses to drown the cries of the dying. But the Poles held them in a vice, and after ten days even Bogun concluded he must save at least a remnant of the Cossack force.

That night shadowy figures made a brushwood path over the marshes to the rear of the battle-scarred *tabor*. In silence, most of the Cossacks crept out along it. Awaking to find themselves betrayed, many peasants panicked and rushed headlong into the marsh to be sucked down. The Poles broke into the camp and set about the remaining rebels and camp-followers sparing neither women nor children. Eighteen guns, twenty standards, Bogdan's war chest and regalia of office fell into Polish hands.

Isolated groups still held out in the marshes for a time. A

band of three hundred fought on till only one remained alive. He manoeuvred a boat along a creek and there shot down his assailants one by one, until his powder ran out, then defended himself with a scythe. For three hours this Cossack held out 'against all assaults',[17] refusing the King's offer to spare his life. A German mercenary's pike ran him through at last, and when his corpse was examined they found no fewer than fourteen bullets in it. Such was the stuff of a Cossack. But for all their courage, it was a disastrous summer for the Cossacks. Berestechko was their greatest, but not their only defeat. Kiev, the pearl at the centre of Bogdan's short-lived empire, was occupied. And then the plague came to scourge the Ukraine.

Weeks later Bogdan re-appeared at last. He found the country in turmoil. A 'black' assembly called in his absence had repudiated him, and roaming bands of partisans still refused him recognition. But the wily politician had not lost his old persuasive powers, and realising that he was the man most likely to salvage something from the wreck of Cossack fortunes, the majority came to accept his authority again, albeit less enthusiastically than before.

Meanwhile, the King had returned to Warsaw, and many of the gentry, having discharged their feudal duties, followed him. Vishnevetski, the old scourge of the Cossacks, died soon after Berestechko and though the Polish army moved forward still, they were finding food increasingly difficult to obtain, and, hampered by guerrillas and reduced by disease, the impetus went out of their advance.

Bogdan, by contrast, had recovered his old energies. The old amorist, now in his mid-fifties, had collected a third wife, Anna Zolotarenka, sister of the Colonel of Korsun. The marriage had reinvigorated him. He collected 4,000 men, and ordered a general muster. Then a force of plunder-hungry Tatars joined him, and the Poles realised that they must offer terms a good deal softer than those of Berestechko.

Nevertheless, the treaty Bogdan negotiated at Belaya Tserkov in September with the King's emissary, Adam Kisel, displeased both the peasants and the Cossacks. The register was to be reduced to 20,000 who must all reside in the province of Kiev, which angered Cossacks resident outside it. The rights of the

Bogdan Khmelnitski, *from a contemporary portrait*

Circassians and a Kalmyk, *Seventeenth Century print*

Ciras - Tartars

Orthodox Church were confirmed, but Jews were to be allowed to return. Direct exchanges with the Tatars and all foreign governments were forbidden. But these were the best terms he could get. Bogdan duly swore allegiance to the King with great show of humility and copious tears, which, in the words of a French commentator, 'he had always ready to shed, when the necessity of his affairs required'.[18]

So far from breaking the agreement, he never carried it out. The situation was beyond his control. There was a fresh wave of peasant attacks on the gentry, and a mass emigration east across the Dnieper. Bogdan was forced to submit a register of 40,000 Cossacks. The Sejm refused to confirm it, and he refused to make another. He dared not. His association with the unpopular treaty made him fear for his position. Henceforth he kept a wary eye on popular colonels like Bogun who might exploit the growing opposition. He was to have at least three of his potential rivals killed.

But the suspicious Bogdan retained his dynastic ambitions. Since the Cossacks' defeat, Lupul of Moldavia had called off the marriage arranged between his daughter and Bogdan's son, but Bogdan was determined it should still take place and in May 1652, only eight months after concluding the agreement, he set out to enforce the marriage contract, in open contravention of his undertaking to the King. Polish troops barred his way, but at the battle of Batog he swept them aside. The army rode on, and Timosh led his bride back in triumph to Chigirin.

Home again, Bogdan coolly applied to Warsaw for forgiveness, displaying a modern grasp of the techniques of manipulating facts by explaining that the battle was caused by the Polish commander attacking his son. Unnerved by this latest defeat, the Poles did nothing. It was stalemate again. But there was no reconciliation and by the spring of 1653 the King was building yet another army with which to destroy the Ukrainian vipers' nest for good.

Meanwhile Lupul, Bogdan's kinsman now and his ally once again, was proving a liability rather than an asset. Invaders from Transylvania and Wallachia threw him out of his capital, Jassy, and he called for Bogdan's help. Timosh rode out to the rescue, threw the intruders out, but then pressed his luck too far by invading Wallachia. Trapped in the fortress of Sochav, Timosh sent for his father, but before Bogdan could arrive, Timosh was wounded, a truce was arranged, and the Cossacks left for home. On the way, Timosh's wound developed gangrene. Instead of a beleaguered army, Bogdan met a cortège. His cup of sorrows, twice filled already, overflowed again.

Bogdan had left the Ukraine virtually unguarded but the Poles had started late. Now he stirred himself from mourning, called up the Tatars and the Zaporozhians, and marched off to meet the King. No great battle was necessary, however. It was late autumn and turning cold, and the Polish army, inadequately provisioned and with no winter clothing, was dissolving away. The King could not go on. So, again, he bought the Tatars off, promising to pay them tribute and to observe the terms of Zborov. Bogdan was not a party to the agreement, but he seemed content.

Yet, after six years of destruction, plague and famine, with vast once prosperous districts reduced to derelict graveyards, it was clear that the Ukraine could not support an independent status. Though it was rich in natural resources, could manufacture gunpowder, had a nascent iron industry, and was potentially the granary of eastern Europe, it could not meet its needs in time of war. The Cossacks had won no major battle without Tatar aid, and had had to import armaments and even grain from Muscovy. To develop its economy it needed peace and this the Poles would never allow.

Time and again Cossacks and peasants had united against the enemy, but in peace they were split into many factions, which even Bogdan, with his consummate political ability and well-timed ruthlessness, could barely control. For all his brilliant attempts to balance aspirations at home and pressures from outside, he knew that the Ukraine could not survive much longer on an almost permanent war-time footing. He must find a strong protecting power.

But the Khan was unreliable and Turkish protection would rouse all Christendom against him. An alliance with Moldavia, Wallachia and Transylvania would prove too complex and too weak, and Sweden was too far away—a strategic essential Bogdan understood but which Mazepa was later fatally to ignore.[19]

There remained only Muscovy. She had given moral and economic support throughout the struggle. Her people shared the same religion, common origins and customs, and fundamentally the same language with the Cossacks of the Ukraine. And at last it seemed that she would take them under her wing.

In October 1653 the Zemski Sobor—the great assembly of the free classes of all Russia—recognised the Ukrainian Cossacks as a 'free people', no longer bound by their oaths to the Polish King and called for them to be brought under the Tsar's protection. At the end of December the Tsar's envoy, Buturlin, came to Pereyaslav. Bogdan arrived there a few days later and summoned an assembly. The town became an ant-heap as thousands of black-coated Cossacks scurried into the central square. Then at eleven on the morning of 8th January 1654, Bogdan's stocky figure emerged, an aigret glinting in his turban, orb and sceptre in either hand. He recommended that the Cossacks give their loyalty to the Tsar, and when the *esaul* of the Host called for their decision, the shouts of agreement—'We want to be under the eastern Tsar!'—were overwhelming.[20]

A procession formed, and wound its way to the church to take the oath of allegiance. Then there was an unexpected check. Bogdan asked Buturlin to swear first that the Tsar would keep faith with his new subjects. The ambassador was amazed. The Tsar, as autocrat, could not have obligations to his subjects. The Cossacks must trust to his favour, which they would undoubtedly receive. There was an awkward pause. The feeling for Muscovy was not shared by Teterya, the *esaul*, nor by Bogun and some other Cossack leaders. But the crowd outside was impatient, intolerant of subtleties. In the end only Bogun refused to swear.

The Ukrainians had a new master. The Zaporozhians' ataman had no objection to the arrangement so long as their own liberties were not endangered. He even proposed that his own people should follow the Ukrainians' example, but they refused, and events were ultimately to prove them wise. By the following March, the details of the Union had been hammered out. Bogdan got most of what he asked. The Cossacks' rights and freedoms, as they had existed 'for ages in the Army of Zaporozhiye', were confirmed. They would be subject to their own justice, and elect their own Hetman, though he must be confirmed in the office by the Tsar and must not treat with foreign states without the Tsar's permission. Sixty thousand Cossacks would be registered[21]—more than ever the Poles would have conceded. They would be paid rates, ranging from three rubles for a private to a thousand ducats for the Hetman, out of taxes to be raised in the Ukraine itself.

But while the Cossacks were granted autonomy as a class the peasants got nothing. The Tsar rewarded members of the Cossack oligarchy with 'perpetual and hereditary ownership' of lands, villages and towns, but peasants were ordered to return to service. The rule could not be immediately enforced. Feeling ran so high that many of the new Cossack gentry dared not enter their new estates and Teterya went so far as to beg the Tsar's emissary not to announce his grants for fear he might be lynched. Bogdan was slow to draw up the register. Some months after the conclusion of the agreement he had inscribed only 18,000 names, reporting that it was difficult to ascertain which of the 100,000 claimants were really Cossacks, and which were peasant runaways. Delay saved embarrassment and trouble. But in time the peasants were brought back under control and a new gentry class of Cossack elders was to take the place of its Polish predecessor.

The Pereyaslav agreement did not bring peace to the Ukraine. The Poles were furious at the news and denounced the Cossacks as perjurors.[22] But the Tsar had expected as much and now embarked on a pre-emptive war. Cossacks and Russian troops, already stationed at Kiev, marched north to Lithuania; more Russians, under Buturlin, and Cossacks under Bogdan, mounted an offensive to the west. The war was marked with the same ferocity as its predecessors, and though this time the Tatars fought with them, the Poles soon sued for peace.

The Cossacks were excluded from the conference table. Unable to suppress his taste for diplomacy, Bogdan had tried to inveigle Sweden into attacking the Poles. This had discountenanced the Tsar who never fully trusted him again, and with justice, for Bogdan continued to spin his webs of international intrigue.

In 1657 Ukrainian Cossacks again invaded Poland, this time with Transylvanian aid. Buturlin arrived at Chigirin to remind

Bogdan of his obligation not to embarrass the Tsar. The Hetman was dangerously ill and his aids tried to keep the Russians at bay, but he insisted on approaching the sickbed. There Bogdan promised to withdraw his men from Poland, and when a Polish emissary came to propose a Ukraine independent of both Russia and Poland he gave him no satisfaction. Too near the other world to break more oaths, the old intriguer, it seemed, had given up his plots at last.

Concerned above all now for his family and his successor he struggled out to address his last assembly. His farewell speech was an occasion for emotion. He thanked the Cossacks for their support through turbulent years, then offered up his sceptre and the other symbols of his authority. They were free to choose a successor. Tearful Cossacks begged him to remain, but Bogdan was insistent. There must be no interregnum on his death. He recommended candidates to them—Vygovski, Secretary of the Host, Teterya, the *esaul*, and others—but the Cossacks would have none of them. They wanted Yuri, his sixteen-year-old son. Bogdan warned of his youth, of the dangers of the times. But they insisted. Fearful and yet content, an enigma to the end, Bogdan was helped away while the crowd hurled their hats into the air and fired off their muskets in one final, heartfelt tribute.

For five days he lay paralysed in his bed. Then a stroke ended all resistance. They buried him in the church near his old house at Subbotov. Seven years afterwards, during yet another incursion, the Poles had his bones dug up and thrown to the dogs. The Ukraine was still to know no peace.

The years that followed were ruinous. The solidarity the Cossacks promised at Bogdan's last assembly dissolved almost immediately. Within a month of his death young Yuri was ousted by his guardian Vygovski[23] and sent scampering to the shelter of the Sech. Vygovski threw his hand in with the Poles, showed contempt for the interests of the poorer Cossacks, and in 1658 used Tatars and German mercenaries to suppress a popular revolt against his rule. Yuri returned next year on a tide of anti-Polish feeling and Vygovski fled to Poland. But the divisions among Ukrainian Cossackdom yawned ever wider. Faction fought faction, groups intrigued against each other, while wolfish neighbours backed rival groups. The Ukraine had become the cockpit of eastern Europe.

The almost continual war between Poland and Russia which swung to and fro across the Ukraine soon resulted in its being torn in two. Teterya became Hetman of the western area, orientated towards Poland and the Russian-dominated east fell under a rival Hetman, Bryukhovetski, who quickened the conversion of the Cossack oligarchy into a class of landed gentry. The Tsar created him a boyar, ennobled his chief collaborators and sent in Russian troops to help suppress the underprivileged Cossacks and peasants who rebelled against him.

The peace concluded between Poland and Russia in January 1667 established an official frontier between the east and the west Ukraine. Though the fighting flared up again, the division proved lasting. Coup followed coup and puppet followed puppet, but under Muscovy all vestige of Cossackdom in the Ukraine was to disappear.

The decline was not sudden. Long before Bogdan's birth the Cossacks there had been infiltrated by an alien social structure which came, insidiously to influence their own social patterns and values, and give them a radically different form from those of Cossack communities farther to the east. The Secch had remained egalitarian, Bogdan had served there as a young man and he had retained ties with it, but he had also been an heir to property and was by class a member of the gentry. Though he led a brief Cossack resurgence, the short-lived state which he created was hardly a Cossack one.

His great revolution had come too late. The lines dividing the poorer Cossacks from the peasants who aspired to Cossack status and the richer Cossacks from the Polish gentry, were already blurred. Even at the height of his power, Bogdan could not reconcile their differences. After him, the trend to inequality merely became more marked.

Mazepa, often cited as Bogdan's spiritual successor for leading a revolt against Peter the Great, was to rebel in the interests not of Cossacks but of a group of gentry who happened to have Cossack origins. Whatever his own motives, and the facts leave plenty of scope for speculation, Bogdan's revolution was more than this. He had proved himself capable, as none of his predecessors or successors were, of holding the disparate elements of the Ukraine together if not of reconciling their differences. A better general, a shrewder politician, it was due to him that the year 1648 showed the Ukrainian Cossacks united, determined to die rather than accept alien authority and alien values. It was not an isolated case. The Don, the Terek and the Yaik Cossacks also reacted violently against each new step an expanding state took towards controlling them. Everywhere Cossacks fought doggedly to preserve their own traditions, for freedom and the right to rule themselves.

'Cossacks of Razin, light of his people,
Rise, rise, O red sun,
Warm us poor people'.

—Traditional ballad

5 Bandit into revolutionary: the career of Stenka Razin

Shortly before Bogdan and the Ukrainian Cossacks swore submission to the Tsar, a young and deferential Cossack from the Don stood for the first time in a muddy Moscow street. Stenka Razin did not look like a budding outlaw as he stared up in wonder at the Kremlin's glinting cupolas and towers, yet he was to be the most famous of them all. As lithe and slender as Bogdan was corpulent, as ignorant as he was lettered, and as impetuous as he was statesmanlike, this was to be a rebel of a more devil-may-care breed, the Russian image of the swashbuckling pirate, a Robin Hood, a Giuliano of the steppes. And yet in retrospect he was to become a national hero of another type—a romantic, charismatic freedom fighter, canonised by the Soviet order as a sort of non-intellectual Che Guevara, a folk precursor of Lenin, the master revolutionary.

Still, so far this was a conformist, a privileged young man, protégé of the influential, respectable class in his community. His godfather, Kornili Yakovlev Cherkez, was to become Ataman of the Don Host, and young Razin himself was being groomed for leadership. Now, as a part of that programme, he was one of the chosen few to pass through Moscow on a pilgrimage to the far north of Russia, to the famous monastery of Solovetsk.

In 1658 he visited Moscow again, this time as a member of a Cossack embassy which returned with money, supplies and six cannon with which to defend their capital, Cherkassk, against the tribesmen of the steppe. Three years later, still firmly in the ranks of the establishment, Razin was sent to negotiate with some Kalmyks—'the most ougly and misshapen People in the World', as a contemporary Dutchman once described them,[1] who had been moving their black felt tents dangerously near the Don Cossack settlements of late. He acquitted himself well, established that for the moment at least, both Kalmyks and Cossacks feared the Tatars more than they did each other, and returned with 500 of their warriors to join in a Cossack attack on the Tatars at Azov. The same autumn, Razin set out for Moscow yet again and early the next year was once more sent as envoy to the Kalmyks.

He proved a competent soldier too. In 1663, in command of a Cossack troop, he was sent to intercept a Crimean Tatar war party returning, plunder-laden, from the Ukraine. Leaving thirty of them dead upon the field, he returned home with 2,000 horses, 600 sheep and 350 captives, whom the Tatars had carried off to sell as slaves. Yet this promising 'insider', the discreet negotiator and dashing commander, the man of the world who knew Moscow and Solovetsk, the man destined, some thought, to be Ataman of the Don Host some day, was soon a rebel outcast, the terror of officialdom.

One clue to his unexpected change of course involved his brother Ivan, who, in 1665, was in the Ukraine serving with a Don Cossack contingent in the Tsar's army. That autumn, Ivan and his men, 'esteeming to have done good service . . . desired to be dismissed',[2] but the Russian commander, Prince Yuri Dolgoruki, would not release them, and Ivan, who, as a free Cossack, regarded himself as beholden to no man, and

E*   125 certainly not as a feudal underling to be ordered about by a Muscovite, simply rode away for home. He was chased down by Dolgoruki's soldiers, and hanged as a deserter. His brother's execution must have coloured Razin's attitude to Muscovite officialdom, but he does not seem to have turned outlaw simply out of personal interest or lust for vengeance. A contemporary insisted that it was Razin's 'malicious and rebellious temper'[3] that moved him on to lawless roads; others see him as a social rebel, a rebel out of principle, moved by the sufferings of others. In particular, his concern was for the mass of starving immigrants who were pouring into the Don as a result of the upheavals in the Ukraine and a new wave of oppression in Muscovy.

The reasons for these new oppressive policies ran deep. After the accession of Tsar Alexei in 1645 the pace of Muscovy's territorial expansion quickened considerably. So did the development of her standing army on which ever greater emphasis had been laid since the Times of Troubles and the Polish invasions. But the state's preoccupation with military affairs necessitated policies in other fields which had profound implications for the free Cossack communities and for their relations with Muscovy.

The government was finding difficulty in paying for its military machine. The extra funds had to be raised from taxation which ultimately derived from the amount of land under cultivation. But this, in turn, depended on keeping farm labourers on the land—and too many Russian peasants, saddled with increasing obligations, were trying to leave it. The state reacted by extending Tsar Boris's legislation.

The Russian peasant rentier, once a free man, was being made a slave. The Muscovite government had recently compiled a sort of Domesday Book, ascribing peasants to their landlords, and enacted a series of draconian laws to ensure that they stayed with them. The peasant's status and obligations were made hereditary. Landlord and labourer were becoming, in effect, the owner and the owned. A man who lived three months on a landowner's estate could now be pressed into his permanent service. The time limit during which a runaway peasant could be searched out and returned to his former master was gradually increased and finally abolished altogether. In 1658 flight was made a criminal offence, and the law prescribed severe punishment for anyone who helped a runaway. Landlords came to control not only a peasant's labour, but his property, his person, his wife and children, even his brothers and nephews, and soon nine out of ten Russians were the serfs of the church, the gentry, or the Tsar.[4]

But many peasants still preferred to risk the punishment for running away, and most of these now headed for Siberia, or, since the Moscow government could not obtain the return of the fugitives from them, to the Cossack lands. The Don in particular, still immune from punitive search-parties, became their principal refuge. The majority of the immigrants went there as individuals or in family groups, but sometimes the entire population of a village would load their few belongings on to carts and set off for the Don, knowing that if they ever reached it they would be safe and able to live in freedom.

The large influx of newcomers transformed the economy and the social fabric of the Cossack communities. The middle stretches of the Don especially filled up with runaways who came to form a distinct class of Cossack poor, known as 'the naked ones' in contrast to the established 'householders' living further downstream. Most of the newcomers were destitute. Living in villages of makeshift hovels beside the curving middle stretches of the river and its tributaries, they had virtually no means of subsistence. Many lacked ploughs or seed-corn, and in many a case it was hardly worth a man's while breaking the virgin ground when he might starve to death by harvest time. The newcomers were accepted into the community, but excluded from the rich fishing and the more generous hunting grounds of the established Cossacks further down the river, who took most of the insufficient grain and money the Tsar sent to pay the Don Cossacks for their services. As a result there was 'a great hunger on the Don'[5] and, lacking alternative means of support, many of these new Cossacks took to brigandage.

Many of the old-established Cossacks in the south, who exercised most influence in the assemblies and retained a virtual monopoly of the chief offices, were sympathetic to their poorer comrades. But their interests, strategic as well as economic, diverged. The chief threat to the 'householders' was presented by their Tatar neighbours. They needed Muscovite support to guard the prosperity they had been building up since the ruinous times of Azov, and were predisposed to accommodate the Tsar. On the other hand, the fears of the newcomers upstream were orientated chiefly towards Muscovy. They were afraid that the government might sooner or later send forces to fetch them back to their old homes and punish them for their piracy, and that in pushing its borders even farther to the south, the state would gobble up the land which they were beginning to cultivate.

Moscow tried to pressurise the established Cossacks in all communities to curb their wayward comrades and to cease harbouring peasant runaways. In 1645, for instance, the Yaik and Don atamans reporting to Moscow had been told to 'persuade' the 'robbers' in their respective communities to come to order. But such exhortations did not always procure the desired effect—in 1695, for instance, the ataman of the Yaik was to be slaughtered by his own men for accepting an order not to grant asylum to new arrivals into the community. The Don Cossacks resolutely refused to extradite condemned men, and for the moment, they did nothing to curb the Cossack brigands.

In 1659 there was an entire township of 'robber Cossacks' on the northern Don. Led by their ataman, Vasili Prokofiev, they preyed on shipping passing along the Volga and in 1660 they mounted a raid which ranged right down to the Caspian Sea. Moscow now put pressure on the Cossack elders in Cherkassk, who had so far turned a blind eye to these activities. Though the elders were torn between their sympathy with the Cossack poor and their fears of offending the Tsar on whose pay and protection they were coming increasingly to rely, in the end self-interest tipped the balance. They duly knuckled under to the government, had the robbers' base burned down and several of their leaders hanged. But the Don elders were to suffer more crises of conscience.

The other traditional feeding ground of new Cossacks, the Black Sea, was now also closed to them. In the summer of 1660 a Turkish fleet disgorged an army of workers and soldiers at Azov, and soon two towers of stone had grown up to dominate the mouth of the Don, and the great iron chains slung between them stopped any would-be plunderers from entering the Black Sea. With all Russia suffering from famine and yet more people fleeing to join the Cossacks of the frontier, the hunger on the Don was biting even harder by the spring of 1666. The old-established Cossacks down-river were hardly affected. It was the new-comers who suffered—the propertyless poor, the *golytba*, 'the naked ones'.

At the brink of despair 500 of them, under their leader Vasili Us, marched northwards into the Russian province of Voronezh. Hungry peasants flocked to join them. Houses were burned down, estates plundered, landowners and bailiffs slaughtered. But it was the peasants who were responsible for the worst of these disorders. The Cossacks 'took food, but plundered nothing else, and committed no murders'.[6] All they wanted was govern-ment subsidies in return for service, such as the old-established Cossacks of the lower Don enjoyed. The authorities tried to buy Us off. But since they insisted that he surrender all the peasants with him and consent to his Cossacks being inscribed in a register, and since the peasants were ready to fight rather than be handed over, Us moved on to Tula, hardly more than a hundred miles short of Moscow itself. Only when a strong force of troops was sent against him did he withdraw.

By now, Muscovy was seriously concerned about the restless Cossacks of the upper Don. Not only did they constitute a threat of disorder in the border provinces, they were a magnet to hungry peasants all over the realm. In panic at the decline of the rural population, Muscovy now demanded the return of all who had fled to the Don since 1661. The Cossack leaders in Cherkassk did nothing about it, and they dealt lightly, too, with Us and his men, making great show of depriving them of pay which they were not receiving anyway. This particular storm seemed to have died down, but a much greater one was on the way.

The year Vasili Us marched on Tula was the year of the Great Fire of London, the year Shabbatai Tsvi proclaimed himself Messiah of the Jews, the year pious Russians were shaken to the core by the religious changes promulgated by the Patriarch Nikon. It was a terrible year, a year of plague and penance. Farms were running fallow for lack of hands to tend

129

them; in some districts women and children outnumbered men ten to one. God's wrath seemed to have descended upon Holy Russia. Many expected the end of the world, and many were to wish it had, for in 1667, the year of Antichrist, Stenka Razin threw his hand in with the Cossack poor.

An established, well-fed Cossack, Razin need not have concerned himself about these newcomers. Yet in the words of an old Cossack song 'he did not think thoughts with the great gentlemen. . . . [He] thought his thoughts with the poor'.[7] Razin was a man of rumbustious energies, a stormy-head who in another age, in another society, might have sought an outlet in tycoonery or on the wilder shores of politics. Whether or not the course on which he now embarked was an act of social conscience; whether he turned bandit and killer from some base motive, or like Schiller's 'Robber' to avenge society's injustice, in the spring of 1667 he gathered six or eight hundred destitute Cossacks together, including the remains of some bandit gangs recently broken up by the authorities, and led them out on the most spectacular of all the Cossack pirate expeditions. As he later explained, he took them out 'to feed themselves', since they had 'nothing to eat or drink' and the government was 'mean in the money and grain' it sent them.[8] But this may not have been the completely independent action of a maverick. Razin had the unofficial blessing of several Don Cossack leaders and there is reason to suppose that Ataman Yakovlev, his godfather, and some elders of the Host supplied him with boats and with powder from the official armoury—less out of fellow-feeling for their poorer comrades, perhaps, than out of a desire to deflect the robbers' attention away from themselves. Whatever else he needed he seized, or secured by arrangements from passing merchants and trading people from neighbouring Voronezh. Then, with four black-tarred, sea-going barges, several smaller boats, and a quantity of arms, lead, powder and other supplies at his disposal, he was ready to set out.

With the Turks barring the mouth of the Don, he decided to head for the Volga, and his men set about dragging the boats over the melting snows, across the narrowest neck of ground that separates the Don and Volga rivers. But there was no easy way out here either, for at this point stood the citadel of Tsaritsyn

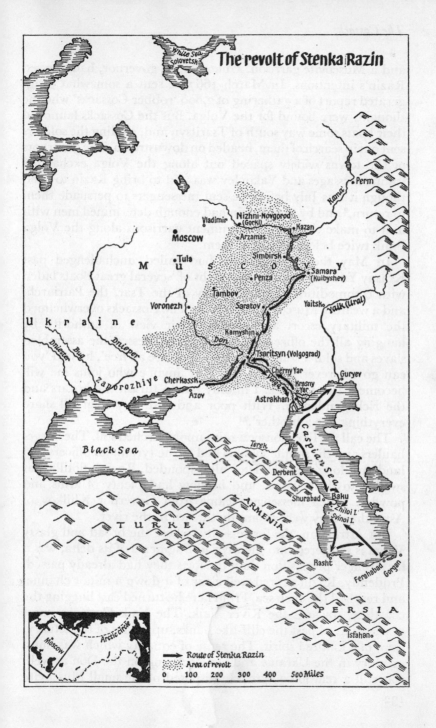

The revolt of Stenka Razin

White Sea
Solovetsk

Perm

Kama

Vladimir
Nizhni-Novgorod
(Gorki)

Kazan

Moscow

M U S C O V Y

Arzamas

Tula

Simbirsk

Samara
(Kuibyshev)

Penza

Tambov

Voronezh

Saratov

Yaitsk

Yaik (Ural)

Ukraine

Dnieper

Bug

Dniester

Kamyshin

Don

Zaporozhiye

Cherkassk

Azov

Tsaritsyn (Volgograd)

Cherny Yar

Krasny
Yar

Astrakhan

Guryev

Black Sea

Terek

Caspian Sea

TURKEY

Derbent

ARMENIA

Shurabad

Baku

Zhiloi I.

Svinoi I.

Rasht

Ferahabad

Gorgan

PERSIA

Isfahan

Moscow

Arctic Circle

→ Route of Stenka Razin
∴ Area of revolt

0   100   200   300   400   500 Miles

and a Muscovite garrison. Unkovski, its governor, had guessed Razin's intentions. In March 1667 he sent a somewhat exaggerated report of a gathering of 2,000 'robber Cossacks' who, he thought, were bound for the Volga. But the Cossacks launched their boats some way south of Tsaritsyn and, eluding the soldiers sent out in search of them, headed on downstream. The governors of the towns widely spaced out along the Volga exchanged frantic messages and Yakovlev was told to bring Razin to heel, though it was July before he sent messengers to persuade them to return,[9] and by then Razin had enough determined men with him to make the small government garrisons along the Volga think twice before engaging them.

In May the pirate flotilla had sailed unchallenged past Krasny Yar and soon came in sight of 'several great Boats laden with commodities',[10] the property of the Tsar, the Patriarch, and a wealthy Muscovite merchant. The Cossacks overwhelmed the military escort and showed their view of authority by hanging all the officers. Then Razin addressed the assembled slaves and soldiers taken prisoner. 'You are all free', he said 'you can go wherever you like. . . But anyone who joins me will become a free Cossack. I'm only out to thrash the boyars and the rich gentlemen. With poor and ordinary men I'll share everything like a brother'.[11]

The call fell like monsoon rains upon parched soil. The barge-haulers and the simple soldiers had borne tyrannous officers and landlords long enough. They all responded. Razin's flotilla was swelled to thirty boats, and he now had plenty of arms and powder. When messengers came from Governor Khilkov of Astrakhan they were promptly thrown in the river.

But Astrakhan, the fortress city, where the broad and glassy Volga is shattered into the myriad fragments of its delta, was a far stronger proposition than the forts they had already passed. Prudently, Razin steered well clear of it down a minor channel and reached the open sea. From here he turned east hugging the coastline, towards the River Yaik. The Yaik Cossacks, most of whom lived past the cliff-like banks, upstream of the estuary, were of a kindred spirit. The sense of equality which was but a memory in the Ukraine and fast declining on the Don as well, was still a real force here. He disposed of the small Muscovite garrison in the unprepossessing town of Guryev, the most southerly settlement, and spent the winter on the Yaik. But the community was small and poor, and he knew that Khilkov, the ineffectual governor of Astrakhan, had been replaced by the more determined I. S. Prozorovski who already had 2,600 regular troops under his command and was mobilising the Volga district. Prozorovski was out to catch Razin. The Cossack brigands must move on.

Envisaging an adventure on the grand scale, Razin had sent appeals for support out far and wide, and men came great distances to join him. Cossacks came from the swift-flowing Terek, as well as from the Yaik; Ataman Boba brought 400 Zaporozhians, and the call even penetrated the small garrison of soldiers stationed near Cherkassk, who, fired by the general trend to go Cossack, fled to the upper Don and down the Volga to the sea. But most of them were Cossacks of the Don. In the spring of 1668, Sergei Krivoi set out with seven hundred men, and in June 300 more, led by Vasili Us himself, took the river route past Astrakhan.

By then, Razin had left Guryev and camped on an island near the Terek—a convenient base from which to intercept shipping bound for the Volga. Joined here by Boba's Zaporozhians and Krivoi's men, he soon had a whole fleet of swift, manoeuvrable 'seagulls' and over two thousand fighting men—the largest force of Cossack pirates ever assembled in the Caspian Sea.

Still, so many men could not be fed on the proceeds of chance attacks on shipping, and so the armada sailed south into sunny Persian waters.[12] Razin had fixed the important trading town of Derbent as his first objective. The Cossacks drew into the harbour, leapt swiftly ashore, and tore like an avalanche through the narrow alleys of the town. The cannon, jutting out of the castle walls, stood silent, the gunners unable to distinguish friend from foe among the surging mass below. Pistols cracked and sabres slashed as the Cossacks rampaged their way into the market. Stalls were upturned, doors crashed down, and flocks of sheep, released from their pens, tottered bleating through the streets while the raiders looted, burned and slaughtered.

Then, suddenly, the Cossacks were gone. A terrible silence fell over Derbent—a silence unbroken for two years, men said, until the terrified survivors at last ventured back to their deserted homes from the shelter of the nearby hills. There followed attacks on a string of minaretted towns and villages along the once quiet and pleasant coastline of the Caspian, and soon the Cossacks, sated with plunder, must have thought of sailing home. But new arrivals from Russia warned of military preparations. The pirates, it seemed, might never reach the Don alive. So Razin thought of an alternative and sent messengers across the mountains, to the Shah in distant Isfahan.

The scruffy aliens who rode into the Persian capital, loveliest city of the east, and prostrated themselves before its ruler, told a glib story. They came in peace, they said, to offer their services, hoping that 'so great a Monarch' would be so generous as to 'afford 'em Sanctuary and assign 'em lands for their Habitation'. The Persians were astonished. The Cossacks were armed intruders; they had wrecked their towns, massacred their citizens. Ah, but they had been 'forced' to this, the Cossacks answered coolly, 'not meeting the hospitality they thought customary'.[13]

The Persians stalled Razin's ambassadors, instructed the Khan of Rasht meanwhile to exchange hostages with the Cossacks and to supply them with the food and clothing they requested.[14] Then, when the Tsar confirmed that the intruders were but thieves and runaways[15] and offered help in destroying them, the Shah had the emissaries clapped into gaol and ordered the Khan of Rasht to attack Razin's camp.

Several hundred Cossacks were slaughtered; the survivors cut their way through to the boats and put hastily out to sea. Now they sailed across the Caspian to Ferahabad, where they began to trade their remaining loot in the market. Commercially naïve, they sold ridiculously cheap, and the Persians 'caress'd the *Cosaques* at a high rate, finding 'em such admirable customers'. But the merchants were soon to repent their profits. On their sixth day in Ferahabad, at a prearranged time, the pirates drew their swords and sacked the town. Breaking into a palace, they found a 'vast Treasure'—dishes of porcelain and china, cornaline and agate, coral and amber; cups cut whole out of crystal of the rock and 'sundry other samples of the finest eastern craftsmanship'. All they thought valuable they carried away; the rest they smashed to fragments.[16] By the time they left, Ferahabad was in ruins, hundreds of its citizens slain. But Persian troops were soon on the way to avenge the massacre. They caught up with Razin at his winter camp by the bay of Gorgan and forced him to take to sea again.

The pirates were in difficulty. Fresh water and food supplies were running low; many a good man had been lost and no more recruits were reaching them now since Ataman Yakovlev had been replaced by a Cossack elder, Samarenin, who had taken effective steps at last to stop more Cossacks leaving the Don. Now Razin attacked settlements north-east along the Persian coast, then swung about, and made camp on an island, forty miles south of Baku. But he was allowed no rest. In June 1669, a great fleet approached, carrying nearly 4,000 of the Shah's soldiers.

Preferring to fight at sea, Razin led his little boats in close under the looming prows of the Persian ships and grappled with them. Pirate gunners hammered away at point-blank range and sweating Cossacks cut into the sides of the Persian ships with axes, while Persian warriors, waving scimitars, leapt down onto the pirate decks. Many a Cossack sank bloodied into the sea; and weight of numbers would have told against them had not the Persian commander chained his ships together, intending to trawl up the Cossack boats like so many mackerel. At first the tactics seemed to be succeeding. Then a lucky shot crashed into the Persian flagship's powder magazine. There was a deafening explosion, a huge spurt of flame. The ship, clouding smoke, began to list, then settled in the water. As it sank, the chains on either side of her clanked tight and the ships abeam of her heeled over, dragged down by her weight. The admiral escaped to another ship and ordered the chains to be cast off. He was too late. The Persians were doomed, and only three ships escaped. The rest glided down to the bed of the Caspian or were captured by the Cossacks.

The plunder was considerable, but victory had been bought at grievous cost. Five hundred Cossacks had lost their lives, and fewer than half the 1,200 survivors were fit for action now. Persia had become too hot for them, Razin decided. They must head for Russian waters and risk their fortunes there.[18]

Early in August the pirate fleet beached on an island near Astrakhan and used it as a base from which to waylay shipping and to raid the mainland. But it was not long before a Cossack look-out saw a Russian armada heading for the island.

Razin's desperadoes suffered no sudden nemesis. The Muscovite government had problems enough, not least with other Cossack communities. With peasants streaming to join the Cossacks of the Don, and the fractious Hetman Bryukhovetski making trouble in the Ukraine, it was anxious to bring Razin to heel by means short of fighting. Prozorovski mounted a daunting show of force. The approaching ships carried upwards of 3,000 soldiers, but packed so tight they could hardly move, still less fight. The Governor had little confidence in them anyway. Too many of them had heard the tale of Razin's exploits which had reached Astrakhan and grown in the telling. Men said he was a wizard, that bullets could not touch him. The Cossacks were offered a pardon if they would return peaceably to the Don. It was immediately accepted, and Prozorovski was as relieved as Razin at this avoidance of a fight. But he made great show in escorting the pirates into Astrakhan.

As the motley fleet approached the lofty walls and stately buildings that rose up from the grey green waters of the delta, the twenty-two guns of the *Orel*, the first real warship of the Russian navy, thundered out in salvo. The Russian soldiers fired their muskets into the air, and the 500 brass cannon in the towers around the city belched out their salute. The welcome, intended for the pirates' captors, turned into a triumph for Razin and his men, who, not to be outdone, started to fire off their guns as well. Crowds had rushed to the quayside to watch the spectacle and the din and pandemonium were so great that the master of one ship fell overboard from sheer excitement.

For several days the Cossacks wandered about the bustling city—past the foul-smelling shops of tanners and tallow-boilers, the great barges loading with salt bound for Moscow, and the huge piles of fish being cured. They drifted through the alleys under the shadow of the great cathedral, strolled past stalls filled with melons, oranges and grapes from the orchards and vineyards around the city and fish and water-fowl of a hundred varieties brought in from the myriad streams and marshes. They fingered cloths and carpets offered by merchants come from Persia, Armenia, Bukhara, and India to trade in Astrakhan. It was one great emporium. Peoples from half the world rubbed shoulders there—from thickset, little-eyed Nogais from the steppes, to the exotic strangers from England, Germany and Holland working on the ships of the Tsar's new navy.

The Cossacks were welcome for they had goods for sale and at moderate prices. They sold silk for a third of its proper value and a Dutchman bought 'a Gold-chain of one of them which was almost a fathom long, and in joynts like a Bracelet, between each piece were precious stones'. He paid 'not fully 7 pound *sterl.*' for it.[19]

The ragamuffins who had slipped past Astrakhan two years before were now 'dressed like kings; in silk, velvet and cloth of gold: some of them wore . . . crowns of pearls and precious stones'. Razin did not stand out from the general glitter, but was recognised by the honour the Cossacks did him. They called him 'little father' as indeed he was to them, having given them hope, led them to riches and dutifully divided it equally among them. But this tall, well-proportioned swashbuckler with a not unattractive pock-marked face, was not only the Cossacks' hero, he was becoming the idol of all the poor in Astrakhan. He tossed handfuls of coins to them as he strode about the city, and stopped to listen to their tales of grievance. He felt the people's pulse and prescribed a remedy. He promised to return one day, and free them from oppressive government.[20] He was to keep that promise.

Razin had already surrendered captive Persian officers, some banners, guns and his horse-tail banner as a sign of submission to the Tsar. But though pressed to do so he was disinclined to concede more. The boats and the remaining guns would be needed for the journey home, he claimed. The negotiations were protracted and tough, and when the Governor demanded a list of his followers so that the army deserters and serfs among them could be weeded out and handed over, Razin burst out in a fury: 'Nowhere does Cossack law allow a list of Cossacks to be made!'[21] Prozorovski had to give ground. Astrakhan was a long way from the nearest Russian garrison and four of his regiments were due to return to Moscow before the end of the year. He could not afford to let the talks drag on too long.

But Razin seemed in no hurry to leave. After the rigours of the expedition he wanted pleasure and in particular, more of the company of a captive girl he had brought with him. 'Her attire was of rich Cloth of Gold, richly set out with Pearls, Diamonds and other precious Stones. The Lady was of an angelical Countenance and amiable, of a stately carriage of Body, and withall excellently well qualified as to her Parts.'[22] People were sure that she was a Persian princess. But her hour of glory was to be short enough. The time came for the Cossacks to leave Astrakhan, and traditionally, they never carried women with them on such journeys. The interests of the brotherhood had to come first—and besides Razin already had a wife back on the Don.

The parting was described by a Dutchman living there at the time. Razin sits fondling his princess at a great feast. The Cossacks are drunk, almost to the point of helplessness. Suddenly he disengages himself from the girl's embraces, and sweeps her up in his arms. '*Well*', he says striding out towards the dappled surface of the Volga, '*thou art a noble River and out of thee have I had so much Gold, Silver and many things of Value. Thou art the sole Father and Mother of my Fortune and advancement; but, unthankful man that I am? I have never offered thee any thing: well now, I am resolved to manifest my gratitude*'. And with these words he lifts his mistress high above his head, and casts her into the water— 'with all her rich Habit and Ornaments',[23] his sacrifice to the inscrutable river god.

On 4th September 1669, the Cossacks set out on their homeward journey up the Volga. There were only 500 of them now, the rest having gone separate ways or stayed behind in Astrakhan. But the ranks were soon swelled with new recruits. Not far out Razin persuaded the accompanying escort of fifty soldiers to join him. Prozorovski sent a Captain chasing after them, to accuse Razin of breaking his agreement and to demand the return of the soldiers and his guns. Razin was adamant. 'The Charter . . . said nothing . . . about giving up . . . guns'.[24] As for the soldiers anyone was free to become a Cossack if he chose. When the Captain threatened him, Razin lost his temper.

'*How dare you make such an impudent Demand? shall I then betray my Friends who have out of a pure inclination to me . . . deserted their nearest Allies and Fortunes? and shall I be threatened with loss of Favour to boot? Prethee, go tell thy Master that I equally value him and the Emperour and let him know that I shall be with him ere he be aware, and reward him for this Protervity!*'[25]

It was no empty warning. Razin's concern to ensure a Cossack's right to find a livelihood was already broadening into a concern to bring that right to everyone. Indiscriminate brigandage became transformed into a tool with which to subvert the whole fabric of the state. The change in emphasis first noted at Astrakhan was obvious before he reached the Don.

Near Tsaritsyn he heard that Governor Unkovski was misappropriating taxes and charging too much for monopoly goods—a common enough story in Russia at that time. But unlike most men, Razin refused to accept public dishonesty as an inevitable fact of life. When his own men were charged twice the proper price for vodka, he took them to the Governor's palace and battered down its doors. Confronting the trembling Unkovski, he settled the matter there and then, without the use of further violence. The Cossacks moved on homewards, and, as if disgruntled at being denied an excuse to start a riot, plundered two merchant boats and tossed a Government messenger on his way to Astrakhan into the river.

The hard, upstream haul was over at last. The Cossacks pulled their boats out of the Volga and dragged them over the portage to the Don, then headed downstream. They stopped two days' journey short of Cherkassk, put in at an island, and there they made camp. They laboured in the days that followed, felling trees, clearing undergrowth, digging and building until a village of long log huts had risen up.

Of those who had originally set out for Persia only a fraction had returned. But the 500 who left Astrakhan had become 1,500 by the time they reached the upper Don and though many of the original band drifted back to their old homes, the population of the village steadily increased as new recruits flocked in day after day. Young bloods who had heard of Razin's reputation as a pirate chief arrived from as far as Zaporozhiye and the hungry too came, having heard that Razin was dividing the last of the plunder among the newcomers as well as his fellow brigands. By November 1669 he had 2,200 followers. By the following spring he had 4,000.

Razin set out to establish the new community as an economically viable entity in touch with the outside world. Merchants sailing past towards Cherkassk, capital of the established Cossacks downriver, were intercepted and forced to trade their cargoes of food and other necessities for the trinkets and bales the pirates had accumulated and which were useless for their day-to-day existence. This interrupted the trade on which the Cossacks downstream depended and immediately aroused their resentment. Muscovite officials were quick to exploit their concern, warning them that the robber Cossacks would gobble up the pay and the essential grain and supplies which the Tsar sent down to them every year. Then at the beginning of 1670, a Muscovite envoy, Gerasim Yevdokimov, arrived in Cherkassk to address the Don Cossack assembly.

Suspecting that the Muscovite would try to rouse the assembly to take action against his own community, Razin burst in, denounced him as a spy and accused the Tsar of wanting to deprive the Cossacks of their freedom. Many of the rank and file applauded and Razin sensed that the tide was running in his favour. In contempt of Ataman Samarenin and those Cossacks who wanted compromise with Moscow he called an assembly of his own upstream and dragged Yevdokimov off to face it. The Tsar's ambassador was beaten up and then drowned, and the Cossacks of the lower Don did nothing, not daring to move against so popular figure as Razin now was. When the Ataman and some of the elders tried to calm him Razin answered brusquely: 'You look after your people and I'll look after mine'.[26]

Having cut himself off from the Cossack leadership he now declared war on the Muscovite government, proclaiming a new crusade 'against the enemies of the state'—'the traitorous nobles and advisers'. He would march, he said, 'from the Don to the Volga and from the Volga . . . into Russia' to bring 'freedom to the poor'.[27] Razin the brigand had become the Russian Spartacus.

In a sense it was inevitable. Sooner or later, necessity would have forced the poor Cossacks of the Don out on another pirate venture. Though Razin had brushed with the Tsar's men once and been forgiven, he knew he would receive no second pardon. So he had to build up sufficient force to render him immune from punishment and since the Cossacks of the lower Don were too dependent on Moscow's material support to dare anger the Tsar, he could turn only to the Muscovite peasants. These were not strangers. Most of his own people had been peasants not long since. What, then, was a peasant if not a prospective Cossack? What could he offer them?—freedom from authority, a transformation of the social structure. The means?—a grass-root revolution.

The call met a rousing response. Reports of Razin's valiant deeds, his dashing personality and his promises had travelled far and fast. At a time when search parties were combing the country for runaways, knouting suspects, and dragging priests of peasant origins from their churches and returning them unfrocked to their old masters; at a time when once prosperous state peasants groaned under an unprecedented weight of taxation, this was exciting news for the legions of the oppressed, and for the army, too. The soldiers were in a rebellious temper. Their pay was mostly overdue, and when it arrived, it was devalued by clipping or paid in copper instead of silver coin.[28] The dragons' teeth of Muscovy's incessant wars with Sweden and with Poland were sprouting fast.

The discontent was not limited to social and economic causes. The Patriarch Nikon's moves to bring the liturgy of the Russian Church more closely into line with the original model of Greek Orthodoxy, were alienating millions of religious conservatives. The old prayer books were purged, the liturgy altered. Henceforth processions went to the left instead of to the right about in church; and the sign of the cross was made with thumb, index and middle finger, instead of two fingers. Such apparently trivial changes were regarded as catastrophes. The age-long rituals had been the chief support, perhaps, a Russian could cling to in times of tempestuous change and personal misery. Millions accepted the reforms, but despite draconian measures to make them conform, millions abided stubbornly by the old beliefs. And the religious issue was bound up with the social one, for many of the Old Believer monasteries sheltered debt-slaves and serfs. They were becoming centres of passive, and occasionally active, resistance to the authorities.

Razin was to exploit the religious situation to the hilt. The monks of Solovetsk, whom he had met as a young pilgrim, were prominent opponents of the reforms, and he himself may have been disturbed by the substitution of new truths for old. At any rate he began to show scant respect for the established church of the new model. When monks came begging for funds to rebuild their burned-down monastery, he laughed in their faces and asked what purpose clerics served. The Muscovite officials reported that the 'robber and traitor Stenka Razin and his friends have lost their fear of God ... Stenka talks disparagingly about Our Saviour, Jesus Christ. He ... has driven the priests away'.[29] He discouraged his people from marrying in church and, instead, had them 'goo (*sic*) several times round a Tree dancing',[30] according to more ancient custom.

In order to strengthen the military core of his revolutionary army and extend the area of operations, Razin approached the Hetman of the Ukraine with a view to forming an alliance. But the Ukraine was torn apart in chaos, Hetman replacing Hetman as rival parties gained a momentary ascendency, and nothing came of the proposal. Razin was more successful with the war-like people of the Volga—the Kalmyks, Mordvins, Chuvash and Bashkirs, and with the Tatars of Kazan and Astrakhan. Many of these had a status similar to Cossacks, with freedoms conditional upon service, but they were disgruntled at being denied rights in their ancestral lands, and many promised their support. But it was chiefly on his own Don Cossacks that Razin had to rely, and formidable warriors they could be.

In the spring of 1670 when the ice on the river Don began to melt, Razin's little army moved out towards the Volga and the walls of Tsaritsyn. The new Governor, Turgenev, had barred the gates, but the rebels surrounded the city and began to shout slogans across the walls. The propaganda worked well. Already there were murmurings of revolt within Tsaritsyn and the townspeople remembered the way Razin had rated the previous Governor for overcharging. The rebels did not have to wait long. On the night of 13th April the gates were opened. Turgenev was taken alive. Insulted and jeered at by the mob, he was trussed up, weighted and thrown into the Volga.

Razin introduced the people of Tsaritsyn to Cossack government, grouped them into tens and hundreds, and told them to elect atamans. Tsaritsyn rejoiced at the new regime and Razin found many recruits there, besides a whole arsenal of military supplies. But government forces were already converging on the city from Kazan in the north and Astrakhan in the south. A council of war was called. It decided to deal with the northern threat first.

As the 800 troops passed within seven miles of the city, they came under heavy fire from the men Razin had stationed on both banks. Instead of fighting back, the soldiers rowed on all the harder towards Tsaritsyn which they believed still to be in government hands. But when they reached it the rest of the rebel forces greeted them with a hail of cannon shot and rattling musketry. This new onslaught proved too much after their losses in the ambush and their exhausting row. The survivors, less than 400 of them, surrendered.

The Cossacks tortured the commander and then executed him together with all but one of his remaining officers and NCOs. Most of the rank and file joined the rebels and were sent upstream to Kamyshin, to pose as loyalist troops. The gates were duly opened to them. They persuaded the townsmen to join them and then upon a pre-arranged signal, admitted a party of Cossacks lurking outside.

So another town had fallen to Razin, and he used the same Fifth Column techniques successfully when he turned downstream to Cherny Yar. There was another slaughter of officials here and another proclamation of a Cossack democracy. But Prince Lvov was drawing near with 4,000 troops from Astrakhan, the mutilated corpse of a tortured rebel dangling on a gibbet at the head of his armada. The motley rebel force, about 9,000 strong, moved downstream towards him.

There was to be no battle. Lvov's men had no inclination to fight so popular a hero and one whose generosity many of them had experienced. Instead, they turned on their own officers and deserted *en masse* to the Cossacks. Lvov, himself, was fortunate to escape.

His return to Astrakhan brought Governor Prozorovski near despair. The Prince's dishevelled presence was proof that the Volga, the city's umbilical cord, had been cut. No messenger could reach Moscow or Kazan by the direct road now, and though Prozorovski sent runners out by devious routes he knew that if they arrived at all they would be too late to bring relief.

Still, he had 12,000 troops and 500 guns at his disposal, the great ship *Orel* and a number of eight-gun sloops—and the enemy was but a half-organised rabble. But the garrison had too little food to withstand a lengthy siege, the troops, who had not been paid for months, were restive, and the common people in the city were all for Razin. They smelt the scent of victory, and savoured it. As John Struys, the sail-master of the *Orel*, reported, 'it was no rare thing now to see the Rabble assemble togethers in heaps, and before the Doors of the Magistrates to cry out with infamous and bitter Railings, *Now, now the times begin to alter, it will be our turn next to Lord it, you villains come out and show your-selves to the World*'.[31]

Desperate times require desperate measures and Governor Prozorovski dug into his own purse to find 600 rubles to pay the troops. The Monastery of the Trinity contributed a further 2,000 and the soldiers were persuaded to re-affirm their oaths. The weather had turned unusually cold for June; a storm of hail-stones beat down on Astrakhan; it seemed a bad omen. Then, on the 18th, fishermen brought news that the enemy was near. Most of the foreign merchants and sailors in the city set sail for Persia. Those who remained helped prepare the defences. The gates were bricked in: great stones, and cauldrons of boiling water were dragged up to the 30-foot battlements.

'On Sunday, *June* 22 came the *Cosacks* within sight of *Astrachan*', reported a Captain Butler. They 'sent a *Cosac* Trumpetter with a *Russian* Priest to demand the Town. The said *Cosac* had also a letter for me in *Dutch*, wherein I was advised not to fight with my Men, if I hoped for Quarter, or Mercy at their hands.'[32] Prozorovski snatched the letter out of Butler's hands, and had the messengers killed. The Governor would fight.

As prayer-chants echoed round the incense-ridden churches, the streets were filled with scurrying figures. Old men crept down to the refuge of dank cellars; women gathered up their children and went in search of safer hide-aways. Prozorovski made a last inspection of the walls.

The Cossacks 'with about 300 Keels, great and small' landed 'near the Vineyards that ly about half a League from the Walls'.[33] The bells rang out, the trumpets blew, and Prozorovski donned his armour and took up station at the Voznesensk Gate, on the western side of the city. He chose his place in error. Advised by deserters, Razin made only a show of force there, and prepared to mount his main attack from the south.

In the middle of the night his men raised their ladders silently to the walls. Shadowy figures leant out to help the rebels over. Astrakhan was being betrayed by its own soldiers. A loyalist gunner fired. The iron-clad commanders on the western wall sprang suddenly to life and clanked their way across the city. But the signal had come too late. Thousands of Cossacks were already running through the streets. Soldiers turned their great halberds menacingly towards their officers and soon the five-gun signal of surrender boomed out over Astrakhan. Prozorovski's loyal bodyguard fought on and were cut down almost to a man. The wounded Governor sought refuge with a congregation of priests, officers and officials in the Cathedral. This merely postponed the reckoning a little. By dawn all resistance had ceased; Prozorovski and his supporters had been rounded up and placed under arrest.

At eight o'clock the gay figure of Stenka Razin strode through the excited crowd massed on the Cathedral square. He ordered the Governor to be brought out to face trial before the people. Within moments Prozorovski was pushed forward, stumbling, to fall at Razin's feet. The crowd saw Razin whisper something in his ear and the Governor shake his head. He was taken back into the cathedral. Soon his figure was seen again, high up, limbs outstretched, hurtling from the belfry. There was a grim thud; a grisly mess upon the pavement. The crowd cheered.

The other prisoners, some arrogant, some abject, were brought out one by one. And the crowd, venting the pent-up spite of years, yelled out their verdicts like proletarians at a Roman circus. There were calls to free an honest official or an officer who had treated his men well. But mostly they shouted for execution. The methods employed for this were spectacular. Prozorovski's elder son was roped by his feet from the battlements and swung like a pendulum against the city walls before being mercifully loosed into the river. The younger son was tortured almost to the point of death, then returned to his mother. Officers and clerics were hung up on hooks like pieces of meat. At night a mass grave was dug to hold the 341 victims of that day's work.

The rich man trembled but the pauper took a holiday. The Cossacks and their friends went mad with delight—feasted, caroused and danced about the streets. Gaols were unlocked and prisoners released. Eager crowds burst into public buildings and cheered themselves hoarse as criminal records and taxation papers went up in flames. Set on destroying every vestige of the old regime, they rushed to the docks, and burned the *Orel*, pride of the Russian navy, down to its keel. Churches, warehouses and private moneybags were rifled and the proceeds divided up. Soldiers were given the value of two months' pay; doles were distributed to the poor.

But the time of joy merged into a reign of terror as mob rule took a hold. Witch hunts were mounted; the malicious paid off private scores. Innocent citizens suffered death or mutilation; their wives and daughters were given over for rape. The atmosphere was such that men were afraid to succour their friends. Butler saw men 'hanging up by the Feet, others with their Feet and hands chopt (*sic*) off left in the open street to shift for themselves, none daring so much as put forth a finger to help them'.[34]

Razin meanwhile basked in a sun of adoration as the inhabitants of Astrakhan flocked to swear him loyalty. But he insisted that 'his purpose was not to rule as Lord and Soveraign but to live with them as a Brother to revenge that Tyranny and Oppressions which They had for so many years, and their Progenitors for so many ages past, suffered against all Reason and the Law of Nature'.[35] They must continue to serve the Tsar, he insisted, but govern themselves grouping themselves in tens and hundreds and choosing their own atamans. And those who would follow him would help rid the country of Russia's real traitors—the nobles, the governors, all people in authority.

On 20th July 1670, leaving Vasili Us and two other trusted lieutenants in command of the city's defences, he went north from Astrakhan to liberate all Russia. An armada of two hundred boats moved slowly up the Volga, eight thousand pairs of arms straining at the oars; two thousand horsemen on the bank easily kept pace with them. At Tsaritsyn, Razin sent his brother Frolka and Ataman Gavrilov westwards to rouse the Don, and then moved on, past Kamyshin, towards Saratov. News of his coming had preceded him and the people delivered up the city without a fight. The governor was executed, official records burned, and a primitive democratic government established. The triumphal voyage continued north and the wooden town of Samara with its stone monasteries and churches fell into rebel hands. And all the time fresh volunteers swelled the ranks of Razin's army—peasants, soldiers, priests and motley bands of tribesmen on the prowl for booty.

Though appeals to the Crimean Khan brought no response, and the Persian Shah still threatened to hunt Razin down like wild boar, there were some established leaders who saw prospects of furthering their own political ambitions by joining him. The Ukrainian Colonel Dzikovski of Ostrogozhsk kept in secret touch, sent food, and even offered to open his town to Razin's men.[36] But the overwhelming proportion of support came from the common people, and Razin did not scruple to play on traditionist instincts and loyalist sentiments to draw them in. He fitted out a boat in red plush for a young Circassian prisoner who posed as the Tsarevich Alexei. In another vessel, decked in black velvet, he installed a spurious Patriarch Nikon. No matter that the real Tsarevich had died several months before; that Nikon had lain in prison four years since. News travelled slowly and people accepted what it pleased them to believe.

His agents flitted through the land with the most stirring messages,[37] with slogans in the names of Don and Yaik atamans, of God and Tsar, and 'of the most saintly Mother of God', of 'all the saints' and of 'the faith of Orthodox Christians'. But the chief of the 'mischievous devices . . . set on foot by *Stenko* to ruin the Russian Empire, and to seduce the common people', was his claim to come 'by order of the Great Czar to put to death all the Bojars, Nobles, Senators, and other great ones ... as Enemies and Traytors of their countrey'.[38]

Razin had mixed a strong potion and even the supporters of Tsarist law and order could not deny its effectiveness. 'People ... have been humouring the robbers, and rejoicing in the lies they put about. News has spread that the robbers have been killing soldiers and the people have been glad to hear it'.[39]

With the whole of the Volga already up in arms, in August Cossacks invaded Voronezh. The peasants of Pensa, Tambov, Nizhegorod, Ryazan rose up and soon the rebellion 'began to burn not above twelve miles from *Mosko*' itself. In the capital the poor 'began to speak openly' in Razin's praise, 'as ... a person that sought the publick good and the liberty of the people'.[40]

By the time he reached Samara, he had as many as a quarter of a million men behind him. But they were not an effective fighting force. A Cossack expedition had become a peasant free-for-all. It was only general sympathy, not any chain of command that connected Razin's immediate followers with the other rebel bands, and most of the men with him were armed only with scythes and axes. Brilliant successes had been achieved without the need to fight. Town after town had been betrayed by their rebellious inhabitants. But meanwhile the government was rallying its strength; and organisation, modern equipment and the military skill of trained men led by foreign officers was soon to tell against the mob.

In the first months of 1671 news filtered through to western Europe that 'the rebels ... commanded by Stephan Razin had given the Empire's troops a great defeat'. He was 'very potent', it was said, and 'had put the Emperor into great fear and disorder'.[41] But by then it was all over.

The turning point had come at Simbirsk. Razin had arrived there in September 1670 hoping to press on along the Volga through bustling Kazan and Nizhni-Novgorod, and then westwards overland to the ancient city of Vladimir and the capital itself. He had already covered two-thirds of the immense distance between Astrakhan and Moscow, and when the people of Simbirsk opened the gates to him his prospects seemed good. But this time the garrison remained loyal. Led by the Governor Miloslavski they barricaded themselves in the castle.

Razin tried every Cossack ruse and tactic to break in. He

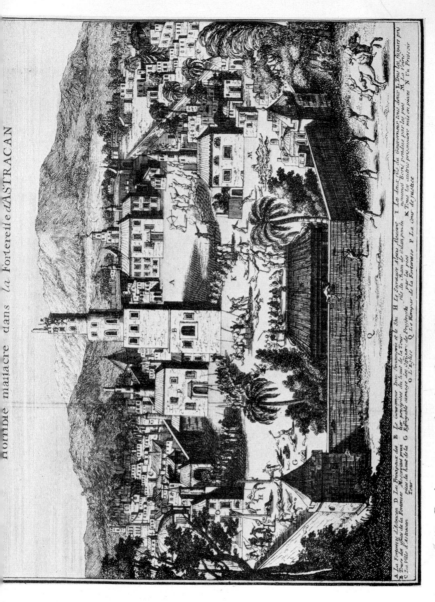

horrible massacre dans *la Forteresse d'ASTRACAN*

Razin captures the city of Astrakhan, *from a Seventeenth Century Dutch print*

his Brother

Razin and his brother, Frolka, being led to execution, *from a Seventeenth Century English print*

built a siege wall all around it, turned the guns of the outer perimeter against it, had flaming torches hurled at it—and all in vain. The fires were dowsed, the walls proved strong, the soldiers incredibly stubborn. Four times Razin ordered a general storm, and on each occasion his people were sent reeling back with heavy losses. Nearly a whole frustrating month had passed when news came that 1,500 efficient troops under the command of Prince Baryatynski were on the march towards them from Kazan.

Razin led a variegated crowd of Cossacks, townsmen, peasants and nomads, out to meet them. The two forces halted within fifty yards of one another. The red-coated *streltsy* in their neat ranks and the heaving, raggle-taggle opposite, with their flint-locks and pitch-forks sticking out at all angles, eyed each other for several moments. Then the rebels rushed forward.

They were sent crashing back. Razin rallied them, and led them in another furious advance—foot, horse and guns all mixed up and packed so tight together that most men scarcely had space to wield their weapons. The cold, disciplined, regular troops cut into them like harpoons into blubber. Razin himself was slashed by a Muscovite sabre, then hit in the leg by a shot from an arquebus. As he fell the rebel lines were breaking. He was alive on enemy ground, when a Cossack troop wheeled about, charged a wedge into the red-coats, snatched him up and galloped him back towards Simbirsk. By dusk Baryatynski was advancing on the city. Razin had mustered his men outside the Kazan Gate. As the red-coats came on they could see him gesticulating wildly, trying to restore his crumbling positions. Then fire broke out in the rebel camp and all sight of him was lost in the smoke and the confusion. When the Muscovites at last occupied the camp, Razin was nowhere to be found.

The Governor of Kazan reported triumphantly to Moscow: 'The robber, Stenka, was overcome with such a panic that . . . at about five hours before dawn he ran for the boats accompanied only by the Don Cossacks. He left the men of Astrakhan and Tsaritsyn and Saratov and Samara behind . . . and [so] betrayed them'.[42] Like Colonel Bogun at Berestechko, Razin had abandoned the rabble to save a core of good fighting men.

The disastrous defeat at Simbirsk had been heralded in September when the same Prince Dolgoruki, who had executed

Razin's elder brother years before, routed 15,000 rebels at Arzamas. By January 1671 Tsarist troops had broken up most of the larger rebel bands. Razin was still at liberty and bands of brigands would roam the countryside for a year and more to come. But the eye of the storm had blown out at Simbirsk.

The government extracted a vicious price for the disorders. The vast tract of south-eastern Russia, where thousands of landowners and officials had been butchered during the warm summer months, became the scene of innumerable retaliations as the ground grew hard under the winter frosts. Dolgoruki, brutal champion of order, turned the Arzamas district, in the words of one Westerner,[43] into 'the Suburbs of Hell', sown with gallows, drenched with blood. Tens of thousands were executed, more mutilated—some by due process, most without trial. Women suffered as well as the men, including the remarkable Alena, female 'Ataman' of several thousand peasants. And months later, Astrakhan capitulated upon the cynical promise of an amnesty, which was not kept. Razin's revolt was born of bitterness and it left bitterness behind.

After Simbirsk, Razin, chased unremittingly, was given no time to gather strength again. The Church declared him excommunicate; people became afraid to consort with him; his band of followers melted away. He headed for Saratov, then to Samara, but the gates of both cities were closed against him. He went on, homewards, to the upper Don—only to find he had become a stranger in his own land. His godfather, Yakovlev, was ataman again, but under too great a pressure from Moscow to follow his old policy of non-involvement. Nevertheless, perhaps out of some residual sympathy for his godson, the ataman seemed reluctant to move against him. He merely reported Razin's movements to Moscow and gave assurances of the Don Cossacks' loyalty. But the Tsar was adamant: the rebel must be captured. And so, in April, loyalist Cossacks marched north and, after a brief mêlée, led Razin and his younger brother, Frolka, in chains back to Cherkassk. Within a few days they were taken on to Moscow.

Now the days of doubt were over, Razin showed his spirit again, comforting the miserable Frolka with the thought that, when they arrived in Moscow, 'they should receive great honour, thousands of people and the greatest of the Land being (doubtless) ready to meet, and to see them'.[44] He was right. As they approached the city on the 4th of June 1671 the crowds stood thick beside the road. But the authorities did not want them to see a dashing hero. A few miles out they had stripped Razin of his silken habit and now they brought him in in rags, chained by the neck and limbs. The reluctant Frolka tethered like a dog to the same cart came stumbling along behind. Yet the Cossack brigand kept his bearing and his gay demeanour. It was a brave show; a triumph of a sort.

Two days later they were led out through another huge and noisy throng, past lines of gleaming halberds, to mount a tall scaffold. An official stepped forward and began to read out a long indictment, listing all their crimes.[45] Razin seemed to bear this cheerfully enough. Then they laid him down between two beams, and the executioner did his work.

The poor Cossacks of the Don had lost their idol, the repository of all their hopes. For years afterwards they mourned his passing in song:

It was at dawn, then, my brothers, at the break of day,
Just as the little red sun was rising
At the set of the bright sickle moon . . .
The *esaul* strolled round the settlement . . .
And he roused the splendid brave fellows:
Good lads, arise. Get up, my brave lads,
Cossacks of the Don arise!
It's a bad day for us on the Don.
The glorious, quiet Don has grown dim
From its source right down to the Black Sea,
Right down to the Black Sea of Azov. . . .
Our leader is with us no longer.
Stepan Timofeyevich who was called
Stenka Razin is no more, is no more.
They caught that Cossack brave and good,
Tied up his white arms in cruel bonds, and
Carried him off to stony Moscow.
And there, there, on the famous Red Square,
They struck off his tempestuous head.

The establishment may have cut off Razin's stormy head, but they had not torn up the roots of revolution. Other rebels would arise and when, more than thirty years later, Bulavin led the Don Cossacks in another great revolt, his supporters included men who once had followed Razin.[46]

Stenka Razin was the last of the great Cossack pirates; the first great protestor against Tsarist domination, which the Cossack elders were beginning to accept. Though his crusade to preserve the Cossack freedoms and to re-introduce democratic forms of government into central Russia had failed, all the power of the Tsar's men could not break his legend. Representative of that gay, unbridled, adventurous vitality which had marked the Cossack out from earliest times, his name became symbolic of the resistance to Moscow's efforts to stifle that free spirit. He had been the hope of the common people, and now he was dead they built their aspirations into his legend. Peasants as far north as Archangel, toilers in a score of Russian provinces, sang of him for centuries to come as they laboured their lives out for their masters.[47] They did not wait for the Messiah, they waited for Stenka to return.

Many refused to believe he was dead. Some said it was not Razin, but another who was executed in Moscow.[48] His sins were so great, said others, that the earth would not receive him. He had to remain alive, suffering perpetual torments, like some new Prometheus. Two hundred years and more after his death people still talked of him with bated breath. In some parts of Russia they were afraid even to pronounce his name. 'They are afraid to talk', said one nineteenth-century historian, 'as if he were not a legend of ancient times, but an important criminal, who has escaped from prison and is wanted by the police.' Razin had not died. He was shut inside a mountain ready to return. Razin, 'the scourge of God', would come again. 'He must come, he cannot fail to. He'll come on judgement day. Ah, hard times are on the way', men would say. 'God grant that no good Christian should live to see the day when Stenka comes again.'[49]

'But what he *did*, was to lay on their backs,
The readiest way of reasoning with Cossacques'.

—Byron, *Don Juan*, Canto XCIII

6 The Cossacks in transition

Razin's revolt, in calling up visions of another Times of Troubles, had terrified the Muscovite authorities. Not content with Razin's execution and the utter crushing of the insurgents, they embarked on a much tougher policy, began to take measures designed to preclude any possibility of such a rebellion bursting out of the Cossack lands again. The days of diplomacy were over. Henceforth if economic pressure seemed too slow to take effect Muscovy was always ready to use direct political interference and brute force as methods of curbing Cossack waywardness and self-will.

On 29th August 1671, Ataman Yakovlev returned to the Don with the Tsar's pay. This was welcome enough, but he also brought unwelcome orders for the Cossacks to swear oaths of loyalty to the Tsar and the younger men fought against it for three days in the assembly before they were finally brought to heel. Of itself, the oath of 1671 did not herald a period of obedience. Only three years later, the Don Cossacks ignored orders to build a fort on the river Miuss, and the following year, when they were told to surrender a troublemaker, the rank and file forced the loyalist leadership to back down, and threatened that if the Tsar 'should send a great army to the Don' to enforce his will, they would throw in their hand with the Sultan and the Khan and 'kill the elders . . . who . . . are friendly to the Tsar'. The embarrassed elders tried to shrug the whole thing off. 'Some drunken Cossacks in the settlements upstream are getting excited', they reported, but most of them 'never had any such evil intention'.[1] But even the elders, predisposed to recognise Muscovite authority, were coming to be viewed less sympathetically by the Tsar.

In the 1660s a Muscovite official had complained that not only were runaways, even men condemned to death for robbery, immune from the law once they reached the Don, but that 'when they come to Moscow . . . honour is accorded them as if they were foreigners'.[2] In 1673 the government formally denied the Don the right to harbour fugitives and despite this, Cossack officials and rank and file alike still continued to give them shelter. But this situation would not be tolerated much longer.

The only factor which restrained the Tsar's hand was an appreciation of the Cossacks' function in border defence and their use as campaign auxiliaries. He could now call on the services of a whole chain of Cossack communities along the southern frontier, west to east. But they were not politically reliable and total reliability was what the state was coming to require.

Only in Siberia were the Cossacks subject directly to Muscovite governors, but then the Siberian Cossack had evolved into a quite different type from the rest. True primary Cossack forms still persisted among them—property was often held in common, and the inmates of isolated blockhouse stations would work jointly, dividing their profits among themselves at the end of the season's hunting. But, rather than forming close-knit territorial groups, they were spread wide over the countryside, acting as official tribute-collectors, guides and militiamen. Unlike the Cossacks of the free communities, the Siberian Cossacks were paid individually, though from 1640, in commutation of their pay, allowed to hunt and trade on their own account once they had discharged their duties as agents for the state. Nevertheless, the freedoms these Siberian Cossacks enjoyed were personal to them as individuals, not communal.

The Muscovite government created a new mutation of the Cossack type in the 1650s, founding a military community between the Ukraine and the Don in the forests and marshes around Kharkov and Belgorod known as the Slobodskaya Ukraine. Migrants from the Ukraine proper had been settling there since the 1620s and in 1651 Tsar Alexei inscribed many of them as Cossacks with an obligation to guard a line of defensive entrenchments against Tatars and occasionally against marauding Zaporozhians, leaving the rest as peasants to support them. The Cossacks were apportioned to five 'regiments', 600 or 800 strong, on a territorial basis, each with its colonel, who was initially elected but then held command for life. He could apportion land in heredity, to himself as well as to others, though his powers were limited by a council of 'elders'—a chief of staff, a judge for civil affairs, a military *esaul* and a secretary for civil and one for military business.

The system of internal government, which bore striking similarities to that of Bogdan's Ukraine, was carefully controlled by Moscow. The election of every officer down to the rank of centurion had to be confirmed, and many were simply appointed by the authorities. The character of the experiment was primarily military and the regiments of neo-Cossacks were eventually converted into regular hussars.[3] They were the precursors of the military colonies which were founded later and a model to which the government was soon trying to make the free Cossack communities conform.

In the war-torn Ukraine itself, the Cossacks were soon tamed. True, the urge to solidarity had gained force once more when Peter Doroshenko became Hetman of the Polish sector and with Tatar help led a celebrated and successful campaign both against the Poles, and against Bryukhovetski, Hetman of the Muscovite sector. In 1668 he had become Hetman of a reunited Ukraine. But this success was short-lived. Pro-Russian Cossacks chose a new leader, Demyan Mnogogreshny, and Doroshenko was forced to turn to the Turks for support, becoming a vassal of the Sultan, who added the words 'Protector of all the Cossacks' to his titles. Turkish troops helped Doroshenko drive the Poles out of Podolia and Galicia, but his domain was ultimately limited to the provinces of Bratslav and southern Kiev, and his regime did not prosper. Increased taxation and land appropriations encouraged a steady drift of emigration, and, in 1676, having lost all popular support, he submitted to the Tsar who, curiously enough, made him governor of Vyatka.

Mnogogreshny was exiled to Siberia and in 1687, after an unsuccessful Russian campaign against the Crimea, his successor, for a short time Hetman of all the Ukraine under Muscovite tutelage, was accused of treason and given the same sentence. The Tsar continued to deal as he liked with the Hetmans. If the present incumbent suited him, he would keep him in office far beyond his three-year electoral term; if the Tsar disliked him, he broke him at once. The last Hetmans were not even to be Cossacks, but governors sent out from St. Petersburg, and in 1764 the office was to be abolished altogether.

By then, Cossackdom itself had long since ceased to exist in the Ukraine. In the latter years of the seventeenth century, Muscovy allowed a register of 30,000 Cossacks. But though, officially, peasants and burghers could be registered, established Cossacks naturally wanted places reserved for their own children, and, as the population increased and more serfs fled in from the Polish-dominated west Ukraine, the register proved totally inadequate. Anyway, as Moscow drew the economic and political bonds steadily tighter, the registration question became ever less important. Speeding the process begun by the Poles, Muscovy ensured that the acquisition of landed property turned a few Cossacks into a gentry class with interests markedly different from the mass of poorer Cossacks and aspiring peasants, and it was through this upper crust that Moscow exerted its squeeze on the rest. Despite a succession of risings, the old Cossack traditions gradually disappeared in the Ukraine, and in 1699 the Tsar felt able to abolish registration altogether.

But it was no easy task to bring the remaining Cossack communities into line. The Zaporozhians, nestling in their Sech beyond the rushing Dnieper waterfalls, remained relatively immune from governmental interference. Tsar Alexei encouraged them to raid Turkish positions by the Black Sea and to ride with Russian troops against the Crimean Tatar army, but he did not insist on a register as he did in the Ukraine. Nevertheless the Zaporozhians were largely dependent on Muscovy for munitions, and Muscovy used this need as a lever to control them, much as it had done with the Yaik and Don communities. Then, in 1663, the Tsar had sent 300 serving men to the Sech, ostensibly to help defend it against the Tatars, but with secret orders to watch developments and report. And there was enough to watch in the kaleidoscopic changes of Zaporozhian opinion, which veered now one way and now another in response to the struggles between the Turks, Tatars, Poles, Ukrainians and Moldavians surrounding them—and to the bribes that came their way. But for the most part the Cossacks of the Sech regarded the Crimean Khan and the Turks as their traditional enemies, and in this they were encouraged by the Tsar.

The Zaporozhians had become such an uncomfortable thorn in the flesh of the Turks that the Sultan ordered a large force of janissaries and the army of the Crimean Khan to march on the Sech and destroy it. The fate of this expedition became the subject of one of the most popular tales in Cossack folklore. According to the story, the Tatars surrounded the Sech one winter's night, unnoticed by the sentries who were sleeping the deepest of Zaporozhian sleeps after a riotous drinking bout. It was only by chance that a Cossack called Shevchik happened to wake up, glance out of the window, and not attribute to his hangover the sight of armed strangers creeping silently between the barrack blocks. Stealthily he roused his comrades. The would-be ambushers were themselves surprised, and utterly routed.

The attack on the Sech was accounted particularly underhand, so the story goes, because the Sultan had recently offered the Cossacks his protection. Now the jubilant Cossacks composed a letter in reply, distorting each of the Sultan's high-sounding titles into a foul-mouthed, blasphemous insult. It was a masterpiece of crude ridicule:

'Thou Turkish Devil', the letter ran, 'Brother and Companion of Lucifer himself! Who dares to call himself Lord of Christians, but is not! Babylonian cook! Brewer of Jerusalem! Goat-keeper of the herds of Alexandria! Swineherd of Great and Lesser Egypt! Armenian Sow and Tatar Goat! Insolent Unbeliever! The Devil take you! We Cossacks refuse every demand and petition you make us now, or which you may in future invent.'[4]

Though apocryphal, the letter embodied something of the Zaporozhian spirit—earthy, cruel, and yet engaging—and Russians have enjoyed it ever since. Two centuries later, it provided Repin with the subject of his most popular painting over which he laboured thirteen years; and the story of the Zaporozhians' letter was to become a favourite joke of Stalin's.

Serko, Ataman of the Sech at the time, was an archetypal Zaporozhian war lord. He fought for the Polish King and the Russian Tsar in turn, was sent to Siberia, then suddenly bounced up again to lead a great raid on the Crimea at Muscovite behest. The Sech still harboured renegades and refused to surrender at least one pretender to the Muscovite throne. The Russian garrison posted there was set to flight in 1686, and though the Zaporozhians were persuaded to join Don Cossacks and regular troops under Prince Golytsyn in his Crimean campaign in 1687, and to fight for the Tsar more frequently than for any other outsider, they remained as volatile, as mercurial as ever.

Their neighbours, the Don Cossacks, on the other hand, seemed more amenable, thanks largely to the continuing pressure put on them by the continuing border war. In 1675 Kalmyk tribesmen made a devastating attack on several large settlements on the lower and middle Don, setting ablaze the hay-fields all around them, destroying modest fortunes built up by years of toil and thrift. The Don Cossacks stood nervously on the watch, ready at a moment's notice to save what they could of their household goods and livestock, ferrying them over to islands in the river. It was chiefly the richer Cossacks who were affected. The 'new' men up-river had less to lose anyway, and were much more concerned with the menace from the north. In 1682 these poor Cossacks were concerned in another uprising which spread into provincial Muscovy before the Don elders could bring it under control. But the tensions between richer and poorer, between Muscovite and anti-Muscovite parties were not the only factors which led to storms within the community in the 1680s.

The more prosperous men were split among themselves, especially over the religious question, for many of them were Old Believers. In the end it was Muscovy's line which prevailed again. Its spokesman was Ataman Frol Minayev who at an assembly in 1687 officially condemned the schismatics, had several dissident elders arrested, and mounted a general campaign of persecution against all non-conformists.

The faithful Minayev did the Tsar sterling service in his campaigns against the Turks and Tatars. In 1695 he led 6,000 Don Cossacks to join Russian troops in an unsuccessful attempt to storm Azov, and again the following year when Azov fell. Though it was to revert to the Turks again for a period from 1711, henceforth the threat to the Cossacks from the south declined.

This success reduced one danger only to intensify another. Peter the Great, the new, expansionist, modernising Tsar, anxious to consolidate the southern gains was encouraging the boyars to extend their estates into the middle Don at the expense of the Cossacks who had settled there. Members of some of the great princely houses of Russia—Repnins and Dolgorukis— were prominent among those who had already pressed their holdings to the very edge of the Don country. On the other side, Cossacks had begun to solidify their hold along the middle Don itself, and in the Khoper, Medveditsa and Donets valleys by beginning to scratch a living out of the soil. In 1685 the Governor of Tambov had reported that Cossacks there 'have been ploughing . . . and sow grain'. The Don elders had become concerned at the development of arable farming and in 1689 they had forbidden it on pain of execution. But if the Abels down river could make a reasonable living from stock-farming and fishing, the Cains to the north could not, and the number of arable small-holdings continued to increase despite the warnings.[5]

The Cossack leadership's antipathy to arable farming was based largely on tradition, but the government itself could not have liked the development of farming in areas into which Russian landowners hoped to extend their holdings. A clash was bound to come and in 1700, the state began its campaign in earnest, ordering Cossack settlers along the Khoper and

Medveditsa to move south, closer to Azov. Five years later settlers on the northern Donets were also told to move out. Moreover the government was still concerned at the rate at which peasants were fleeing to the middle Don valley to farm for themselves. The Cossacks still honoured their tradition of asylum and repeated demands for the return of fugitives met with a spontaneous response of passive resistance. The settlements on the middle Don continued to grow.

Tsar Peter was not a man to be baulked. In 1703 officers arrived on the Don to round up runaways 'their wives and children and all their livestock'. One in ten of those caught was taken for forced labour to Azov where an imperial fleet was being built, the rest were flogged and sent back north in chains. Peter interfered in other matters too, decreed that some Don villages should come under the administration of the Admiralty office at Voronezh, declared the mouth of the Don out of bounds to Cossack fishermen, made dried fish products his own monopoly, and forbade Cossacks from mining salt near the upper Don. The autonomy of the Host was being steadily eroded, its affairs interfered in by a governor based initially at Azov and then at Voronezh, and the government took into its own hands the settlement of boundary disputes between the Don Host and its neighbours—the Zaporozhians, Kalmyks and the neo-Cossacks of the Slobodskaya Ukraine. The process was to go into reverse for a time after the failure of Peter's Pruth campaign in 1711 and the consequent loss of Azov, but at the beginning of the eighteenth century Don Cossacks were bristling at a treatment they had never previously experienced. In 1702 the Austrian ambassador to Moscow remarked the 'danger of a Cossack revolt is growing with every hour'[6]; in 1704 a Don Cossack rising was generally expected in southern Russia. But the revolt against the Tsar Peter flared up first, not on the Don, but in another place, not even among Cossacks, but in a city at the extremity of Russia, where the memory of Razin was still very much alive—in Astrakhan.

In 1705 Astrakhan threw out its governors again and elected its own leaders, Cossack style. The people had had enough of Peter's financial demands, his ruthless authoritarianism, his determination to impose Western styles and customs on traditionalist Russia immediately and by force. More peasants were crushed by taxation; serfs and slaves freed by their masters were now drafted into the army or sent back to their captivity; the *streltsy* resented their fall from the status of Muscovy's Praetorian guards; millions of Old Believers were hounded, and pious and traditional people all over Peter's empire were appalled at his wholesale importation of godless foreign customs, the ban on the old style of dress, and the compulsory shaving-off of beards. Old Muscovy was suddenly being changed into a new, un-recognisable Russia. The people did not like it.

Though the Cossacks were exempt from these innovations, Peter, afraid they might join in the Astrakhan revolt, suddenly relaxed the demands for the return of runaways and the expulsion of Cossacks from the middle Don. But in 1706 the Astrakhan rebellion was crushed. The need for Muscovy to tread softly disappeared and the demands for the surrender of recent runaways were not only renewed but back-dated to 1682. When they were ignored, Prince Yuri Dolgoruki and 1,000 troops marched south to the Don country.

Village after village was subjected to Dolgoruki's inquisition. 'Runaways' were winkled out by means of terror. Houses were burned down, old men knouted, suspects had their lips and nostrils slit; all who resisted were hanged. Dolgoruki had soon accumulated about 3,000 people to send back to their 'owners' in the north. Many others had already fled to the extreme west of the Don region. Dolgoruki followed, but on the night of the 8th–9th October 1707 he was attacked by 200 Cossacks. His soldiers were overwhelmed; and he was killed. The five Cossack elders who were acting as his guides escaped in their nightshirts through the dark.

The man who led the attack was Kondrati Bulavin. Born in 1660 the son of a village ataman, he had fought with distinction against the Crimean Tatars and had become ataman of Bakhmut, one of the settlements on which the Dolgorukis and other landowners were casting greedy eyes. In 1704 Bulavin had taken the lead in combatting the neighbouring Izyum regiment of the Slobodskaya Ukraine which was disputing his Cossacks' rights to exploit salt pans which lay between the two settlements, and now he took on the leadership of the recent runaways and planned to resist the intruding Muscovites. Having dealt with Dolgoruki, he issued a call to the whole Don Host to rise up, free the exiles labouring at Azov and Taganrog, and then march with him on Moscow. But the loyalist Ataman Maximov issued sanctions against Bulavin, collected a scratch force together, and at the end of October, with the help of soldiers from the garrison at Azov, managed to disperse the rebels. Bulavin escaped to the steppe and then arrived in Cherkassk disguised as a monk to sound out some elders whom he knew to be sympathetic to his cause. They reckoned that an immediate rising would be premature, and Bulavin headed east towards the Sech.

Many of the Zaporozhians were keen to join him; not so their Ataman, Finenko. But in January 1708, when the Tsar called on him to hand Bulavin over, the Zaporozhians deposed Finenko, ignored the order and when Bulavin set out for the Don, 3,000 of them went with him. It was March 1708 when Bulavin called on the Don Cossacks to join him. He did not limit his appeal to runaways and poorer Cossacks. His messages promising action against 'the evil boyars, governors and officers' were to spread into the Ukraine, the Slobodskaya Ukraine, the Volga region and many provinces in central Russia.[7] He was to call on people 'everywhere' to organise themselves 'according to Cossack customs . . . electing atamans and *esauls*' and for every village and stanitsa to send him twenty men. He soon had about 9,000 men at his command. But Ataman Maximov had not been idle in the meantime and early in April he marched against the rebels at the head of 8,000 supposedly loyalist Cossacks. Many of them went over to Bulavin when the two sides met. The loyalists were defeated and Maximov fled back towards Cherkassk. Bulavin arrived there on 23rd April to find that the place had been barricaded against him. But numerous Cossacks in the town were for him and some of the elders, including I. G. Zershchikov whom Bulavin had consulted the previous October, recognised that the loyalists could not hold out against him, and prudently joined the rising. On 1st May the gates were opened, Bulavin rode into Cherkassk and had the loyalists quickly rounded up.

An assembly was convened to try Maximov and his chief

supporters. They were charged with throwing elderly Cossacks into the river, burning down settlements, providing Dolgoruki with guides, misappropriating pay, and enclosing common-lands for their private use. They were executed. Bulavin was elected Ataman in Maximov's place and one of his first acts was to confiscate 20,000 rubles from the local churches for distribution among the Cossack poor. He had letters issued to the Tsar and nearby Muscovite governors explaining the change in leadership, protesting his loyalty and begging them not to march against the new regime, but by the end of May he knew this line was unavailing and forbade mention of the Tsar's name on pain of death.

An energetic government gave him scant opportunity to dictate the course of the revolt, to choose his targets and his timing. Tsar Peter made haste to mobilise a force of 32,000 gentry militia and, having thought of leading the expedition in person, entrusted it to Major V. Dolgoruki, brother of the slain Prince Yuri. The choice of a vengeful brother to bring the Don to heel was deliberate, and Peter personally instructed Dolgoruki to carry out a reign of terror, to 'go round the Cossack towns and burn all of them down and slash down and hang the people'. The reason? 'You know how much we need the land.'[8]

Some of the elders who had joined Bulavin were soon smuggling out information about his plans. Yet Bulavin's strategy was far from clear. The rebels could not decide whether to march north straightway or to deal first with the garrison at Azov, which threatened their rear. In the end Bulavin divided his forces. He sent Nekrasov north-east to the Volga with some of the 'inn-scum' of Cherkassk, as the government saw his supporters, to take Tsaritsyn and besiege Saratov. Others were sent to help rebel atamans already skirmishing with Dolgoruki's men in the north, while the main force, including the Zaporozhians, marched on Azov. The strategy was disastrous. The Cossacks were defeated in the north and thrown back from Azov with heavy loss. Loyalist conspirators in Cherkassk drove their horses out into the steppe which reduced the rebels' mobility, and as Dolgoruki came on down-river, the bodies of one in ten of his prisoners swinging from the mast heads, many rebel Cossacks in Cherkassk took fright. In the hope of allaying retribution, they hurriedly abandoned Bulavin, sacked many of his supporters among the village atamans and elected the more 'respectable' Zershchikov to take his place as Ataman. Surrounded by Cossacks trying to arrest him, Bulavin shot himself through the head.

Dolgoruki duly arrived in Cherkassk, but the rebellion had spread as far as Tver and Smolensk, and was still raging in the Don outback. Yet before the end of the year the partisans in the north were defeated, though many of them escaped to the Sech, and the government forces had set methodically about the task of dealing with the others. Realising the position to be hopeless, Nekrasov led a caravan of 2,000 Cossacks, their wives and children into voluntary exile beyond the reach of Russian power. He went south-east to the Kuban river, where some Cossack Old Believers, despairing of the grip the new orthodoxy was taking on the Don, had settled some twenty years before. He was soon followed by another thousand Cossack families, and together they built up a new life under the protection of the Sultan. They were to continue the fight from the Kuban, making repeated raids into southern Russia until, in 1722, the Sultan, in his turn, pulled the reins in on them. Their descendants were moved to the Danube and settled ultimately near Istanbul, where some were still living after 1945.

Some 7,000 Cossacks perished as a result of Bulavin's revolt— in battle or in the aftermath of execution. Among them was the elder Zershchikov who had first seemed friendly to Bulavin and had then betrayed him. Forty-four settlements in the Khoper, Medveditsa and Donets valleys were destroyed, and nearly 4,500 square miles of territory on the northern and western Don were incorporated into Russia proper. The Dolgorukis had got their extra lands at last.[9]

The territory of the Host was now considered part of the Russian province of Azov, and though the Cossacks retained a large degree of internal autonomy they were subject to careful government scrutiny. In 1709 Tsar Peter secured the election of the reliable Peter Ramazanov as Ataman, and in April he made the long journey to Cherkassk in person to inspect the decomposing heads of Bulavin and Zershchikov, and to receive the cringing protestations of loyalty of the Don elders, who were henceforth defined by Muscovite standards as 'the known and the wise'.

But though the Don was subdued, the Cossacks had not done with Peter yet. His programme of dragging a backward Russia into the eighteenth century by the scruff of its neck was producing a volley of opposition from the borderlands. Had the rebellions all come at once they might have done for Peter. Only the volley was ragged, unco-ordinated, allowing Peter to deal successively with the rebellion in Astrakhan and then with the Don. Yet the latest threat, deriving unexpectedly from Mazepa, Hetman of the Ukraine, seemed the most dangerous of all.

The romantic picture painted by the poet Byron of a naked Mazepa sent galloping over the steppe bound to the back of a wild horse as punishment for making love to a Polish courtier's wife, is unfortunately unsubstantiated. The son of a Ukrainian gentleman, Ivan Mazepa had received a good Polish education, made a wisely profitable marriage, and changed his allegiance repeatedly and advantageously during the anarchic times that followed Bogdan's death. A politician of the Machiavellian type, Mazepa could trim his sails to meet any political winds of change. He had been a henchman of virtually every Hetman since Khmelnitski, contriving to align himself successively with each rival party as it came to the fore. He had been Poland's man and then Russia's, and having insinuated himself into the favours of the powerful Prince Golytsyn, was finally appointed Hetman of the Russian Ukraine.

After more than twenty years in office, he had accumulated a vast fortune, acquiring considerable estates with thousands of peasants in Russia proper as well as in the Ukraine. Members of the Cossack oligarchy who filled the chief posts under him also prospered, the more successful landgrabbers among them becoming aristocrats, preserving hardly a trace of their ancestral traditions. During the past two centuries the Cossacks had been gradually stratified on class lines, and under Mazepa the process was accelerated. The rank and file either became gentlemen farmers or were depressed into the peasant class, and though there was no serf legislation in the province, peasants who dared to leave the elders' estates were often searched out, beaten or hanged, and many were relegated to the position of serfs regardless of law.

Mazepa was presiding over the final liquidation of Ukrainian Cossackdom. He was not popular. There were repeated rebellions against his rule and in 1687 he had had to call in Russian troops to stand guard over his residence in Baturin. But he was the trusted friend, as well as the puppet, of Tsar Peter.

Mazepa's greed and ambition did not diminish with old age. An offer of the title Prince and the lordship of Vitebsk, Polotsk and Courland made by Charles XII, King of Sweden, with the connivance of the Polish King, proved attractive enough to buy his loyalty. In return for this Mazepa promised to help Charles in his war with Russia. A loyalist called Kochubei got wind of the plot and warned the Tsar. But Peter would not believe it. Kochubei's daughter had been compromised by the old Hetman, and Peter imagined Kochubei had fabricated the story in hopes of obtaining revenge, and had him executed. Even when Charles marched south and Mazepa, ordered to join Peter with his forces, refused to move, pleading various excuses, the Tsar could still not believe that Mazepa had turned traitor. Only after weeks of dissembling did he realise the truth and send an army marching towards Baturin.

Mazepa hurried out to join the Swedes, though with fewer than the 20,000 men nominally at his call. But a good many Zaporozhians joined him. Though they had long disliked Mazepa because of his social policies and his constant support for the Tsar, his warning that Peter intended to transport them together with a large body of Ukrainians to the wild lands beyond the Volga, his calls for freedom from Muscovite tyranny and his judicious distribution of hard cash, won them over. In March 1709 the Zaporozhian Ataman Gordiyenko left the Sech to join Charles and Mazepa, raising a further 15,000 Ukrainians on the way.

The rebel propaganda was countered vigorously by the Tsar. His promises secured the loyalty of the majority of the Ukrainian elders. Then Mazepa saw his hopes dashed in a single day on the battlefield of Poltava. The Swedes and the Cossacks were utterly crushed and Mazepa fled south, clutching two barrels of gold coin, to find a refuge with the Turks.

Peter had regained control of the Ukraine, and now it was the Zaporozhians' turn to suffer. Despite their usefulness as frontier guards against the Tatars, they had dared to join Mazepa. For Tsar Peter the Sech had become 'an accursed place, the root of the evil and the hope of the enemy'.[10] He would tolerate its existence no longer. In May 1709, two months before his victory at Poltava, he sent troops into it. The Zaporozhians held out for three days, then succumbed. Every barrack block, every building on the Sech was ransacked and burned down, and many Zaporozhians, including Gordiyenko, escaped downstream to settle under the protection of the Crimean Khan.[11] Here they fell in with the plots of Mazepa's ex-secretary, Pilip Orlik, who was living nearby at the Turkish fort of Bender. Orlik assumed the title of Ukrainian Hetman-in-exile and the Zaporozhians hoped he might bring them home again. But as time dragged on the prospects of a victorious return faded away. In 1714 they replaced their ataman, Gordiyenko, and, though a hard core of anti-Muscovites stayed beyond Peter's reach, many began to drift back to their old haunts in Zaporozhiye and make their peace with the Russian state.

Mazepa had tried to rouse the Zaporozhians to his cause by warning them that the Tsar intended to transport them to distant corners of the empire. The warning was to be vindicated, and the Zaporozhians were not the only Cossacks to be affected. Anxious to secure its fast extending borders, the state forced many Cossacks to pull up their roots and set them down again in strange soil. In 1712, for instance, the Grebensk group of Terek Cossacks were moved to the north bank of the river to form the basis of a cordon line against the increasingly hostile peoples of the Caucasus. Then to secure the gains of the successful war with Persia in 1722, the line was moved southwards and a Cossack colony was stabilised on the Agrakhan peninsula near the Terek delta, and since reinforcements were needed, 1,000 Don Cossack families were ordered to leave their homes and settle there.

Transportation was only one of the ways in which the state could disrupt Cossack lives these days. Peter's incessant wars kept the younger men away from home for years on end sometimes. Of the 51,000 men who won the Persian war, 20,000 were Cossacks, nearly half of them from the Don. Don Cossacks took part in the siege of Riga in 1711, in the Pruth campaign the following year and were with Sheremetyev's army the year after. The Yaik Cossacks were just as heavily engaged, fighting at Poltava, on the Pruth, in the Kuban and at Kharkov. In addition, 1,500 of them and 500 Terek Cossacks made up a third of the force Prince Bekovich-Cherkasski led out on the disastrous Central Asian campaign of 1717. They set out bravely enough on horses and camels to cross the desert steppe to Khiva, but few of them returned and those who did, it was said, did so with their hair turned grey from the experience.

If most Cossack communities were almost continuously embroiled in warfare on their own doorstep, the Yaik Cossacks were particularly affected. Charged with the pacification of rebellious Bashkirs and Kalmyks and the hunting-down of runaway *streltsy*, they were in constant peril now from Kirghiz warriors. Every fishing and salt-gathering expedition needed the cover of a strong guard. And despite the value of their service, the government consistently added to their burdens and turned a deaf ear to their requests for extra aid.

They were kept short of artillery necessary for their defence and in 1719 and 1720 were allotted no military supplies at all. They refused a pay offer which was sufficient for only 600 men. It was increased, but then reduced to the lower figure again. High-handed officials prowled the Yaik in search of runaway serfs; Cossacks were barred from selling their surplus salt, and when they visited Russian towns to trade, officials would sometimes confiscate their fish, and turn the entire contents of their carts on to the ground, ruining their goods, as they searched them.

Three times Ataman Rukavishnikov of the Yaik journeyed to St. Petersburg to complain. He was given little satisfaction. One official was put on trial, and the Yaik Host was presented with new colours, studded with imperial eagles. But these were hollow gestures. The shortages, the searches and the insults continued and on his third visit there in 1722 Ataman Rukavishnikov was arrested and taken back to the Yaik under guard of 300 dragoons and deposited in gaol. Colonel I. Zakharov, in command of the dragoons, had instructions to draw up a register of all the Cossacks, including children, and to inquire into complaints lodged, not by the Cossacks, but by the governors of neighbouring Kazan and Astrakhan.

Peter's new military system with its heavy tax burdens and exact registrations had been driving ever more people to lawlessness. Bands of outlaw robbers roamed the land, and, between 1719 and 1727 alone as many as 100,000 peasants fled to the frontiers, chiefly to the south-east and east now rather than to the Don where the government had at last succeeded in restricting the flow of runaways. But the state was still obsessively afraid of another Bulavin or Gordiyenko arising with an appeal to the old Cossack values which could spread havoc through the Empire. It clamped down on the Cossacks at the merest hint of trouble.

When Colonel Zakharov arrived in Yaitsk in March 1723 the Cossacks were at the point of rebellion. He forestalled it by a sudden purge. Many arrests were carried out, anyone suspected of being a potential trouble-maker was hauled in, and the remaining Cossacks, duly chastened, were assembled to take their oaths of loyalty, Zakharov having orders to hang one in ten of all who refused. Then the inquisition began. Every man on the Yaik was questioned, those who were insufficiently co-operative were tortured. Some elders who were still at liberty managed to contact Ataman Rukashnikov in gaol but he had given up hope of any effective opposition. A centurion called Chuvachennikov planned to follow the example of Nekrasov of the Don and 'escape downstream to the sea and find some likely place where we can settle'.[12] But a plot to free Rukavishnikov was set aside in favour of a petition for the prisoners' release. It did not succeed. The new Ataman, Merkulev, who had had his own brushes with authority in the past now decided that obedience was the only way of survival. Oppositionist leaders still at liberty were arrested, questioned, and duly sentenced together with those already in custody. Rukavishnikov was quartered; two others were publicly hanged.

In due course Zakharov produced his lists, naming every Cossack and his origins, whether peasant, runaway, tribesman or soldier. He counted only 3,196 Cossacks. The rest all lost their rights. The Yaik simmered down. The Cossacks retained

169

some political autonomy, but it was only nominal so far as the more important issues were concerned. They were allowed to elect their own Atamans, but the government insisted on confirming them in office, and, once installed, they could no longer be removed at the will of the Cossack assembly.

The Zaporozhians and the Yaik Cossacks had already been crushed. So were those of the Don. When Ataman Ramazanov died in 1715 the government's candidate, Frolov, was duly elected and three years later when the assembly decided that Frolov had held office long enough and elected another Ataman, Tsar Peter immediately made it clear that Frolov had been confirmed as Ataman and that Ataman he would remain. In 1723, when the office became vacant again, the Cossacks elected the man who had led them on the Persian expedition the year before, but any popular Cossack choice was unacceptable to Peter. He cancelled the election and ordered the Cossacks to choose his candidate.

The Cossacks whose delegations to the Russian capital had once been welcomed with the respect due to foreign ambassadors went there now to receive orders, and it was a brave Ataman who dared register a complaint. They still dealt with the *Posolski Prikaz*—from 1718 the College of Foreign Affairs—but on 3rd March 1721 even this token privilege was denied them by the bald statement to the effect that henceforth 'the Don, Yaik and Grebensk [Terek] Cossacks will be administered by the College of War'.

Neither mass uprising nor subtle politicking had succeeded in holding the state at bay. The rampaging, democratic Cossack communities were no longer the free societies they once had been. The old institutions of self-government survived but they were gradually sterilised of all real content. The Ataman became a mere delegate for a Ministry in St. Petersburg; the assembly, which was to meet ever more rarely, became a rubber stamp to endorse decisions already made, and ordinary Cossacks took less and less part in its proceedings. Elders were still elected, but came to hold office for life. Cossacks were ruled more and more by imperial whim and less and less by their own customs and traditions.

The free-ranging, devil-may-care, self-sufficient, rampant

Cossacks were on the way to becoming servile minions of an autocratic master. Resistance did not cease, but it went underground. The old spirit would flash again, but already there was a sense of fatalism. Cossacks who used to boast that they had 'never bowed to the heathen, nor asked Moscow how they should behave', now sang a quieter, a more furtive, tune— 'live, brothers, while you may; when Moscow finds out it will go hard with us'.

Their independence lost, the Cossacks' old spirit of solidarity was gradually eroded by accelerated economic and by social change. Few things reconcile a man more to political impotence, perhaps, than a fat increase in his standard of living, and, their political freedoms curtailed, the Cossacks began to concentrate on their personal affairs and fortunes. Some of them grew too rich to be daring, and the Russian government was able to exploit the growing differences of interest between them and the Cossack mass, and encourage them to identify their interests with the state's. To preserve their liberties, Cossacks came to struggle as much among themselves as against the Tsar. This was true for all the Cossack communities— Zaporozhians, Yaik, and Don Cossacks alike.

By 1728 the Zaporozhians had had enough of living in exile under Muslim protection and had humbly petitioned the government to be allowed to return. Their request was eventually conceded and they were granted 20,000 rubles a year and supplies of grain, powder and shot in payment for their obedience and true services,[13] though, just to make sure, Russian troops were stationed close by to keep an eye on them. But the fire seemed to have gone out of the stormy Zaporozhians. They were even reduced to bribing officials. In the words of a member of a Zaporozhian delegation to St. Petersburg, 'without presents we would have got nowhere, achieved nothing'[14] and, in all, they were soon reckoned to be 'so thoroughly subdued . . . that they cannot for a long time be in any condition to revolt'.[15]

In fact they were too busy accumulating wealth. Though still primarily a bachelor society their population was increasing— mainly by accepting runaways and to some extent by kidnapping children—and by 1762 they numbered 18,000 adult males. The menace of the Crimean Tatars had declined, allowing the

171

Zaporozhians to operate far from the environs of the rebuilt Sech, and their activities had spread from the river Bug in the west to the borders of the Don in the east. Indeed, the Don Cossacks were soon complaining that the unscrupulous Zaporozhians were rustling their horses and poaching in their waters.[16] But though privateering still played a part in their economy, they were becoming primarily a community of farmers. Sheep-rearing was popular since it needed little labour, but they also raised cattle and horses, kept bees, tended gardens and orchards and sowed 'the fields with various grains'. They enjoyed a remarkable rate of economic growth. In the 1730s they had to import 80,000 bushels of corn a year; by the seventies they were exporting a grain surplus.[17]

Trade increased. Tailors, bootmakers, brewers and other tradesmen set up shop outside the Sech, and merchants came from afar to buy their produce. By the mid-fifties as many as 1,500 wagons, loaded with salt and fish, left Zaporozhia every year for the Polish Ukraine. Such a caravan—'many carts piled with various kinds of salted fish, dried spinal cord of sturgeon, and fish-oil'—came to Uman for the fair in 1762 and having sold their goods for a substantial profit the Cossacks 'made merry in Uman for a long time'.[18] They also exported grain, oil, tobacco, wool and hides to Russia, Poland, Moldavia and Wallachia, importing metal and leather goods, arms, cloth, dyes, medicines, sugar, pepper, tobacco and a variety of household goods in return. Indeed, the Zaporozhians became such avid businessmen that they even traded with the Crimea when it was in a state of war with Russia, and overcame their ancestral prejudices to the extent of providing Jews with special protection to come and trade with them.

Small fortunes were made out of milling and fishing enterprises, or purveying wines, fats and other commodities to the Russian army stationed in the south, and some warriors of Zaporozhiye soon became substantial men of property. One such, called Kalnishevski, who sold horses as far afield as Prussia, accumulated a considerable fortune in livestock—639 horses, nine buffalo, 1,076 cattle, 14,045 sheep and goats, as well as some pigs, asses and camels and about 40,000 rubles' worth of property.[19]

Kalnishevski's house was carpeted, its walls were hung with icons, gem-encrusted sabres, and fire-arms of French and English, as well as of Russian, manufacture. Crystal and china-ware adorned his table, and his larder was stocked with large quantities of rice and olive oil, sugar, wine and dates. He had treasure chests containing rolls of expensive cloth, fine furs, various objects made of gold, silver, enamel and pearl, as well as quantities of coin and a bible. Kalnishevski also owned a telescope and, somewhat out of character for a discerning man of property, a couple of imitation gold watches.[20]

Other Cossacks also acquired their status symbols—framed pictures, wall-clocks, tables weighed down with sausages and foreign wines, and the dashing ceremonial costume of the Zaporozhian—loose breeches, golden cummerbund, red tunic, white silk coat, and a tall fur hat topped with silk and hung with a golden tassel.

But there was another estate in Zaporozhiye—the poor. Many Cossacks were unable to profit from the boom, lacking sufficient capital to build a shack in the outback, take a wife perhaps, and start farming, fishing, or carting on their own account. These belonged to the *seroma*, the bachelor class which made up the garrison of the Sech. The Sech, itself, besides administrative buildings, consisted of a few dozen wooden barracks (*kureni*). Each had between 200 and 500 Cossacks ascribed to it, though only a fraction of its members, generally the poor, actually lived there. Life in the barracks was communal, and the food was free, but a *kuren* was more of a Dickensian doss-house than a knightly hall. Run by an ataman who often contrived to make an unofficial profit out of the communal fund, it was a dark, cold room furnished with long tables on which the Cossacks slept and where their meals—generally consisting of just a mess of gruel—were served. There was no cutlery and anyone with a taste for fish or meat usually had to provide it himself. Some of the Cossacks who lived here were old hands, others boys as little as eleven years old, who suffered frequent thrashings from the barracks ataman.[21] There was a school on the Sech but it had very little impact on the literacy of the community.

A Cossack could usually leave the Sech after a period and try to make his fortune. He would generally start by selling his services as a hired hand to some richer Cossack in the outback. But the odds against his saving enough to start some farm or business enterprise of his own were considerable. Rates of pay were low—on a farm rarely more than $3\frac{1}{2}$ rubles a year plus keep and sometimes keep alone; in a fishery anything from five to twenty rubles a season. A man was fortunate to make a profit of six or seven rubles a year and this was barely enough to equip himself for the military service which was required of him, for a good horse cost as much as fifteen rubles and a rifle three; an ordinary shirt cost nearly half a ruble, a pair of boots at least that, a decent cap nearly twice as much.[22]

As a result, about 4,000 Zaporozhians could only afford to serve on foot,[23] and some could not afford to serve at all. These either lost their privileged status as Cossacks altogether or had to serve as substitutes for richer Cossacks who were not prepared to neglect their private affairs by going on campaign in person. Nor did the hirers equip their substitutes as well as when they went to war themselves. The rich man took warm blankets, ornate saddlery, a carbine, lance and sabre, wore a pair of pistols in his belt and carried two more on his saddle. The poor black-shirted Cossack on the other hand rode a nag, and was armed only with a lance, sabre and some sort of firearm which might or might not fire.

Most Zaporozhians were neither rich nor poor, but there was a definite polarity within the community which was reflected in the political as well as the economic aspects of their life. A very high proportion of the 'elders'—the Ataman and his fifty assistants at the central chancery at the Sech, the thirty-eight barrack atamans and the colonels in charge of the five up-country districts (*palanki*)—came almost exclusively from the ranks of the well-to-do. Free elections to these offices were still held annually but the frequency with which certain elders got elected—I. Malashevich was elected Ataman nine times and the prosperous Mr. Kalnishevski in no fewer than ten successive years[24]—indicates the use of bribery, rigging and probably of intimidation too.

The burdens of office were heavily outweighed by the rewards. Since the elders were responsible for the distribution of land and of fishing rights they were in a position to ensure that they and their friends were allotted the best. The sharing-out of the grain and pay—which tended to settle at the sum of 5,550 rubles[25]—and the storing of the other supplies furnished by an appreciative monarch, presented them with splendid opportunities for misappropriation, and their responsibility for enforcing the few rules that regulated the society put them in the way of bribes.

On the whole the rank and file were not very much concerned. This was an open society, economically and socially, in which any man could make his way. Only those in danger of losing their status, those whose very penury made it almost impossible for them ever to become financially independent, were dissatisfied, and their needs were too immediate to resort to politics as a means of redress. It was these poor Zaporozhian bachelors—men who 'not only own no horses or cattle but not even the clothes on their backs'[26]—who formed the core of the notorious *gaidamaks.*

These 'thieves and vagabonds who subsist on nothing but rapine',[27] would ride north into the weakly guarded Polish Ukraine where, joined by vengeful peasants, they would terrorise the countryside, murder officials, Poles, Jews, and the richer peasants and carry off such plunder as they could find.

The *gaidamaks* have been characterised as patriotic freedom fighters by the Ukrainian poet Taras Shevchenko, though in fact they were illiterate and quite innocent of the ideologies of nationalism; and as religious rioters by the Jewish historian Simon Dubnow, though there were Jews among the *gaidamaks* and at least one gang of Jewish bandits which operated in the *gaidamak* style.[28] Traditional hatreds certainly played their part, but the *gaidamaks* were primarily in immediate and primitive search of subsistence and rough justice. They were organised criminals, like the professional kidnappers of Sardinia; they were also rebels bursting out against a society which treated them too hard—like the rural bandits of nineteenth-century Hungary, the Argentinian *gauchos*, the outlaws of Mexico and the anarchistic freebooters who terrorised southern Russia and the Ukraine after 1917.

Using tactics in line with the best guerrilla doctrines of

Chairman Mao and General Vo Nguyen Diap, they would retire to hide-outs in Zaporozhiye when things became too hot, then ride out again in bands of anything from a dozen to two hundred men. Their operations were generally small-scale, hit-and-run affairs, but sometimes they attracted enough runaways, deserters and poor Ukrainian farmers to mount much bolder campaigns.

In 1768 a Zaporozhian called Maxim Zelezhnyak collected a force of 1,000 *gaidamaks* and slashed, burned and terrorised his way right up to the gates of Uman in the Polish Ukraine, where many Jews and Polish gentlemen had run before them to take shelter. The garrison of Polish service Cossacks under Ivan Gonta went over to the *gaidamaks* and in the outbreak of mindless violence which followed, thousands were massacred. The movement spread like wildfire and soon threatened to engulf Russia, too.

The government took brisk measures. It already had troops stationed in Poland and it ordered them to catch Gonta and Zelezhnyak. Pressure was also applied to the Zaporozhian elders, despite their protests that the *gaidamaks* were not Zaporozhians at all, but 'brigands calling themselves Cossacks'. In fact a roll-call revealed that 649 Cossacks were missing from the Sech. The rest were made to swear to fight the *gaidamaks* and posses were organised to track them down.[29]

As troops began to restore order in the Ukraine, large bands of *gaidamaks* appeared in Zaporozhiye. Reports came in of attacks on outlying farms, of local revolts against the elders, of crowds, marauding, knives in hand. As winter approached the disturbances became more serious and on 26th December a revolt was staged in the Sech itself. According to Ataman Kalnishevski, 'the poor Cossacks' wanted to kill him, together with all 'the elders, past and present, and after them the worthy Cossacks'.[30] Together with other leaders he bolted to the Russian garrison nearby. Its commander handled the situation with extreme adroitness, encouraged the rebels to elect a spokesman, then persuaded him to get them to disperse. Only a minority refused to do so. There was a sharp and bloody encounter, and the outbreak was quelled.

This was not to be the last challenge to the Zaporozhian

leadership. In December 1769 following several violent incidents in the outlying districts, there was another, less serious, rebellion in the Sech. Next year, many Cossacks refused point-blank to do military service because of inadequate pay; *gaidamaks* were active again in 1773, and in 1774 army units on their way from the Turkish front were attacked as they passed through Zaporozhiye.

The government was running out of patience with the entire Zaporozhian community. Although the elders and the more prosperous Cossacks had nothing to do with the disorders, for years past they had been sheltering runaways despite repeated instructions not to do so. The conclusion of a successful war against the Turks and of a treaty which brought the Crimea— that age-long obstacle between Russia and the Black Sea—into the Russian sphere of influence made the Zaporozhians seem no longer to be needed, and in June 1775 Russian troops surrounded the Sech and, heavily outnumbered, the Cossacks gave in without a fight. The elders were arrested and Kalni-shevski, the last Ataman, was transported to end his long life in the Arctic monastery of Solovetsk.[31] Zaporozhiye was incor-porated into 'New Russia', the people subjected to military rule. Every building on the Sech was obliterated. It would never be rebuilt, though within twenty years the irrepressible Zaporo-zhians were to rise again in another place.

On the Don life was quieter than in Zaporozhiye, but social and economic change had been having a similar impact on the fabric of society. The Tatar menace had declined, prosperity was increasing, and, with it, the scale of farming and fishing opera-tions. Cattle-raising had become a more reliable source of income, and by the 1760s there were over 100 fish-processing factories on the Don. Lumbermen went out in gangs near Azov to cut timber, and in some southern settlements vines were found to thrive. In the north, grain-farming was paramount, but hunting still added to many a household's purse, and Cossacks also grew melons, cucumbers and sunflowers outside their cabins. Surpluses of fish, caviare, cattle and horses, wool and grain attracted Greek, Turkish and Persian as well as Russian mer-chants,[32] fairs thrived and the Don soon boasted over 500 shops. The number of villages and townships had increased to over a

hundred and by the end of the century the Cossack population
had grown to about 200,000.

Newcomers accounted for much of the increase. Emigration
from the Ukraine was not banned until 1783, and runaways still
came from Russia proper. The government issued over a hundred
orders during the course of the century in its attempts to stop
this traffic, but unofficial asylum was still granted by the
Cossacks, particularly by the richer men who needed labour
for their enterprises. The newcomers were generally admitted to
Cossack status after a time, though many of them continued to
work as hired hands, and they were joined by established
Cossacks who were unable by working on their own account to
accumulate enough for a horse and the military equipment
necessary to maintain their Cossack status. Poverty on the
Don even gave rise to something like *gaidamak* movement,
though on a much smaller scale.

The large majority of Cossacks were not touched by poverty
however, though they had to be vigilant in guarding what they
had—and not only against robber gangs. Complaints flowed
into the Host chancery of unscrupulous men grabbing a neighbour's land or rustling his cattle. When the authorities, as often
was the case, failed to take official action the injured party often
took the law into his own hands, drove off the offender's livestock
or burned down his house or barns.

A small class of prosperous oligarchs formed the top of the
social scale, and from these the elders of the Host were mostly
drawn. A number of these families developed into dynasties
who, backed by the state, came to dominate the Don, politically,
economically and socially. One of them, Danilo Yefremov, was
chosen by the Empress Anne to be Ataman in 1738. Danilo had
his picture painted, dressed in the finest silks and brocade and
wearing a huge portrait of the Empress hung by a chain around
his neck. He looked the personification of the wealthy Cossack
oligarch. He decked his wife out, too, with the costly rings and
bracelets, the jewels and the stiff, embroidered gowns favoured
by the new rich. Danilo was proud of himself, servile to the great
men in the capital and contemptuous of the Cossack assembly.
He shut the mouths of all who challenged his authority or the
government's rulings, and was showered with rewards for his

services—made a Major-General and raised to the rank of privy counsellor, which, for a Cossack, was unprecedented. When he retired in 1753 he was succeeded by his son Stepan.

Stepan Yefremov became even richer than his father, came to own several trading establishments and managed to acquire over 500 male serfs. Other wealthy Cossacks were also influenced by the Russian landlords who founded estates on the Don in the eighteenth century and were settling peasants on them. They, too, were beginning to acquire serfs to supplement the free labour available on the Don, which was in short supply and consequently more expensive. But their rights in this respect were limited. Their social aspirations were to reach such a point that, so far from asking for more autonomy for the Host as a whole, the Cossack leadership was to press hardest of all to be put on a par with the Russian landed aristocracy. It was symptomatic of how far members of the aspiring class, impressed by the privileges and opportunities enjoyed by the Russian gentry, were becoming estranged from the Cossacks of the rank and file, and from the old Cossack ideals.

The stresses which underlay society in Zaporozhiye and the Don had also developed on the Yaik, though it was less well placed commercially and its economic development still retarded by incessant border warfare with Kazakhs and other tribesmen. Like the Israeli frontier *kibbutniks* the Yaik Cossacks had to go out armed to gather in their hay harvest and organise full-scale convoys to protect their annual expeditions for salt. Nevertheless some of them managed to profit from the conflict to the extent that they could capture more livestock from the nomads than the nomads did from them. In 1760 they drove off 8,000 horses and when the authorities ordered their return, Ataman Borodin surrendered only half of them.[33]

The robber instinct was still strong. But plunder was declining in comparative importance as a means of income, and though Yaik Cossacks had begun to plough early in the eighteenth century, and some rice, cotton and water melons were grown, arable farming did not account for much either. It was cattle-raising and fishing which remained the major sources of income, and grain, metal goods, cloth, and other necessities had all to be imported.

As many as a quarter of the Yaik Cossacks were unpropertied and though their pay, of between ten and thirty rubles, was higher than in Zaporozhiye it was barely enough for a man to equip himself for service, buy forage and food and keep his family as well. As a consequence Russian officers inspecting the cordon line noticed many deficiencies. In 1745, for instance, only fifty-one out of a command of 1,000 men were found to have sabres—and here, too, many a poor Cossack, unable to find his own equipment, had to hire himself out to a richer man.

On the other hand there were Cossacks who owned as many as 10,000 sheep, 500 horses and 700 head of cattle, men who could afford to build a neat stone house in Yaitsk, and dress their wives in gaudy headdresses, shoes and bright silk stockings while most womenfolk went bare-foot. The private ranches and fisheries belonging to such men came to vie in importance with the old co-operatives and even the administration of the communal fishing was less egalitarian than it once had been. Every Cossack registered for service was issued with a ticket allowing him to participate, but by the middle of the eighteenth century atamans got four tickets, elders three and junior officers two apiece, and, since the tickets were transferable, the rich could take an even larger share, while a poor man might not be able to use his single ticket because of the high cost of the equipment needed. A sizeable boat and nets up to 200 feet long were necessary to bring any considerable return from the spring season, while in the December season seines up to a thousand feet long were used and though friends might band together to find the capital to equip themselves, a hundred rubles, which was what it cost, was still a lot to find.

Since the state required that atamans and elders should be men of financial standing, political power became the purlieu of certain prosperous families like the Borodins, the Tambovtsevs and the Merkulevs who used office to grow richer still. They made illegal profits out of communal hay-reaping and fishing, pocketed official pay, insisted on 'fees' before enrolling new-comers to the community, and even used servicemen for their own purposes, posting Cossacks detailed to cover the communal hay harvest in 1748 as guards over their private herds of cattle.

Yet they had their problems too. As their herds of livestock

How the State
punished
dissidents,
Dashkov collection

Pugachev, *Eighteenth Century portrait*

Seal used by Pugachev, and his
attempt at a signature

grew, the demand for labour outran the supply. Circassian slaves could occasionally be bought and captured tribesmen set to work, but in 1724 only 308 workers were employed by 285 Cossacks. More were doubtless hidden from the registering officers, and the statistic takes no account of seasonal Cossack labour. Even so, labour was chronically short, and runaways came to be welcomed with open arms. In particular the Yaik became a known refuge for Old Believers. Most Yaik Cossacks shared their creed, prayed at home rather than in the established churches, and they often suffered for their beliefs. Hundreds— including both runaways and elders—were arrested in the 1750s of whom several drowned or froze to death on the way to prison and more on hunger strike.

Religious fellow-feeling and economic self-interest combined to encourage Cossacks to employ runaways on their farms. But while, as Soviet historians emphasise, a patriarchal concern often masked an exploitation of labour that was sometimes vicious, some Cossack employers were prepared to risk severe punishment in the runaways' defence. One day in 1759 a lieutenant, a corporal and three soldiers, accompanied by an elder of the host, rode into the farm of another elder called I. Loginev, in search of runaways. Loginev immediately mustered his hands, and striking 'a soldier ... on the head with a cudgel' and stabbing him 'in the left arm with a lance', chased the intruders 'out of the yard', afterwards threatening that if the lieutenant, or any other governmental representative, should trespass on his property again, he would shoot him dead with his pistol.[34]

Conflicts arose between the elders and the rank and file and among the elders themselves as venal atamans followed one another into office by means of rigged elections and shameless governmental interference. In 1738 when Ataman G. Merkulev lost the election by a large margin, the government immediately sent in troops and had the new leaders carried off to Astrakhan. The Russian commander then connived with Merkulev and his friends, to instal Vasili Prytkov as Ataman, 'by their own will', as the Cossacks said, 'and not by our common decision'.[35] The government now insisted on nominating the Ataman, from among three 'God-fearing' candidates submitted to it. The Cossacks did not always knuckle under, but their opposition

G

was futile. Even when they murdered Ataman Borodin, Prytkov's successor, in 1748, he was only succeeded by his brother, who misused the office even more outrageously.

Prominent among the new Ataman's opponents was the same Loginev who had used violence in defence of the runaways he was sheltering. Loginev journeyed all the way to St. Petersburg to lodge complaints against Ataman Borodin, but, achieving nothing, returned to the Yaik in 1761 and issued an open challenge to the leadership, calling Borodin and his cronies 'thieves', who pocketed all the communal pay and paid out nothing. The Ataman promptly bolted to the Russians to report a 'rebellion' and the government set up an inquiry, as a result of which Loginev was deported to Siberia and several other 'troublemakers' were exiled, flogged or sent to the unpopular post of Guryev at the southern end of the Yaik defensive cordon.

The government at last decided to dispense with Borodin's services, only to replace him with another of his kind. The army commandant at Yaitsk duly ordered an old aide of Borodin's to be 'elected' Ataman and when the Cossacks refused, he had several of them clapped in irons. The dissidents sent another delegation to the capital and another commission of inquiry was appointed. But obedience came before justice in the government's scale of values and a martinet, Major-General Cherepov, was sent out to restore it.

The Cossacks were mustered on the square outside the chancery. Surrounded by dragoons, they were ordered to recognise their former elders and to sign a declaration admitting 'guilt'. 'Please, your Excellency', the Cossacks protested, 'we know of no guilt on our part'. But Cherepov was impervious, and determined. He ordered his dragoons to open fire on the defenceless ranks. Shots sang into the air above the Cossacks' heads. Still they would not submit, and the furious General barked again. The soldiers were told to fire into the crowd this time. But a sergeant called out for the order 'to kill innocent people' to be put in writing. There was an ominous silence. Cherepov slowly turned an apoplectic red—then grabbed for his sword. A tactful major quickly ordered a salvo to be fired, aimed at the Cossacks' knees, and when the smoke cleared away three or four men lay dead and half a dozen wounded on the ground.

Since the outraged survivors obstinately maintained their innocence, they were kept to attention on the square all night long. It was winter. By the following morning their blood had cooled and they were at last prevailed on to admit their 'guilt'.[36]

Cherepov was soon replaced by a Guards Captain who rightly concluded that the trouble had been caused, as the Cossacks had always maintained, by the elders pocketing communal funds. But this was no Daniel come to judgement, no enemy of corruption. He ordered fresh elections to be held, but showed himself ready enough to be bought, and the new Ataman, Peter Tambovtsev, promptly rewarded him with 5,000 rubles for securing his election. Like his predecessors, Tambovtsev treated the office as a means to profit. He sold privileges, and was even prepared to intercede on behalf of Loginev and the other exiles in return for a suitable fee. He was also a reliable friend of the government. In 1769, when young Cossacks ordered to the Terek refused to go, saying that their parents were withholding the usual blessing from them because of the godless new styles of dress they would be required to wear, Tambovtsev had 400 of them arrested and applied for the removal of 620 disobedient Cossacks from the register.

Rumours spread that the government was about to convert the free Cossacks into hussars, subjected to regular army discipline, and, what was anathema to Old Believers, make them shave off their beards. So in 1770, when an attempt was made to draft Yaik Cossacks into the new Moscow Legion, they called it 'sinful' and refused to join. Two thousand found guilty of disobedience were conscripted, given extra periods of service, or knouted. But several ring-leaders, condemned to life servitude in government factories, avoided arrest and disappeared into hiding.

Meanwhile the resentment against Tambovtsev was growing, even among prosperous Cossacks and some elders. A Cossack centurion led a delegation to the capital to complain of being denied fishing and hay-reaping rights and of receiving no pay for six years. He had the privilege of being beaten up by the Minister for War Count Chernyshev in person, and although the complaints were eminently justified, Catherine pronounced the petition to be a tissue of lies and ordered the delegation's arrest.

Somehow the centurion managed to escape and early in 1772 he returned to the Yaik.

Meanwhile, Major-General von Trauenberg had arrived to supervise another orgy of whippings. But a convoy of prisoners had been ambushed and released and, sensing that armed rebellion was near, the General sent for reinforcements. At this point the centurion returned and spun a story to a Cossack crowd to the effect that Chernyshev had suppressed the Empress's order restoring self-government to the Yaik, and called for the Ataman and some of the elders to be replaced. He got strong support. The number of dissidents grew from hour to hour as disgruntled Cossacks armed themselves and galloped into town. They refused to disperse upon request and, without his reinforcements, Trauenberg dared not make them. He withdrew to the chancery building under cover of his thirty cannon.

It was bitterly cold, but the excited crowd stayed in the streets all night. By the morning of 13th of January the place was teeming with Cossacks come in from the line, and a huge procession, including many women and children, formed up. With icons borne before them, they walked first to the church to take oaths of mutual loyalty, and then towards the chancery building, a group of spokesmen and a priest going on before. Met by Captain Durnov, they asked that their official leaders be removed from office and that von Trauenberg withdraw in accordance with Catherine's supposed 'order'. Durnov promised consideration of their request and to provide an answer within ten days provided they disperse, which they refused to do. By now the square was crammed tight with people, the side streets, too. Only the guns and a thin line of soldiers stood between the angry crowd and the trembling elders and officers in the chancery. The tension mounted higher.

Then a nerve snapped. A stray shot sounded out and von Trauenberg gave the order to open fire. Furrows of blood tore into the crowd. With an angry roar the Cossacks surged forward.

The guns were soon overwhelmed and Trauenberg and the elders and officers went scurrying for shelter to a house nearby. But the crowd smelt blood now. Within a few moments they had torn down the door, hacked General Trauenburg to pieces, murdered Ataman Tambovtsev and several of his cronies. The gaol was broken open, the chancery records went up in flames.

Once they had calmed down, the Cossacks tried to make their peace with the government. They were pathetically naïve in their approach, sending presents of fish and caviare to General Reinsdorp at Orenburg. But Reinsdorp, unmoved, stayed cautiously still. They explained to the wounded Captain Durnov that Trauenberg had started the trouble by firing on peaceful demonstrators bearing icons and asked him to accompany a delegation to St. Petersburg. He was in no position to refuse. But whereas Durnov was allowed through to the capital, the delegation was arrested at the nearest post and in March the government sent General Freimann out to quell the mutiny.

The news reached the Yaik early in April and the Cossacks set about preparing for a war of secession. Towards the end of May, an advance guard left Yaitsk; the main force of about 2,000 followed later. General Freimann approached with 2,500 dragoons and over 1,000 Kalmyks and Orenburg service Cossacks. The two sides came face to face across the river frontier on 1st June. At dawn on the 3rd Freimann crossed.

A blood-chilling scream pierced the still, spring air, and in answer to the signal, knots of horsemen cantered down from the surrounding hills. As the Cossack artillery opened up they broke into a gallop and charged in against the methodical Russian square. Making no impression they wheeled away again. Again and again they attacked but to no effect. Their cannons were firing too high to be of help, and their supplies of powder were beginning to run short. Spirits were still high enough that night, but next day Freimann occupied the hills and despairing of holding out any longer, the Cossacks decided to burn Yaitsk down and emigrate *en masse* to Turkish territory.

While a few members of the elders' party took advantage of the confusion to slip through to the Russian lines and protest their loyalty, thousands of Cossack families loaded their belongings on to carts, and driving their livestock on before them set out across the river, like Israelites from Egypt towards the promised land. But unlike the Red Sea, the waters of the Yaik would not swallow their pursuers. The bridges behind them were still intact when Freimann arrived, and his troops were soon across them giving chase. The refugees were quickly rounded up the more easily because of a cynical promise of amnesty which the authorities had no intention of keeping. Martial law was imposed, and patrols of soldiers and loyalist Cossacks paced the streets of Yaitsk. The assembly was suspended and a temporary government set up under a military commandant with whom various members of the old oligarch families including Tambovtsevs and Borodins were only too happy to co-operate. A great purge was carried out 1,774 Cossacks being declared guilty of treason. A further 2,461 rebels were pardoned, but saddled with a crippling fine of 20,000 rubles.

A report into the causes of the rising referred to 'abuse' and 'injustice' on the part of officials, misappropriation of official pay, partial justice and oppression of the weak.[37] But the government did not make the admission public. In the autumn sixty-seven ring-leaders were sentenced, all but thirteen of them to death. Six were later reprieved and the remaining sentences commuted to thrashings, slit noses, hard labour in Siberia and exile to various other distant and insalubrious spots. The community fine however was increased to 37,000 rubles, the Host was reorganised into ten regiments, and a permanent garrison of 800 regulars was stationed in Yaitsk. But the people were not cowed. 'You've not heard the last of us', cried the exiles as they left, 'We'll shake Moscow yet.' The promise was kept. Within a few months the Yaik Cossacks were following the most famous of all the Cossack rebels.

'A storm has blown up here on the Yaik.
Our little river Yaik has turned cloudy
Right from its source to the dark-blue sea,
To the dark-blue Caspian Sea . . .
Our Cossack assembly has risen up in arms,
Every man, from oldest to youngest'.

—Cossack song

7 Pugachev: the peasants' 'Tsar'

Pugachev is a prime example of a man hounded by authority
along the road to revolution. For all his quirks of character
and the split personality consequent upon his calling himself
'Tsar', he was in many respects a representative rank-and-file
Cossack of his age. His tribulations were those of his class;
his reactions personified the reactions of the Cossack mass.

Born in 1742, Yemelyan Pugachev was the son and grandson
of Don Cossacks.[1] He grew up with a brother and two sisters
helping to tend the family's little farm while their father was
away fighting with the Russian army. When he reached the age of
seventeen, it was his turn to register for service. It was also time
to marry for when a young lad went to war in those days another
strong pair of hands was needed on the farm if the household
was to stay above the bread line. Young Pugachev dutifully
married Sofia Dmitriyeva, a girl from a neighbouring village,

and a few weeks later, decked out with sabre, rifle, horse and saddlery at his family's expense, he kissed her farewell and rode west to fight the Prussians then ruled by Frederick the Great.

Denisov, the colonel of the regiment, liking the look of the young recruit, chose him as his orderly. But Pugachev's first experience of battle proved rather less than glorious. He had been entrusted with Denisov's horse, and during a skirmish with Prussian troops it became excited and bolted. The enraged colonel had him whipped for carelessness. This may not have been Pugachev's first encounter with the hard end of authority; it was certainly not his last.

The Empress Elizabeth of Russia died as her armies were on the brink of victory. Her mad German successor Peter III hastened to conclude a peace and Pugachev rode homewards with his regiment. On the way, news came that Tsar Peter had been ousted by his wife Catherine, and along with his comrades, the young Cossack swore his oath of loyalty to her. He thought little of it at the time. Tsars and empresses were way beyond his limited horizons. Yet Pugachev would break that oath, and Catherine would hear of this obscure Cossack and fear him.

The next few years he spent at peace beside the quiet Don, begetting children, ploughing the land, reaping the crops and fishing in the river. He started a modest river-haulage business in partnership with another Cossack and, in all, seemed well set on the road, if not to riches, then to relative prosperity. True he was called out for short spells of military duty from time to time, but never far from home, and they did not interfere too much in the progress of his affairs. But in 1768 all his prospects, all his hopes, were dashed when he was called to fight in a new Turkish war. He had to leave his wife and children, his farm and his business, not knowing when, if ever, he would return, nor how they would manage in his absence.

Pugachev fought well, and was promoted to the rank of cornet for bravery at the siege of Bender. After the fortress fell in 1770 his unit was moved into winter quarters and there Pugachev took ill. As a result he was granted home leave, but had to find a substitute to serve out the remainder of that year's campaign on his behalf. He found a poor Cossack, called Biryukov, who was prepared to do so. But the price

Biryukov asked was high—two horses, a saddle, a sabre, a cloak of blue cloth, saddlebags of food and twelve rubles—and Pugachev's illness persisted. He was still sick, with sores on his arms, legs and chest when, early in 1771, the time came for him to return to his unit. This he was not inclined to do. Why should he go away again to risk his life in return for a pittance and uncertain opportunities to loot, while his family had somehow to fend for itself? At last the village ataman advised him to go to Cherkassk and apply to be retired, issuing him with a passport, without which, by then, even a Cossack could not travel. But winter was no time to make a journey, and Pugachev waited until spring came and the grey Don began to flow swiftly again, before rowing down to the Don capital.

The officer who interviewed him at the chancery of the Host was not sympathetic. Pugachev pleaded sickness, but the officer was not convinced. 'You can't be retired early', he told him.* 'You'll have to go into the infirmary for treatment. If they can't cure you, then you'll be released.' But Pugachev was too old a soldier to risk staying in a death-trap army hospital. 'I'd rather cure myself at home', he said. The officer shrugged his shoulders. Once he had recovered he must return to his unit.[2] It was an angry Pugachev who walked out of the chancery building.

He did not go home. Instead, he lodged for a few days with a local witch who had a reputation for curing illnesses, and then, since his pass held good as far as the new town of Taganrog, he went to see his sister and her husband, Pavlov, there. Pavlov was as bitter as Pugachev about the way officialdom had treated him. He grumbled incessantly. Why should Cossacks like him be forced to take up their roots and move to strange, uncomfortable spots like Taganrog? Why did they teach Cossacks to behave like hussars, instead of letting them fight in their traditional styles? Why did atamans and *esauls* not behave like Cossacks any more, but demand to be addressed as colonels and captains? The new forms of service were too long, and too hard. A Cossack was pushed around from pillar to post these days. Revolt had failed, but surely there must be some corner of the earth a man could

* This conversation and those that follow are based on the reports of the interrogations of Pugachev and others carried out in 1774. The author has turned occasional passages of reported into direct speech.

escape to and live a decent, free existence. The only question was where. Regular troops guarded the frontiers with other countries. The Zaporozhian Sech perhaps? Cossack fugitives were always welcome there—but not with wives, and life would be tedious without a woman. Pugachev had heard that the Cossacks of the Terek still accepted newcomers. He told Pavlov so. One could build a new life there, and a good one. The idea immediately excited Pavlov. He, his wife and three of his friends decided to flee there. Pugachev could act as guide.[3]

His sister obtained a pass to visit their mother, and they set off together. But the old woman wept at the thought of Pugachev's going with them and made him promise to take them only on the first stage of their journey. He ferried them across the Don, showed them the way across the Nogai steppes and then turned back. But within a day or two the emigrants had lost their way, and Pavlov was soon in custody, telling the whole story to the authorities.

Getting wind of the news and 'knowing it had been explained to all Cossacks . . . not to take runaways across the river',[4] that a man could be hanged for crossing to the 'Nogai side of the Don',[5] Pugachev galloped off into hiding. But when he heard that his mother had been arrested and sent to Cherkassk, he followed her there. Though he managed to convince the authorities that he had not run away, they would not release his mother, and when Pavlov continued to insist that Pugachev was implicated, they ordered his arrest. But when they came for him, they found him gone. Pugachev had escaped, but his name was on the black list. Henceforth he was a wanted man, a fugitive.

He succeeded in reaching the Terek, which his querulous brother-in-law Pavlov had failed to do. He was accepted by the Cossacks there and was soon agitating the more recent arrivals among them to protest about the inadequacy of their pay. They elected him village ataman and in February 1772 he rashly set out for St. Petersburg to plead their cause. But the new roots were shallow. He was detained at Mozdok and though he broke gaol he could not resist returning home to see his wife again.[6] He stayed with her for several weeks, ready at a moment's notice to gallop off into hiding, but the fragile period of liberty did not last long. He was soon under arrest again. The local elder detailed to guard him offered to get him out of trouble for 100 rubles. Since Pugachev had no such sum he was sent on towards Cherkassk under escort. But on the way he had the good fortune to be put in the custody of an old friend of his father's, who gave him a horse, a sabre and an old blue caftan and told him to make a dash for it. This time Pugachev headed west.

In his absence, another storm had broken out on the Don. Discontent had been growing among the Cossack rank and file for three years, ever since the government had called for 'volunteers' to move to Azov and Taganrog. Ataman Stepan Yefremov, sympathetic to their cause for once, had fought in vain against these forced migrations. But now rumours began to spread that Cossacks would be drafted into the regular army. Ataman Yefremov was again sympathetic to them, and the rift between him and the government yawned wider when the Cossack-tamer General Cherepov, who had suppressed the Yaik Cossacks in blood six years before, arrived on the Don. The government had sent him to crush the opposition and when he appeared at their assembly, the Cossacks' mood turned ugly. 'You want to inscribe us as soldiers', they roared. 'We'd all die rather than let you do that.' They stoned him, tore off his hat and the tails of his frock-coat and only Yefremov's intervention saved him from being thrown into the river. The Ataman, riding high on a crest of popularity, was obviously amused at the arrogant Cherepov's bedraggled appearance. 'This is the Don Host', he taunted him, 'not the Yaik you know.'[7]

The Cossacks did not disperse and regular troops marched towards Cherkassk. It seemed as if another Cossack rebellion was on the way, but with the help of some loyalist elders, a detachment of dragoons spirited Ataman Yefremov, the figurehead of the resistance, away to the fort of St. Dmitri of Rostov. A group of Cossacks broke into the chancery building, accused some elders there of treachery, beat them up, and galloped off to rescue their Ataman. The fort was too well guarded and they rode away threatening to return in greater numbers, but that night the authorities hustled Yefremov away to the north. The Ataman was deposed, his property was confiscated, and he was sent into exile. Having removed Yefremov, the government soon regained control. Yet another Cossack resistance movement had collapsed.

Pugachev, meanwhile, had found shelter in a monastery at Starodub near the Ukrainian border. There he heard that Old Believers who had fled into Polish territory to escape religious persecution were now being allowed to return, provided they settled as pioneers in certain distant Russian provinces. Equipped with a forged pass made out for a Don Cossack returning to his unit, Pugachev crossed into Poland, then went along the border, turned up at another frontier post and, posing as an Old Believer, applied to enter Russia. On 12th August 1772 he was issued with an official passport entitling him, after spending six weeks in quarantine, to settle as a free citizen on the Irgiz, the desert area in south-eastern Russia, near Orenburg.

He spent his quarantine with a local Old Believer merchant called Kozhevnikov, who paid him a couple of rubles and his keep in return for his doing odd jobs. Another fugitive, a deserter called Alexei Semenov, worked with him. Semenov kept watching Pugachev, and one day, over their meal he told Kozhevnikov: 'You know, this man looks the double of Peter III' —the Tsar who had been deposed and killed nine years before.

Pugachev laughed. How could he, a shabby bearded figure of five foot four, his swarthy face disfigured by great white scrofula scars, and several teeth missing from a punch on the jaw[8]—how could he be mistaken for a Tsar? 'I'm not joking', Semenov insisted. 'I say you're the splitting image of Peter III.' After all, he had been a guardsman in St. Petersburg, he should know. Pugachev, however, was only interested in discussing where else he could settle than on the Irgiz where, he had heard, life was grindingly hard. Perhaps the Kuban, on the eastern shore of the Black Sea, just beyond the Russian border, was a good place, where a man could build a free life. But the shrewd Kozhevnikov, who had noticed Pugachev's bearing and discerned a certain dignity in the man, had been dreaming up other plans for him. He went warily, anxious to lead Pugachev on, and did not tell him all he had in mind.

'Listen, my friend', he said, 'you can't run there all by yourself. . . . Since people here think you look like Peter III, why not say that you are?' The Yaik Cossacks, many of them Old Believers, lived near the route he must take to Irgiz. He should go to them, proclaim himself Tsar and get them to go to the Kuban with him. Semenov would convince everyone that he was the real Tsar and the Yaik Cossacks would be predisposed to accept the idea because they were being persecuted by the government. Anyway he should promise to give them twelve rubles each. He could give Pugachev some money; other Old Believers would stump up more if he would take them with him, for, as he said, 'it is hard . . . for us Old Believers to . . . bear this ceaseless hounding'.[9]

Pugachev at last accepted the proposition, and when his quarantine had expired he and Semenov started on their way. Kozhevnikov had given them money, food, and letters of introduction to Old Believers who lived along their long route from the Ukraine to the Urals. Passing along this chain of contacts they came at last to the Volga where they sheltered in a monastery. The abbot, Philaret, did not think Pugachev resembled the Tsar in the least. 'But that doesn't matter', he told him. 'Life's bad for the Yaik Cossacks nowadays'; they would want to believe it.[10] Another pretender to the title, Bogomolev, had roused some Cossacks on the upper Don and Volga recently. He had soon been caught and packed off to Siberia, but the rumours that Peter III was still alive had persisted, and had spread to the Yaik.

Semenov disappeared, but Pugachev went on until, towards the end of 1772, posing as a fish trader, he arrived at the crowded little Cossack town of Yaitsk nestling in a steep bend in the Yaik river and called at the house of Denis Pyanov. Pyanov, a fifty-year-old Cossack Old Believer, was yet another disenchanted man. He told Pugachev the whole unhappy story of the Yaik, of the Cossacks' recent rebellion, the cruelty with which it had been put down, of how many of them had wanted to flee to the protection of the Turks rather than live under Russian rule. 'Look what we've come to', he complained, 'we've not even enough bread for dinner.'[11] Pugachev, thinking that Pyanov could be trusted, began to tell his story. He had been advised by Philaret to put a high colour on it, and he did. He began by saying he was really a rich merchant who had travelled to

Constantinople and to Egypt, that he was worth thousands of rubles abroad. He offered to lead a migration of Yaik Cossacks to the Kuban, to pay twelve rubles to every Cossack who would follow him. Then he said he was Peter III. It was his double who had been assassinated, he claimed. He himself had fled to Poland, and then gone on to the East. Now he had come to the Yaik.[12] But the authorities had heard that a suspicious 'foreign merchant' was in town and soldiers soon came knocking at Pyanov's door. The house was searched, but the 'merchant' had gone.

In December 1772 Pugachev was arrested in the village of Malynovka as a suspicious character. He was tortured, and then sent to Kazan on the Volga river where he was imprisoned in a government blockhouse. Then the local cell of the Old Believer underground moved into action. The guards were offered bribes for his release. They refused, although he was only one of many suspects and did not seem particularly dangerous. Since no instructions had yet come through about his case they were eventually persuaded to let him out into the town occasionally, and a local merchant called Druzhinin set to work on a rescue plan. One day Pugachev was brought into town under escort to see a priest. The priest offered them all a drink and began cautiously to sound the two guards out. One seemed ready enough to desert but not the other, and the priest saw to it that his glass was constantly refilled. By the time a cart driven by Druzhinin's son drew up outside the house an hour or two later, the more dutiful guard was thoroughly inebriated. Pugachev and the other soldier pushed him aside, dashed outside, leapt on to the cart and were driven quietly out of Kazan. By the time orders came through for the prisoner to be whipped and exiled with hard labour, he was far away again.

The lonely Pugachev was on an escape route to nowhere. 'God knows where I have been and what . . . I have suffered', he would say, 'I have been cold and hungry, and spent too long in prison'.[13] He had borne enough; he was tired of constant flight, of sleeping light, of living constantly in fear. Yet there was only one alternative to exile or punishment. The logic of a hopeless situation was leading him inexorably along the road to violence, to revolt. And there were thousands who felt like him.

The 'disobedient' Yaik Cossacks in particular were in an angry mood. The Government had just announced a long list of sentences—executions, beatings, impressments into the army—for their revolt the year before. They were now ready to welcome a 'good' Tsar and Pugachev decided to test his appeal in that role.

He appeared again in August 1773 at a farm about twenty-five miles from Yaitsk. The autumn fishing season was about to open and many Cossacks would soon be outside the heavily guarded town. A few were brought to meet him. They saw a lean, broad-shouldered man of average height, dressed in a camel skin and a blue Kalmyk cap. He did not look a Tsar, though he embroidered his tale convincingly enough. But he was not to labour the pretence to everyone. 'Everywhere people say that Tsar Peter III is still alive', he confided to one conspirator, so 'if I use that name I could take Moscow itself. For on the way I shall collect many people' and with most of the army fighting the Turks 'there are no forces in Moscow at all'.[14] The idea of leading a migration to the Kuban was already receding. Recognising the likelihood of mass support for a revolt from the miserable people he had seen in his travels across Russia, and flattered by the hand-kissing and general adulation he received from those who believed he really was the Tsar, Pugachev's horizons had broadened. Anyway a real Tsar would not declare himself merely to lead a grand retreat abroad, he would go to the capital, take his rightful place upon the throne. What the conspiratorial Kozhevnikov had planned was coming about at last. Pugachev was ready to head a revolution.

Yet he and his supporters seemed strangely out of touch. He would march on Moscow, but for three generations St. Petersburg had been the capital of Russia. He talked of oppression by the boyars, but they had been replaced by a new aristocracy years since. Even the idea of raising a revolt in the name of an alternative Tsar dated back two centuries.[15] Still it was to prove effective, for though a demented German princeling, such as the late Peter III had been, seemed a strange figurehead, people knew him to have released the gentry from the service obligations imposed by Peter the Great and, with innocent logic, assumed that he had been about to liberate the peasants as well, when

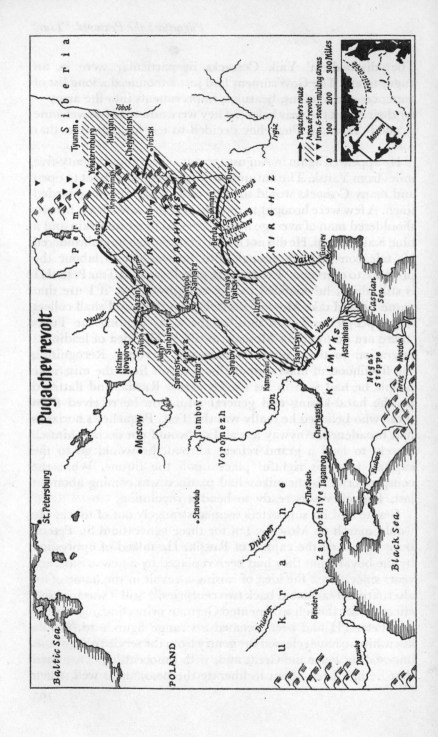

Pugachev revolt

he was toppled from the throne. This was to be a backward-looking revolution, promising the restoration of an old idealised age; its appeal was to be no less attractive for that.

But for the moment 'Tsar Peter' did not feel safe. Nor was he. One night a Cossack got drunk in Yaitsk and talked too much. Next day soldiers rode out to the farm where Pugachev was staying. Once again, the quarry had vanished. Then Simonov, the Russian commandant of Yaitsk, got wind of his new hide-out, and on 16th September a troop of soldiers rode out towards it. But a Cossack galloped wildly on ahead of them to give warning. The conspirators took to horse and rushed away to another Cossack homestead about sixty miles from Yaitsk. The time had come for Pugachev to act, and he moved fast.

Riders flew out over the steppe with messages for Cossacks and the local tribesmen. Tolkachev, the owner of the farm, sped round his neighbours and told them of the Tsar's arrival and Pugachev told the Cossack Pochitalin to take pen, paper, ink and sand and write down a manifesto, which he would dictate. When it was finished he told Pochitalin to sign it for him. 'The Tsar' could not write.

Armed Cossacks began to arrive at Tolkachev's cabin. They came in in twos and threes, tethered their horses to the posts outside and clumped in to see their new leader. When about forty had assembled Pugachev addressed them. He wore a crimson cap, a caftan with a silken sash and held a musket in his hand. He told them of his wanderings. 'I have been in the Ukraine, on the Don and in many towns in Russia', and every-where he had seen the people ruined. His audience too, suffered 'insults and impositions'.[16] His elongated swarthy face, had come alive, the hazel eyes flashed. 'Listen, little children to what Pochitalin will read'. His secretary read out the manifesto:

> 'From the Emperor Autocrat, our great Lord Peter Fedorovich of all the Russias, etc., etc., etc.
> 'This is my decree issued to the Yaik Host: Just as your fathers and grandfathers served the former Tsars to the last drop of their blood, so you, too, my friends, will serve your fatherland and me, the great Lord Emperor, Peter Fedoro-vich. Your Cossack glory will not die if you serve your

fatherland to the very end and so it will be with your children. I, the great Tsar, will reward you—Cossacks and Kalmyks and Tatars. I, the Lord Peter Fe[do]rovich, do forgive those who have sinned against me. . . . And I grant you the rivers from the mountains to the sea, and the land and pastures, and pay of money and lead and powder and of food.

'I, the Great Lord Emperor [will so] reward you,
'Peter Fedorovich
'1773, September 17th'.[17]

The expression might be imperfect but the tone was excellently judged. There were to be rewards for the tribesmen, but the Cossacks, he promised, would be his 'leading people'.[18] Then he asked them 'Well, is it good? Did you hear?', and they all cried out: 'It is good and we heard and we're ready to serve you.'[19]

They were told to spread the news and return at dawn the following day. Next morning about sixty more Cossacks rode in bringing an assortment of workers from nearby farms and a few Kalmyks with them. They were invited to swear allegiance: 'We promise before God to serve you faithfully . . . to the last drop of blood.' But Pugachev swore, too—'to love and reward the Yaik Host as Tsars did of old', to give them the Yaik and its tributaries, with 'fishing rights, land, hay fields and all the fruits thereof without payment of duties,' and to abolish the hated restrictions on the salt trade.[20]

The same day an emissary arrived from Nurali, Khan of the Kirghiz-Kaisaks, in response to a letter written by Baltai Idovkin, a Cossack of Turkmen origin. He brought Pugachev gifts—a sword, a silver-ornamented axe, a gown of Bukhara silk and a fine bay horse—but no warriors. Nurali was not convinced of the veracity or strength of 'Peter III'; besides the Yaik Cossacks were the traditional enemies of his people. He was trying to stand aloof.[21] Pugachev had to move without him.

A hundred horsemen trooped out of Tolkachev's farm in the direction of Yaitsk, four Cossacks and a Kalmyk riding at their head, pennants streaming from their lances. Hour by hour as they cantered along, dark forms on horseback, with guns slung

across their backs, fell in behind them. By the next day Pugachev's army had swollen to 200 armed men. The fugitive would
soon be the pursuer.

Colonel Simonov, commandant of Yaitsk, sent out 500 service
Cossacks with infantry and two guns to deal with them. The
vanguard, 200 strong, under Captain Krylov was met by a
solitary Cossack waving a letter in his hand. Krylov's service
Cossacks demanded it to be read, and when they had heard it
half of them declared for the Pretender and, leading several
loyalists by the reins, rode on to join him. The rest of the force
turned back. Next day, Pugachev, having hanged eleven of the
loyalists, approached Yaitsk. But once it was apparent that
Colonel Simonov would not surrender without a fight, the
Cossacks passed on to another outpost where a Cossack assembly
was convened. Andrei Ovchinnikov was appointed Ataman and
he and the other officers elected kissed Pugachev's hand in
homage. Then they rode on again to the next in line of the
stockade forts, built to keep the tribesmen in order.

They came to Iletsk, some ninety miles north-west from Yaitsk
and seventy-five short of the great citadel of Orenburg, on the
21st. The local people responded immediately to the Old
Believer slogans and to the manifesto. Two priests emerged
bearing the traditional welcome of bread and salt; the 300
Cossacks of the garrison dipped their banners in salute, and the
bells of the little church pealed out a welcome. But the local
ataman was a loyalist. He was hanged, and Pochitalin elected in
his place. Of the regular officers, one was hanged 'at the request
of the inhabitants', another spared, the people insisting he was 'a
good fellow'.²² Loaded up with supplies from the armoury, the
Cossacks pressed on to Rassypnaya, fifteen miles away.

Here Pugachev, as befitted a 'Tsar of all the Russias',
broadened his appeal to 'all classes of people', promising to
reward them 'with the rivers and the seas and all their produce,
with pay, provender, powder and lead, rank and honour
and . . . liberty for ever'.²³ As a result a number of regular
soldiers and 150 Cossacks of the garrison came over and the
officers, the commandant's wife and the local priest were soon
swinging from a makeshift gallows. Pugachev pushed on twelve
miles to Ozernaya. It capitulated within two hours of his arrival.

Its commander, Major Kharlov, was killed, his young wife raped by the mob.

At Tatishchev, which they reached on the 27th, the Cossacks encountered more serious opposition. They galloped round the walls like the Israelites at Jericho, trumpeting calls to the garrison 'not to heed the boyars',[24] but the fort's ten guns continued firing, and only when they set fire to the stockade and succeeded in breaking in, did the 600 garrison Cossacks mutiny. All the officers were hanged, the commandant's wife was murdered, and another woman strangled, though Pugachev spared the commandant's daughter.[25] A few loyalist soldiers were shot, the rest shorn of their pigtails, and allowed to join the rebels. News of their progress was carried before them. The commander of the next fort, Captain Nechayev, was a man of discretion: he surrendered. But his serving girl made a complaint against him and he swung like the rest.

In barely a fortnight Pugachev's tiny band had become an army of over 2,500 men. He had taken half a dozen forts and twenty guns with hardly a shot being fired. But ten miles short of Orenburg, he decided to skirt round it and headed towards Sakmara, eighteen miles the other side. Pugachev was welcomed there in style. Carpets were laid down and the priest came out to greet him with the cross and holy icons. As he rode inside the bells pealed out and the people bared their heads. When he 'began to dismount . . . they all fell down upon their faces'. Pugachev 'prostrated himself before the cross, kissed the bread and salt', then seating himself magisterially upon a chair, allowed them all to kiss his hand. He was beginning to enjoy being a Tsar. But next day he ordered his men to march again. They asked him what supplies they should take with them. He told them just to 'take a crust of bread each'. They were only going as far as Orenburg.[26]

General Reinsdorp, the cautious German commander of the citadel, knew he was cut off. But he also knew that, though Pugachev had sympathisers within the city, they were not numerous nor confident enough as yet to show their hand. The garrison, 3,000 strong with seventy guns, prepared for siege. It was to be a long and hard one.

The first snows of the winter fell on the 16th October and two days later Pugachev set up his headquarters at Berda a mile or two from Orenburg. During the next few weeks acres of tents and earthen huts sprouted up to house the hordes of Bashkirs, Kalmyks, Tatars and Russians, who wandered in to join him. The army grew to 10,000 and as word of the rising spread, peasants and tribesmen from as far afield as Kazan and Astrakhan began to tread the warpath. Once again Cossack initiative was creating a vast opposition movement; a Cossack was acting as a magnet for the myriad victims of the autocracy.

At last the government was forced publicly to admit the existence of the Pretender, but it could do little about him while the best part of the army was tied down on the Danube, fighting the Turks for the fifth successive year. Catherine, however, did not appear to be seriously concerned. Though she delighted to flirt with progressive ideas, she was a German by birth and upbringing, and, isolated in the narrow circle of her court, she could hardly have been more out of touch with the grim realities that affected so many ordinary Russians. While she chatted to Diderot in her glittering palace in St. Petersburg, the distant storm in the east roared louder; while she exchanged letters couched in the most delicate and delightful terms with Voltaire, an ignorant Cossack who claimed to be her husband threatened to destroy the empire and her with it.

Pugachev set about knitting his new army together. He founded a 'College of War' modelled roughly on the Russian war ministry. Headed by four 'judges' it dealt with finance, discipline, arms and supplies, forage, reinforcements and intelligence, and administered the ranks and awards which Pugachev instituted. Though only Tvorogov of the judges and the Secretary, Maxim Gorshkov, were literate, the College employed several scribes and translators, and issued manifestos and proclamations in Arabic, Tatar and Turkic as well as Russian,[27] to spread the good news to all the polygot peoples of Catherine's huge empire.

The Cossacks of Yaitsk, Iletsk, Isetsk and Orenburg formed the core of the army, but the others were also roughly divided into regiments. The soldiers who had deserted made up units of 'state Cossacks', and the large contingents of Bashkirs, the Kargalinsk Tatars, the baptised Kalmyks of Stavropol, 500

Cheremis, and some Kirghiz-Kaisaks were also brought under a crude system of command, each segment having its own scribe or mullah. The artillery formed a separate section, and there was a special ordnance and repair unit.[28]

An increasingly important part of the army was made up of maltreated industrial peasants from the Urals. The mines and metallurgical industries here had developed rapidly to become the most important in all Russia. Thousands of peasant runaways had come there hoping for the status of free labourers, only to find themselves and their families tied in perpetuity to the industrialists for whom they worked. Conditions were bad, wages low, the treatment brutal. Some workers were housed in miserable barrack blocks, others fetched hundreds of miles from their homes every year to work their quota of days. In reaction there had been strikes and violence, and though troops had frequently been called in and massive reprisals taken, the unrest of the factory peasants had continued, and now Pugachev offered them a new, more hopeful outlet.

Their leader now was Afanasi Solokov, nicknamed Khlopusha, the Cracker. He had been in consistent trouble and bore the horrible marks of it. Scarred by countless knoutings and brandings, his nose torn off to the bone, Khlopusha was sensitive about his appearance and kept his face covered by a net.[29] But he was able. He had raised a successful rebellion among the workers of the Urals, organised them, and brought them to Pugachev. Now he was arranging for him to be supplied with guns, money and food from the Ural district.[30]

That October large quantities of stolen metal, money, clothing, muskets, cannon, powder, horses, cattle and grain were brought in. Three thousand sheep, some horses and oxen were intercepted on their way to Orenburg. But by December the army had grown to between 15,000 and 30,000 men, and the supply of equipment could not keep pace. Most of the peasants were armed with bayonets, pitchforks or knives lashed to staves, sometimes only with cudgels or with sticks; the Bashkirs had their traditional bows and arrows and even the Cossacks did not all have muskets.[31]

Pugachev himself was always surrounded by a personal guard of at least twenty-five well-armed Yaik Cossacks. Wearing a magnificent red coat trimmed with gold lace he would sit in his imperial chair of judgement, sceptre in one hand, his silver axe in the other, while supplicants knelt and kissed his hand. He would walk among his troops flinging them coins which were the more welcome since only Cossacks and Kalmyks received any regular pay, and practise his oratory on new recruits. 'O children', he would cry. 'God brought me ... to reign over you ... I was in Jerusalem, in Constantinople and in Egypt.' The gestures were grand, the promises grander. He would reward them all with 'lands, waters, forests, the cross and the beard'—the rights of Old Believers—'and all freedoms'.[32]

But he was shaken out of his euphoria by news that troops were on their way to relieve Orenburg. In the second week of November a cluster of red and yellow banners, sewn with Old Believer crosses and the images of Christ and St. Nicholas, swirled away from Berda, leading the rebels out to engage them. Colonel Chernyshev's troops were cold and hungry, his Kalmyks and Cossacks not disposed to fight. They were quickly overwhelmed. Chernyshev and thirty-two of his officers were captured, stripped naked and brought to the gallows one by one, Pugachev waving a handkerchief to signal execution. The soldiers, their hair cropped, were made to swear loyalty, and to make the sign of the cross Old Believer fashion with two fingers, on pain of having them cut off. The rebels celebrated an easy victory, but a more serious threat was already on the way—a task force under Major General Ker. Pugachev sent Ovchinnikov against him with about 3,000 men and a few guns. Ker's troops, mostly old men or inexperienced recruits, immediately formed a square and began to retreat. Ovchinnikov followed, his men dragging the guns from hill to hill to keep them constantly under fire. But after seventeen miles they ran out of powder and Ker, having lost more than 300 men including some who had been intercepted on their way to rendezvous with him, made good his escape.

Among the grenadiers captured by the rebels was an officer called Shvanovich. His life was spared at the request of his men, and when Pugachev heard he knew French and German he asked for a written sample of his skill. 'You write well', he said, scanning the papers as if he could read. 'You must serve in my College of War. Whatever needs to be written in foreign there, you write it.' Shvanovich's first task was to write to Reinsdorp, Governor of Orenburg, in German, inviting him to surrender. No reply was received.[33] The siege was now into its second month and the food shortage in Orenburg had already become serious. Only the rich could afford flour at twenty-five rubles a bag; the poor were driven to making bread out of roasted horse hides, to eating any rubbish they could find. Sickness was spreading and the insurgents outside were always nagging them to come to their senses and serve the Lord Peter Fedorovich, bribing them with promises of wine. But the garrison of Orenburg held on.

The victory over Ker improved the rebels' confidence and induced many tribesmen who had been waiting on the sidelines to throw their lot in with them.[34] The news sparked off violent uprisings in districts far from Orenburg. It seemed that the peasants of Russia, long since reduced to the status of serfs, were just waiting for a Pugachev. With life short and miserable for so many of them, there was no shortage of men who welcomed the opportunity of a little loot and pillage and of enjoying something of the Cossack comradeship in arms. This was clearly the time for Pugachev to extend the front. But he refused to start a general advance on the Russian capital as Razin had done. Instead, the rebellion spread outwards from Orenburg in a series of formless secondary campaigns. Khlopusha marched east over the snows to take the forts of Verkhne-Ozernaya and Ilyinskaya, and at the end of November Zarubin-Chika, one of the original conspirators, led another horde north to Ufa. Linking up with rebel groups, he soon had as many as 15,000 men besieging Ufa. In January Chelyabinsk to the north-east was to fall, then Kurgan on the river Tobol. By the end of 1773 the province of Orenburg and Perm, part of Simbirsk and most of the ninety-two Ural mills were in rebel hands. Yekaterinburg was soon threatened. The peasants of Tyumen, in the country Yermak had conquered two centuries before, rose in arms, and rebel propaganda whipped along the road to Tobolsk as far as Irkutsk in central Siberia.[35]

The Bashkirs, terrors of the steppe of Orenburg, forgot their old enemies and joined in, deciding that 'we Russians and

Bashkirs shouldn't quarrel and ravage each other'.[36] Many Chuvash, Mordvins and Tatars also discovered an identity of interest with the revolutionaries. Bands of robbers roamed the countryside about Kazan and Nizhny-Novgorod in the north and west and Astrakhan in the south. Rebellion took root in the areas of Kama-Vyatka, Pensa, Voronezh and the fringes of the Don. And one day a Yaik Cossack called Perfilev arrived from St. Petersburg to tell Pugachev that in the capital itself the poor were whispering rumours of his coming.[37]

The Pretender was in an expansive mood. 'You can see for yourself... that my followers are as numerous as grains of sand', he told Perfilev. 'The time will come when we'll deal with them in St. Petersburg. They won't pass through my hands. I know full well that the poor people everywhere will welcome me with joy.'[38] Still, he refrained from marching west, though he did begin to formulate his aims more clearly. 'If I manage to take Orenburg and Yaitsk', he told his henchmen, 'I shall go on to Kazan with just the cavalry and, when it has been captured, to Moscow and St. Petersburg.' Once there he would 'make the Empress into a nun',[39] though at another time he did think of putting the Grand Duke on the throne, claiming 'I don't want to reign myself'.[40] But he was always insistent that Russia must be led by a 'good peasants' Tsar',[41] and he would ensure 'that the people are not burdened'. The upper orders would be destroyed, 'the land . . . taken from the gentry'.[42] 'A man who kills a landlord and destroys his house should be rewarded with a hundred coins', said Pugachev, and 'a man who destroys ten houses of the gentry shall get 1,000 rubles and the rank of general.'[43]

His men would ride into estates like Bolshevik agitators a century and a half later, saying they had been sent 'by the Lord Peter Fedorovich to destroy the landowners' houses and to give freedom to the peasants'. 'Don't do any sort of work for the landlord', they warned them, 'pay him no dues. If we find you doing the landlord's work again, we'll thrust you all through.'[44] The slogan 'land and freedom' was sweeping through the countryside now,[45] sped on by the neatly written 'charters' and manifestos churned out by the 'College of War'. Pugachev explained his failure to sign them by saying the 'time had not yet come', that he would only write his name when he mounted the throne. But although some of his closer followers came to believe he was illiterate and Cossacks inside Orenburg refused to come over without 'at least a line' in the Pretender's own hand, the wide currency and credit of the manifestos was beginning to worry the government seriously.[46]

The rebels' organisation was more sophisticated than in Razin's time, and though the social programme of Cossack equality was much the same, Pugachev laid more stress on the messianic hopes and liturgical preferences of the people than Razin had done. He was presented as the king-saviour; he harked back to the deep-rooted old religious beliefs, offended by Nikon's reforms over a century before and by Peter the Great's programme of westernisation; he appealed to the traditional piety and the earthy patriotism of the people. In contrast to the Emperors and Empresses, some of foreign origins and all with foreign advisers and with foreign ways, Pugachev was demonstrably a Tsar sprung from Russian soil. 'If God wills that I should have the kingdom', he announced, 'I shall order everyone to follow the old faith and to wear Russian clothes. I shall not allow beards to be shaved and I shall order people to have their hair cut Cossack style'.[47] And so he attracted peasants and paid his debt to the Old Believers who had sheltered him in harder times.

Yet for all his political shrewdness, his ambitions and pretensions, Pugachev remained parochial at heart, a child of the backwoods, playing at kings and queens. He had promised that 'when . . . all Russia is won, the Yaik will be made St. Petersburg and the Yaik Cossacks will be promoted to the highest quality for being the cause of raising him to the Kingdom'.[48] The Yaik Cossacks still provided his most reliable support and, of course, he had to please them above the others. But he also began to hold court at Berda, giving his closest companions among the Cossacks the titles of Catherine's own courtiers. Zarubin-Chika became 'Field Marshal Count Chernyshev', Shigayev and Ovchinnikov 'Counts Vorontsov' and 'Panin'. Soon Berda became 'Moscow', the Tatar village of Kargal 'St. Petersburg', and Sakmara 'Kiev'. It was only half in jest.

As he learned more about the real St. Petersburg he embroidered his story of how, as Peter, he had lost his throne and then returned. 'The boyars' were against him he said, because he had been living with Elizabeth Vorontsov, so he had to flee the city. When they sent men after him and swore loyalty to his wife, 'the Lady Empress Catherine Alexeyevna', he took ship for Germany with sixty men. He lived there three years, and then for a year on the Kuban before returning to Russia where he wandered about to find out how ordinary people lived and what they suffered from the authorities.[49] The Cossacks at his court might be sceptical, but in public they bared their heads, and prostrated themselves before him.

Pugachev lived half in reality, half in a dream world. He would use high-sounding phrases one moment and coarse provincial epithets the next. He would consort with the wives of Tatar chiefs at Kargal and entertain his cronies to lavish meals, cooked by two Russian girls in his household, where he and his Cossacks behaved as brothers, drinking and singing songs together. He would ride before his flock dressed like an emperor wearing the red sash of the Order of St. Anne under a handsome red coat and a large silver medal pinned to his chest. But he would suddenly lapse from his dignified pose and begin to wink.[50]

Though the leader, the figurehead, Pugachev relied largely on the Cossacks of 'the College of War', which laboured on in its amateurish way, to provide administrative backing to the revolt. It lent credence to its governmental claims by using seals fashioned by rebel silversmiths, including one with a Tatar inscription and at least one other with an imperial double-headed eagle.[51] To increase morale it distributed medals bearing the portraits of bygone Tsars, and to keep the rebels fed it sent foraging detachments ranging far and wide, confiscating grain from official storehouses and the private granaries of land-owners and peasants hostile to the revolt. Produce taken from friendly peasants was paid for, though sometimes in worthless promissory notes. Further and further afield they rode to tap new sources of supply until in March 1774 two atamans leading collection drives were driven back by government troops.

The 'College' kept a treasure chest which it dipped into to pay the Cossacks and grant special bounties and to allow the Ural factory workers to buy raw materials and repair broken machines. But the supply of money was too short to maintain the economy of the rebel areas and Pugachev issued no coinage of his own.[52] Though the College had a few howitzers cast and some ammunition manufactured, the important armaments industry in the Urals soon ground virtually to a standstill. Nor could the College concert the operations of rebel bands operating at any distance from the Yaik, Orenburg and Ural areas.

Pugachev had his tens of thousands ranged over the thick snow around Berda, most of them still armed with axes, spears, sticks and balls and chains. And he would not move into central Russia until Orenburg and Yaitsk had fallen. On 13th January 1774 Reinsdorp attempted to break out from Orenburg, and was beaten back with heavy losses but the garrison continued to hold out. On 20th January Pugachev turned his attention to Yaitsk.

He supervised the operation in person, had a sap dug forward and a mine laid near a particularly harmful gun emplacement. He lit the match himself. It was a misfire. Cossacks stormed forward through smoke and dust to find the walls as solid as ever. For nine hours the battle raged, Pugachev swearing to hang the officers in Yaitsk and their wives and children, but at last having lost more than 400 men, he called off the attempt. In a furious temper he had the Mordvin who had laid the mine shot for incompetence.

While still waiting for Yaitsk to fall, Pugachev met a Cossack girl called Ustinya Kuznetsova, and though so far as he knew, his wife, Sofia, was still alive, he expressed his intention of marrying her. The girls' parents were astonished. She was 'not a princess or a queen. How can she be for you'? they asked. 'If he's really Peter Fedorovich', whispered local gossips, 'how can he marry with his wife, Catherine, still alive?'[53] and even the priests felt they needed confirmation from the local synod before they could include Ustinya in the 'royal prayers'. But Pugachev was insistent and early in February 1774 the 'marriage' took place.

Ustinya was called 'mother Tsarina' and allotted a quota of 'ladies-in-waiting', but, however beguiling, she remained the simple country girl. Once when she heard the Cossack women talking of the coming march on Moscow, she burst into tears. 'When Peter Fedorovich takes Moscow', she sobbed, 'I'll have to leave you, my dear ones, and live there.' 'How foolish you are, Mother Tsarina', the gossips replied consolingly. 'It is the Yaik which will be Moscow'.[54] But before Pugachev was ready to march on Moscow, Moscow marched on him. It was the end of February when he heard that troops were heading for Orenburg, and he again rushed back to Berda.

In December 1773 General Bibikov, who had been charged with quelling the revolt, had arrived in Kazan to find all senior government officials gone. Briskly he had set about restoring loyalist morale. He rallied the local gentry and organised them into a militia. He sanctioned the recruitment of 'healthy people as Cossacks' to be sent 'under reliable officers against the rebels',[55] and, though hampered by snow and poor communications, began to redeploy the scattered forces put under his command.

In January he had turned to the offensive and by February his men had taken Kurgan and relieved Yekaterinburg. Troops were sent east to make Siberia secure; more, under Mansurov, marched west to the Samara line. Government forces approached Ufa, and Major General Golytsyn set out from Kazan. Joined by Mansurov, Golytsyn tramped on to Orenburg. The net round Pugachev was closing in.

The Pretender set out towards Golytsyn with 10,000 picked men. They attacked at night, were repulsed, and withdrew by a roundabout route to Tatishchev, where they prepared their positions with a competence that surprised the Russian general. They stood firm under his artillery barrage and under several attacks, but Golytsyn's units were not obsolescent troops of *streltsy* such as Razin had encountered, but part of a highly trained and efficient army, probably the most effective in Europe. On 22nd March the rebels suddenly broke and ran. The Russian cavalry tore after them. At least 2,000 insurrectionaries were killed, another 4,000 wounded or taken prisoner.

Pugachev and sixty Cossacks, their horses foaming, galloped into Berda followed by a straggling train of survivors. He immediately had the barrels of spirits lying about the place smashed in an attempt to stop widespread drunkenness and help restore at least some semblance of discipline. But rebel morale had collapsed. Most decided to get out with what they could. Khlopusha fled towards Kargal, trying to save his wife and son—only to be betrayed and beheaded three months later. Shigayev tried another road of escape, sending a secret message to Reinsdorp at Orenburg offering to hand Pugachev over in return for a pardon. The cautious Governor pondered the offer for an hour or two, and meanwhile Pugachev burned the 'College of War' archives and, taking his war chest and ten guns, moved out of Berda, accompanied by Shigayev, Pochitalin, Gorshkov and 2,000 men.[56]

Golytsyn relieved Orenburg on 26th March, then moved off after the rebels. For some days he played the cat to Pugachev's mouse, then he caught up with him outside Sakmara. Here Pugachev lost the last of his artillery, and most of his remaining men. Shigayev, Vitoshnov, President of the 'College of War', and Pochitalin, who had penned Pugachev's first manifesto, were all captured. Calling out 'save yourselves, children. All is lost',[57] Cossacks galloped madly along the road to Yaitsk with news of Pugachev's defeat. Russian cavalrymen came pounding down behind them and Ovchinnikov and Perfilev, who tried to bar their way, were swept aside.

The Yaitsk garrison, driven to eating cats and dogs after three and a half months of siege, were at the point of collapse when they noticed a stir among the besiegers camped on the freezing ground below. A cloud of vapour was rising in the distance, and soon a crowd of rebels, carrying the trussed up figure of Tolkachev came hammering on the gate, praying for forgiveness. On 17th April 1774 Mansurov brought relief at last and poor Ustinya was led away under guard.

It was spring, and as the rivers shook themselves free of ice, the dead of Tatishchev began to float downstream. A crowd of wailing women gathered along the banks, and tried to pick out their missing husbands and sons. The Yaik was in mourning—but Pugachev was still alive and at liberty. He tried to break out south to Guryev, but finding the route blocked, he headed up-river again with a handful of followers, into the southern Urals.

Troops were scouring the country for him; everything seemed lost. Yet, suddenly, he rose again like a phoenix from the ashes of misfortune. First, Ovchinnikov and Perfilev, bringing 300 Cossacks, joined up with him,[58] then a few hundred factory workers, and the Bashkirs rallied to his cause again. The whole area took flame as Russian serfs, Tatars and Mordvins committed 'all kinds of crimes' and generally behaved 'like barbarians'.[59] With the pursuing troops slowed down by muddy roads and overflowing rivers, village after village surrendered to Pugachev, and by the time he reached the fort of Troitski on the 19th May, he had a new army of 10,000 men and thirty guns.

But on the 21st General Dekolong arrived and dispersed the rebels. Pugachev, who had been nursing a wound incurred in a previous skirmish, tried to rally his forces, but at last, he, too, was forced to flee. He thought of heading east into Siberia, 'I don't know those places' he told his retainers 'so lead me wherever you want'.[60] Then, two days later, Colonel Mikhelson who had been tracking across the Urals through deserted Bashkir villages rounding up isolated bands of rebels, ran into him. After a sharp fight, Pugachev, having lost all but 500 of his remaining men, took to his heels again.

He headed west, then north towards Chelyabinsk, adopting a guerrilla strategy—always on the move, always changing direction, avoiding battle, except against forces much inferior to his own. None of the larger army units could keep pace with him, only Colonel Mikhelson kept up the pursuit. But the quarry was elusive. Once Mikhelson sighted the rebels across a river, but the bridges were down and they escaped him. He made contact a little while later but Pugachev disappeared again, and with ammunition down to two cartridges a man, Mikhelson turned away to Ufa for fresh supplies.

Pugachev reached Krasnouifimsk, where he was joined by 3,000 Bashkirs and then moved on westwards to the Kama river. By the time he reached the fort of Osa in the middle of June he felt powerful enough to risk a confrontation with its garrison. It resisted strongly. But Pugachev had acquired a capable tactician in an ex-bombardier called Beloborodov. He sent several carts of straw hurtling, blazing towards the ramparts followed by a crowd of men, and the men of Osa were soon calling for a truce. One was soon arranged. An old guardsman took one look at Pugachev and returned to Osa to assure his comrades: 'Have no doubt, lads!' he shouted, 'This is your natural lord Peter Fedorovich'.[61] The commandant was persuaded to welcome Pugachev upon his knees, and his 1,000 men were formed into the 'Kazan Regiment' of the rebel army. Then one of his officers discovered him trying to get a message through to the governor of Kazan. The commandant was hanged and the informer, Mineyev, promoted colonel by Pugachev.

For more than a week now the Cossacks, excited by the new upsurge in their fortunes, had been pestering Pugachev to march on Moscow. He was still reluctant but agreed at last to take a decisive step in its direction, to move on Kazan. Mineyev promised to guide them by the most direct route.

This latest move threw the government forces completely off balance. Kazan had been reckoned safe, and Major General P. S. Potemkin, member of a secret commission formed to investigate the rebellion, had set up his headquarters there. The Governor hurriedly armed 6,000 citizens and sent out the cavalry under Colonel Tolstoi to meet the rebels. But on 10th July, Tolstoi was killed, his men scattered, and next day Pugachev set up camp outside Kazan.

He had 20,000 men with him, but the core of experienced Cossacks was much diminished, and the force consisted almost exclusively of tribesmen and poorly-armed peasants, who, despite Beloborodov's efforts, were hardly more effective than the rabble led by Stenka Razin 100 years before. They were divided into four divisions, administered by a new 'College of War' under the Cossack Tvorogov. But the new 'College', too, was much less effective than the old. Many of the more capable administrators had been lost, and since it was constantly on the move, it functioned only as a very primitive campaign headquarters. Still Pugachev decided to take Kazan by storm.

On the morning of 12th July, Beloborodov entered the outskirts at the head of his peasants. He occupied the Governor's summer house, captured a gun almost bare-handed, and advanced into the suburbs, his men pushing carts of hay and straw before them. Another division attacked, and a third, of Bashkirs, put

Ataman Platov

Pugachev captured, *contemporary print*

An English picture of the ideal Cossack, *Gilray, 1814*

up a swishing barrage of arrows and advanced behind it into the streets. Fires broke out, and as the mob closed in on all sides, generals, soldiers and burghers retired into the castle.

The rebels broke into shops, set fire to houses and rode into churches and monasteries where they shot holes into icons, tore religious pictures out of their frames to use as saddle-cloths, knocked nails into crucifixes and broke open graves. Bashkirs roamed about flailing their whips, and anyone found dressed in the detested western style was immediately slaughtered. The fire spread to the gaol and Cossacks hastened to release the prisoners.

Among those who emerged into the street was Pugachev's first wife, Sofia, brought to Kazan for questioning with her three children. The youngest of them, a girl, had never seen her father and little Trofim, the eldest, could barely have remembered him, but he had heard much talk about Pugachev. Suddenly he began to tug at his mother's sleeve. 'Look over there, Mummy', he shouted excitedly, 'there's daddy riding among the Cossacks!' Sofia, who had heard not a word from Pugachev since he had fled to the Ukraine, who had had to sell the house for twenty-four and half rubles to keep her brood fed, responded immediately. 'What a dog,' she spat out, 'what a faithless villain!'[62]

Pugachev could not mistake the voice, but he proved equal to this unexpected and embarrassing challenge. He ordered his family to be installed in a tent near to his own and coolly informed his suspicious companions that Sofia was 'the wife of my friend, Yemelyan Pugachev, who was tortured in prison on my account during an inquiry. But since her husband, Pugachev, has earned my gratitude, I shall not desert her'. With tongue in cheek, Sofia saw Pugachev being wined and dined in imperial seclusion, watched him surrounded by Yaik Cossacks who called him 'Your Majesty'. But she kept her mouth shut, for fear, as she said later, that 'the dog might . . . cut me down or hang me'.[63]

Meanwhile the fires in Kazan had got completely out of hand and the rebels withdrew to their camp setting more houses alight for good measure as they left. A storm blew up, and sped the flames on towards the castle. Sparks ignited the wooden roofs inside. Then a wall collapsed, in a thundering roar,

H

crushing men beneath it. The garrison prayed as never before as the flames lapped ever closer. Whether or not in response to the fervent intercessions of the Metropolitan Benjamin, the wind veered round that evening; the storm, and the fire, died down. But already twenty-five churches, three monasteries and nearly three-quarters of Kazan's 2,867 houses had been gutted. The smoking city itself stood empty, dead.

Rebels were still staggering into the camp with their loads of booty or herding prisoners in front of the guns and forcing them to their knees to beg for pardon. Many citizens of Kazan volunteered to serve the Pretender and assembled cheering before his tent. The Kazan Tatars also arrived, bearing gifts and their respects, which Pugachev received in imperial style. But the rebels' euphoria was soon dispelled by the sighting of government troops. Pugachev met them four miles outside the silent city, but having lost 1,000 men he withdrew, thinking he was facing a whole army. In fact it was only the indefatigable Mikhelson's small force, which came on again dealing with the gangs of drunken plunderers who reeled across their path. Pugachev, discovering his error, returned to the attack, but Mikhelson's guns held him off and he fell back towards Kazan to regroup his forces.

On the morning of 15th July he at last announced his advance on Moscow and the army now 25,000 strong, crashed forward again, churning up a huge cloud of dust. As Mikhelson and his 800 men approached it, he heard a rumbling and the rumbling swelled into a chorus of wild cries as the peasants and tribesmen careered into the attack.

They cracked at the first collision and turned into an irresistible retreat. Mikhelson occupied their camp and took thousands of prisoners, including the officer Mineyev, who was forced to run the gauntlet until he fell dead, and Beloborodov, who was knouted and taken off to Moscow for execution. Pugachev was on the run again. He hid in woods for a few days with Sofia, the children, a few hundred Cossacks and some Bashkirs. Then, having shaken off his pursuers, he crossed the Volga. The clumsy Russian army machine changed gear again, the weary troops, marched this way and that. But Pugachev was too swift and slippery for them.

The light of rebellion flickered and threatened to go out. Then for the third time it flared up again. Its strength, which had come first from the Yaik Cossacks and then from the factory workers of the Urals and the Bashkirs, now derived chiefly from the peasants of the Volga estates. Pugachev made the appropriate modifications to his programme. He offered to treble the soldiers' pay, he fixed the price of salt at two kopeks a stone, declaring it free for the poor, and on 18th July at the little town of Tsyvitsk he issued a manifesto promising the Volga peasants free use of land, forests, fishing rights and salt pans, and urging them to hang their landlords—the real disturbers of the peace and 'ruiners of the peasants'.[64] This was Razin country and village after village welcomed their saviour come again—and waited for the distribution of captured money, grain and wine.

Soon Pugachev was less than three weeks' march from Moscow, but he was headed off south towards Alatyr. He reached it on 23rd July and then marched southwards through Saransk towards Pensa. He had about 2,000 supporters now and more were joining him every day. Another manifesto was issued. The peasants were 'granted' the right freely to practise the old faith 'and to be Cossacks for ever'. There would be no more recruiting, no more poll taxes, no more duties, no more 'burdens . . . imposed by criminal nobles and corrupt city judges'. The social order would be turned upside-down. The property-owning gentry— 'these enemies to our authority and rebels against the realm'— were to be hanged 'just as they, these men without Christianity, used to treat you peasants'. Once the gentry had been liquidated as a class, everyone would 'enjoy peace and tranquillity and a quiet life, which will last for ever'.[65]

Pugachev set the example himself. At Saransk he hanged 300 gentlefolk, men and women, old and young. At Pensa he burned down the governor's house with the governor and twenty members of the gentry inside it. The youngest Pulawski, fighter for Polish independence, who had recently joined him, left Pugachev in disgust, but the garrison of Saratov mutinied and opened the gates to him. On the 9th August he proceeded on his triumphant way, Mikhelson dogging him like a shadow, just two days behind.

Judgement day had come—and not only to the Volga.

Agitators spread the good news from village to village, far and wide, and peasants in provinces east and south of Moscow acted straightaway on Pugachev's promise of the kingdom of heaven come upon earth, stringing gentlemen up on a thousand lynch gallows. But the movement spread too fast, and lacked the organisational backbone which had existed in Orenburg. Attempts were made to set up governmental organs in the liberated areas, but they were episodic and local in character. Though the rebels were becoming more numerous than they had ever been, they were less capable of effective military action. The 10,000 or so Chuvash, Mordvins and tributary Tatars, soldiers, serfs and peasants actually with Pugachev represented only a small fraction of all those engaged and only a fifth of them were properly armed. The 'College of War', vainly striving to be an efficient quartermaster, was only a shadow of its old self.

But Pugachev was now approaching the Don, where he hoped to find a new military core for his movement. Already more than a hundred Don and Volga Cossacks had joined him—and 600 mounted Zaporozhians and Ukrainian bandit *gaidamaks*.[66] On 13th August he issued a manifesto to the Cossacks of his native Don. They were 'blinded', he warned them, by the blandishments of 'that cursed stock of gentry who, not satisfied with enslaving Russia, want to demean the native Cossack armies . . . and destroy the Cossack stock'.[67] They must make a final effort to repulse the creeping attacks on their autonomy. Pugachev must have known that, two years before, Ataman Yefremov had challenged Catherine's new rules for the Don Host and been arrested and replaced, that a surge of support among the Cossacks on the upper Don for another pretender, Bogomolev, had been quickly suppressed. Now the reliable Ataman Sulin and a cohort of elders, carefully chosen for their loyalty to Catherine, were in command. They warned the people against Pugachev, and had his old house ceremoniously burnt down. But though, in December, it was to be reported that many of the more disaffected Don Cossacks, 'in their naïveté' were drawing conclusions about Pugachev other than those they were fed with by the government's propaganda,[68] they had little chance to lend him active support. The local police were on the watch, regiments had been brought back from the Turkish front to cope with the possibility of Pugachev's appearance, and new forces had been raised locally in readiness for emergency. Fifteen hundred 'reliable' Cossacks and Kalmyks were soon on their way to fight him and with security so tight, few of Pugachev's agitators could get through to the Don, and those that did met with little success.[69]

Pugachev clashed with the loyalist Cossacks and Kalmyks along the Volga between Kamyshin and Tsaritsyn, but the Kalmyks, who had much the same grievances as the poorer among their Cossack neighbours, came over to him at the first shot, most of the others followed. The Cossack commanders fled for their lives. A delighted Pugachev had presents of cloth and money, looted on the way from Kazan, handed out, and had medals distributed, made out of silver rubles minted by the real Peter III. But he was apprehensive of being recognised by some old comrade among the new recruits, and tried to turn his face away from them. A Don Cossack had shouted out 'Hello there! Yemelyan Ivanovich' and that had been passed off. But it was not long before another called out in surprise: 'That's our Pugachev!'[70] Surrounded by hordes of the faithful as he was, his old comrades dared not make a scene but that night 100 disillusioned Don Cossacks packed up and left and on the next night about 400 others followed them. Even Yaik Cossack believers were beginning to realise that the Don Cossacks had recognised, not the Tsar, but one of themselves.

On 22nd August the rebels moved on down the Volga, further away from the Don. On the way Pugachev chanced across the astronomer Lowitz and had him hanged so that he might be 'nearer the stars'.[71] But nemesis was already close at hand. One morning late in August Mikhelson came in sight of the rebel caravan. Next day, Pugachev turned to greet him. A cloud of peasants drifted up against the thin wall of the troops. Some carefully placed cannon shots blew the cloud away again. Mikhelson sounded the advance, and the peasant army began to disperse leaving over 2,000 corpses and a scattering of upturned guns and carts behind them. Pugachev, unable to stop the rout, put Sofia and Trofim on horseback, lifted his two small daughters onto a cart piled with loot, and fled like the rest, but the cart overturned in the rush, and Sofia was lost among the crowds jostling their way to safety. Pugachev sped on south, with his boy Trofim and 400 Cossacks, who beat off all who tried to join them fearing they would slow them down. With Mikhelson breathing hot upon his heels, they began to cross the Volga forty-two miles from the scene of battle. There were only four boats and many who tried to swim across were drowned. Fewer than 200 joined him on the other side, and soon most of them had fallen by the wayside.

Ideas of possible refuges competed with each other in Pugachev's mind. He said first that he was making for Astrakhan, then thought of Zaporozhiye, or of following the route to Turkey Nekrasov had taken after the Bulavin revolt and again of the Kuban. But his comrades insisted on heading home to the Yaik and they went on into the desert steppe. Burned by day, shivering by night and desperately hungry, they passed slowly across the dreary landscape of sandstone, salt lakes and the curious ancient shellstone formed in the wake of a retreated sea. The desolation of the country reflected their own approaching doom—Mikhelson was still in pursuit, Golytsyn and Mansurov barred their way ahead and General Suvorov, hero of the Turkish war, was soon only a day or two behind them with a troop of cavalry.

Pugachev now wanted to head for the steppes south of Orenburg where, since May, the Kirghiz-Kaisaks had been on the rampage. But the Cossacks said they must first go to the Yaik to collect their families. On 14th September, Pugachev reached the tiny Old Believer settlement of Uzen where most of his remaining companions deserted him. Besides Trofim only Tvorogov, Chumakov and one or two others remained and their minds were already turning to the possibility of pardon—and to the price of 28,000 rubles on Pugachev's head.

On 8th September three of them were discussing the position with Pugachev. While he was describing a new plan to head for Guryev and the Caspian they were trying to lure him away from the gun he always had beside him. At last they said they had followed him far enough, that it was time he followed them. 'Enough blood has been shed', protested one. 'If you're really the Tsar, ride then with us to Yaitsk and justify yourself and us.'[73] Pugachev refused, grew angry, accused them of betrayal. Then they rushed him.

He struggled desperately for some moments, then suddenly stretched his hands out towards Tvorogov and told him wearily to tie them up. Tvorogov did—behind his back. Pugachev protested. They might betray him, but at least they need not treat him like a bandit. They relented at last and loosened his bonds. Pugachev immediately grabbed a sabre and managed to wound one of his captors, before he was overpowered again. On 15th September they brought the shorn Samson into Yaitsk. The rebellion had come full circle.

Handed over to Colonel Simonov and a member of the investigation commission, Pugachev immediately admitted his guilt: 'God has been pleased to punish Russia through my sinfulness', he said, 'I am guilty before God and her Imperial Majesty.'[74] But this was no bold Razin, cheerfully taking all responsibility upon himself. He blamed the Yaik Cossacks for starting the revolt, claimed that everything he had done was at their behest and against his own will, presented himself as a pawn, used and exploited by malicious men cleverer than he.

Next day they put him into a specially constructed cage on wheels and carried him like an animal to Simbirsk. He arrived there on 1st October and was immediately taken to Generals Potemkin and Panin for interrogation. Panin greeted him on the porch. 'How dare a thief like you call yourself Tsar!' he shouted. But Pugachev would not admit he was the chief, the only culprit. 'I'm not the real raven', he replied 'only a little one. The raven still flies.' Panin hit him several times about the face; Pugachev fell to his knees calling for mercy. Little Trofim burst into tears.[75]

For five days they questioned him, then they sent him to Moscow. 'Peter III' arrived on 4th November to find himself a person of importance still. Crowds flocked around the prison hoping for a glimpse of him; potentates hurried down from St. Petersburg to investigate his crimes and prepare a great show trial. A thorough purge was instituted. His old associates, practically every stray acquaintance from years back, were also gathered in—Zarubin-Chiki, Shigayev, Perfilev, Pochitalin, Gorshkov, Pyanov, old Philaret, Sofia and many others. Reports piled up and huge dossiers were formed as every available participant, every witness, every officer the authorities could find, told what he knew, if necessary under torture, and their stories were investigated and cross-checked.

Pugachev himself received the most attention. He was interrogated for days on end, almost without rest. They made him tell his story over and over again from the beginning. The result was a series of retractions and contradictions, though usually on minor points. But his inquisitors seemed never satisfied. They were determined to find evidence of foreign plots. Messages were passed daily to a xenophobic Empress who could not conceive that so great a rebellion, a rebellion involving about a fifth of the population, was possible without inspiration from abroad. They discovered that a young Polish freedom-fighter, Pulawski, had joined the Pretender after Kazan though he had left soon afterwards, disgusted at the rebels' cruelty. But they had to abandon ideas of a Polish plot. Suspicion was aroused by the discovery of a banner of the real Peter III's Holstein Guards among the captured rebel standards, and Voltaire had chipped in with the idea that Baron de Tott, French military adviser to the Turks, was the *eminence grise* behind the whole affair, encouraging the poor Empress, who had vaunted herself as such a liberal and enlightened ruler, in her self-deception.

Alienated from her people, sheltered always from the seamy sides of Russian life, Catherine simply could not credit that the revolution had been born of grinding poverty and by the evil cruelties inflicted on the great mass of the Empire's inhabitants by the Russian gentry, with her connivance. Extraordinary tales of foreign intervention were to be spread abroad, but Pugachev himself denied he ever received outside help. 'What use was that to me? I had as many men as I wanted, only they were irregulars.'[76] The interrogators drew a blank in testing every theory but the obvious one, and at last, on 16th December, they asked Catherine for permission to proceed with the trial, and she consented.

At nine o'clock on the morning of 30th December 1774 the twenty-nine judges took their seats in the throne-room of the Kremlin. There were fourteen senators among them, four

members of the Holy Synod and the heads of several ministries
besides a strong contingent from the Secret Chancery. For all her
talk of abolishing capital punishment, Catherine herself fore-
cast the death sentence,[77] though, bearing in mind the possible
effect on her reputation in western Europe, she had told the
judges to be measured in the numbers convicted and their
punishments. Pugachev was brought in on the second day, in a
state of exhaustion, a drained man.[78] He added nothing, just
prayed for the intercession of God, the Empress and of all
good Christians. At the end of the day the sentences were read
out. Pugachev was to be quartered and then beheaded. His
divided body was to be put on display, then burnt and the
ashes scattered. The fate of his companions ranged from quarter-
ing to deportation. His wife Sofia and his mistress Ustinya were
found innocent but Sofia and the children were nevertheless
incarcerated in a fortress in the north, where his two daughters
were still detained fifty-two years later. The men who had
betrayed Pugachev were pardoned.

When the judges met again the members of the Holy Synod
refused to sign the warrants out of considerations of
'Christian mercy'.[79] But they knew their endorsements were
unnecessary, and on Saturday, 10th January 1775, the convicts
were led out two by two, towards the scaffold, where the executioners waited, drinking wine.

Pugachev, in a huge sheepskin coat and holding a candle in
each hand, brought up the rear of the procession. He rode on a
tumbril, flanked by priests, and bowed low in all directions.
The sentence was read out. Pugachev crossed himself. Then
they excommunicated him, took off his sheepskin coat and led
him, shivering, towards the block. In a moment the head of
Catherine's 'Genghis Khan' was being held up high for all to
see.

The executioners entertained the huge crowd with a truly
splendid show. While they cut up the quivering carcass and
lashed the pieces to wheels which were to be exhibited at the
city gates, three men were hanged at corners of the scaffold.
Whippings and brandings provided a background while Perfilev
received the same treatment as Pugachev in the centre of the
stage, and by kind permission of the generous Empress, the

H*   221 citizens of Moscow were treated to the dainty spectacle of men's nostrils being torn out. The executions began shortly after eleven; it was evening by the time they were finished.[80]

The rebels had killed over 3,000 people and the forces of law and order were not to be outdone. The formal executions were numbered only in hundreds, but many of the punitive units escorting terrified gentry back to their estates were egged on to slaughter defenceless peasants out of hand.[81] Some of the tribal groups were pardoned provided they surrendered their captives; some were punished by the confiscation of a few thousand horses.[82] The Volga Tatars even benefited in that the Government began to restrain the Church in its campaign forcibly to convert them, and some limits were placed on the powers of the Ural factory owners to punish their workers. But the aftermath of Pugachev's revolt saw the culmination of the process by which the free Cossacks were finally shackled by the state. Those of the Yaik were policed by a huge force of regular troops; those of the Volga were transported to the Caucasus, and the distant Zaporozhians sent packing from the Sech.

The revolt made Catherine shrink back from her dalliance with the idea of liberal reform. Indeed, the spectre of Pugachev so haunted her that in March 1775 she issued a manifesto consigning Pugachev's name and deeds 'to everlasting oblivion and deep silence'.[83] The village in which he was born was razed to the ground, rebuilt on the far bank of the Don and re-named Potemkinskaya after her latest lover, Grigory. Even the word Yaik was expunged from the atlases. The river became the Ural river; Yaitsk, Uralsk; the Yaik Cossacks, the Ural Cossacks.

But she could not blot out the memory. All the propaganda presenting the rebellion as an outburst of gratuitous viciousness fomented by 'disloyal' elements could not obliterate the image of a naïve attempt by men for whom violence provided the only means of social protest, of escape from an intolerable existence. Not everyone accepted Pugachev as the villain of the piece. Years afterwards exiled Russian liberals and revolutionaries adopted his slogans[84] about restoring the peasants' rights to the land, and bringing democratic Cossack government to all the people. Intellectuals noticed with regret that the Boston Tea

222

Party had coincided with the start of the revolt—and the time of Pugachev's capture with the signing of the Declaration of Rights in Philadelphia.

And in the areas affected by the revolt Pugachev was remembered fondly and with respect. Pushkin, questioning peasants about him sixty years later, was told by an old Cossack woman that though it was still 'a sin' to mention his name 'we have no complaint against him. He did us common people no harm.' If he was cruel, it was not his fault; 'it was our drunkards who led him astray.' And an old inhabitant of Berda retorted: 'It may be Pugachev for some people, your honour, but for me he's our Father, Tsar Peter Fedorovich.'[85]

'Too soon the time will come for you
To live a rough and martial life,
Boldly to put foot in stirrup
And to carry a gun . . .
And I'll watch you go
And wave goodbye,
And then that night
Many a bitter, furtive tear I'll shed'.

—Lermontov, *A Terek Cossack Lullaby*

8 The Cossacks harnessed

The Pugachev revolt had stemmed from a general crisis among
Cossackdom. Pugachev knew the Terek; he had been in the
Ukraine during *gaidamak* outbreaks, and, above all, he had
been conditioned by his own experience on the Don. His
attempted revolution was the last great and furious outburst
against Tsarist government to emanate from the Cossack
borderlands, and its failure brought the domination of the
Cossacks by the state to its point of culmination.

Following the unconcerted Cossack rebellions in the seventies,
the state smashed all potential resistance in the old frontier
communities. The Sech was destroyed, the very name of the
Yaik obliterated, the community of Cossacks which had been
formed on the Volga was transferred wholesale to the Caucasus,
and the Don Host was placed under the rule of Catherine's new
favourite, Potemkin. The last vestiges of effective democratic

government finally disappeared; power which once had sprung from the grass roots of the Cossack masses now derived entirely from above, and a chain of Cossack officials from Ataman to village leader stood ready to implement every minute instruction issued from on high.

Even in Pugachev's time, Cossacks were ordered about from pillar to post, made to fight the state's battles when they were young, and when they were past service age to ride post and maintain roads and fortifications. Now, the only reason Cossacks were still allowed to exist as an element separate from the rest of the population was that, with their traditional warlike skills and the toughness imbued in them from early youth, they were a necessary supplement to the armed forces at a time when Russia was more often at war than not, and ideal pioneer settlers to defend the vast new tracts of territory being incorporated into an expanding empire.

War, red war: the Cossacks were never without it. They were a warrior class now, a caste of *Samurai* and as proud as the *Samurai* of their martial traditions, which distinguished them from the common peasantry. Like the Texas Rangers they provided their own clothes, mounts and arms, and, in return for a coin or two, they went out to kill and die for Russia. They fought the Swedes, the Poles, the Persians and the Turks, and as Russian arms entered the western European scene, against the Prussians and the French as well. There was no war, hardly a skirmish, in which Cossacks did not participate. They were the eyes and ears of the army, the screen which fanned out before the advancing regulars, the rearguard which covered their withdrawals, the pursuers and devastators of a retreating enemy. At the end of the long war against the Turks in 1775 Marshal Rumyantsev reported that 'their exploits . . . were an outstanding factor in hastening all the glorious successes of Russian arms. . . . They were daunted neither by want nor by disadvantage. . . . In both small and large-scale encounters . . . they were the first into the fire, distinguishing themselves with outstanding bravery'.[1]

Their natural role was to act as scouts and light cavalrymen, but commanders would use them for almost any purpose when proper specialist troops were lacking, and with no regard for the heavy casualties they might sustain. When the famous

General Suvorov was short of infantry for the great storm of Ismail in 1790 he had them dismount, cut down their lances to use as spears and rush the heavily defended walls of the citadel. Bogged down by their long cloaks in the muddy approaches, they were mown down in their hundreds, and yet the survivors fought on like demons and at last carved their way to the centre of the city.

Cossacks had been in the thick of the first battle between Russians and Prussians at Gross Jägersdorf in 1757 and three years later they had galloped into the streets of Berlin itself—an exploit which helped to create the Germans' lasting fear of 'the eastern menace'. This war marked the arrival of Russia as a great European power, and stimulated unprecedented western interest in the Cossacks.

From the start their reputation was unenviable. In 1757 an English journal reported that as a result of Cossack activities many of the 'inhabitants of *Prussia* have been hanged, others have had their legs cut off, or been ript up alive and their hearts tore out'. At Memel over a hundred women were said to have thrown themselves into the sea rather 'than submit to the brutalities offered them by these monsters'. Cossacks were accused of burning towns and of the wholesale slaughter of children, and westerners expressed surprise that Russia 'should employ in its armies barbarians to whose inhumanities it cannot put a stop'.[2]

Such horror stories contained exaggeration, but so did the denials of later Cossack apologists. Not only were Cossacks less susceptible to discipline than regular troops, they had been trained in war against the Tatars and the Turks where excesses were not only allowed, but actively encouraged. In Europe their commanders tried to wean them of the habit. General Apraksin had Cossack officers given 200 strokes of the knout, from which one or two died, for 'committing irregularities in *Lithuania* and *Prussia*'.[3] In Poland Suvorov 'reprimanded certain units ... especially among the Cossacks' for brigandage and had some men thrashed for it with rods.[4] But such punishments had only a limited effect. The Cossack was not only a plunderer by tradition, he needed plunder more than other troops. His pay was meagre and the commissariat generally expected him to live off the land. He had to feed himself and his horse, and often plunder could mean the difference between survival and disaster for his family at home.

There were times when lengthy service so disrupted family life and the family economy that Cossacks would go on strike. In 1769 twenty Don regiments refused point-blank to go on campaign and two years later, when another regiment of Cossacks was mobilised out of turn, the men ignored orders to march to the front. Attempts to subject them to the discipline of ordinary troops produced mutinies even on active service. Equality between Cossacks had become a thing of the past, and a man complained of ill-treatment at the hands of Cossack officers only at his peril. Zaporozhians who had a taste of such treatment while fighting the Turks in 1774 reacted by arresting their officers and compiling a charge-sheet of all their misdemeanours. And Cossacks on service were constantly nagged by fears of what might be going on at home. In 1795 a rumour circulated among Don Cossacks stationed in the Crimea that 'their families were being ruined, their houses burned and their children taken as soldiers'. With what an official report described as utter tumult and impertinence, they rode off towards home, taking the regimental banners and a number of officers with them as hostages.[5]

The most serious disturbances, however, were triggered off by compulsory resettlements. Russia counted her wealth in people, and the Cossacks, valued for their particular qualities as warrior-farmers, continued to be uprooted from their homes and transplanted to colonise virgin lands and defend new frontiers. In the thirties and forties Don Cossacks were shipped out wholesale to form the new communities of the Volga and Astrakhan and to reinforce the Terek line, and the scale of resettlements became ever larger. In 1791 six whole regiments were ordered to move with their families to the Kuban. They protested to the Ataman and a petition was sent to St. Petersburg. When the order was confirmed, the affected villages raised a considerable rebellion which was not brought under control until 1794, when over 6,000 Cossacks were fined, re-settled on the Kuban, or deported to Siberia.

The government, more than ever obsessed with the problems

of administering the new empire, transported Siberian service Cossacks east of the Altai Mountains, along the Yenisei and the Mongolian frontier and when their numbers were insufficient, drafted in rebellious Zaporozhians and convicts from the Don or Ural to join them. When the supply of Cossacks ran short, they would be created by the simple device of giving other sections of the population Cossack status. Peasants had been settled in virgin areas of western Siberia in 1736 and, reinforced by some Yaik Cossacks, became the new Cossack Host of Orenburg. Retired soldiers, exiles, orphans, immigrants from the Polish Ukraine, and even tribesmen were merged into existing Cossack communities. Kalmyks and Bashkirs, tribesmen of the borderlands, were given land and duties as frontier guards. Tunguses and Buryats were formed into regiments according to the Cossack pattern.

Potemkin, Catherine's one-eyed lover, and reorganiser of her army, even had the notion of forming a Cossack-style host to guard the road between St. Petersburg and Moscow against the Swedes. Nothing came of this particular idea, but other vulnerable areas saw the development of new Cossack armies and one of these, the Kuban Host, was to become the largest Cossack community, next only to the Don, now that the Ukraine had ceased to be Cossack at all. The Kuban Cossacks were born out of the need to develop and protect the area immediately north-west of the Caucasus mountains, won from Turkish protection in 1775. The destruction of the Sech in the same year made many Zaporozhians available for the purpose, but in the sophisticated Russian state system the peg did not find its hole at once.

Many Zaporozhians, having had enough of Russian rule, soon left their old haunts to settle on the Danube under Turkish protection.[6] Of those who remained, some were given the status of crown colonists, a few became serfs. Potemkin was now the overlord of the new south lands. Master planner and the great showman of Catherine's Russia, it was Potemkin who was to organise the Empress's celebrated tour of the newly annexed south lands during which she drove through the streets of handsome new villages and towns, not realising that the fine buildings she passed were just façades to hide the ugly mass of hastily-built hovels that lay behind them. Potemkin had great ideas for developing Zaporozhiye. He introduced serfs and land-lords into the area, ordered the outlying Cossack farmers to move into villages, the more easily to keep an eye on them, and even made them site their houses in accordance with set plans. Those who conformed received privileges of two years' free trading and fishing rights, and a few richer Cossack petitioners were granted rank, estates and serfs.[7]

One of those to be privileged in this way, an ex-elder called Anton Golovaty, had conceived the idea of re-establishing a Cossack order acceptable to the government. His first petition to Potemkin met with a rebuff. 'You Zaporozhians can't be re-strained', he was told. 'You've done serious mischief and there's no way you can be of use.'[8] But together with two other ex-elders, Sidor Bely and Zakhari Chepega, Golovaty persisted, and in time the government began to view the proposition in a new light. When the Crimea rebelled in 1783, Potemkin authorised Golovaty to raise a thousand ex-Zaporozhians to serve as marines, and in 1788, just after the outbreak of another war with Turkey, Catherine ordered the mobilisation of a whole army of 'faithful' Zaporozhians with Bely as its Ataman. The flags and regalia confiscated when the Sech was destroyed were handed back and many elders of the old force made officers in the new 'Black Sea Cossack Host'.

They acquitted themselves well in the war, fought at Kinburn and Ochakov and took part in the terrible storming of Ismail in 1790. Some reward was due. Many had already settled between the rivers Bug and Dniestr, but the land was overcrowded and it was difficult to build up their shattered fortunes there. They needed some wider foot-hold in the world. For its part, the government was anxious to put a greater distance between them and both the landowners of south Russia whose peasants might seek shelter with them, and the renegades of the Danube Sech. And so, when Golovaty and Chepega fell on their knees before the Empress and begged in their quaint provincial accents to be granted lands on the eastern shore of the Black Sea between the Kuban river and Azov, their plea was granted. An unofficial migration to the Kuban had already begun, when in August 1792 Colonel Bely landed at Taman with 4,000 Cossack marines. A long train of family Cossacks led by Golovaty soon followed overland to join them.

The territory was a near wilderness demanding all the qualities of the Cossack pioneer. It was hot, marshy, humid and misty, and good water was hard to find in it. But there were salt lakes, an abundance of game and fish, and much of the land proved fertile. The Cossacks, nearly 13,000 strong, set to work with a will and soon established three townships and the foundations of a cordon line along the Kuban river to protect the land against the bellicose tribesmen who inhabited the other shore.

Every man had his military duties to perform, but otherwise the rules were few. Any serving Cossack could carve out a farm for himself, build, plant, till, or breed livestock as, where and as much as he pleased, though fishing rights were at first reserved for those who had actually fought in the Turkish war. There was land in plenty; only labour was scarce, and after a severe outbreak of plague in 1796 even scarcer. So newcomers were enrolled as Cossacks with few questions asked, and the Kuban was soon notorious as a refuge for army deserters. By 1803 their numbers had doubled and the government had noted 'many complaints . . . of runaways being . . . hidden' on the Kuban.[9]

The capital of the host, Yekaterinodar (Catherine's gift), became a boom town. In 1794 its inhabitants numbered less than 600 men—administrators, merchants, and a variegated collection of other artisans including two icon painters and a couple of musicians— most of them living in crude earth huts. Yet within eight years the population had expanded ten-fold and scores of solid-looking houses were rising up along its muddy streets. Yekaterinodar's prosperity reflected the development of the region as a whole. Men of enterprise were extending their farms, going into fishing on a large scale[10] and developing carting and trading businesses, borrowing capital from Crimean Greeks, or less wisely, from fellow Cossacks who lent at double the rate.

Comfortable fortunes were made within a very few years. When a nephew of Ataman Chepega died in 1807, he left a house in Yekaterinodar and a farmstead up-country where he kept 338 horses, 262 head of cattle, an apiary, and a number of pigs and poultry. The contents of his barn showed him to have been a mixed farmer of the more progressive kind, for besides a carriage, two ox-carts, forty spare wheels, some of them broken, five yokes, a Circassian nomad tent and a clutter of pitchforks, sickles, chisels and hammers, there were two new ploughs with iron shares besides two normal wooden ones, and two harrows with iron teeth.

There were a number of other buildings—a smithy, two mills, an ice-house and dwellings for his workers. The farmhouse itself had a cane roof, but was comfortable enough inside, heated by green-tiled stoves and furnished with three tables, and several chairs, two of them upholstered. There were two portraits on the walls, eight other pictures, glassed and framed, and no fewer than thirteen icons to demonstrate his appreciation of his good fortune.[11]

Such pious gratitude was not always evident. When the authorities, anxious to encourage the established religion, ordered Cossacks to build a church in every village, they grumbled at having to spend their labour and hard-earned savings to such non-utilitarian ends. They did not resent their local defence duties so much, since they stood to lose if the Circassian raiders got through, but they were impatient with the orders forbidding them to cross the Kuban and retaliate. Only in 1809 did an official war party of 5,000 men ride out on a punitive expedition to burn down eighteen Circassian villages and drive off thousands of sheep and cattle.

The Kuban was ruled by a small clique of bosses—ex-Zaporozhian officers of the Turkish war—who held on to power by ingratiating themselves with their superiors. In 1794 the government confirmed Chepega as Ataman, Golovaty as chief judge and Timofei Kotlyarevski as Secretary to the Host. When Chepega died three years later Tsar Paul chose Golovaty to take his place, and Kotlyarevski was to succeed him. There was no general assembly as there had been in Zaporozhiye; the colonels were appointed by the Ataman. Only the local atamans were still elected, and an order of 1798 laid it down that these must be 'respectable', 'God-fearing' and 'loyal'.[12] Russia generally was noted for the corruption of its administration but the Cossack leaders were second to none in the venality and corruption with

231

which they carried out their duties. Under their rule in the Kuban the substitution system thrived; officers who actually went on campaign often contrived to make a profit from it at the expense of their men, and senior officials of the Host did the best of all.

Early in 1796 Golovaty led 1,000 Cossacks east to fight the Persians. On the way, he hired them out to work for the commander-in-chief at Astrakhan to his own private profit. The men got nothing. Later, at Baku, during the intervals between the fighting, Golovaty set them to work as dockers, salvage-men and foresters. Though pay was promised for these services few Cossacks ever saw any, and even their rations were sold off by their commanders, who pocketed the proceeds. Of three barrels of corn liquor apportioned to the force, for instance, only three measures were ever issued. Golovaty kept the rest. As a consequence of his lining his own pockets at their expense, some Cossacks died of sickness hastened by malnutrition, many deserted, usually to the enemy, and barely half of the original number returned to the Kuban.

Arriving at Yekaterinodar they were thanked for their service and then dismissed. But they refused to budge until their grievances had been rectified, and in the succeeding weeks they virtually took over the town. The change of scene from Zaporozhiye to the Kuban had done nothing to change these Cossacks' rumbustious spirit. When Dikun and Shmalko, two of their leaders, were arrested their comrades promptly stormed the prison and released them. The elders tried to calm them down and asked for more evidence of the alleged injustices, but when they tried to make them swear fresh oaths of loyalty the Cossacks swarmed round the church, protesting that guilty men were being shielded. Cossacks called up from the cordon line to deal with them simply joined the demonstrators and rushed through the streets brandishing their weapons, and beating up every elder they could find.

At last two companies of regulars arrived, but when it was announced that Kotlyarevski was to succeed Ataman Golovaty who had recently died, the Cossacks flared up again. Kotlyarevski was tarred with the same brush as his predecessors; they wanted none of him. The Colonel in charge made him swear not to maltreat them, but still they were not satisfied. At last they were persuaded to draw up a petition and send a delegation with it to St. Petersburg. Like so many hopeful Cossack delegates before them, they were promptly arrested on arrival.

A government inquiry which reported three years later granted the justice of the Cossacks' case, found they had been treated improperly on campaign and that at home salt and forest rights controlled by the Host had been let out by the elders only in return for bribes. In December 1799 Ataman Kotlyarevski was retired, ostensibly because of old age. But Russian imperial justice made a point of protecting the strong against the weak. The bureaucracy's sense of identification with functionaries lower down the scale made it strive all the harder to support the corrupt elders of the Host. The need for discipline outweighed all other considerations and so the leaders of the demonstration were beaten, branded and sent out to Siberia as serfs.

The government began to supplement brute force with a public relations campaign to tame the Cossacks. Catherine the Great in 1775 had sent for sixty-five of 'the best and most distinguished' Don Cossacks to form her bodyguard during celebrations of the peace treaty with Turkey,[13] and in 1793 she came on a state visit to Cherkassk, issuing a gracious charter granting the Don Cossacks their land 'in perpetuity'—though her successors felt it necessary to repeat the act. Such empty gestures—'imperial favours' as they were called—came to be highly valued. The psychological harnessing of the Cossack was to be just as complete as the physical take-over had been.

Mesmerised by the grandeur and mystique surrounding the throne, the Cossack leaders were becoming ever more responsive to its will; captivated by the Russian world of privilege, they sought to accumulate privileges to themselves. War service had opened their eyes. Having mingled with regular officers on campaign and seen how well they lived, Cossack elders determined to catch up with the Greater Russian Joneses. The government encouraged them. In 1775 it granted the more senior Cossack officers substantive rank and the privileges of minor nobility which from 1796 their children were allowed to inherit. In 1798 junior Cossack officers were also given gentry status and peasants residing on the elders' estates were formally tied down as serfs. The distance between elders and ordinary Cossacks was growing wider and to ensure that the latter kept their distance, the Don elders actually ordered their Cossacks to treat them with great respect.[14] By 1802 the Don boasted fifteen generals and over 1,000 other officers—a social upper crust of about two and a quarter per cent. A once homogenous community had already been stratified on class lines, but henceforth rights of inheritance ensured the perpetuation of these differences.

It was not only a new class that had arisen; it was a new breed of men. Its prototype was a Cossack called Platov. Born in August 1751 into a prosperous Don Cossack family, Platov was enrolled for service at the age of thirteen, commissioned six years later, and had his blooding in war in 1771, when Russian forces attacked Perekop, the gateway to the Crimea. Transferred to the Kuban he first earned distinction in command of a supply convoy which was attacked by a vastly superior force of Tatars. Swinging the wagons round to form a corral, he managed to beat off seven swarming attacks and hold out till relief arrived. A man of unquestioned valour, Platov never doubted his allegiance; he marched willingly against Pugachev, rode through the provinces of Voronezh and Kazan searching for rebels and killed many of those he found without a tremor.

He was raised to the rank of elder for his zeal. And once he reached the rank of Major in 1784, his military career progressed by leaps and bounds. He became a lieutenant-colonel in 1786, a full colonel a year later. With Russia almost constantly at war, the qualities of dash and courage were quickly recognised, and Platov was a man of the hour, almost constantly in action. He fought at Bender and at Akkerman, was created a knight and promoted brigadier. At the bloody storming of Ismail in 1790 he won the third class of the coveted order of St. George besides a severe wound in the stomach, and at the conclusion of the peace was promoted to the rank of major-general.

The awards continued to flow in. His services in the Persian campaign of 1796 earned him a diamond-encrusted sabre, and on the accession of the Emperor Paul he was made a Commander of the Order of St. John of Jerusalem.[15] A professional warrior, ambitious to rise in the hierarchy of the larger Russian community, Platov was the faithful servant of autocracy, the dedicated enemy of revolution. But in 1799, when Don and Ural Cossacks marched against the armies of revolutionary France, he was not among them.

Cossacks spear-headed the way to a series of astounding victories, which cleared the French out of Italy. This sudden success provoked delight in England, Russia's partner in the anti-revolutionary alliance, and stimulated a new wave of interest in Russia. The spot-light fell on the Cossacks in particular.

'The Cossacs', one British newspaper assured its readers, 'are amongst the fiercest people on the Globe'. The picture of them as Asiatic demons, dating from the Seven Years' War, was softened now that they were fighting on the side of the righteous, against the revolutionary French. They seemed more like the knights of old, bore lances, 'couched as in the days of ancient chivalry'. The officers, at least, gave an impression of being polite and even cultivated, and their predatory exploits came to be praised as admirably intrepid when used against the French. As the campaign progressed, the Cossacks became 'charming . . . young, well built [and] in appearance . . . not unlike the English'.

With their oriental dress and fine bushy beards they looked 'more picturesque and romantic than formidable'.[16] But formidable they certainly were, as they proved when Suvorov had to turn north into Switzerland that winter. On foot, in mountainous terrain, leading their horses, piled high with stores, stumbling along perilous Alpine tracks, they were quite outside their natural element. And yet they fought as eagerly as ever and huddled over their horses' necks, and almost covered with snow, they guarded the army's terrible retreat over the mountains. Many of them failed to emerge from that frozen hell. They died of starvation and of exposure; not a few slipped, screaming, over the edge of a precipice, or were swallowed up silently by a hidden crevasse.

Battered in Suvorov's grand retreat over the Alps, they were depressed by the fiasco of the Helder campaign when Cossacks had sailed from England as part of a joint Russo-British expeditionary force to land in Holland. They had held on there for some weeks. But due to mismanagement they had failed to advance against insignificant opposition and had then embarked again, the generals blaming each other for their humiliating failure to accomplish anything. But the fighting Cossacks had yet another trial in store. Tsar Paul had withdrawn from the coalition and now turned a greedy eye south, towards the British possessions in India. The distance, the deserts and mountains that divided Russia from India did not daunt him in the least. No thought was given to the resources necessary to such an undertaking. The Don Cossacks were simply ordered to march and promised 'all the riches of India' as their reward.[17]

Platov was put in command of the expedition and at the end of February 1801 he led it out at a speedy trot—22,000 men, each with two mounts, and carrying six weeks' supply of food scraped from the larders of the Don. There were no maps but in the event this did not matter. They had barely crossed the edge of their own territory when trouble overtook them. Already shivering with cold, their imperial banners swirling madly about in the snow storm, they reached the Volga. The ice broke as some of them were crossing, and in the Irgiz desert beyond the Volga there was no feed for the survivors' horses. But still the loyal Platov led them onwards like Gadarene swine, towards inevitable doom. Then, on 23rd March, a courier caught up with them. The Tsar was dead. His successor had called the expedition off. The column turned back gratefully towards the Don.

Platov's duty was rewarded again. He was promoted lieutenant general and made Ataman of the Don. He proved an energetic administrator, rationalised and Russianised the system, breathed new life into the Chancery, established a local police force, and added a touch of pageantry by forming a special Ataman's Regiment—in all, fashioned the community to serve the more effectively as a military caste.

About 50,000 Cossacks, about half of them of the Don, were now available. Two-thirds of these were horsemen—two-fifths of Russia's entire cavalry arm. In the succeeding wars against the Swedes, the Turks and, above all, against Napoleon, there was not a campaign nor a sector of the front in which they did not serve. They fought at Austerlitz, and at Jena and distinguished themselves particularly at Eilau in 1807, though they still maintained their reputation as the vultures of the battlefield. When the French Cuirassier Guards broke into the Russian centre Cossacks instantly bore down on them and not only drove them out, but reappeared a few minutes later wearing the Frenchmen's armour. Later they raided Murat's advance posts, inflicting many casualties and taking 1,600 prisoners, captured Marshal Ney's baggage train, and covered the army's retreat from Friedland.

There was no comparable body of fighting men in Europe. Yet their capabilities derived, not from drills and mass discipline, but from their qualities as individuals bred in a peculiar martial tradition. Most of them were used to horses from early childhood—ponies which might look unprepossessing, but could walk at five miles an hour for days on end, and when touched by their riders' wrist-whips 'dispute the race with the swiftest'.[18] They were well looked after, their saddles lightly drawn so that they could graze at will; and they never felt the bit or spur.

Like his Tatar predecessors the rider was as hardy as the mount, could stay in the high saddle, day and night, even sleep in it. He moved fast and in absolute silence for he wore nothing that could give a betraying ring—no chain to his bridle, no button to his coat. As a scout the Cossack was without compare, could tell the direction of gunfire twenty miles away, find his way unerringly across unfamiliar country, track 'with the assurance and the indefatigable ardour of the instinctive bloodhound'. Nothing could 'elude his activity, escape his penetration, or surprise his vigilance'. He could steal upon an outpost and whip away a prisoner with his lasso before the enemy was roused, was adept at laying booby traps, and knew 'as if by instinct, the situation fit for ambuscades'.[19]

Good shots with musket and carbine, the Cossack made effective *tirailleurs*, but their usual weapon was the lance—an immense instrument, sustained by firm wrists and impelled with swift and devastating force. At a disadvantage when charged by regular cavalry, Cossacks were vicious in attack themselves. They would advance in dispersed order, like a swarm of bees, making 'a thousand curves, galloping in every direction with incredible rapidity', the snaffle bridle allowing the horses to twist and turn at full speed through intricate terrain, which could be most disconcerting to stiff-trained regulars. Yet the mercurial Cossacks could also keep together like a chain, bear in on the enemy in broad single rank, then reform on the centre 'with the rapidity of lightning and almost without word of command'.[20] A master of surprise and stratagem, with superb field-craft and a reputation for never offering quarter, the Cossack trooper usually had the psychological advantage over the enemy. His talents and loyalty were never more needed than when Napoleon's Grand Armée crossed the Russian border in 1812.

The Don mounted fifty regiments and several batteries of horse artillery—nearly 30,000 men dressed in uniform blue coats with red turn-ups, and white-frogged cuffs, caps made of the skins of unborn lambs, and long Circassian cloaks. Cossacks were on the march, too, from the Ural and Orenburg, the Terek and the Kuban. Most of them were parcelled out among the various commands, but fourteen regiments made up a special 'flying corps' commanded by the veteran Platov himself, now raised to the rank of General of Cavalry.

Platov's flying corps was engaged from the first day of the war, covered the withdrawal of Bagration's Second Army, breaking down bridges to delay the French advance. With Platov was a British liaison officer, Sir Robert Wilson, who as he passed through eastern Poland, found 'not a single village or cottage inhabited' the peasants having 'fled to the woods for fear of the Cossacks'.[21] They were leaving a trail of devastation behind them; but Russia was being invaded and the hated foreigner must be denied the means to live.

The generals, however, seemed more engaged by squabbling among themselves. General Barclay de Tolly hated Bagration, and Bagration—and Platov—resented the 'foreigner' Barclay. In June 1812 Barclay accused Bagration of intriguing with Platov 'thus putting the latter general, who . . . is but little developed and completely uneducated, into a muddle'.[22] He asked for Platov's dismissal. But he remained, and Wilson, who thought Platov would have been 'one of the first men of the age, as indisputably he is one of the most eminent warriors' had he but had a 'liberal education', joined in on his side, wheedled for reinforcements, and pressed for the Cossack corps to be made independent.[23]

So the armies tramped back through Smolensk to Borodino, where Platov's Cossacks played a brave and crucial part in the battle and were the last Russian troops to leave the bloody field. But the retreat left Moscow unprotected, the ancient capital of all the Russias was occupied by foreigners again, and, by ironic chance, almost exactly two centuries after the Poles had occupied the Kremlin.

Murat attempted to rouse up their old anti-Tsarist feelings, but Cossacks rallied round the Tsar with a unanimity they had never shown before. Napoleon drew them all together—men of the Kuban and the stormy Terek, of Orenburg and of the Ural. The whole of the quiet Don stirred, and when Platov called for volunteers, hoary veterans and boys barely in their teens flocked in to sacrifice themselves for Holy Russia.

The government dared not arm the peasants, for fear of a rebellion, and it had no plans to raise a Cossack levy either. This was Platov's own idea and it was swiftly and efficiently carried out. A register was made of all fire-arms on the Don and the police ensured that prices did not rise in response to the sudden demand. The local gentry donated 1,500 horses and Cossack traders 93,000 rubles to equip men who could not afford to mount and arm themselves, and soon 15,000 Don Cossacks—old men and their grandsons—were riding north at thirty-six miles a day, towards the Russian camp at Tarutino.

They found their comrades in a poor state. Some regiments had lost three-quarters of their complement, and now they were bivouacked miserably in frosts twenty-five degrees below zero. But in October Napoleon abandoned Moscow and as the long streams of dispirited men moved westwards, away from the fire-torn city, Platov was ordered to give chase.

He took part in defeating the sullen Marshal Davoust at Vyazma, but generally the Cossacks operated in small groups, buzzing like hornets round the straggling columns. There was no need for a major battle. Kutuzov, the wise Russian commander, was content to let the winter smash the invaders.

The Cossacks were loosed merely to hurry them on their way.

Once a band of Cossack raiders smashed their way into a French encampment and were so eager to carry off the cannon they found there that they ignored a plump little man wrapped in a fur coat. And so they lost their chance of capturing Napoleon. But they took upwards of 50,000 other prisoners that winter, and slaughtered many more. Napoleon could call the Cossacks a 'disgrace to the human species', though he had to admit their skill in guerrilla warfare.

The remnants of the Grand Armée continued its retreat, and as Marshal Ney's rearguard were crossing the Dnieper, the ice broke and two-thirds of them joined the mighty legion of the lost. Many Cossacks, too, had frozen to death or died of sickness. Some Don regiments were reduced to sixty men and one with a quarter of its normal complement was reckoned strong. Still, the survivors had a field-day stripping the frozen corpses of the enemy. They sent a ton of silver, which the French had taken from the churches of Moscow, home to the Don, traded a mass of lesser spoils with Jewish traders as they passed through the Ukraine, and, as the campaign progressed, they crammed so much loot under their saddles that, head-on, they seemed to be riding on the horses' necks. So the Cossacks' sabres whistled on, beyond the Russian border—to Bautsen, Dresden and Leipzig, and in January 1814 Platov crossed the Rhine and soon Cossack bivouacs were sprouting up along the Champs Elysées and upon Montmartre.

Europe could now inspect the Cossacks at leisure, and Englishmen were treated to many a conflicting story of this strange wild breed. Reports reached London of Hamburgers asking some into their homes, and actually surviving. In Dresden, Cossacks were said to sit in church for hours, entranced by the sound of the organ, and the quest for music led some of them to break into a house where a young lady was playing the piano, and pay for the pleasure with a gold coin when they left. Elsewhere, these ferocious men of war were domesticated to the point of doing household chores for the housewives they were billeted upon, though in Berlin and Nuremburg they allegedly refused rooms in the best hotels in favour of straw beds in the stables, and turned up their noses at recherché dishes, preferring to prepare their own cabbage soup on the pavement.[24]

Parisians suffering occupation by these uncivilised invaders might be expected to shudder at their 'uncouth appearance, their singular physiognomy', and their 'barbarous costume', but everywhere property had to be watched when the Cossacks were about. They were said to treat pictures or statues of a religious nature with a great respect which, however, did not prevent them spiriting them away. And the disposal of their booty was well organised—a great chain of post-stations stretched right across Europe to facilitate its movement to the Don.[25]

But the English were spared their excesses. To them the Cossacks were allies, great fellows, and Londoners were agog when in March 1813 a real live Cossack, an immense steel-tipped lance sprouting from between his thighs, drove up to the Post Office accompanying dispatches. Six feet tall with a long, curly, grey beard, this was a private Cossack of the 9th Don regiment called Zemlenukhin. He was fêted for a week. The publisher Ackermann had two portraits made of him, he was cheered at Lloyd's Coffee House, entertained to a cold collation at the Mansion House, and stood beside the Lord Mayor on the balcony of the Royal Exchange where the Tsar and Wellington were toasted. Asked if he had killed any Frenchmen Zemlenukhin coolly replied: 'three officers; besides the fry', and patriotic Englishmen were delighted with his answer. The City raised a subscription for him and the Prince Regent presented him with a sabre and sword belt in silver and black velvet.

Next year, heralded by much publicity, Ataman Platov arrived in London. His fame had preceded him; he had become the symbol of Russian resistance. Gossips told of his weeping as Moscow burned, of his vowing to give his daughter to the Cossack who captured Boney. Now he was in England to attend the great review in Hyde Park on 20th June 1814. It was a great occasion. The Prince Regent, the Tsar and the King of Prussia were all there. But of the 15,000 troops on parade it was 'Hetman Platoff' and the small Cossack detachment which received the loudest cheers.[26] He was showered with gifts and honours—a sword worth 200 guineas from the city, a gem-encrusted portrait from the Prince Regent, and from Oxford an honorary degree. And for his services both in war and in consolidating the Don Cossacks' in loyalty round the throne, the Tsar raised him to the dignity of Count.

When Platov died in 1818 a period of transition in Cossackdom had reached its point of completion. The larger communities were in sight of a prosperity unimagined a century before; a distinct class of 'gentlemen' had emerged, and the ignorant elders of a past age were already being replaced by young officers with a smattering of education. Above all, Cossack attitudes had been transformed. In 1812 when he called for volunteers, Platov had told his people of their obligation 'to sacrifice everything for the defence of . . . the August Throne'.[27] Such an appeal might have been hooted at even half a century before, but now it touched the Cossacks' hearts. They had accepted the Tsarist bit at last. Once the core of resistance to autocracy, henceforth Cossacks could be relied on to stamp out defiance to the Tsar.

'We heed one command alone;
And what our father-commanders have commanded us
We obey . . .'.

—Cossack song

9 Servants of the Tsar

As if to symbolise the break with the rebellious past, in 1805
Platov had ordered that the Don Cossack capital be moved to a
new site. Old Cherkassk had looked picturesque enough from a
distance, with its spires seeming to rise straight out of the water,
its canals and its quaint wooden houses standing high on piles.
But summer and autumn the place was scattered with foul-
smelling pools, and too often the river rose up so far that Cossack
dignitaries were forced to remove themselves hurriedly from the
little cluster of public buildings that stood on the higher ground.
Still, the new town, Novocherkassk, though placed in a more
elevated position, was badly sited from a trading point of view.
Merchants were especially reluctant to move there, and it was
never to achieve the commercial importance of its predecessor.

Primarily an administrative and social centre, Novocherkassk
was soon a lively enough place, where 'a wealthy and enlightened

society' enjoyed 'the refinements . . . even the luxuries of the most civilised nations'.[1] Foreigners, however innocent their curiosity, might be carefully watched by the police, and the streets might be disfigured by ragged prisoners in clanking chains let out of the town's six prisons to beg, but the chief impression on a visitor was one of grace and prosperity. Cossack officers with martial brows and flowing mustachios, girls, charming in silk tunics and yellow boots, went about their daily rounds. Stately Cossack matrons in caps as tall as mitres and decorated with flowers or pearls passed in and out of houses whose parlours were stacked with porcelain and plate, and where jewels worth thousands were hidden away in private boxes. And on Sundays all the finery was shown off in the main church where the banners of the Host, the silver-headed staves of bygone Atamans and the ancient horse-tail banners were now outshone by gold faced, diamond-studded icons, rich altar cloths and massive pieces of gold and silver—the tithes of the rich and the gifts of pious Cossacks returned laden from the wars. Gold pieces of every European currency were common tender in the shops and in no other Russian province did good coinage seem to be so plentiful.[2]

Life still flowed along the rivers rather than overland across the steppe, where lonely Cossacks galloped, carrying the mails. And for the sight of really bustling commerce, one went to Rostov at the time of the fair. Cossacks from as far as the Caucasus and the Kuban, and Kalmyks riding camels, drove huge trains of cattle into market here. The river bank was lined for miles by barges carrying timber and cow-grease, grain from Saratov and iron from Siberia. And plying in between them, came the little boats from the by-ways and shallows of the quiet Don—dug-out canoes bearing quivering piles of glinting trout and sturgeon, perch and tench, enormous crawfish, tortoises and carp like porcupines.[3]

With the once fearsome Kalmyks absorbed into the system and bearing service like the rest of them, Cossacks were now safe to pluck the fruits of a temperate climate and a prodigal nature, to brew their spirits, and generally profit from a free commerce and access to the sea. In the north, men still bent over ox-drawn ploughs and threshed their grain with iron chains, but they made

Cossacks of the Don, *above, from an Ackermann lithograph*

The wife of a prosperous Kuban Cossack, *Nineteenth Century*

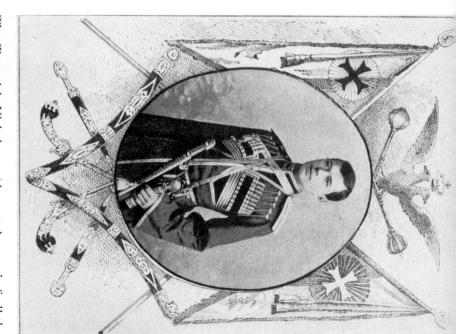

The Tsarevich Nicholas as 'August Ataman' of all the Cossacks

a better living than in Razin's time. Ten thousand sacks of grain arrived every year still, by courtesy of the Tsar, but the Don could feed itself these days. Fifty thousand tons of fish were being hauled out of the rivers each year, a million head of cattle, over 250,000 horses and about two and a half million sheep grazed on the generous pastures of the steppe, and the vineyards in the south produced heavy crops of grapes. Enterprising Cossacks had brought vines back from France and even the method of making champagne, and by 1843, 750,000 gallons of wine mostly rough, was being produced, which found a steady market in Moscow.

Farming, fishing and viniculture were not the only stays of the Don Cossacks. About 64,000 tons of salt were annually produced, coal had been found, there were several brick works, and an iron foundry had been established as early as 1795. By 1860 there were over 200 factories, a pig-iron works at Rostov, an agricultural machines factory in Novocherkassk, and the Grushevka coalfields were producing 60,000 tons a year. But the biggest growth of all, thanks largely to the abolition of the English Corn Laws, was in arable farming, and especially in wheat.

Cossack merchants anxious to profit from this growth of trade and stand up to competition from Russians, Armenians and Greeks, had found that military service interfered too much with business. Some of them had therefore pressed Platov for exemption from military duties and this had been granted, in return for an appropriate contribution to the Host treasury. In due course a guild was founded—the Society of Don Trading Cossacks. Its numbers were limited to 500. Each member had to have capital of at least 5,000 rubles and pay 200 rubles a year for the thirty years for which exemption was required. It was a small price to pay for a good chance of making a fortune.

By the nineteenth century there were comparatively few really poor Cossacks on the Don, for, from the age of seventeen, every man was entitled to a share of land. This was allocated on a local basis every year by the village ataman according to need and to service obligations. Bribes sometimes secured extra plots or land of better quality, and it was not unknown for the names of children to be registered in order to obtain a share. Yet on the whole, by comparison with the Russian peasant, the Cossack was well off.

Nevertheless of the thirty-eight and a half million acres at the disposal of the Host in 1823, only forty-two per cent was at the disposal of the ordinary Cossacks. The Kalmyks had another four and a half million acres, a million was allotted to community purposes, chiefly horse rearing, six and a half million was held in reserve, much of it let out to the profit of the Host as a whole, and ten and three-quarter million acres was the privately owned —much of it by members of the official class.

Of these, a few were very rich and powerful. Martynov owned 20,000 head of cattle and the Yefremovs employed 3,000 of the 70,000 peasants who had been imported into the area in recent years, though barely 1,000 of the 8,000 officers of 1823 owned land with peasants.[5] A handful of other oligarchs—Ilovaiskis, Denisovs and Isayevs—were also numbered among the rich, and about two dozen other families came not far behind. Together they constituted a charmed circle from whom the Tsar generally chose his atamans.

Social distinctions between ordinary Cossacks and the officer-gentry class were growing, but the gap was still narrow by comparison with peasant-gentry relationships in Russia, and although advantages of rank and wealth tended to be handed down from one generation to the next, status was not irrevocably fixed. A Cossack from a plain family could be commissioned and a general's son remain in the ranks. A son could lose his father's fortune, and even a family of staff rank could lose its noble status if the sons and grandsons failed to be commissioned.

Ironically, it was the state, which had encouraged serf-owning and the growth of privilege in the first place, which now determined to set a limit to them. When Platov had applied for permission to found class-distinctive institutions for the gentry on the Don, he had been refused. A government commission found that 'this new class of people', the Don gentry, had already 'caused harm' and that any further increase would endanger 'the homogeneity' of the community.[6] It was proposed that personal gentry status should be accorded only to Cossack generals and staff officers, not to everyone who reached commissioned rank.

The government had realised that the creation of a social

and economic system such as obtained in Russia proper would destroy the Cossacks' peculiar military qualities and their ability to support their service. As early as 1801 the War Ministry had become concerned at the unequal sharing-out of land on the Don. It was proposed to guarantee the common lands by charter, but the Host authorities protested. Larger farming units, so they claimed, were necessary to increase the prosperity of the region, and much of the land in question was not irrevocably lost in any case, only leased out. But though they denied that the interests of poorer Cossacks were being harmed, in fact the richer men who had first imported peasants to compensate for the lack of labour in the region, had been continuing to import them, and so were being driven to acquire even wider tracts of land, ultimately to the Cossacks' detriment. The government toyed with the idea of turning the Don serfs into Cossacks and then dropped it but in 1816 it forbade landowners from buying in more serfs from outside.

But the process had already gone too far. The tracts of free, virgin land, were already beginning to run out and willy-nilly, communal lands intended for the support of ordinary Cossacks were being eaten into. As a result some Cossacks allotted plots too small or of too poor a quality, reached such an impoverished state that they had to be equipped at the expense of the community, and too many were reporting for duty with poor clothing and equipment, sometimes even without a horse. The government made a sincere attempt to stop incursions into common land. But the opposition was still strong. Cossack officials 'covered up for others . . . turned a blind eye at . . . the abuses perpetrated by people like themselves'.[7] Cossacks who complained of common land enclosures, of being fined for grazing their cattle on it, or of it being let out for private profit often found their complaints passing through the hands of men who were guilty of similar offences and by 1824 about 13,000 unresolved cases of land-grabbing had piled up on the desks of Host officials.

The administration of the Host was overhauled. The Chancery was abolished and the Ataman appointed from St. Petersburg given full powers of a provincial governor under the Ministry for War. The land problem was also dealt with. From 1835 land-owners were limited to forty acres per serf, though in practice many still got more, and limits were placed on the sale of land, though this rule was later to be waived. Even though considerable differentials were soon introduced, officers being given over 500, colonels over 2,000 and generals about 4,000 acres, the government laid it down that every Cossack must be allotted eighty acres for his family's support.

The reforms were not entirely successful. In 1850 the Don authorities applied to St. Petersburg for permission to make loans to 1,800 destitute Cossack families, whose local communities had refused to stand security for them, thinking they would never be able to repay. But by and large the rot had been stopped. Poverty was much less marked among the 250,000 Cossacks, than among the peasants who formed a high proportion of the 175,000 'foreigners' living on the Don. In 1818 they rebelled and it took two years to put them down.

The Cossacks themselves had left rebellion behind. On the whole they were better off than they had ever been. True, in return for his plot of land, a Cossack had to serve twenty years with the colours, much of it abroad, and then a further five years in the militia. But this in itself encouraged stability. With the young men away, the Cossack household, as the Cossack village, was ruled by the over-forties, by men who had themselves undergone a twenty-year indoctrination course in the glory of Russian arms and the privilege of serving the benevolent Tsar.

The new myths and traditions were deliberately fostered by the granting of 'royal favours'—charters which bestowed no material benefits but which were redolent of propaganda, permission to name regiments after selected Cossack heroes like Yermak. And in the spring of 1818 Alexander I had come in person to the Don intent on raising enthusiasm to a new pitch. He presented a banner commemorating the victories over Napoleon, and made a speech. 'We hope', he said, 'that this recognition . . . by Us of the Faithful and Beloved Don Host will direct them . . . in holy obligation, to strive with fresh zeal towards fresh achievement at the first call of the Fatherland.'[8] The assembled Cossacks were flattered by references to their glorious forefathers, impressed by the florid verbiage, hypnotised by the pomp which gave a god-like image to the autocrat.

In 1827 Nicholas I granted the Cossacks another great favour.

He made his nine-year-old son Ataman of the Don, Ural and Terek Hosts. Ten years later in another Tsarist spectacular, he introduced him to the Don Cossacks. Twenty-two Cossack regiments were drawn upon parade and the royal party was greeted by loud hurrahs and pelted with flowers. Gifts were gravely presented—another set of charters, standards and imperial regalia. The Cossacks were exhorted to emulate their 'glorious ancestors and earn the gratitude of their fatherland',[9] and in response to the Tsar's signal act of generosity and condescension in appointing the heir to the throne as their leader, the bells of Novocherkassk pealed out, the guns roared, the crowd broke out in renewed hurrahs, and the senior officers of the Host crept in fawning submission round their 'August Ataman'.

The same year when the youthful Ataman made his debut in Uralsk a group of ancient Cossacks rushed forward, grasped the wheels of his carriage and dragged it to a halt. When a pale Alexander emerged from it, they prostrated themselves before him and humbly begged for their old freedoms to be restored. They were seized and imprisoned. The Don, too, still harboured a few men who cherished the old faith in democracy—men like Colonel Ivan Turchaninov who emigrated in 1858 and reached the rank of General in the Federal Army in the American Civil War.[10] But for the overwhelming majority a religion of unquestioning loyalty replaced the memory of their free and stormy past. The Cossacks were being held fast in the smothering embrace of the paternal Tsar.

The psychological enslavement of the Cossacks, favoured by the patriarchal family structure, inculcated by military service and fostered by propaganda ceremonies, was now strengthened by an educational system. A school had been opened in Cherkassk in 1790, then a secondary school, and in 1827 a college of higher education.[11] But for the most part educational opportunities were confined to the one-room village elementary schools, where besides reading, writing, arithmetic and the catechism, Cossack boys learned about their duty to the Tsar and the Church, and imbibed the elements of an anthropomorphic form of history. According to the history books Cossacks had always considered themselves subjects of the Tsar, who had granted them all the freedoms they enjoyed. Loyalists like Platov were idolised, rebels like Pugachev blackened or, when possible, ignored. The reading was dull—full of formal addresses by monarchs and generals, lists of banners presented and church plate donated, and the whole overlaid with a thick coating of religious sentiment.

The community's narrow values and the prevalent desire to please superiors were not conducive to the formulation of independent thought. Nor was the constant barrage of propaganda aimed at them. Cossack folklore, recognised by the critic Belinski as the richest in all Russia, had more influence on poets and intellectuals in Russia proper than on its direct heirs of the Don. Collections were made of Cossack ballads—tales passed on by mouth across the generations—lest they be forgotten and lost altogether. It was the new revolutionaries of the north who took up the torch of freedom from failing Cossack hands. Many of the officers who conspired to launch the 'Decembrist' revolution of 1825 admired the way Cossack elders had governed in accordance with the general will. But when the revolt broke out in December 1825 the Cossack Guards Regiments in St. Petersburg staunchly refused to join it.

Cossack minds hardly stirred at all. When they did, the impetus came from outside. A few young men, nominated to places in Russian universities, returned with a smattering of new ideas, but they were chiefly technocrats. The first literary society in Novocherkassk was founded, not by a Cossack, but by a regular officer. The old pattern of trade by which the Cossack imported food and exported revolution was reversed. The Don exported food now—and imported its ideas.

It also imported fashions. Bookshelves might be rare in the homes of leading Cossacks in Novocherkassk, but many a game of whist was played in them and many a quadrille danced. And the society of the town went to the theatre—or rather 'the *featre*' as the poet Lermontov called it, having attended a performance at which the orchestra's deaf conductor-violinist had his coattails tugged whenever it was time to start or finish and was eventually sent flying headfirst into the drum by a bass player.[12] The sophisticates of the Don were more successful at the arts of the table at which dishes were served smothered in sauces and washed down with Veuve Cliquot.

Some old warriors sighed for the days before civilisation, champagne and education. The historian Bronevski snorted that Cossack gentlemen might soon be expected to appear in frock-coats and with eyeglasses, which Count Platov would never have stood for in his time, and in 1843 a German visitor was assured that though the old virtues survived only in the far south of the Don and in the Manych steppes, for the rest 'everything has changed'. Bankruptcy, fraud and adultery were of the order of the day. Fifty years before, an illiterate child of the steppes, with a bloody sabre and a hungry eye for silver, would have been treated with respect by Ataman Platov himself. But now formality and rank counted for everything. The new men were graduates of the cadet school and commissioned in the Guards.[13]

Even the old cameraderie between Cossacks of different communities was on the wane. A Don Cossack could now describe the Cossacks of the Kuban 'as a lawless set of banditti'.[14] But though more backward than the Don, the Kuban was subject to the same changes. As early as 1799 the elders of the community dressed in cravats and shirts with huge collars and cuffs, and allowed their hair to grow in cultivated ringlets—a style old Zaporozhians would have spat at. And the same economic forces were at work in the Kuban as well. While some Cossacks lacked the capital to start a farm on the open steppe or were burdened by loan repayments, others went on to make fortunes. Enterprise, hard work, profitable marriage and thrift were not the only ingredients of success. Bribes were paid, rank pulled and suspicion cast on competitors as politically unreliable. Brute force was also used, and attempts by private farmers to enclose common lands could lead to bloody conflicts.[15]

In 1826, for instance, Esaul Ivan Savitski bought a farm and proceeded to dig a ditch round an extensive strip of neighbouring pasture which local Cossacks claimed was commonland. When they continued to graze their livestock on it, Savitski coolly rounded up the intruding animals, branded them and added them to his own stock. Cossacks who tried to retrieve their property were beaten off with whips, and when they called a village meeting to discuss the situation, Savitski rode into town himself, threatened to 'shoot anyone' who dared take action against him, and, having no weapon on him at the moment, made for them with his fists. The Cossacks did complain to the authorities but Savitski was, after all, an elder of the Host, and they got no redress. So they retaliated in kind, carried off the hay in the meadow and drove their cattle through his property to trample down his crops.[16] But on the Kuban possession was ninety-nine parts of the law.

The few rules of the game were bent by means both subtle and violent. Where a bribe failed, the mutilation of a rival's cattle or the terrorising of a village ataman would often succeed, and even shootings were not an uncommon way of settling a dispute. A richer farmer might help out a poorer comrade after a poor harvest, but by and large this was an open society which hardened any man who hoped to make his way in it.

A certain Lieutenant-Colonel Bursak was one who emerged successfully from this free-for-all. He acquired several extensive farms, on which he grazed 3,000 sheep, and 2,000 excellent horses, and owned over 200 serfs, whom he treated abominably, besides employing a considerable number of seasonal labourers. Bursak had the scruples of a man determined to get on in life, enough piety to consider his soul saved, and over 200,000 rubles banked at St. Petersburg.

Rank and connections had helped him to amass his fortune, but wealth counted even more than rank and it was Bursak's misfortune to run up against an even richer villain than himself. The man was an ordinary private Cossack at that. A dispute developed between them, as a result of which the man drove his cattle all over the colonel's crops. Bursak laid an official complaint, but the private had more influence. The complaint lay untouched on functionary's desks for over ten years. By then the Colonel was dead.[17]

As some climbed up this dubious ladder of success, others fell. There were even some officers who proved unable to support their position in the end. Many a Cossack was reduced to selling his labour, and some became destitute, and had to send their wives and children to labour for keep and clothing in the cloth mills of the Host, the Kuban equivalent of the English workhouse.[18]

The bachelor traditions of Zaporozhiye were virtually dead,

though the institutional barracks, the *kurens*, still existed for the unmarried men. And although lands were allotted to them, many inmates still joined runaways and family Cossacks, who, anxious to supplement a meagre income, travelled from place to place to earn their keep. Since labour was at a premium now, a man could earn a silver ruble a day gathering in the harvest or rounding up cattle from their summer pastures. Generally their work was seasonal, though a few settled down on the farms of richer Cossacks. Others, particularly the runaways, worked in the coastal fisheries, which, after struggles marked by the same viciousness as the grabs for land, were largely controlled by the elders and the rich. Here, by tradition, the workers divided half the gross produce between them, but usually this amounted only to twenty paper or seven silver rubles a season and sometimes even less.[19]

Another source of income, service as a substitute, was abolished in 1820 when every Cossack was obliged to serve in person. At first some men contrived to circumvent the rule by paying extra sums into the messing group to induce their comrades to make up their time while they went on permanent leave. But in 1823 the authorities put a stop to this dodge as well.

Cossacks on service who owned homes and farms were allowed home on furlough, provided that no more than ten per cent were absent at one time. The others were released only at harvest time and for the express purpose of earning money 'to improve their uniform and arms'. And they were watched by 'reliable' comrades to make sure they did not squander their pence. Such measures were necessary. General Paskevich, the Russian commander in the Caucasus, saw 'Cossacks without horses, without proper arms . . . almost without clothes and without bread. In a word poverty of the highest degree', and in 1836 the clothes of the poorer servicemen manning the cordon line was found to be 'scant, slovenly', giving little protection 'against the cold and the hardship constantly undergone on service'.[20]

The Kuban was a risky Eden for anyone with a farm near the border. The trees and the thick belts of reeds along the river provided good cover for bands of Circassian marauders, who despite the sixty observation posts and 100 pickets guarding the north bank, regularly got through to plunder farms and villages.[21]

The border conflict was marked by an intractability and an atmosphere of animosity not dissimilar to that obtaining between Israel and her Arab neighbours. In the words of an old Circassian warrior, the north bank of the Kuban had once been inhabited by the Nogais, 'a people whose customs and religion were in union with our own—with whom we could trade, associate and war, it might be, all on a neighbourly footing'. But in 1792 the Russians had driven them from 'their rightful homes', and established Cossack settlers in their place—'gaiours like themselves and whose way of life is to us an abomination'. The tribesmen mounted something like a *fedayeen* war against the Cossacks who protested that they had always wanted to farm in peace. But the Circassians disputed this. 'When they say . . . (liars as they are), that we will not remain at peace with them it must be with a view to justifying their own barbarity.'[22]

The pressure of the tribesmen was so severe that although only a third of all Cossacks of military age were supposed to be on duty at any one time, double that number were often needed, and sometimes all of them. In their absence, the countryside was left to women and children, and fields remained untilled. Under the single-crop method prevalent until about 1850, half the land lay fallow in any case and harvests from the rest were poor. The thirty acres allotted to each serviceman—less than half than on the Don—was apportioned in scattered strips which reduced the effective utilisation of pasturage and encouraged the spread of thorns and bushes. A Cossack was not allowed to sell his plot, and if he could not afford to till it, the land simply ran to seed. In the late twenties, General Paskevich saw the Kuban area 'waste away from day to day; the population decreasing in alarming proportions'.[23]

The Kuban Cossacks, so the government decided, had to be reinforced, and during the first half of the nineteenth century, it drafted in about 100,000 people of both sexes, most of them Ukrainians. Families set out full of hope with a cart and a horse or two, a bag of millet, some fodder, and three or four rubles in cash. But, cheated by officials in the towns through which they passed and forced to sell off their last pitiful possessions, many were reduced to 'the most terrible poverty' by the time they arrived.[24] Charitable regular officers raised subscriptions for them, but they were losers from the start.

The man would be granted his thirty acres. But often he had to borrow in order to buy the simple implements and the seed he needed, and depend on the generosity of neighbours for the loan of a plough and ox-team. After the spring ploughing, he would probably be called away to serve, which earned him a few rubles, but left his wife to harvest the crops, or obliged him to call a neighbour in to reap it for a percentage fee. The immigration, so far from increasing prosperity, tended to reduce it.

By the early forties, some 20,000 Cossack homesteads held an average of only twenty-seven acres of arable land apiece. True a further five and a half million acres provided grazing for more than 40,000 horses, nearly 100,000 head of cattle and over a quarter of a million sheep, but the bulk of these belonged to the private sector. By 1851 the number of households had increased to nearly 27,000. This made the thirty-acre standard impossible to fulfil, yet the property of richer private farmers, who were specialising more and more in stock-raising, increased by over fifty per cent.[25]

Unable to control the inroads the private cattle farmers were making into land intended for the arable plot-holders of the rank and file, in 1862 the authorities extended the area of the Host to include lands south of the Kuban river which had recently been secured from the tribesmen. A land fund was created. Families which were prepared to settle there, and so help to relieve the pressure on the old acreage, were granted fifty-five to eighty acres, officers 540. As an extra inducement, private Cossacks were offered an additional thirteen to twenty-six acres, officers seventy to 135, in hereditary ownership. Land suddenly became so plentiful that in 1869 the Cossacks were allowed to sell their allotments—preferably to Cossacks, but to others as necessary—and, as a consequence, the number of non-Cossack farmers in the Kuban began to grow.

The end of the fifty-year Caucasian war relaxed the pressures which had checked the economic development of the Kuban, though the problem of the poor was never completely solved. But, whatever the hardships involved, the war had consolidated the old frontier virtues, which were declining on the Don, and it had sharpened the techniques of the Kuban Cossacks to a very fine edge. Their horsemen learned the gravity-defying tricks the Caucasians called *djigitovka*, and the infantry (*plastuny*) became splendid trackers, practised in moving silently through marsh and undergrowth, hiding from Circassian warriors, or stalking them down.

These skills were particularly in evidence, too, on the eastern flank of the Caucasian line, among the Cossacks of the Terek. Dressed in their colourful baggy clothes and armed with silver-ornamented weapons captured from the Circassian braves, these Cossacks seemed the most romantic of all, and their handsome self-reliant women, whose dark features betrayed their tribal as well as Russian ancestry, captivated many a visiting Russian officer. Everything about them seemed picturesque—their villages hedged in by walls of earth and brambles, their thatched and gabled cottages standing high on stilts, the vines, pumpkins and water-melons which grew in their gardens, the cows and buffalo browsing in the meadows, and the verdant forests nearby where partridges, stags and wild boar could be hunted. And the grandeur of the snow-capped peaks of the Caucasus which rose up sheerly in the distance provided just the right romantic backdrop to their scene.

The Terek Cossacks kept a constant watch across the turbulent river. Bare-chested, shaven-headed Circassian braves—men who only a day or two before, perhaps, had come to the village to sell a horse or to trade in some honey and some nuts or a few furs or vegetables—might always be lurking in the reed-covered creeks beyond the grey sandbanks, waiting to pounce. A Terek Cossack knew danger from his earliest childhood and was often a soldier by the time he was twelve. But it was precisely the uncertain quality of life that imbued him with the qualities which visiting novelists and poets so much admired.

Dumas the elder, who took a rather superficial view of them in the fifties, saw them as 'agile, gay and war-loving, always laughing, singing or fighting',[26] and the youthful Tolstoi who lived two years among them tended to see them through a rose-coloured filter. The characters he describes in his novel *The Cossacks*—the proud, bare-footed Cossack girls, whom he tried to ravish, and Yeroshka, the veteran, who stinks of vodka, sweat, gunpowder and blood—were drawn from life. Indeed, Yeroshka has been identified as Yepishka Sekhin—horsethief, hunter, Circassian fighter and gargantuan drinker. Tolstoy's Cossacks show contempt for the tobacco-smoking 'heathen Russians' sent among them and are too proud to salute their own officers, though ready enough to haggle over a captured rifle.

But on the Terek, too, the gap between officers and Cossacks were growing, and not all the villages were as comfortable as those Tolstoi describes. The land allotments were generous enough. But though a private was entitled to 135 acres, a staff officer was granted over 1,000. Cattle plagues and hard winters could impoverish whole villages, as happened in 1839, and many farming cooperatives, though well supplied with land, lacked the capital equipment with which to exploit it. It became quite usual for rich Cossacks to lease communal plots or simply take them over—the resultant inequality in land holdings was, in effect, confirmed by regulation in 1869—and many a Cossack was too poor to buy a horse. Military service and border raids disrupted the economy and though exempt from general taxation, the maintenance of local services put heavy demands on a Cossack's purse and time. Post-stations had to be manned, veterinary surgeons and chemists paid, roads and bridges repaired, and funds made available for education, the upkeep of local government, and the church. And besides all this bed and board had to be provided for passing army units.[27]

While the Cossacks held the lines of the Terek in the east and the Kuban in the west, more Cossacks had been drafted in to secure the central Caucasus from the mountaineers who threatened communities with Georgia. In the thirties and forties, as a military highway was laid across the Daryal pass to the city of Tiflis, new cordon lines were formed, held by Ukrainian regiments specially drafted in, and new settlements constructed, from which punitive expeditions were mounted against the refractory local tribesmen.

The Don Cossacks made a considerable contribution to the war, and fighting side by side with the Cossacks of the line they, too, picked up Caucasian ways—wore flowing cloaks, sewed dummy cartridge pockets slant-wise on their chests, learned the wild trick riding and how to emit spine-chilling Circassian war cries. But the station was unpopular. Three-year tours of duty often dragged on long beyond their proper time, and though lives could be lost, there was little booty to pick up. As for the officers, they were bored, and whenever they could, joined regular officers in Yekaterinodar where they consoled themselves 'through drink, love affairs and games of chance'.[28]

At last in 1859, Shamil, the great leader of resistance in the eastern Caucasus was subdued. Before long, both eastern and western flanks were quiet. The Don Cossacks went home and the military settlers were consolidated into the Terek and the Kuban Cossack Hosts. The area between the Black Sea and the Caspian was now secure, but Cossacks were still needed to guard other borders of the Empire. By the end of the century Cossack communities formed an almost continuous chain stretching nearly 5,000 miles—from the Don, over the towering mountains of the Caucasus, along the desert fringes of Central Asia, through Siberian marsh and highland, to Lake Baikal, and thence along the Amur river to the coast of the Pacific.

Cossacks were the cheapest means of holding new territory. They were virtually self-supporting; they could develop agriculture and maintain defences at the same time. With the Russian Empire expanding as never before, the government continued to tempt, draft, or exile men from established communities to virgin or vulnerable areas and, when they were too few, to give Cossack status to people of other classes. Peasants, retired soldiers, baptised Tatars and Bashkirs, even military convicts were drafted out to join the Cossacks, and completely new Cossack hosts were founded by government decree. Men from the Don formed the basis of the Astrakhan community, Ural Cossacks sired the Orenburg Host; and the old town service Cossacks of Siberia provided the core of the Siberian Cossack Host.

But side by side with the creation of new communities, old ones were abolished. The Azov area being safe, the Azov Host was disbanded. The remaining descendants of the Siberian service Cossacks, many of whom, vegetating in outlying areas, still demanded private tribute, and even women, from the natives, were deemed to have outlived their usefulness, and though a few were retained as policemen, guides or interpreters the rest had their pay discontinued and were gradually merged with the peasant population.

But more Cossacks were created than were disbanded. With the occupation of Central Asia, Cossacks of the Siberian Host were drafted in to form the core of a new community, the Seven Rivers Cossack Host, established in 1867 to keep order in the area. Siberian Cossack families were also grafted off to create the Transbaikal Host, formed in 1851 on the Chinese frontier, to which 29,000 peasants and a number of Tungus and Buriat tribesmen were soon added. And the Transbaikal Cossacks, in their turn, were used to found a new community still farther east, along the Amur.

The man who supervised the development was General Muravev, a Russian proconsul fired by the same spirit that drove on his British, French and German contemporaries in their nineteenth-century quest for empire. In the 1850s Muravev set out to colonise eastern Siberia and to establish an effective Russian military presence along the Chinese frontier. The culmination of his achievement was to be the creation of the power base of Vladivostock on the Pacific. The Cossacks played an important role in his scheme, and with their help he succeeded in colonising the lower stretches of the river Amur. But the success was bought at a dreadfully high cost in human suffering.

The supply lines of Muravev's force along the Amur broke down. Fresh food perished in the hot Siberian summers and some men were caught in the extreme winters without any food at all. An officer called Bogdanov, who was sent down the Amur in the autumn of 1856 to bring relief to returning troops and Cossacks, found the blackened corpses of starving men who had gorged themselves to death on an abandoned barge of flour. Others he came across were 'half dead', clad only in greatcoats and caps, having eaten the leather of their packs and boots. And, further along the shining river, Bogdanov encountered the grisly sight of corpses with their hind parts cut off. Men had been reduced to casting lots to decide who should provide a meal for the others. And yet their commander, the ambitious Muravev, was not the least deterred.

That same autumn he called on the Transbaikal Cossacks to

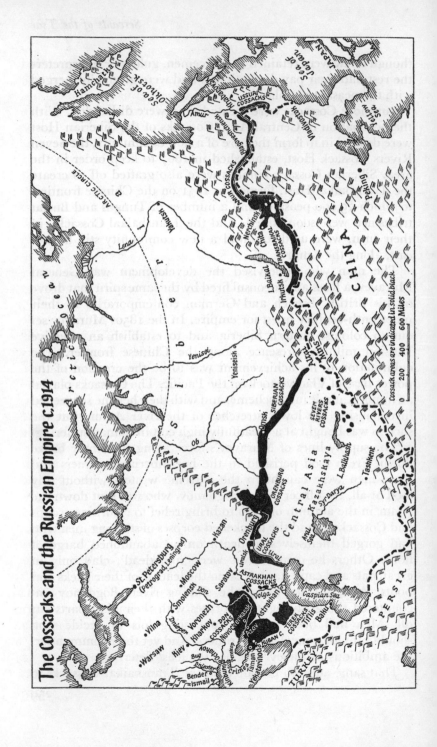

The Cossacks and the Russian Empire c.1914

Cossack areas are indicated in solid black

0 200 400 600 Miles

provide volunteers to settle along the Amur. He promised exemption from service, full maintenance for each man and half maintenance for his family, an allowance of fifteen rubles, and the timber of the raft which would take him there. But just in case sufficient volunteers were not forthcoming, lots were to be cast for the privilege, though a rich Cossack so chosen might send a substitute if he provided him with a horse, a cow and 'everything necessary for farming'.

So, in the spring of 1857, a fleet of river craft carried the migrants eastwards into the Amur, past the bones of the men who had perished the previous winter. Muravev went with them, pointing out the sites for Cossack villages, and giving them names. Many of the sites he chose were prone to flooding and regardless of the Cossacks' difficulty in building up homes and farms from scratch, he ordered them to build churches as well.[29]

Nevertheless, by dint of the sheer size of the migration, the new Amur Cossack community was soon thriving. Before long 12,000 Transbaikal Cossacks were settled there and in the early sixties they were reinforced by a number of peasants and soldiers. And Muravev's determination brought immediate results so far as his imperial ambitions were concerned. Peking was persuaded to give ground. In May 1858 the Chinese government recognised the Amur as her frontier with Russia and in 1860 agreed to extend the line east along the Ussuri to the Pacific. The new frontier needed guarding and, predictably, it was Cossacks who were designated to fulfil the task, 6,500 men and women of the Amur Host being hived off to settle along the Ussuri.

Important though the Cossacks were to frontier settlement their contribution to the army was still greater—far greater proportionately than any other section of the Russian population. In 1826, there were 70,000 Cossacks on active service—a tenth of their entire population. And their numbers were growing fast both by natural increase and by adoption. In 1838 there were fewer than a million Cossacks of both sexes, by 1859 over a million and a half, and by the eighties almost a million more.[30]

Each community provided men in rough proportion to its numbers, from scores of regiments on the Don to the Kamchatka

Cossacks' two platoons. By the nineties there were about 300,000 Cossacks fit to bear arms, including horse artillery and infantry, which was furnished by the Kuban and Transbaikal. But the cavalry was by far the most important. In 1881 Cossacks accounted for almost forty-five per cent of the Army's total cavalry complement of 92,000 men, and a German expert reckoned that they would furnish seventy per cent of the cavalry Russia could field in a European war.[31]

Terms of service varied, but in 1835 one in four of the entire population of the Don and Ural Hosts was reckoned ready to serve. A Cossack joined up at seventeen and served for thirty years, twenty-five if an officer. The first two years he spent in training and on local public works. Then his service proper began—three years on duty and three on furlough, more in wartime, till he reached the age of forty-two; then five years as a reservist. But by the end of the Caucasian war, during which Cossacks had often been kept on duty beyond the normal three-year stints, the detrimental effect on Cossack livelihoods of this crippling weight of service was recognised at last. Following the introduction of conscription into Russia, the Cossacks were given a fairer deal.

In 1875, a Don Cossack's service liability was reduced to twenty years, and similar arrangements were made for the Orenburg, Siberian and the Terek Hosts. A Cossack was now enrolled at eighteen, spent three years in training, twelve in the line, only four of them actually away from home, and then a period on the reserve. Each regiment of about 1,000 men was numbered in a sequence corresponding to its availability for duty. On the Don numbers one to seventeen were on active service, and numbers eighteen to fifty-two on leave, at second or third call.[32] However, new compulsory annual exercises and the time spent marching to and from their service stations cut quite significantly into the furlough periods.

Clergymen were exempt from service altogether, teachers, doctors, veterinary surgeons and some other categories were excused in peacetime, graduates had a reduced commitment, and the Don traders could still buy themselves out. And since the birth rate varied, there were years when the numbers of lads reaching call-up age exceeded requirements, allowing others to buy out too. On the other hand, in 1874 only less than half the usual number of 10,000 Don Cossacks were called to the colours because of the low birth-rate during the Crimean war of 1854–6, and when men were short in the field category, others were sometimes called up out of turn, usually chosen by lot and given some pecuniary compensation. Exemptions were highest in the Siberian Host where as many as one in five was listed unfit or excused by payment, and lowest in the Ural, where service obligations were actually increased, which resulted in riots, and the transportation of nearly three thousand men to Turkestan.[33]

Despite the granting of commissions to Cossacks, by no means all the officers in Cossack units were Cossacks themselves. In fact early in the century there had been widespread opposition to Cossacks being granted commissions at all, and a good deal of prejudice against those who were. One Russian general opined that a Cossack was unfitted for rank on account of his 'extreme ignorance' and because, once so honoured, 'he abandons himself to all the vices of a parvenu'. He thought Cossacks should be commanded by Russian officers since they had 'more intelligence' than Cossacks.[34] Regular officers were often drafted in, and, on the Terek, Cossacks could only reach the rank of subaltern. But as educational facilities improved, Cossacks were able to provide enough qualified officers themselves, most being chosen from NCOs who could pass an elementary written examination, though heredity was a major factor in selection. By 1880 there was a Junker school on the Don. The Don, Kuban, Orenburg and Siberian Hosts each had a cadet corps, and there were officer-training facilities for Cossacks of other Hosts.

As for the ordinary Cossack, he still had to provide his own horse, saddlery, uniform and arms for service, though Cossack Guardsmen were issued by the state with everything except a horse. By the seventies it cost a man about 200 rubles to fit himself out, and predictably, many Cossacks, not all of them poor, tried to do it on the cheap. Nicholas I had been shocked to find so many Don Cossacks shoddily turned out, when he reviewed them in 1837, and the officers were not the least culprits, though in 1841 he refused their request for a pay increase which might allow them to turn themselves out in the style he desired.

Much more serious than poor turn-out were the short-comings in arms and horses. Many Cossacks opted for re-conditioned muskets which cost a fraction of new ones, and an inspection of Cossack units in 1855 revealed that most of them carried inefficient and sometimes totally useless fire-arms which had been assembled from diverse parts of various, often anti-quated, makes. Cossacks called to serve in Poland in 1863 arrived with 'old worn-out uniforms, rusty guns and sabres, cords in place of straps in the saddlery' and on small, weak horses.[35] And almost a third of the 32,000 Don Cossacks re-called for the Turkish war of 1877–8 had to be granted subsidies averaging fifty rubles each to bring them up to the minimum standard.

Attempts were made to rectify these shortcomings. Since many Cossacks were still using ancient flintlocks the standard M73 rifle was made general issue, but these had to be returned to armouries before the Cossacks left for home, and so their marks-manship tended to deteriorate. The problem of mounts proved more intractable since, except in the Ural, the quality of breeding had declined, and was only revived towards the end of the century. Anyway few Cossacks wanted to invest in good horses which might be killed in action. So the authorities offered to pay remount money for animals lost on active service. But Cossacks saw this concession merely as a way of making good the deficiencies of pay, for though the officers got regular rates, the men earned only three and a half to six and a half rubles. As a result many Cossacks returning from duty sold their horses to men coming to relieve them, and then claimed the compensation.

Inadequate pay and the heavy obligations to equip them-selves expensively helps to explain the Cossacks' bad behaviour while on service. During the Napoleonic wars it was sometimes 'impossible to bring half the men under fire', not because of cowardice, but because they were out looting.[36] At Balaklava, having prudently fled headlong before the charge of the Light Brigade, allowing the Russian artillery to cut the Englishmen to pieces, the Cossacks promptly wheeled round and set about catching riderless horses which they then sold.[37] Even in Russia, in time of peace, they were hardly more restrained. Cossacks quartered on military colonists in 1831–2 forced the inhabitants to slaughter their livestock, and demanded excessive quantities of butter. They also acquired a habit of sticking the nearest pig for dinner whenever they felt hungry while out on patrol, and in 1854 Cossacks of another unit plundered villages and the mansions of the local gentry in the neighbourhood of their camp.

Officially forbidden to touch civilian property at home or abroad, they were always asking their officers with a beguiling, wide-eyed innocence: 'May we look for things here, your honour?' In Hungary in 1849, they stole anything they could lay their hands on, often selling it for next to nothing, and in 1823, the Tsar had been so amazed when a Cossack patrol brought back four Turkish civilians with their money intact, that he gave them a fat reward.[38]

The Cossacks' reputation for thievery made them prime suspects and regular officers were none too scrupulous about pinning offences on them. An army regulation of 1830 had banned knouting and branding with the specific exception of the Cossacks, and, in general, they were often grossly discriminated against by military authority. They found it difficult at times even to preserve their personal dignity. The once fiery Cossack warriors were employed on various menial duties, used as baggage carriers and orderlies. Virtually any clerk could authorise their use as messengers, groom and carters, and they were sent riding hundreds of miles on errands 'without receiving a penny for food', having to depend on the charity of their 'half-starving brethren at the posts'.[39]

Too often, the military authorities regarded the Cossacks 'as a surplus that can be sacrificed to the preservation of the ease and security of the regular troops', and with so many of his men detached to other units or on personal service, a Cossack commander was sometimes left without anyone to command. All this had a severe impact on their military capabilities. Once, when the 41st Don regiment was mobilised the colonel apparently knew so few of his subordinates that he had to pick men for staff duties from their general appearance. Men forgot their drill, officers the words of command, and Cossacks called out to serve in 1863 were reported to have not the least idea of military discipline. Yet the misuses continued, and in the Turkish war of 1877–8 Cossack units were again split up to such an extent that in some regiments 'only the commandant and the officers remain with the colours'.[40]

But for all the mismanagement of them, Cossacks had lost none of their individualistic skills as scouts, pickets and patrolmen. In the judgement of one officer no one was 'shrewder, quicker, and in some cases, bolder and more rash than they'. Yet a Cossack had no wish to be killed or taken prisoner and so risk his family being reduced to poverty or the work-house. 'To die, standing uselessly in one's place is not valour according to their views. . . . To evade the enemy, by any means whatever, they regard as a good deed and not a disgrace.'[41]

If their stock as cavalrymen had fallen this was largely because of unimaginative leadership, and their fall from grace, never complete, was only temporary. Some units still distinguished themselves, notably at the battle of Plevna, and Governor Perovski of Orenburg who led an expedition against Khiva in 1840 had nothing but praise for them. 'Cold and snowstorms are nothing to them. . . . They have very few sick and almost no dead. . . . They work harder . . . and more willingly than anyone else. Without them it would have gone badly for the whole detachment.'[42] The military reforms of the seventies improved their capabilities as cavalrymen, though apart from a single independent Don Cossack division, Cossack regiments were thrown in with dragoons, hussars and lancers to form regular cavalry divisions. Horses learned to respond to bugle calls and whole regiments to execute drills and evolutions as one man. There were serious misgivings not only among the Cossack authorities hitherto responsible for administering the units, but among some regular officers, too, who feared that these formal drills might destroy the Cossacks' inimitable fighting qualities. But the fears were to prove groundless, and by the end of the century Cossack morale, their tremendous pride in arms, had reached a new high point.

By then Cossacks were required to mount and dismount bareback and at full trot, and encouraged to learn such tricks as shooting to the rear while jumping a fence or while clinging to the underside of a galloping horse. Don Cossacks could be as adept as the *djigitovka* experts of the Terek or Kuban, and an American was astonished at the performances mounted at a Don Guards battery field day competition early in the First World War. It began 'with such simple things as standing up-on the saddle at full gallop . . . two men picking up a third dis-mounted comrade, and a dismounted man leaping behind a galloping companion'. There followed 'such gymnastics as I have never seen in any circus, the men swinging from the pommel of their saddles while the horses were in full gallop . . . leaping from one side of their horses to the other side, and turning somersaults'. Then, as if this were too tame, a six-foot, 180 pound sergeant 'performed all these things with a sabre clenched in his teeth'. Only the last trick—picking up a handkerchief from the ground at full gallop—'was very badly done until the colonel of the battery . . . put five rubles in each handkerchief'.There were no more failures after that.[43]

Despite their roles as frontiersmen and soldiers, the reformist government of Alexander II had questioned the value of con-tinuing to preserve the Cossacks as a separate caste. If serfdom was anomalous, perhaps Cossackdom was too. The Cossack districts looked untidy from the point of view of centralist administration and were virtually exempt from state taxation. The Don Host in particular had no frontier or colonising function to fulfil and so, in the sixties, its abolition was seriously con-sidered. The War Minister made his calculations: abolition would bring in nearly nine million rubles more in taxes every year. But to replace the 310 Cossack cavalry squadrons presently available would cost an additional ten million rubles a year. The idea of abolition was quickly dropped.[44] For all their 'privileges' the Don Cossacks showed a profit to the state.

The efforts continued to seal off the old Cossack communities from the populations surrounding them. From the thirties, no one not belonging to the Don Host could be inscribed as a Cossack. The caste was to be purely hereditary,[45] and an attempt was made to limit the influx not only of runaways and labourers from central Russia but of any more 'foreign blood' into the Don province. In 1838 Don Cossacks were forbidden to import 'any outsider of either sex and of whatever status' when returning

267

from duty,[46] though even after 1850 Cossacks would return from campaign with Turkish or Bulgarian girls, and in the Caucasus, intermarriage with tribeswomen had always been considerable. Cossacks were only allowed to marry non-Cossack girls with the permission of their Ataman. But the chief threat to the preservation of the Cossacks' military spirit and of their economic viability, with which Alexander II was now so concerned, was the alarming growth of non-Cossack communities in the Cossack provinces.

Serfs had first been introduced into the Don in small numbers in the eighteenth century. They had multiplied, and in 1861 they had been emancipated. The expansion of commerce and industry was attracting more outsiders to the fast-developing towns, and the Cossacks were soon in danger of becoming outnumbered in their own land. In 1877 the outsiders (*inogorodnyye*) had formed less than forty per cent of the Don population, but by 1895 they had nosed ahead with 50.39 per cent, and the trend continued. The Terek and Kuban Cossacks were soon outnumbered as well[47] and Yekaterinodar was to become a predominantly non-Cossack town. The increase in the number of outsiders created a land-shortage, particularly on the Don, and triggered off conflict between the Cossacks and the non-Cossacks living in their midst.

When they were emancipated most of the serfs were allotted about ten acres per family, though some got as little as two and about 35,000 males remained landless. Yet though the Cossack minority held on to three-quarters of the total land area on the Don,[48] the population explosion had reduced their standard holding, laid down by the authorities, to a mere thirty-five acres per household. Ordinary Cossack families owned only their houses, gardens or vineyards outright, their stakes in village common lands being reviewed for reallocation according to need every two or, at most, every six years. Much of the general land reserve, which might also have been allocated to make up deficiencies in the common land available for individual households, was leased out by the Host authorities at low rates, chiefly for horse-breaking. And by 1881 this reserve had been virtually eroded away altogether by its apportionment by the government in private ownership to officers and officials.[49] Communal village land could be let, though not sold, and there was at least one *stanitsa* in 1899 which leased out 2,000 of its 2,500 land shares.

As a result, some Cossacks could not receive their full allotments, and many even of those who did found it hard to make ends meet. A survey of ten Don settlements in 1899 showed a fifth of their households to be comparatively prosperous, but one out of three to have little property or none at all. Not a few families lived from hand to mouth, and had to turn to the moneylender each autumn in the knowledge that for every five kopeks they borrowed they must repay as much as a ruble in the spring.[50] The majority of the Don peasants, however, were still worse off, and they were beginning to protest about it, calling for equal rights to land and for an end to Cossack privilege.

The fears, prevalent among the Don Cossacks at the time of emancipation in the early sixties, that the government would convert them into peasants were soon dispelled, but fiscal and political measures were introduced which aroused considerable resentment. The Cossacks seemed little concerned about the removal of some vestiges of autonomy—the debasing of the *krug* (general assembly) to the point of denoting a parade on a public holiday, the appointment in 1848 of a non-Cossack general as Deputy Ataman—in fact a military governor—the fact that Cossacks were now ineligible for top executive office, or that, from 1891, Cossacks under the age of twenty-six could take no part in village politics. What most concerned them were the changes which hit them in the pocket and affected their position in relation to the despised outsiders.

So far, the Cossacks had been virtually free of taxation. The Host commanded a central fund which it disbursed on churches, roads, fire-fighting and other services, improvements in mining and agriculture, the maintenance of a reserve of horses and other military purposes, officials' salaries and pensions, and a little on education and on the poor. Over half the income had derived from leasing the land reserve; the rest was provided by the state, though this took the form of a rebate on those taxes, notably on liquor, from which Cossacks were not exempt. Local taxes were also raised for community services—aid for the wounded, support for destitute families and the like.[51] But this was a tax fixed by Cossacks for Cossacks, and when, in the mid-seventies, the *zemstvo* was introduced there was a tremendous outcry. The *zemstvo* amounted to a new system of local government for the Cossacks. Not only did they impose a fairly high incidence of *per capita* taxation, but Cossack representatives on them were often outvoted by outsider landowning and commercial classes.

The Cossacks were outraged. The chief of their 'privileges', as they well realised, had always been their treatment as a class superior to the peasants. Now, it seemed, they were being placed on a par with them. It was a nasty shock to Cossack pride. Moreover their lands, as they claimed, had been won by their forefathers, and well earned by their services to the state. Many of them were finding it hard enough to make ends meet in any case, and it seemed quite unjust that they should be required to bear this extra burden of taxation.[52]

In several districts, Cossacks refused outright to pay their *zemstvo* dues and, early in the eighties the administrators at last bowed before the storm. The *zemstvos* were abolished on the Don, even though, as the War Minister was to complain in 1891, the local *stanitsa* administrations were 'slack and venal'. But this hardly affected the state's interests. What concerned the War Minister far more was the fact that Cossacks were becoming 'demoralised', losing their 'sense of religion, discipline and respect for their elders'.[53]

The Cossack provinces could not be insulated from the outside world, nor, ultimately, could the Cossacks themselves, hard though the authorities tried. The quality of life around them had been changing faster than ever before. During a very short period around 1860, the first steam-boats had ploughed their way down the Don, the first train had crossed the steppe, the first public library had been opened, and the first secondary school for girls founded in the province; private newspapers began to appear and the first morse telegraph office was opened. There was a sudden boom in industry, based on coal and iron ore found in the western Don basin, and by 1892 some 15,000 workers were employed in nearly 400 factories in the province producing about nineteen million rubles' worth of goods a year.[54]

The growth of industry, the introduction of the strange

innovations of the modern age, began to impinge on the sluggish flow of life in other Cossack provinces as well. Oil was struck in the Kuban and on the Terek, and the beginning of the Trans-Siberian Railway in the nineties promised to bring the isolation even of the Cossacks in the Far East to an end.

But the Cossacks were slow to adjust to such developments. Indeed, most of them failed to adjust at all. Soon after the arrival of the railway on the Don it was decided to move the line outside Novocherkassk because it obstructed access to the river Aksai and the movement of local cattle out to pasture. It was decisions such as this which ensured that the Don capital would be overtaken by the non-Cossack commercial and industrial centre of Rostov-on-Don. Two ways of life now existed side by side on the Don and each tried hard to ignore the other.

The Cossacks, with official encouragement, left town and industry to the outsiders and remained obstinately rural themselves. In the 1880s there were only fourteen Cossack towns in all the Empire with populations of more than 5,000. The Don had only three of them. On the Kuban and Terek, where tribal raids earlier in the century had encouraged settlements of larger size, most people lived in villages of two or three thousand. But of the 1,900 Don settlements three out of four had fewer than 500 inhabitants.[55] Though by 1880 the Don had nearly 600 miles of railway line and sixty-one railway stations, the Cossacks hardly used them. Few of them went beyond the next village except on service, and then usually by river and by road. But there was hardly a bridge across the Don, and the roads were merely tracks. From early November until late spring there was no communication at all, at least not by carriage, and in spring and autumn travellers by road could 'hardly wade through the mud'.[56]

Only the small class of trading Cossacks took much advantage of the changes, and only in arable agriculture did other Cossacks benefit from the boom. The Kuban, the Terek, Orenburg and Transbaikal all had their trading Cossacks now, even the tiny communities of Astrakhan and the Seven Rivers, and by 1870 there were 3,000 Don Cossack merchants, half of them members of the Trading Society exempt from service, and many with business interests in St. Petersburg, Moscow and other cities far beyond the borders of the Don.

The development which affected the ordinary Cossack was the new world demand for grain. In response to increasing prices, wheat production in the Don, and to a lesser extent on the Kuban had shot up. The expansion was achieved partly by improved methods but mainly by taking more pastureland under cultivation. Arable land farmed by the average Cossack family rose from thirteen and a half to thirty-two and a half acres in the course of the 1880s, and by 1905 the total area under seed had increased by a further 350 per cent, much of this in the private sector. There was a corresponding rise in land prices—from five and a half rubles an acre in 1860 to twenty in 1889—and by 1900 the Don took the lead over every other European Russian province as a grain producer with a surplus in 1898 of nine bushels per head of the population.[57]

The cultivation of grapes and the tobacco crop also increased in importance. In 1883 the vineyards east of Novocherkassk covered a mere 6,500 acres; by 1900 23,500, and orders for Don tobacco came in from places as far afield as Amsterdam, Egypt and Japan. But the biggest growth was in wheat, and with almost ninety per cent of the land under cultivation the number of livestock inevitably fell.

This trend was common to all the more westerly Cossack provinces, though not in those to the east, where labour was short and world ports less accessible. The drastic decline in horse-breeding which followed from the switch to wheat would have had a deleterious effect from the military point of view had not the Ural Cossacks compensated with fantastic expansion of their studs, reckoned the best in all Russia, as well as of their herds and flocks. By 1880 there were 140 horses, 362 cattle and 544 sheep per hundred inhabitants in the Ural Host, whereas the Don was down to thirty-one horses per hundred, the Terek to fifteen and the Kuban to seventeen. Fishing also remained important on the Ural, while elsewhere it was in relative decline. In 1877, 24,000 tons were exported from the Ural, including the usual gift of caviare and huge sturgeons for the Tsar, and two years later the industry earned almost two and a half million rubles or fifty-eight rubles per head of the population.[58]

Despite their new prosperity, the Ural Cossacks remained the most traditional of all. While other Cossack communities had long conformed to the official orthodoxy, they were still mostly fervent Old Believers. Religious fashions may have swept the Don early in the century and strange sects flourished among the Cossacks in the Caucasus, but periodic waves of religious fervour were a feature among the Ural Cossacks. In 1898 they raised a subscription to send three devout Old Believers on a pilgrimage to Constantinople and Jerusalem, and as far as India, China and Japan, in search of 'the true orthodox faith'. They searched in vain. But meanwhile Russians had been travelling other roads to find a new heaven upon earth, and many had been looking to the stormy Cossack past for inspiration. Herzen had considered that the Zaporozhians' 'Cossack republic' with its 'democratic and social base', was 'the most suitable form of state for the Slavonic peoples'; Bakunin saw Razin as 'the first and most terrible revolutionary in Russia';[59] Nechayev, mystic proponent of violent rebellion, had looked forward to the anniversaries of Razin and Pugachev, and intellectuals toured the Don in hopes of finding cadres to mount a revolution.

But Razin's bicentenary was ignored. Instead, Cossacks were persuaded to celebrate occasions like the 300th anniversary of the Don Host's first service to the Tsar. Yet despite the un-remitting campaign to persuade them of their ancestors' supposed perpetual loyalty, the occasional shaft of independent thought was threatening to penetrate even their close world. The Cossacks were becoming more literate and literacy was dangerous. It was still far from universal. In the Siberian Host, only three in 10,000 attended school in 1887, and even on the Ural, only thirty. But by 1900 about a third of Don males and about a twelfth of the females were literate and one male in forty received a secondary education though only one in a thousand had been to college. The general emphasis might still be on religion, gymnastics and quasi-military skills, but pupils of at least one grammar school dared to discuss the rights of man, and in 1886 the head of the gendarmerie reported that there was not one secondary school in Novocherkassk 'which might not be a breeding ground for revolutionary ideas'. Within two years an end was put to 'all the unseemliness',[60] by steps which included the cutting back from 166 to forty-five the bursaries available to Don Cossacks to attend

universities in Moscow, St. Petersburg, Kharkov and elsewhere.
No effort was spared to douse the memory of what Cossackdom
had really been. Every village ataman exercising the powers of
a police commissioner, kept careful watch, and the calls to
glory and for blind obedience were shouted ever louder. At all
costs, the government had to insulate the Cossacks from the
rising swell of social discontent and intellectual ferment, and
enmesh them totally in the toils of the reactionary system.

It was not that the government feared a Cossack revolt. But
it had to preserve the morale of men they were employing so
frequently now to suppress revolutionaries throughout the
Empire. Some attempts were made by means of counter-
propaganda to wean them away from their loyalties. Polish
émigrés in Paris in 1848 had incited 'the warriors of the Don and
Ural' to fight with them 'as a free people', and throughout the
eighties revolutionaries tried to smuggle pamphlets through to
the Don, asking the Cossacks to help the Russian people.[61] They
had no discernible effect.

Along with other troops, Cossacks had crushed repeated Polish
risings, put down peasant and tribal outbreaks all over Russia
and were being used increasingly against student demonstrators
and striking workers. Stationed in St. Petersburg, Warsaw, Vilna
these ignorant men, inculcated with legion prejudices from
earliest childhood by parents who had themselves been conditioned by official Tsarist myths, were more than ever subjected
to intensive indoctrination, forced into the belief that it was
their 'holy duty' to fight not only Russia's foreign enemies but
'internal enemies' as well—be they students, socialists, trade-
unionists, nationalist minorities, or Jews.

And they were conscientious in fulfilling their duties. In
Poland they fired on a procession bearing crosses, galloped
through Warsaw laying into peaceful crowds with iron-tipped
whips. They beat up and killed defenceless students in St.
Petersburg, trampled down demonstrators from the Universities
of Moscow and Kiev and attacked a meeting of women workers
at Rostov. Cossacks, supposed to back up the police in keeping
public order, provided cover for Black Hundred rioters, and
themselves assaulted Jews in the Ukraine and Lithuania, broke
into their houses, stole their money and on occasion murdered

them. Cossacks so rarely responded with any promptitude to calls to protect the victims of the Black Hundreds, that, when they did so, grateful Jews would present them with illuminated scrolls or gifts in recognition of unexpected favour.

They did not merely obey orders; they 'carried their obedience to . . . inhuman lengths'.[62] Cossacks came to serve as the very symbol of Tsarist repression. In the words of a socialist pamphleteer of 1902 the term 'Cossack' had come to be used throughout Europe 'as a scarecrow, to represent all that is most terrible and monstrous'. The people who had once 'valued freedom above all else in the world', had been turned into 'blunt and brutalised' scourges, into centaurs, wielding whips upon women, children and old men.[63]

Yet, however fierce he was on station, on his home ground, by his beloved Don or Kuban, the Cossack was a gentle sentimental creature, and even on campaign he could demonstrate remarkable softness of heart. Maurice Baring saw the Cossacks fighting in the Russo-Japanese War, where, under the atrociously incompetent direction of Russian officers, they showed great heroism and suffered many casualties. To Baring they appeared 'a delightful race of people, good-natured, long-suffering'. He saw them 'bullied by the Chinese, and yet . . . bear the exasperating treatment with the utmost forebearance'. He saw Cossacks at the front go out to look for Japanese wounded, bring them back to their fire and ply them with tea and cigarettes before going off to fetch a doctor. These Transbaikal Cossacks might be a different breed from those of the European Hosts, but Baring could not believe that even their reputation for brutality and cruelty was deserved.[64]

Yet, though there was exaggeration in the charges made against them, the Jekylls of the Don and Kuban could become the Hydes away from home. It was understandable that Cossack farmers, called away to suppress rebellious peasants or military colonists, might well vent their anger on the miscreants rather than on the authorities who ordered them out. Most soldiers can behave badly in alien surroundings. But the Cossacks could outdo the worst. It was their isolation, both at home and on active service which helped most to forge them into bludgeons of oppression. At home they formed inward-looking societies,

275

encouraged to view the outsiders living around them as inferior
and the cause of all their grievances. Stationed outside their
native environment, they lived just as insular a life. Their
barracks were tight little enclaves in an unfamiliar, hostile
world, where these countrymen, used to the open steppe, felt
claustrophobic and ill-at-ease. Ignorance and homesickness
bound them together; their fear of strange places and unfriendly
peoples, strangely combined with a proud feeling of superiority
to them, gave them a sense of separate identity, as a species
different from other men.

But at the rate at which the lava was heating up inside the
Russian volcano, not even the Cossacks could be kept for ever
in cool obedience. The failure completely to solve their recurrent
land problem led to a certain restlessness, especially on the Don.
Once, regular soldiers had to be called in to quell local disturbances which Cossack servicemen had refused to deal with,
and at the threshold of the twentieth century Social Revolutionaries who came canvassing into Cossack country, managed
to re-kindle just the faintest glimmer of political awareness.

As yet Cossacks were still the most faithful and reliable servants
of autocracy. They still formed the spearhead of Russia's
imperial advances into Asia and did as well as any other troops
in the unsuccessful Japanese war of 1904–5. Before they marched
home again a much larger number of their comrades had been
called out to suppress the most serious rising the Empire had
known since the time of Pugachev. Since 1900 the tide of strikes
and riots had engaged them more than ever before and they
played a major part in defeating the great attempted revolution
of 1905. In doing so they virtually saved the Tsar his throne.
But it was to be their last great service to him. By 1906 even the
Cossacks had begun to turn.

Cossack regimental band

Police and Cossacks dispersing a demonstration

'And when it broke, there was the crowd there,
And the cossacks, just as always before,
But one thing, the Cossacks said:
    "Pojalouista".
And that got round in the crowd,
And then a lieutenant of infantry
Ordered 'em to fire into the crowd,
    in the square at the end of the Nevsky,
In front of the Moscow station,
And they wouldn't,
And he pulled his sword on a student for laughing,
And killed him,
And a cossack rode out of his squad
On the other side of the square
And cut down the lieutenant of infantry
And that was the revolution . . .
    as soon they named it'.

—Ezra Pound, Canto XVI

10 Age of Revolution

In 1906 a grateful Tsar Nicholas rewarded the Don Cossacks
for their loyalty during the troubles with another gracious charter
and permission to wear a white ribbon on their uniforms. The
overwhelming mass of Cossacks had indeed carried out their
duties but though Lenin considered them 'just as monarchical
as before',[1] there had been signs of restlessness among them.

The mobilisation of men on second and third call had put a
heavy strain on the poorer families and provoked some protest.
Men stationed in St. Petersburg wrote to a Don newspaper in
November 1905 complaining of having to protect the capital
'while our homes are going to pot'. Women in one village
protested to the Minister of War that their husbands were only
'protecting the rich' which was 'not state service'; in December
Cossacks of another regiment resisted efforts to get them on the

move saying they were not prepared to serve away from home merely on police work while their own farms were left without hands,[2] and in the same month a Kuban regiment, called out to break a strike, came out on strike themselves, moved off home and held out until February 1906, when they at last surrendered to other Cossack units. Men of the 3rd 'Yermak Timofeyevich' Don Cossack Regiment disobeyed orders in Vilna, a Siberian Cossack unit went on strike at Irkutsk and elsewhere Cossacks refused to disperse demonstrators or to ride against peasants.

Such incidents had reflected impatience with authority rather than sympathy with the rebels. But there had also been occasions when Cossacks had shown solidarity with striking workers, threatened to fire on soldiers if they attacked them, and urged peasants, whose cattle they had been ordered to seize for tax arrears to 'thrash . . . the damned souls in the hairy caps [the police]. Don't pay them anything'. In May 1906 a Cossack platoon refused to move against workers in Novocherkassk telling the police: 'We're not your servants now', that they would henceforth serve the workers. And, here and there, political agitators had at last succeeded in piercing the thick cocoon of Tsarist ideology which encased the Cossacks. A battery at Rostov was said to be 'completely propagandised' and when, in August 1906, a political activist was arrested at one *stanitsa* over 2,000 inhabitants held a protest meeting which Cossacks of the 48th Don regiment refused to break up.[3]

Yet on the whole, these stirrings derived not so much from the general Russian crisis, as from a particular crisis which had arisen in the more crowded Cossack provinces. The Don, especially, was short of land. Too much of this was in private ownership and the population explosion of the late nineteenth century had exacerbated the shortage. By 1906 the Don budget had fallen into deficit to the tune of several million rubles due to the State's failure to fulfil its obligations, and since the government would not help by direct means, the Don authorities had to compensate by leasing large tracts of the land reserve which might otherwise have supplemented the inadequate *stanitsa* lands, and allowed the average communal plot to be increased. The local administrators were not unsympathetic but decision rested with the Military Council and the General

Directorate of Cossack Hosts in St. Petersburg. No Cossacks sat on these bodies and some members of them ascribed the Cossacks' difficulties to laziness and saw in their demands a dark tendency to revolution.

As members of a special caste with strong regional associations, the Cossacks felt that their problems were basically different from those of the rest of Russia, that their difficulties were of a type which a distant government would never recognise, still less solve. And so they began to call for self-government. But on the Don, Cossacks were now in a minority. The *stanitsas* returned only seventy-nine out of 177 representatives to the provincial council. But though the landowning gentry and non-Cossack industrial towns, notably Rostov, were well represented, the peasants were grossly under-represented with only fourteen seats. They shared only ten per cent of the arable land on the Don against the Cossacks' seventy per cent, while on the Kuban 1,339,430 Cossacks farmed sixty per cent of the arable land, the 1,646,901 'outsiders' only thirty-seven per cent, and the average Cossack household owned about three times the number of cattle as its peasant counterpart.[4] Yet Cossack resentment continued to mount against the underprivileged peasant 'outsiders' as well as other 'usurpers and intruders' who occupied lands which were formerly theirs, and, so far as the peasant was concerned, the antipathy was mutual. Moreover the growing towns, equipped with strange innovations and brash with a prosperity he lacked, served further to increase the rural Cossack's sense of alienation, and his determination to regain control. The slogan 'The Don for the Don Cossacks and for no one else' gained considerable popularity.

The sense of caste separateness allied to local patriotism increased in other Hosts as well, even in Central Asia where the Cossacks were often indistinguishable in dress and custom from their Kirghiz neighbours, and it was marked in the Kuban where the land shortage was particularly severe. Inequitable division had resulted in an exportable grain surplus north of the Kuban river and a subsistence economy to the south. Discontent provoked such serious disorders that General Mikhailov, a Ural Cossack and Deputy Ataman of the Kuban, persuaded the Tsar to allow the calling of a Cossack Rada to regulate the question—the first full-scale democratic assembly ever to be held on the Kuban.

It met in December 1906 over 500 strong and elected as as its President a Cossack of liberal education called F. A. Shcherbina. Shcherbina was a student of Cossack history and, fired by ideas of Cossack brotherhood, he saw the occasion as the beginning of a new democratic era in Cossackdom. The assembly agreed on better provision for the poorer Cossacks in the southern Kuban which the Tsar duly endorsed. But it went further. Though expressly forbidden to debate anything but the land question, the subject of the men sentenced for mutiny in refusing to carry out policing duties the previous year was raised, and despite threats to dissolve it, the Rada petitioned St. Petersburg to grant an amnesty to the mutineers.

A wave of liberal idealism was sweeping the educated Cossacks. There was a revival of Cossack self-awareness, a desire to seek political solutions to their problems. At the second state Duma in March 1907, Shcherbina was active in creating a bloc of Cossack delegates and helped to draw up a joint Cossack declaration which was presented by Kaledin of the Don. By the time delegates dispersed Shcherbina considered that representatives of all Hosts had achieved a certain solidarity, that they were 'united, with their feet placed firmly on democratic Cossack ground'.[5] But little could be realised in practice.

The authorities tried to curb this new enthusiasm for democracy and liberalism. Cossack representation to the Don assembly was drastically reduced from nearly forty-five per cent to a mere twenty out of 142 seats, and from February 1908 a property qualification of 550 acres for voters and 1,600 for candidates was introduced for elections to the State Council, which in effect excluded the average Cossack from its debates. And the land problem still remained. The peasants were becoming increasingly restive and were held in check only by increased efforts by the police. Agricultural methods were backward and productivity low. The government reckoned a Cossack needed between sixty and seventy-five acres for his maintenance but on the Don the average was down to twenty-five, forcing many Cossacks to grow grain year in year out, wearing out the soil. Between 1905 and 1911 the average wheat harvest per acre on the Don was only two-thirds the national average, the rye crop only half. Only the large private farmers could afford to introduce modern machinery; sometimes even a Cossack of average means had to sell his pair of oxen or some valuable implements in order to equip himself for service; and a poor man might have to let his land on a long lease for the purpose, and when he returned, rent a plot from someone else or make a living as a labourer.[6] The large population increase and the inelastic supply of land had the effect of driving many Cossacks towards poverty again, and, since there were no fresh fields to move to, some families even began to escape from rural poverty by drifting into the towns to join the industrial workers, the new urban poor. The caste began to show signs of cracking up.

The authorities dared not ignore the situation. Yet when emigration to Siberia was suggested to relieve the land shortage, the government refused to countenance it. Instead, the Don Land Council began a policy of local re-settlement, and from 1909 Cossacks were allowed land on the Host reserve, but much of this was in arid steppe areas and many families, finding no basic necessities there, moved back to their old homes. The Don authorities began to buy out private landowners, but between 1910 and 1916 they acquired only 150,000 acres and at high prices too, and then, instead of giving it to Cossacks, they leased it out for the benefit of the general budget of the province. At last, in 1912, St. Petersburg sanctioned a migration of peasant 'outsiders' to Siberia, but by 1914 fewer than 50,000—only three per cent of the peasant population—had moved out.[7]

Lacking any effective answer to their grievances, Cossacks continued to return a high proportion of liberals to the State Dumas where they combined in Cossack blocs and persisted in calling for local self-government. In 1910 the 3rd Duma proposed a measure of Cossack autonomy and two years later Cossacks were given a bare majority in the Don provincial assembly. But the assembly's powers were themselves restricted. At the 4th Duma in 1913 the creation of a Don assembly was proposed, which would have powers over economic and cultural affairs.[8] But the Duma could only advise; the Tsar's will was still absolute.

With the Cossacks dissatisfied, the lot of the peasants

deteriorating and the new industrial proletariats of towns like Rostov and Taganrog growing belligerent, the scene in the larger Cossack communities was being set for conflict—conflict between the province and the state, between Cossack and non-Cossack, between town and countryside. But it was external events which were to bring these forces to boiling point.

The early summer of 1914 proved to be the last langorous days of peace before the storm. In July of that year, church bells rang out over the Russian borderlands signalling general mobilisation. Once more the cry 'To arms! For Tsar and Fatherland' was heard. Cossacks in the fields dropped their scythes, packed up their harvest lunches and hurried home; the quiet streets of Cossack villages from the Ukraine to the Pacific came alive with rushing figures; men searched out dusty uniforms and took down pistols and sabres from the walls; their women collected such food and comforts as they could find and crammed them under their husband's saddles. Then a state of war was proclaimed. Bugles sounded at the assembly points, Cossacks piled into railway box cars; wives and mothers said their last goodbyes and swore at the officials who held them back from the tracks.

Three hundred and sixty thousand Cossacks went to war and within a few days some of them were riding into Prussia. The German press churned out lurid stories of wild Asiatics looting their way across the fatherland,[9] and the thought of emulating their forefathers by galloping into Berlin could not have been far from Cossack minds. But it was not to be. Hindenburg and Ludendorff took charge of the German 8th Army and promptly turned the tide. The Russian 2nd Army was surrounded. General Samsonov's special guard of Don Cossacks was cut down and other Cossack units sustained heavy losses tearing a way out of the German ring.

It was a crushing defeat, but not decisive, and as the fighting swung to and fro in the months and years that followed, Cossacks were involved in myriad actions, playing their traditional roles, scouting out advances, guarding flanks, and raiding enemy communications. Despite their detractors, these rough riders of the steppes proved more than a match for the Prussian Death's Head Hussars and the vaunted cavalrymen of Hungary. But this was in phases of open warfare, and the opportunities to fulfil their special roles became increasingly rare.

On the eastern, as on the western front, the machine gun and barbed wire gave the static defender every advantage against charging horsemen; the aeroplane reduced the need for reconnaissance on horseback, the motor lorry began to replace the horse as the quickest means of troops in action, and heavy artillery often pounded a battle zone to a sea of mud and craters in which it was impossible to use a horse. Yet while the British and French cavalry was soon sitting out the war in billets far behind the lines, the Russian command did not spare the Cossacks—however unsuitable the conditions. In the first year of the war, at Tarnov, the 3rd Don Cossack Division was ordered to charge German infantry entrenchments across an open front swept by rifle and machine-gun fire and guarded with barbed wire. And despite heavy losses the division gained its objective. In 1915, a Cossack regiment at only half its normal strength was sent at night against an Austrian position fortified with reinforced concrete, thick barbed wire entanglements, and line upon line of well-dug trenches held by crack infantrymen with a generous field of fire. Generals on both sides thought it impregnable, and yet in a sharp and terrible action the three hundred Cossacks managed to carve an opening, and the 1st Don Cossack Division galloped through.

But such success stories were exceptional. Frontal cavalry attacks more often ended in utter failure. Yet those commanders who realised the futility of using mounted Cossacks in trench warfare, only began to use them as infantry instead. Near Vilna in September 1915 two Cossack Guards regiments, pounded by a devastating artillery barrage until their trenches became level with the ground, had to withstand a full-scale onslaught without support. They held out, but at a casualty cost of seventy-two per cent. The Cossacks always bore their share of the brunt and sometimes more. They were still occasionally used as cavalry as during the 1916 offensive which drew German troops away from the Western Front; but increasingly they were given infantry tasks for which they had always been reckoned unsuitable and for which they had received little proper training. They responded extraordinarily well to the challenge as

283

Soviet historians still recall with pride. They languished in trenches, bogged down in mud and often short of rations, and sustained the most appalling casualties. Yet their morale stayed higher than the rest of the army's and prisoners accounted for an unusually small proportion of their losses.[10]

And Cossacks did as well on other fronts, rode south across 'gigantic fields of snow and ice', into Georgia, where they fought scurvey and starvation as well as the Turks, and re-learnt their forefathers' skills in snatching some comfort from the most adverse wintry conditions by making the Kars plateau into a rabbit warren, riddling the ground with snug dug-outs which they covered with grass. Nor were Germans, Austrians and Turks the only enemies that Cossacks were called upon to fight. In 1916 Kirghiz tribesmen of the Seven Rivers area, already resentful at losing land to the local Cossacks, rebelled when called to register for service and attacked the nearby Cossack settlements, slaughtering the garrisons and carrying 5,000 colonists away captive.[11] Cossacks took such a terrible revenge for this that even the conservative Russian press was moved to protest. It did not complain, however, of other instances of Cossack brutality initiated by the state against 'internal enemies'. Cossack veterans were used to quell mutinies at the front, and were called out against soldiers in Petrograd who had sided with steel workers against the police. And such duties were becoming much more frequent.

The seams of the Empire were beginning to give way under the increasing strains of war, and even the Cossack caste, one of the strongest threads, was beginning to fray. In August 1916 the Deputy Ataman for the Don warned that the population— Cossacks as well as peasants and the revolutionary workers of Rostov-on-Don—incensed by 'the exorbitant rise in the cost of living' and agitated by 'extreme leftist elements', might combine to 'shake the whole state structure down to its foundations'.[12]

The authorities might well be worried, but to a large extent they had brought the troubles on themselves. The war had brought a considerable deterioration to the Cossack economy. In 1914 the government had banned the export of agricultural produce from the Don. As a result prices fell and with them

Cossacks' incomes. Agricultural machines factories were turned over to armaments production, so that farm equipment, at a premium now that the major part of the labour force was away, became unobtainable. By 1917 the area of cultivation on the Don was down by nearly a quarter by comparison with 1913. And as the call-up of young men continued more and more households had to borrow money from *stanitsa* funds in order to equip them. In order to repay these loans, many families had to let their land and sell off their tools and working cattle. A survey of 1917 showed that though about a third of all Don Cossack households still owned four or more oxen apiece, as many as a quarter had only one working animal and a sixth having none at all was classed as totally ruined.[13] The autocracy ought not to have relied on the loyalty of such people pressed to the breadline and beyond.

Meanwhile conditions in the battle sectors had grown steadily worse. The supply of food and ammunition often failed, and by early 1917 fever was raging on the southern front and the western front was near collapse. With the prospect of victory receding, and with the occasional letters which reached them indicating distress at home, the Cossacks, too, began to weary of the war, and even those stationed behind the lines in Petrograd were caught up in the general mood of despair. For its part the government was just in process of creating yet a new Cossack community, the Yeniseisk Host of central Siberia, far from the scene of any fighting, when in February 1917 the storm broke.

Petrograd was short of bread. Crowds had gathered in the streets. There was some looting, and Cossacks were called out to help the police restore order. It had all been seen a dozen times before. But this time there was a difference. The Cossacks did not seem disposed to repeat their performance of 1905 and 1916; the *nagaikas* remained on the saddle pommels, the sabres were not drawn. Cossacks were slow to leave the barracks and then showed none of their customary zeal in breaking up the crowds. They just pushed slowly through them showing no sign of action, and this 'immensely cheered the demonstrators'. In the main the Cossacks were indifferent, but some gave deliberate encouragement. A Cossack was seen to wink at rioters, others

K*

'showed a clear tendency to fraternise', and once, when a mounted police inspector made for a troublemaker, brandishing his sabre, a Cossack intercepted him and slashed off his hand.[14]

From indifference the Cossacks moved to sympathy with the rioters, finally to open support. Men of the Nevski shipyards were told: 'Don't be afraid. The Cossacks of the 4th Regiment will join the workers',[15] and the 1st and the 14th Don Cossack regiments soon followed them over to the rebel side. In the judgement of one observer, the Cossacks had had it in their power to conquer the revolution 'with their bare hands'.[16] They chose not to. And the Tsar fell.

After nearly a century and a half Cossacks had begun to think a 'strong little thought with the poor' again, and not only in Petrograd. The Ural Cossacks were among the first to declare for the new régime and when the news reached the Caucasus, the Grand Duke Nicholas's personal bodyguard of Terek Cossacks, 'always regarded as the most loyal', escorted him to the station 'waving red flags and singing the Marseillaise'.[17] Cossacks rejoiced as the news swept the western front. Most squadrons of the Nerchinsk Regiment replaced their battle colours with red flags much to the chagrin of General Vrangel, the non-Cossack commander of the Ussuri Division who had always considered them 'brave enough in battle'. And this was no isolated instance. Unit after unit proved 'rotten at heart', as Vrangel put it, and many came to rule their loyalist officers.[18]

The Cossack communities behind the lines were all touched by the new enthusiasm. The authoritarianism which had enmeshed them suddenly fell away; the legends that had held them in thrall since the eighteenth century lost all their power. A visitor to the Terek found 'rejoicing' everywhere. Cossacks took over the towns, arrested the Deputy Ataman appointed by the Tsar, elected their own Ataman, and passed resolutions demanding a republic. A Rada was called in the Kuban, and the Orenburg and Amur Cossacks soon elected their own Atamans, though those of Transbaikal abolished the post and created district committees instead. On the Don an 'Executive Committee' was formed on which Social Revolutionaries and Mensheviks were represented, and anyone who wanted Tsar Nicholas back stayed silent. In the words of an English corres-

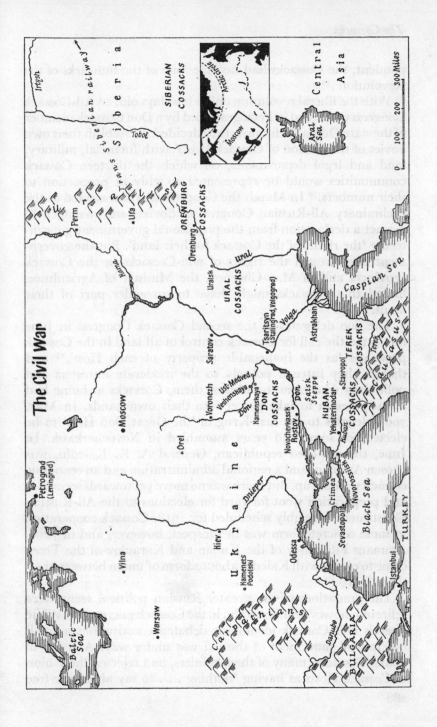

The Civil War

Baltic Sea

Petrograd (Leningrad)

Vilna

Warsaw

Kamenets Podolski

Carpathians

Danube

BULGARIA

Odessa

Kiev

Dnieper

Ukraine

Sevastopol

Crimea

Novorossisk

Black Sea

Istanbul

TURKEY

Orel

Voronezh

Don

Veshenskaya

Kamenskaya

Ust-Medved

Novocherkassk

Rostov

DON COSSACKS

Salsk Steppe

Yehaterinodar

Kuban

KUBAN COSSACKS

Stavropol

TEREK COSSACKS

Terek

Caucasus

Moscow

Saratov

Tsaritsyn (Stalingrad, Volgograd)

Volga

Astrakhan

Caspian Sea

URAL COSSACKS

Uralsk

Ural

ORENBURG COSSACKS

Orenburg

Ufa

Kama

Perm

Ural

Tobol

Trans siberian railway

Irtysh

Siberia

SIBERIAN COSSACKS

Moscow

Arctic Circle

Aral Sea

Central Asia

0   100   200   300 Miles

pondent, the Cossacks had become 'one of the bulwarks of the Revolution'.[19]

With the liberal revolution only a few days old, an All-Cossack Congress was called in Petrograd. Led by a Don Cossack member of the state Duma, Yefremov, they decided to establish their own Soviet of the 'Union of Cossack Hosts' with financial, military, land and legal departments, on which the thirteen Cossack communities would be represented roughly in proportion to their numbers.[20] In March the Congress was represented at the preliminary All-Russian Congress of Soviets and managed to extract a declaration from the provisional government guaranteeing 'the rights of the Cossack to their land'. But the government also stressed the rights of non-Cossacks in the Cossack provinces and in May Chernov, the Minister of Agriculture, hinted that Cossacks might have to surrender part of their lands.[21]

The 600 delegates to the second Cossack Congress in June reiterated the call for Cossack control of all land in the Cossack provinces 'as the inalienable property of each Host',[22] and though they listened politely to the moderate ministers and politicians who came to address them, Cossacks at home had already begun to take power into their own hands. In May, 700 delegates to the first Krug of 'the Great Don Host' to be elected for some 150 years assembled in Novocherkassk. In June, the sad-eyed republican, General A. K. Kaledin, was chosen Ataman, and a regional administration and an economic council were set up. But there was no move yet towards secession, and preparation went forward for elections to the All-Russian Constituent Assembly scheduled for 1918. Cossack cooperation in some concrete form was in prospect, however, and in June, Atamans Filimonov of the Kuban and Karaulov of the Terek came to confer with Kaledin about a form of union between their three Hosts.[23]

The gradations of the greater Russian political scene were reflected, however imperfectly, in the Cossack microcosm. While liberals and Cossack ideologists debated constitutions a small but radical movement of the left was under way. A group of young Cossacks, many of them soldiers, had rejected the Union of Cossack Hosts as having 'nothing . . . to say about the free organisation of working Cossackdom', and set up a rival organisation called the 'Central Soviet of Cossacks', chaired by a Kuban Cossack student called Kostenetski. They followed Lenin's Bolshevik line in opposition to the parliamentary liberalism of the new Prime Minister, Kerenski. Totally absorbed in the dialectics of the class struggle, they aligned the Cossack moderates with the bourgeoisie, and set out to raise the poorer Cossacks to the proletarian cause.[24]

A propaganda war ensued. The Union of Cossack Hosts issued a journal in which it denounced Kostenetski, while Kostenetski's group, soon to be called the 'Party of Working Cossacks', eventually produced its own paper *The Voice of Working Cossacks*. Its influence, negligible in the Cossack provinces, became quite considerable among front-line servicemen, the *frontoviki*, but it failed to shift the allegiance of the Cossacks in the Petrograd garrison.

These remained staunch supporters of the Union of Cossack Hosts, for which they were to vote fairly solidly in the elections to the Petrograd Constituent Assembly at the end of November, and of the Provisional Government. In July, when the Bolsheviks tried to take power, it was the Cossacks of the Petrograd garrison who crushed the attempt, and they were used in the clamp-down on the Bolsheviks which followed, being sent to raid the offices of *Pravda* and of Kostenetski's Cossack Bolsheviks.

The attempted Bolshevik *coup* from the left was followed by an attempted *coup* from the right. In August, General Kornilov ordered the 3rd Cavalry Corps including a Cossack division to move on Petrograd on the pretext of saving it from the Bolsheviks. But many of his men were unenthusiastic, and, delayed along the railway line, they were talked round by agitators, including Cossacks from the Petrograd garrison. Kornilov's attempt petered out into miserable failure, but it triggered off a clash between the Provisional Government and Kaledin of the Don.

This seemed unexpected. True, the Don Krug had called for autonomy, but not for secession, and only recently Kaledin had declared support for a united Russian republic. But though his involvement has since been denied, Premier Kerenski believed

Kaledin to have been implicated in the Kornilov plot. The Don Ataman, who in any case represented only the Cossack minority in the province, was declared deposed and the second session of the Don Krug was banned. But the Krug met and Kaledin stayed on in defiance of the order.[25] The movement for Cossack autonomy had become one of open secession.

With the Russian economy on the point of total breakdown and the Bolsheviks' programme of immediate peace gaining strength with every hour; with martial law being proclaimed in the more riotous areas, and troops—Cossacks wherever possible—being sent out in all directions to restore order, the Government had its hands far too full trying to maintain its own crumbling authority to pursue the issue with Kaledin. And Atamans of other Cossack provinces soon followed Kaledin's example.

But Cossack opinion was far from united. While politicians were trying to create the first Cossack state, and servicemen were preserving order for Kerenski's Provisional Government, many of the younger men at the front, weary of war, were becoming indifferent to the liberal regime which insisted on Russia's continuing to fight the Germans and the Austrians.

The Bolsheviks were subjecting them to a propaganda barrage which won over many of the younger Cossack soldiers. The Bolsheviks also made some progress on the Don itself among the workers and the depressed peasantry, but most of these still supported the Social Revolutionaries and the Mensheviks. While by the end of the year the Bolsheviks could raise over a third of the votes in the industrial Rostov district, the SRs took fifty-one per cent of the poll,[26] and the countryside was still dominated by the Cossack Party. Cossack agitators in the Bolshevik cause had more success among regiments in the Petrograd district. As a result it was these garrison Cossacks, who, albeit by default, aided the success of Lenin's October Revolution.

With power slipping out of Kerenski's hands, a deputation of the Union of Cossack Hosts called on him at the Winter Palace on the night of the 24th October/6th November to insist on a show-down with Lenin's men based three miles across the city at the Smolny Institute. Kerenski agreed. General Krasnov, a Don Cossack, was ordered to the capital from the northern front and messages went out to the 1st, 4th and 14th Don regiments to come to the aid of the Provisional Government. But the Cossacks preferred to 'abstain'. All Kerenski ever got were assurances that they were 'preparing to saddle their horses'.[27] Cossacks already in the streets took no action; those guarding the Winter Palace quietly slipped away.

Kerenski left to join Krasnov who was advancing on the city. There was a desultory exchange of fire outside the capital, but the Bolsheviks' chief defence was propaganda. Cossacks of the pro-Leninist faction were sent out to persuade Krasnov's men to turn back. What success they had is difficult to establish, but the advance soon petered out. Kerenski escaped and Krasnov was arrested, though he was soon released by Trotski on parole.[28]

A second revolution had been effected; the Bolsheviks had taken power. The situation in Petrograd and in the country was totally confused. But the new regime redoubled its efforts to win Cossacks to its side. A new Cossack committee, chaired by a Cossack of the 14th Don regiment called Lagutin, was added to the Executive Committee (VTsIK) of the Congress of Workers' and Soldiers' Deputies, and a Cossack section headed by A. G. Nagayev to its Military Department. The Congress soon added the word 'Cossacks' to its title in recognition of their potential importance to the cause, and further conceded the Cossacks' right 'to their own organisation in accordance with the principles of their way of life' and formed a special Cossack Department,[29] which sent agitators out into the Cossack provinces. Ordinary Cossacks were assured that they would keep their land; Lenin encouraged them to divide up the larger private estates and to form local Soviets,[30] hoping that the 'working Cossacks' might form a Party, which would rally a large segment of opinion to the Bolshevik cause. In this he was to be disappointed. It was also hoped to make the Cossack Committee completely representative of all the Cossack Hosts. But though delegates came in from military units in Petrograd and Finland, the places kept for representatives from the *stanitsa* Soviets were mostly to stay empty.

The Bolshevik leaders were as yet unsure of the line they should take. Trotski praised the 'bravery', and the 'amazing discipline of the Cossack forces', and, admitting that the new government knew 'little of Cossack life and less about its psychology', invited them 'to help the central Soviet authority in deciding all Cossack matters that might arise'.[31]

Bolshevik Cossacks were now represented on the Central Executive and the Military Revolutionary Committees and the General Staff, and the Soviet of Peoples Commissar was soon to acquire a Don Cossack Commissar for Cossack affairs. The new Cossack Department at VTsIK started work on a land reform, plans for civil government, schemes to provide uniforms at government expense and for full compensation for equipment and horses—measures designed to remove long-standing griev-ances and to appeal particularly to the poorer elements. But Russia was withdrawing from the war and since the new govern-ment preferred to form its army from scratch rather than retain the old one, many of whose officers, at least, were of doubtful loyalty, the Department was largely involved in demobilisation. This was carried out with remarkable speed. Most of the service Cossacks at last set out for home, but were disarmed before they left, much against their will.

The Cossack Department set out both to interpret Cossack interests to the new regime and to rouse Cossacks to its support. But it was only an advisory body, often ignored or by-passed by executives pressed to immediate action by the speed of events. It had to campaign for reforms projected for Cossack regions to be referred to it for comment, and for local Soviet authorities in Cossack regions to keep in touch. It tried to brief officials before they set out and to get Cossacks arriving from the provinces to report directly to them.

Meanwhile Kaledin had consolidated his authority on the Don, conducted a purge of Bolsheviks, and proclaimed martial law. Cossacks also took control in the Kuban, the Terek, and in Orenburg where Ataman Dutov defeated the local Bolsheviks with the support of local Mensheviks, Cadets, SRs and Kazakh and Bashkir nationalists.[32] A 'South-East Union', representing the Cossacks of the Don, Kuban, Terek and Astrakhan, the Kalmyks and some north Caucasian tribesmen, was formed, and the Ural and Orenburg Hosts soon acceded to it. It was not secessionist in mood at first. Kharmalov, its President, saw the various provinces as 'states of a future Russian Federation',[33] but as time went on, a 'United Government of the South-Eastern Union' was projected and as the realisation grew that the Bolshevik central government was not merely a nine-day wonder the idea of forming a fringe state independent of Moscow was to gain a certain popularity. The Ukraine, where a democratic Rada had been established with the help of Cossack units serving there, Georgia, and the anti-Bolshevik authorities in Siberia and Central Asia were also attracted to a South-East Union based on Cossack ideology. But there were problems enough even in establishing viable provincial governments in the various Cossack provinces.

The Cossacks of the Don formed only forty-eight and a half per cent of the total population, but owned seventy-nine per cent of the land, and the resentments between them and peasant 'outsiders' threatened stability from the outset. Kaledin, though pressured by his own people, tried to give non-Cossacks a fair deal at least politically. A constitution increased the rights of non-Cossacks and opened up the possibility of their becoming Cossacks themselves. Kaledin's Ministry formed in January 1918 consisted of seven Cossack ministers, some suspected of sympathies to the left of centre, and seven non-Cossacks. He released political prisoners, relaxed the state of emergency, proclaimed freedom of the press, promised to expel counter-revolutionaries, and tried to negotiate with Petrograd on terms for autonomy within the new Russian state. But the land shortage hung like a mill-stone round his neck and there was no prospect of satisfying both Cossacks and peasants. Like its predecessors, the Bolshevik government grew less than ever inclined to countenance any deviation from monolithic unity, and Cossack association with Tsarist officers who were threatening to overturn the Bolshevik regime spurred it on to crush the Cossack movement.

In November and December 1917 a number of Tsarist generals, including Kornilov, Alexeyev, the ex-Commander-in-Chief, and Denikin, had fled south to the Don, intent on building a 'Volunteer Army' with the Cossacks as its nucleus, which would carry them back to Petrograd. Kaledin sheltered the refugees, but banned their appeal for all anti-Bolshevik officers to assemble on the Don and, as his supporters have insisted, tried manfully to pursue an independent course, not excluding an arrangement with the Bolshevik government. If so, it was useless. A moderate Kaledin was trying to ride a tiger, and was inevitably swallowed up by the extremist Whites.

Cossack idealists who had envisaged a time 'when they would have their own government' and, 'setting guards along their own frontiers, would talk as equals, without any cap-raising, with the Ukraine and Great Russia',[34] saw the prize dashed out of their hands straightway. They were not united. General Krasnov, for one, was set against independence, saw the Cossacks as 'the best pearl in the Tsar's Crown' and thought 'they should remain so', but realising that a restoration of the monarchy was impossible, he tried to rouse Cossack servicemen against the new government by paying lip-service to the cause of the old Kerenski regime. Men like Krasnov saw the situation as another Time of Troubles and in which the Don Cossacks must play their patriotic role of 1612 to save the motherland and Moscow.

Lenin, on the other hand, drew parallels with the French Revolution and saw the Cossack borderlands becoming a Russian Vendeé, a base for counter-revolution.[35] Never disposed to countenance secession, he was now able to identify the Cossack leadership with the White Generals, and take action against them. The old Soviet of the Union of Cossack Hosts was disbanded, Trotski condemned the Cossacks' 'counter-revolutionary rebellion', and Antonov-Ovseyenko, briefed by Soviet Cossacks in Petrograd, marched south.[36]

The physical advance was accompanied by a propaganda offensive. A decree announced the abolition of compulsory military and local services, and offered free uniforms and equipment to volunteers for the Red Army. Restrictions on movement were abolished and an immediate settlement of the land question was promised 'in the interests of working Cossacks and all workers', but taking local conditions, traditions and customs into account.[37]

Appeals were broadcast insisting that the Soviet regime was not hostile to the Cossacks and had no intention of depriving them of their 'Cossack liberty'. No, the Cossacks' real enemies were the generals and landowners, who were keeping them in subjection. The Cossack's life, so the message ran, had always been one of 'bondage and hard labour'. At the bidding of authority the Cossack had to ride away on campaign, spending his own hard-earned resources on his uniform and equipment, and when a 'Cossack is on campaign, his farm goes to pieces'. Was this arrangement fair? Of course not. The new government would abolish it but Cossacks themselves must help 'tear off the damned yoke from their necks', form Soviets, and elect representatives of the working Cossacks to replace the atamans, generals and the supporters of the rich. The inequitable system by which some Cossack households had only ten acres and others thousands must also be abolished. Cossacks must not believe the canard that the Soviets would confiscate their lands. This was put about by the rich who knew that 'the Soviets want to hand their land over to you'.

So far the appeal was aimed only at the poorer Cossacks and the majority were neither rich nor poor, but these must be attracted by the prospects of peace. The war had been going on for almost three and a half years, bringing ruin and catastrophe in its train. The Bolsheviks promised peace with honour, peace without annexations. Only the 'criminal rising against the people' led by the atamans and generals threatened catastrophe again. The common people must unite to stop it. 'Down with the war!' shrieked the pamphlets, 'Down with the landlords and the Kornilovite generals. Long live the peace and brotherhood of peoples.'[38] The Bolshevik forces advancing into the border provinces were backed up by the Cossack Department in Petrograd and its agitation unit, and in December 1917 most of its members left for the Don, the Kuban and Siberia to preach the new gospel in person, Cossack to Cossack, man to man.[39]

Kaledin had ordered the mobilisation of a Don Cossack Army, and now withdrew his ban on the generals' appeal for all officers to assemble at Novocherkassk. Their 'Volunteer Army' was allowed to 'remain in existence' provided it did not turn 'against the people' and helped to protect the Don against invasion. But the conditions had no reality. Kaledin was unable to raise sufficient Cossack forces of his own. Few of the men who drifted home from the front showed much stomach for a fight. The 6th Don Regiment arrived in Novocherkassk in good order with no subversive soldiers' committee and with their officers apparently in control. They promised to fight the Bolsheviks, held ceremonial prayers, marched off—and immediately disintegrated. The men had had enough of war; they simply went home.[40] At last Kaledin had to call on the Volunteer Army even to suppress Bolshevik insurgents in his own territory and inevitably the White generals, instead of taking orders from Kaledin, took him over.

General Denikin, arriving in December, found Kaledin downcast. 'I give orders', he complained, 'and nobody carries them out.'[41] Industry and trade were breaking down; all vestige of social cohesion and political unity disappeared. The factory workers were on the point of rising; the peasants began to plunder big estates. The poorer Cossacks were more interested in the land problem than in political independence, and the returning *frontoviki* who had suffered the horrors of the trenches were in no mood to listen to their fathers. There was a split of generations. Kaledin was the patriarchs' man, and the *frontoviki*, many of them benevolently neutral towards the Bolsheviks, had no intention of fighting their battles. The Ataman lost all credence as a leader.

Red units arrived on the Don and in January 1918, a military Revolutionary Committee of 'working Cossacks' was formed at Kamenskaya, seventy miles north of Novocherkassk. Lagutin was there and also a Cossack subaltern called Podtelkov who emerged to prominence. Kaledin's men were arrested, contact established with Bolshevik cells, local Soviets of peasants and Cossacks were formed at various settlements, especially in the north-east Don, and, with the help of Red Guard detachments formed by the Donets miners, the Bolsheviks began quickly to take over the province.

Kaledin called cadets and schoolboys out to fight. Some partisan detachments were formed to hold the enemy at bay. But the Reds closed in relentlessly, and only a handful of the two million Cossacks answered his appeal for service. On 29th January/11th February, a despairing Kaledin committed suicide. Anatoli Nazarov was elected Ataman and, in a sudden revival, Cossacks from the more prosperous southern *stanitsas* rallied to him. But the burst of enthusiasm had come too late.

Ten days later the generals' Volunteer Army pulled out of Rostov and headed for the Kuban. Red Guards took the town on the 24th. Meanwhile a Cossack Lieutenant-Colonel, Golubov, who had been leading Red Cossacks in a series of sharp fratricidal engagements against the partisans, advanced on Novocherkassk. The Krug made one last appeal to the Bolshevik General Sablin. It was rejected. On 12th/25th February Golubov burst into the assembly building, dispersed the krug and had Nazarov shot. One thousand five hundred loyalist Cossacks under General Popov fled to the steppes.[42] The battle for independence had been fought and lost.

The other Cossack regiments also crumbled in much the same way. Three Cossack regiments had refused to fight the Reds at Orenburg and early in 1918 Ataman Dutov had been driven out. The Ural Cossacks held out against the Bolsheviks for a time, but were soon thrown out of Uralsk. The Siberian Cossack Division had promptly dispersed on arriving home at Omsk, and the Bolsheviks took over, though a Cossack officer called Annenkov led away a private army of 1,500 Cossacks on a vicious guerrilla-cum-bandit campaign along the Trans-Siberian railway, through the Seven River district of Central Asia and eventually into China.[43]

While the Bolsheviks overran the lower Volga and took over Astrakhan, anarchy descended on the Terek and Ataman Karaulov was shot dead. A Bolshevik rising on the Kuban forced Ataman Filimonov to flee from Yekaterinodar, and Kornilov's Volunteer Army completing its wintry march from the Don found the Kuban Cossack villagers none too keen to give them shelter, still less join them.

But it kept going, and, joined by groups of Don partisans, some Kuban Cossacks, Circassians and other militant anti-Bolsheviks, by April 1918 it felt strong enough to take Yekaterinodar. The attack was repulsed after several days' hard fighting in which Kornilov was killed. It was a low point in the fortunes of the anti-Bolsheviks, but General Denikin, who took over command, looked forward to success. Seeing 'the Cossacks as our mainstay, if not at present, at least for the future',[44] he ordered his Volunteers to pillage peasants rather than Cossacks wherever possible, and the policy soon paid dividends, for

297

Cossack opinion was already beginning to turn in disillusion against the Bolsheviks.

Having refused to make any deal with Kaledin and the Cossack separatists, the Soviet regime had taken a firm line even with Cossacks who had helped them to power. Golubov, who had hopes of being appointed Ataman, found himself taking orders from non-Cossack officials in Rostov, and early in April, accused of resisting the policies of the new regime, he fled from Novocherkassk with several of his supporters. He was hunted down and shot. The situation on the Don was most confused. A Military Commissar, the Cossack Revolutionary Committee and the Soviets of the towns all competed for authority. The Rostov Rev-Kom proclaimed the Don to be a Soviet Socialist Republic, but the *stanitsas* were still ruled by Cossacks and the confusion was increased by the activity of anti-Bolshevik rebel Cossack bands. One took Novocherkassk in April and held it for several days. Popov's men rode north again, and many stanitsas on the lower and middle Don rose up under General Mamontov against the new regime.

Bolshevik rule on the Don became very unpopular. The Reds stabled their horses in Novocherkassk cathedral and pulled down Yermak's statue. Worse, 'outsiders' were given scope for revenge against Cossacks. Leninist distinctions between workers and non-workers, rich and poor, were being interpreted locally in terms of vendettas and personal hatreds. Then, as the Germans advanced through the Ukraine, Red Army units retreated in disorder across the northern Don, pillaging Cossack homesteads with an impolitic lack of discrimination. As even poor Cossacks were robbed of their meagre stores of grain, and as men who had welcomed Bolshevik rule to the Don were treated as counter-revolutionaries, many of the Cossack *frontoviki* who, a few weeks before, had shot their officers, and marched off home to join the Bolsheviks, now turned against them. Trotski himself admitted that it was 'very possible that in some cases the Cossacks suffered injustice at the hand of passing military units or individual representatives of the Soviet government', and Sholokhov, in his novels, has described how Red soldiers brought 'discredit on the Red Army banner'[45] and alienated potential friends. According to one Cossack who abandoned them, and made his peace with them again later, it was 'only the indiscriminate requisitioning of grain, cattle and fodder carried out at Cossack stanitsas by Red Army Units' which 'produced opposition on the Don'.[46]

So, after less than three months' chaotic rule, the Bolsheviks were ousted from most of the Don province. On May 1st the Germans took Taganrog and on the 6th Colonel Denisov led rebel Cossacks into Novocherkassk. Two days later the Germans occupied Rostov. In the Ukraine, General Skoropadski was proclaimed Hetman with dictatorial powers under benevolent German eyes; and Denikin's Volunteers took Yekaterinodar.

In the spring of 1918 a new Assembly, the 'Krug for the salvation of the Don', was convened, and it elected the authoritarian General Krasnov Ataman. He held out for virtually dictatorial powers and he got them. Grey, elderly and traditional in composition, the krug adopted a flag of scarlet, blue and yellow, revived the old Host seal, introduced a Don national anthem, and left it to the Ataman to lay down the law.

Krasnov set about creating an army and obtaining help from outside. The army, consisting chiefly of youths and middle aged men dressed in motley uniforms with white favours in their caps to distinguish them from the Reds, reached a size of 40,000 by the summer, and, claiming that the Don Host had existed 'as an independent state since 1570',[47] Krasnov approached both the Allies and the Germans, who recognised his regime in June and proceeded to supply it with arms and grain. He forged an alliance with Hetman Skoropadski of the Ukraine and asked the Volunteer Army to return to the Don. By the middle of August virtually all the Reds, concentrated in the larger peasant villages and the rail centres, had been cleared out.[48] But the success was undecisive and bought at an escalating price of terror of which both sides were guilty.

On one side stood the bitter opponents of the injustices bred by rank and privilege; on the other were people indoctrinated in the old Tsarist mystiques, men who believed that privilege was divinely ordained, and in a church which consoled the common people in adversity and taught them to keep their places. The mass of Cossacks wavered between these two uncompromising poles—the one stiff with tradition, the other brash and hopeful.

299

But the struggle was soon to sweep everybody up. Abstention was impossible. Some were to invent slogans of compromise—'for the Soviet regime but against the communes', 'not against the Soviet government, but against the Communists and the Jews',[49] but there was no room for compromise. Men aligned themselves according to personal interest, according to which side seemed to be winning at the moment, or according to which side they unwittingly fell foul of, Red or White. This was to be an ideological war fought among people who only partly grasped the ideas.

The straggling stanitsas of the quiet Don, with their white cottages set haphazard among apple and cherry trees, became scenes of passionate violence as father was set against son, brother against brother, and friend against friend. Mutilations became the order of the day, the bullet the common currency in which every debt of hatred was paid up. In the words of one of Sholokhov's Cossacks, 'It's not a war, but a scourge of God'.[50]

As the concept of class struggle spread, enemies were typed rather than defined. The Whites saw every Red trying to build a new and fairer world as the embodiment of evil, while the new Red morality created its own calendar of saints and sinners typified by the crude caricatures of Sholokhov's early short stories. According to these, a bad Cossack has eight cows, a good Cossack only one. The Bolshevik saints are endowed with all the human virtues, the 'sinners' with every disgusting personal characteristic and vice. A priest's wife is corpulent with thin sarcastic lips, and cracks her fingers.[51] A White officer smells of drink, has stupid, bloodshot eyes and absent-mindedly plucks the legs off a living insect to prove his cold-bloodedness. Position, even dress, came to define political allegiance. A good coat or an officer's cap mark a man out as a White, and Gregor Melekhov, hero of Sholokhov's novel *The Quiet Don*, a Cossack who fought for the Reds, is forced into the opposing camp on his return home only because he has been an officer in the old imperial army and the local Bolsheviks plan to shoot him for it.

Krasnov, brought to power on a tide of anti-Bolshevik feeling, alleged that the Bolsheviks tortured priests, raped girls and tied men to windmills. But he and his fellow generals encouraged a counter-terror which was at least as horrible. A Cossack deserting from the Reds would merely suffer a public beating by village patriarchs, emerge with a rueful smile saying 'my head went wrong and my arse has suffered for it', and be welcomed back into the fold by the crowd's good-natured horse-laughs. But the fate of a captured Red Cossack was death. White officers admitted 'it was necessary to exterminate without any mercy persons who were detected in co-operation with the Bolsheviks',[52] and Krasnov describes with relish a typical occasion 'when the Cossacks at Ponomarev hamlet captured the well-known [Bolshevik] Podtelkov together with the seventy-three Cossacks remaining with him'. A hastily convened 'field court' 'condemned Podtelkov and two of his supporting commissars to be hanged, and the seventy-three Cossacks of the convoy to be shot. Sentence was immediately carried out in the presence of all the inhabitants, and an old Cossack woman of the neighbouring hamlet expressed herself to be 'very sorry she was not in time to see "how the villains will hang" '.[53]

For the moment the weight had swung against the Bolsheviks. There was a new Cossack revival, a resurgence of caste pride and local patriotism, and as men fought for their own homes, Krasnov's slogan 'the Don for the Don Cossacks' carried all before it. By the late summer the Don was cleared of Bolshevik forces and Krasnov's army crossed the borders into the provinces of Saratov and Voronezh.

In the east too, the anti-revolutionary movement, the movement to 'cure Russia from the borders', gained ground as Cossacks who had initially accepted Bolshevik rule now turned against it. Counter-revolution took hold of Western Siberia in June, Transbaikal in August and Ussuri and the Amur in September, and though Ataman Dutov of Orenburg was at last beaten back into the Tugai steppe the Ural Cossacks rose against the Reds and on the Terek, after much fierce fighting, the Bolsheviks were forced into retreat.

The terror affected every region. While Krasnov presided over mass executions on the Don, Annenkov pursued his war of vengeance in the Seven Rivers area, General Shkuro set an example in atrocity to the Cheka men in the Kuban, and unarmed Reds were mown down wholesale in the Urals and Siberia. It was in Siberia that, almost exactly a year after the

Bolshevik revolution, Admiral Kolchak, rising to prominence as the leader of White oppositionists, was proclaimed 'Supreme Ruler', promising the Cossacks, on whose armed support he was largely dependent, a wide measure of autonomy. And while Kolchak was trying to impose cohesion on the anti-Bolshevik movements in the east, attempts were made to create some form of union in the south. Talks were held in Novocherkassk with various groups claiming to represent the Ukraine, Astrakhan and the Caucasus. But Krasnov's own position on the Don was already being threatened.

Even senior officers in his own administration disliked his autocratic grip, and a new Don Krug which assembled in August 1918, much to his distaste, began to discuss a constitution which would limit his powers. The new Krug was more representative than its predecessor and although predominantly made up of semi-educated farmers, included a sizeable proportion of *frontoviki* and old-style democrats.

According to its plan, the Krug and not the Ataman, would be sovereign—make the laws, elect an Ataman or 'President of the Republic' to serve a three-year term, decide the budget, declare war, and conclude peace. The Ataman would be chief executive and commander-in-chief with powers to proclaim martial law and even to declare war 'in an emergency'; he would appoint ministers and also sack them. But he would be subject to the Krug which could impeach him.

Though 'personal freedom' was written into the constitution the equality of rights applied only to anti-Bolshevik Cossacks. Every Cossack was to own some land, but not those who had served in the Red Army or engaged in Red propaganda. And the 'outsiders' were discriminated against. No attempt was made to placate non-Cossack opinion, least of all by Krasnov. When Jews of Rostov applied for wider political rights, he refused them. 'As long as I am Ataman of the Don', he said, 'no one except the Don Cossacks will be allowed to decide the fate of the Don province.'[54]

Resentment of Krasnov was not limited to the 'outsiders'. Many Cossacks disliked his obvious dependence on the Germans who were ferrying arms and munitions to the Don. Yet Krasnov deemed the situation to be beyond the grasp of liberal idealists.

The Don was locked in total war against the Bolsheviks, and its situation was precarious in the extreme. There was not time for philosophising.

The economy was in ruins. Land re-distributed under Bolshevik law was restored to its original holders, but ownership was often in dispute, engendering more local conflict, and much of the land remained unploughed. The fighting had seriously reduced the harvests, just at a time when an exportable grain surplus was more than ever necessary, and Krasnov had to organise grain collection detachments which used much the same methods as the Bolsheviks had done, and gained him further unpopularity. Shortages, already serious, became especially evident in the autumn when the Germans pulled out of the Ukraine. And their withdrawal left the western flank of the Don unguarded. By December 1918 the Don Army, with a strength of nearly 50,000 men, 153 guns and 581 machine guns, had to fight on two fronts against Red Army forces nearly three times as large, and many Cossacks, who, a few months before had been anxious enough to protect their homes, were none to keen to fight away from them.

The situation deteriorated again as suddenly as it had revived in the spring. At Christmas, Bolshevik agitators, bearing white flags, advanced towards Cossack trenches in Voronezh province and the officers could not restrain their Cossacks running out to meet them. The Cossacks' spirit for the war had waned now they were fighting beyond the borders of the Don, and so they stood in no-man's-land and listened to the Bolsheviks' tales about Krasnov selling himself to the Germans for four millions in silver. Hundreds of them responded by driving their bayonets into the ground and marching away, and as the Bolsheviks advanced a second time into the Don many actively supported them. A Cossack called Fomin proclaimed himself Commissar at Veshenskaya stanitsa, and, in October, an elder called Mironov rallied Cossacks of the Ust-Medveditsa district on the northern Don to the Bolshevik cause and, though beaten by troops loyal to Krasnov, escaped to lead a Don corps in the Red Army. Whole regiments were going over to the Reds; the front was breaking up, and reckoning the Krug itself to be 'already half Bolshevik', Krasnov turned over command of the Don Army to General Denikin of the Volunteers. But Denikin, too, was unable to stop the rot and in February 1919, Krasnov resigned.

The Cossack Committee of the VTsIK, now based in Moscow, following Lenin's move to the ancient capital of Russia, had contributed to the new Bolshevik successes, despite the loss of several leaders, including Lagutin, its sometime Chairman, who had been shot when he ventured back to the Don. Reinforced by Bolshevik sailors and 450,000 rubles it had developed its propaganda machine and had tried to strengthen its roots, calling a Congress of Cossack provinces and drafting a decree on the organisation of Soviet power in the Cossack areas which had been confirmed on 1st June 1918.[55] Delegates from Cossack provinces had attended the 5th All-Russian Congress of Soviets, but the Red Cossacks never succeeded in creating a united Bolshevik Cossack movement with authority in the provinces and influence in Moscow. The status and titles of the Cossacks operating at VTsIK was repeatedly changed, but the government still proclaimed reforms affecting Cossacks without taking their views into account, even though a leading Bolshevik like Sverdlov could admit that 'local Soviet authorities in Cossack provinces often permitted mistakes' which now ought to be put right.

The old Cossack Committee had become the Cossack Department of VTsIK, but its chief function was to influence Cossacks at home rather than the government in Moscow. It had trained agitators and sent them out to the Don, Kuban, Terek, Orenburg, Ural and Astrakhan, and its journal, now entitled *The Call of Working Cossacks*, had issued a stream of effective propaganda throughout the summer of 1918. There were cartoons of Krasnov asking the Allies to protect his 'yellow bourgeois dictatorship' against the Red poor, and articles, some of them powerful in their appeal, by Cossacks themselves. 'Having torn up my roots from "The Quiet Don" ', wrote one, 'I think now of my brother Cossacks . . . deceived by the . . . traitorous generals and officers.' The idea of autonomy was merely a blind; Russia must be the market for the Cossacks' produce. But once they turned to the Bolsheviks, they would enjoy a golden age. There would be no more merchants on the Don. *Stanitsas* would sell their agricultural surplus to the cities at fair prices on a co-operative basis and the old sense of freedom and brotherhood would return.[56] The Tsarist generals and the gnomes of international finance were conning the Cossacks into fighting against their own interests, went the central government's message. 'Come to your senses!' it went on. 'Turn the guns, bayonets and machine-guns against the crafty generals and the landlords. Destroy them.'

The 'working Cossacks', an uncertain, undefined quantity, were portrayed as an overwhelming force held in check only by the whips of White officers. But there were admissions, at least by implication, that the majority of Cossacks failed to appreciate the new 'liberating ideas'. In attempting to overcome their ignorance, use was made of Cossack traditions as well as of Marxist values. Bolsheviks were not all ruffians from Moscow and Petrograd, they claimed. They included peasants, too, and Cossacks like them. 'We live in Moscow in the ancient Kremlin and no one encroaches on our freedom.' They still wore their old, proud uniforms and went to church 'and no one says we mustn't'. In fact, so they claimed, they, the Bolsheviks were the real successors in Cossack traditions, not the neo-Tsarist Atamans like Krasnov and Dutov. Cossacks should remember Pugachev and 'the testament of Stenka Razin . . . enemy of Boyars, Tsars and landowners'.[57] They must not retreat into a neutral corner, at a time of world revolution. 'Cossacks of the Don and the Kuban! Wake up!' they cried. 'Surely the thunder of world revolution has stirred your drowsy spirit?' Cossacks must unite, show that 'the blood of Stenka Razin still flows in our veins'.[58]

Such arguments and harangues had affected about half of the Don Cossack Army and had helped to bring the Bolshevik victories of the winter of 1918. Nearly a third went over to the Reds and over a quarter had had to be regrouped because of their unreliability. But the Civil War continued. Krasnov's successor, Afrikan Bogayevski, fell in even closer with Denikin, commander of the White Army in the south, who though fighting a cause that was not the Cossacks' own, succeeded in stabilising the front, partly by bolstering the Cossacks by White cadres and by putting non-Cossack officers of the old Imperial Army in charge of them. As Denikin advanced in a line from Tsaritsyn to Kiev, Kolchak's army, 125,000 strong, had swept on to Perm, Orenburg and Ufa, and with the prospect of the two anti-Bolshevik forces linking up, Denikin recognised Kolchak as 'Supreme Ruler'.

The Bolsheviks were driven from the Urals and defeated on the Terek, but all was not well within the anti-Bolshevik camp. Cossack democrats and White generals never ran happily in harness; dissent was echoed in the army which though predominantly Cossack was controlled by the Whites; and, in addition, friction between the Don, Kuban and Terek administrations, the erection of customs barriers and the imposition of trade exchange regulations between the territories of the allied blocs, hindered the alleviation of a dire economic situation. The Don and Terek Governments did not finally agree the terms of Denikin's supreme command over their armies until 1920 and by then the Kuban was trying to extricate itself from his grip. In June 1919 the President of the Kuban Rada was murdered, possibly with the connivance of extremist White officers. In Denikin's own view Yekaterinodar became the centre of 'the most pernicious propaganda' which lowered morale and led to desertion;[59] Kuban Cossacks, who in the summer of 1919 formed a considerable proportion of Denikin's army, accounted for only fifteen per cent by the autumn, and in November 1919 White troops invaded the Rada building and carried off a dozen 'rabid extremists'.[60]

By then the writing was already on the wall. In June 1919 Dutov's front in the Urals had collaped. Kolchak was forced into retreat. Within four months Irkutsk had fallen and Kolchak, having resigned the supreme leadership in favour of Denikin, was taken prisoner. The fighting was to drag on in the Far East until the autumn of 1922 but the bulk of the Red Army was able to swing south against the Don Cossacks and the Ukraine.

Denikin's offensive had emphasised the need for the Bolsheviks to make their programme more attractive, and together with Kalinin, Makarov, the Commissar for Cossack Affairs, and Stepanov, now head of the Cossack Department, Lenin signed a proclamation addressed to all Cossacks. The government, it claimed, was 'not against the Cossack way of life' and would not 'de-Cossackise' anyone by force. Working Cossacks would keep their farms and the right to wear their uniforms. The Soviet government wanted to ensure that 'each Cossack and peasant should have enough cattle or horses to plough the fields'.[61] And, pressed by the Cossack Department which wanted firm revolutionary policy tempered by a consideration for the 'middling', the more prosperous, though not the rich, sections of Cossacks,[62] these were to be allowed to employ up to ten hired workers and to sell their products on the open market. 'The desecration of churches' and insults to religious observance would be strictly forbidden, and something akin to amnesty would be offered. Cossacks had risen against the workers and peasants but only because dispossessed landowners, industrialists, and Tsarist generals, 'artful foxes' and 'cunning swindlers ... anxious to restore their former life of ease and idleness' had incited them with lies. 'We know . . . that many of you are betrayed by ignorance of what is going on around you. The man who is oppressed or betrayed is not guilty.' Cossacks who would come over to the Red Army would therefore 'be welcomed as brothers who have seen the light'. 'Tens of thousands' of Cossacks had already joined the Reds, but more must follow, join in the struggle against the landlords, merchants, usurers, kulaks and village money-lenders of all countries who had 'fallen in love with the Cossack regions' and were 'trying to turn the free Cossacks ... into police oppressors' once again. Cossacks must stop destroying each other for their sake. Denikin's cause was hopeless. British and French money could not save it any more than German money had saved Krasnov. They must end the conflict and heal the wounds of war, 'come over to the side of the Red Cossacks. '. . . Come into our family'.[63]

The message was taken by agitators to Cossack prisoners and into the Cossack provinces. Between January and October 1919 the Cossack Department sent out 442 men in to the Don, Orenburg, the Urals, Astrakhan, Siberia and elsewhere, and distributed millions of propaganda leaflets and news-sheets.[64] It was the call for peace that was to tell above all else. This, and the massive strength of the new Red Army, guided by the energetic Trotski and welded by the fervour of political commissars, that was to turn a series of brilliant White successes in the south to ashes within weeks.

In June 1919 Denikin had taken Tsaritsyn. Mamontov's Don Cossack raiders tore deep into the Bolshevik rear, and in October Denikin took Orel. This was the watershed. The Reds re-took Orel within a week and began an offensive, which, gaining momentum, swept the Whites out of Rostov in January and out of Yekaterinodar in March.

Huge crowds of refugees, frightened by Red bayonets and scourged by typhus, filled the dirt roads leading towards the port of Novorossiisk and into the Crimea. The new Kuban Ataman, General Bukretov, tried to regain control over the Kuban Cossacks in the White Army, and to dissociate the Cossacks from Denikin's fight for an anti-Communist Russia, but in vain. Denikin refused to the last to submit to Cossack control. 'The Volunteer Army and its Commander-in-Chief', he said, 'serve Russia and not the Supreme Krug.'[65] But with the Reds bearing down and typhus raging the prospects were hopeless. Denikin resigned.

In February 1920 General Vrangel took over, re-formed the disorganised remnants of the White Army and in June sent it northwards from the Crimea. It was the death spasm of a doomed cause. By November they had fallen back again, and those who could piled hastily on to ships to carry them into exile.

At the last, discipline had crumbled away and the White Cossacks had become a robber army. The crumbling of beliefs long held, the uncertain, ever-changing government, and the horrors of civil war had encouraged a recrudescence in all the Russian borderlands of the more ancient anarchic Cossack spirit. In 1919 'ataman' Grigoriev, a Ukrainian in command of Soviet troops, had issued an anti-Bolshevik manifesto, carried out a pogrom, and threatened to flay the Bolshevik governor of Odessa alive. The renegade was gunned down—not by the Reds, but by anarchists fighting under the 'green' banner of Makhno whose private army of Red and White deserters rampaged through the Ukraine like *gaidamaks* 150 years before. Men had changed sides again and again. A Cossack officer called Sorokin joined the Reds who eventually outlawed him for shooting Jews who were prominent local Party men. He was caught at Stavropol and shot. So was another Red Cossack brigand with a contempt for commissars, Ivan Kochubei. Captured by the

Cossack platoon in Kudrinskaya Square, Moscow, during the December, 1905, armed uprising

Cossacks swimming their horses across a river, 1914

Cossack detachments in Palace Square, Petrograd, 1917

White Cossack commander, General Shkuro, he was bribed to turn anti-Bolshevik. And yet another Red Cossack commander, Dumenko, was executed by the Cheka for shooting a colonel who dared protest against his pillaging of Rostov.

Neither White leaders nor Red ever quite trusted their Cossacks. In the summer of 1919 Trotski inspected the new Cossack corps of the Red Army, made up of Cossacks and peasants of the Don and Kuban. He judged its leader, a mustachioed, ex-sergeant-major called Budenny, to be 'the Stenka Razin of today'. But he was none too sure of his reliability. 'Where he leads his gang', he wrote, 'there will they go; for the Reds today, tomorrow for the Whites.'[66]

Nevertheless the recruitment of Cossacks to serve in and train the Red Cavalry went on apace. Horsemen trained on the Cossack model were needed for their mobile war over the steppe-lands, and the word Cossack had considerable appeal in some non-Cossack regions, notably in the Ukraine, where people looked back as to an ideal age to the time, centuries before, when the Ukraine had been Cossack itself. Thus a Red Ukrainian cavalry division was named the 1st Zaporozhian Cavalry Division, and when Ukrainian nationalists formed a 'Vilne Kozatstvo', or 'free Cossacks', the Reds countered with a 'Chervone Kozatstvo' whose units became breeding grounds for future Soviet generals.[67]

Then, with the civil war drawing to a close Cossacks were exhorted to take horse and fight the Poles 'for the independence of the Soviet republic'.[68] And thousands did take to horse again to fight under the red banner. Isaac Babel has described some of them—Kuban Cossacks he served with in the Polish campaign. Rough, ruthless, ignorant, and tragic, they looted their way across the countryside while their Commissars preached about elections. These were men without a cause, caught up by forces they could not understand. For them the struggle between Red and White was often comprehended only in terms of internal family feud. The murder of a Red brother by a White father could lead the surviving son to commit parricide in vengeance for it. Their legion prejudices were tolerated for the moment. But when the time came, Bolshevik rule would 'rub them down with a brush of iron'.[69]

L

Towards the end of 1919 the 7th All-Russian Congress of Soviets admitted that 'working Cossacks' had been 'misused' by 'unworthy representatives' of Bolshevik authority, whom the Soviet Government had punished 'without mercy' and would 'continue to do so'.[70] The promise was also made that Cossacks would not be forced into communes. And in recognition of the Cossacks' role in Russia's revolutionary past, Lenin himself unveiled a memorial to Stenka Razin in Moscow.

But when in February 1920, with victory in sight, he came to address nearly 500 delegates to the 1st All-Russian Congress of Working Cossacks in Moscow, his emphasis was against any idea of Cossack separateness. The Congress decided that the Cossacks were not a distinct national group but an indissoluble part of the Russian people, that 'any attempt to tear the Cossacks away from . . . the Russian working people', was hostile to the interests of working Cossacks.[71] Lenin himself hardly mentioned the Cossacks at all. 'You know what this victory cost us' he told the delegates. Workers in the north had gone hungry when they were cut off from the Cossack grain regions, and people were still starving in Moscow because 'they can't bring up the grain'. The civil war had ruined the transport system, destroyed bridges, steamships and locomotives, and there were no means of rebuilding them quickly. Worse, there was nothing but worthless paper rubles to exchange for grain. But the towns had to live. Since all the starving workers could not buy food, Cossacks and peasants must 'lend' it, against the states promises to supply electricity and other services to the regions some time in the future.[72] The speech rightly warned of the miseries ahead.

The war was over, but the homecomings were far from happy. Poor Cossacks might expect a little more land, most of average resources might expect to hold their shares, but the streaming banners, and the machine-guns treacherously hidden in innocent-looking hay-carts of hay, had crossed the countryside too often. Houses were empty, barns burned down, and fields had run to seed. The Cossack provinces were in ruins.

In terms of lives the effect had been horrific. Between 1914 and 1920 the population of the southern Cossack provinces fell by over a quarter, and the losses were greatest among the young. A generation before the young men had outnumbered the young women. Now there were only four men to every seven girls between the ages of seventeen and twenty-four.[73]

The survivors, even if they could grow more than enough to feed themselves, could do little with the surplus. There was almost nothing to buy—no soap, sugar, paraffin or matches, and worst of all, no salt. Carts creaked for lack of grease and men who wanted the consolation of a cigarette wrapped shreds of home-grown tobacco in strips of paper torn from books and propaganda leaflets.

Cossacks were now put on a par with the despised 'outsiders', the Don and Kuban merged into a commonplace 'North Caucasus Region', but Cossacks cared less about the loss of caste than the difficulties of scraping a bare living, the danger of losing any hard-earned store to the grain-requisitioning squads organised in the autumn of 1920, or their freedom to the pink-capped Cheka men who came searching for anti-revolutionaries.

Peace had not come yet. The grain collections sparked off several local risings and groups of brigands still pillaged their way across the steppes. These were fugitives from the new justice, men who had lost their homes and families, men who after six anarchic years had forgotten how to live at peace. And the spectre of the past haunted every village as neighbours who had worn the Red favour and the White tried to live side by side again. 'If we're going to remember everything', says a character in Sholokhov's epic, 'we'll have to live like wolves',[74] but it was not easy to forget. . . .

Thousands had emigrated, as Cossacks had done after the failure of previous revolts. The chief embarkation had taken place in early 1920 at Novorossiisk. Cossacks of the White Army gathered on the quayside there sang the old songs of freedom and comradeship, about Yermak setting sail. 'All the Don, the Terek, the Yaik Cossacks were there, brothers!' But this time there were not ships enough to carry all of them away, and, when the last had gone, most of those left behind tramped south to Georgia whence they were taken to the Crimea. But after their brief campaign under Vrangel most of these Cossack soldiers, fighting in the White cause to the end, were carried off across the Black Sea to Turkey. From there, carrying tiny bags of Cossack earth round their necks to be buried with should they

311

never see their beloved land again, they began to spread out over the world in search of homes and livelihoods. It was a new Diaspora. In the words of one of Sholokhov's characters, Cossacks were 'like the Jews now—scattered over the face of the earth'.[75]

'And our land is sown with Cossack heads,
Our quiet Don is fair with young widows,
Our father, the quiet Don, blossoms with orphans
And the waves of the quiet Don are full
Of parents' tears. . . .'

'Far away my brave eagles have flown,
My eagles the Cossacks of the Don . . .'.

—Old Cossack songs

11 The end of Cossackdom

History has its ghosts, and in Turkey the Cossack émigrés met just such a haunting survival from their forgotten past. Near Istanbul they encountered a strange little community of fisher-folk and farmers who spoke Turkish but sang ancient Cossack songs, dressed in the Cossack style of two centuries before, had a leader called an ataman and priests who practised the old Russian rites. They were the descendants of the Nekrasovites, rebels of another age, against another centralist regime, who had fled from Tsarist oppression after the failure of Bulavin's revolt in 1708.* With the miseries of exile ingrained into them over generations, they told the newcomers of their sufferings in captivity. The Nekrasovites were a living warning. But the Cossack emigrants, 50,000 strong, did not expect to stay in exile long. They considered their crushing defeat to be only a

* See Chapter 6.

313

temporary reverse and fully expected that, with British and French help, they would soon return and drive the Bolsheviks out of their homelands for good. Their Atamans still held court, military discipline was more or less maintained; they were confident enough. But as the weeks dragged on and gathered into months, their hopes, too, were gradually to recede.

They lived in miserable conditions. The Cossack soldiers and the handful of women and children who had left the Crimea in November 1920 were lodged in military camps at Çatalça, west of Istanbul, and on the island of Lemnos. The roofs of the flea-ridden barracks at Çatalça leaked and the floors were thick with filth. There were no beds, no washing facilities, and those not lucky enough to find a place in barracks had to live in fox-holes torn into the cold earth.

A few found jobs with the French and British armies of occupation but most, having sold off their few possessions, were dependent on the barely adequate rations of bread, biscuit, beans and bully beef provided by the French. Many of these cold, half-starving Cossacks were tempted to join the Foreign Legion; others decided to break camp and make for the Balkans, and in February 1921, 2,500 boarded ship to return to the USSR. In March, the remaining 5,000 were moved to join nearly 2,000 Don and some 16,000 Kuban Cossacks on Lemnos where conditions seemed rather better, where there were even beds and blankets. But the new arrivals were crowded into tents, and the rations were poor again and sometimes underissued. As an epidemic of fleck typhus spread and the underoccupied, frustrated, miserable Cossacks brawled viciously among themselves, Lemnos came to be known locally as 'the island of death'.

The French soon lost interest in supporting a White invasion of Soviet Russia and in March 1921 they announced that they would stop supporting the Cossack army. As the rations were cut down the refugees were faced with a choice of returning to the USSR, of emigrating to Brazil where some doors were opened to them, or of fending for themselves as stateless persons in some other part of an unfamiliar world. The commander of the Don Corps tried in vain to keep his men together; the army was disintegrating day by day and by the autumn it no longer existed. About a third of the Cossacks had returned to Russia, 3,000 had joined the French Foreign Legion, and nearly 1,000 had boarded ship for Brazil. A handful found work locally, helping to build the Allied war cemetries on Gallipoli; and most of the rest headed west into Bulgaria, Yugoslavia and Czechoslovakia.[1]

Strenuous efforts were made to bind the scattered Cossack refugees together, to preserve their sense of community. The Kuban Cossacks had elected a new Ataman, General I. G. Naumenko; a 'United Council of the Don and Kuban and Terek' headed by Ataman Bogayevski Don had been formed in Constantinople,[2] an all-Cossack Congress was held at Plovdiv early in 1922, and a Cossack centre was set up in Prague, where liberal intellectuals like Shcherbina had settled. But, for the most part, mutual aid, and social and cultural activities now took precedence over political aims. Officers in Yugoslavia formed a bureau which hired out Cossacks as lumbermen, building labourers and roadmen. The men wore uniform and decorations, which preserved their identity as a group and proclaimed their generals' intention of one day winning back the homeland. But the old military leaders were becoming discredited, the grip of discipline and ideology was slackening. An attempt to recreate the old way of life in Bulgaria by founding *stanitsas* failed, and more and more ordinary Cossacks began to seek their own salvation in a world becoming daily less strange, or else, unable to bear the separation from their homes and families, made their peace with Soviet Russia and returned.

The Soviet Government, like its predecessors, was anxious enough to have the émigrés back. It promised them amnesty, laid on ships, and in 1922, opened repatriation offices in Prague and Sofia to facilitate their return. Thousands took advantage of this help, and 'bowed their heads before the Soviet government' as their ancestors had done to the Tsars in centuries past. Their recantations were often made public. One wrote a book recounting the Cossacks' bitter experiences abroad, and others wrote to newspapers explaining that they had only gone abroad 'under pressure of the White generals', and, once away, had realised that the Soviet regime was Russia's only lawful government, that Russia was 'the house without which we cannot live'.[3]

But thousands were never to return. Alone or in groups they found their way ever farther afield—to Paris and to Tunis, to Egypt, England and America, while many from the Siberian communities escaped to Harbin and subsequently moved on to Shanghai and other cities all over the Far East. Adjustment was difficult. Many of them arrived destitute, most knew no language but Russian, and some were so demoralised as to become incapable of making any adjustment at all. There were officers who behaved as arrogantly as if they were still in Tsarist Russia. When Egyptians came to barter food with hungry Don Cossack cadets camped beside the Nile, their commanding officer had them beaten up and their wares confiscated, at which the British authorities raised their eyebrows, and though Don Cossack Life Guards serving as porters at the Gare du Nord in Paris worked together as a team, officers and men, at the end of the day they marched off in imperial style to their separate 'messes'.

In Paris, beggar knights of the Cossack exile became night-club doorkeepers and washers-up. Others, with a little capital, set up as taxi-drivers. It was easier for the members of the splendid Cossack choirs and the circus troupes of dare-devil riders which toured Europe between the wars to adjust. These lived by familiar skills and carried the warmth of their homeland around with them. But it was hard for the rest. These were farming people who needed the spacious steppes to hold them. Yet even when land was found on which they could start some cooperative farming venture, the Cossacks rarely settled down.

Towards the end of the twenties the Peruvian Government offered to pay the fares of 500 Cossack families and to settle them on the Apurimak river, where each family would be allotted seventy-five acres, each single man twenty-five. They were to receive a government subsidy for the first six months, repayable at the moderate rate of ten per cent of the harvest value. But transplantation to this distant shore did not succeed. From the start there was bickering among the organisers—a common enough feature at a time, when too many people, used to power, had time on their hands and only petty affairs to meddle in—and though by August 1929, General Pavlichenko had organised two settlements at Tambo and Montagna, the Cossacks at Tambo refused to work and began to drink heavily.

(*above*) Podtelkov, 'Red' Cossack leader, (*below*) Krasnov, 'White' Cossack leader

Djigitovka—a Cossack performing in London, 1938

Soon most of them moved to Montagna, and Pavlichenko, losing interest, organised a troupe of expert riders and took it off with him on a tour of South America.

Those who remained showed no inclination to exploit their opportunity. They cleared no land and built no houses. Some drifted away, some began reluctantly to use the tools with which they had been provided. But most of the Cossacks of Peru rejected the role of pioneer farmers, and reverted to an earlier Cossack pattern. Early in 1930 local newspapers reported that the remaining families at Montagna preferred to live on their government subsidies rather than work, and that they spent their days roaming about brandishing revolvers, terrorising the local Indians and chasing their wives.[4]

Another reversion to an ancient pattern of Cossack life was to be seen among some Transbaikal Cossacks who fled across the river into Mongolia, where they hunted in the wooded highlands for squirrels and wapiti. They lived on friendly terms with the local Tungus tribesmen, each of whom recognised a Cossack as his protector. The system by which a Tungus would sell his furs to his Cossack and no one else recalled the old Tatar tribute system, and there were vestiges of primitive Cossack communism as well, for the Cossacks would hunt in groups, sharing the proceeds of their catch among themselves like Siberian Cossacks three centuries before.[5]

Besides the refugees abroad, there were Cossacks who had become strangers in their own land—men like Gregor Melekhov in *Quiet Flows the Don*, who wanted peace but, branded as a counter-revolutionary, turned outlaw. Like Pugachev, Cossacks like Melekhov had nowhere to turn; they were forced in desperation onto a path of violence. Unable or unwilling to emigrate, afraid to go home for fear of being caught and shot by the Cheka, they joined one of the gangs of bandit fugitives.

These gangs comprised the jetsam of the Revolution and of the wars which followed them. There were Ukrainians and Latvians, anarchists and deserters, as well as Cossacks among them, and together, they brought back something of the old Tatar terror to the Russian borderlands, riding in groups of half a hundred men, like Tatar Cossacks five centuries before, stealing, ambushing, killing and being killed. They robbed

L*

banks, held up transports, waylaid grain collection detachments and conducted a sporadic guerrilla war against the Cheka and the Red Cavalry. Without political aim, and rarely with an objective apart from surviving till the morrow, they sometimes attracted sympathy and support from villagers disenchanted with Soviet rule. In the Kuban especially, groups of renegades managed to hold out for months and years, based in the impenetrable mountains of the Caucasus and in the rolling expanses of the Salsk steppe. But in the last resort they had no future but the grave.

Among the more notorious bandit leaders in the Kuban of the early twenties were Dunko and Vasyuk, two Cossacks who broke out of gaol and carried on a private war with the Bolshevik security forces. Dunko was finally trapped, but true to the spirit of his Zaporozhian ancestors, he held off the forces of order for hours with a Lewis gun and grenades, and when his ammunition at last ran out he killed his wife and then committed suicide. But Vasyuk remained at large. In vain the authorities demanded his surrender. During the winter of 1923, relatives and fellow-villagers of wanted men were sent into the steppes, the forests and the mountains to beg them to surrender. Many responded, but not Vasyuk. Then in 1924 he was shot down in an ambush. His funeral attracted a crowd of a thousand people, as that of his Sicilian counterpart Giuliano was to do. But this time the occasion did not pass without a demonstration by his surviving comrades. Suddenly, in a flurry of dust, twenty-five horsemen broke into the cemetery, scattering the crowd before them. They fired three volleys over the grave in a last salute, then galloped off again as suddenly as they had come.[6]

Since the bandits plundered farms where they were not willingly given food, and since their presence in an area brought local Cossacks under suspicion, the villages began to turn against them. They were exhausted. By now they wanted peace at any price, and, gradually, peace did come to the Cossack lands again. But, like the émigrés, the Cossacks still at home had to make large adjustments, learning how to live within the framework of a new social and economic order.

The Cossacks were a separate caste no longer. There were no more atamans, no distinct Cossack regiments, no separate province in which their demands were given preference over those of the peasants. All this was disturbing. So were the efforts made by the Soviet authorities to introduce equality of the sexes, to bring women into local affairs, hitherto strictly the province of the Cossack male. And more disturbing still was the Soviet insistence on classifying the Cossacks according to the Leninist class typology for peasants. Cossacks were categorised into three grades—poor farmers, who were to receive government approval and support; Cossacks of middling prosperity, who were to be attracted to the new regime; and the rich, the *kulaks*, who were branded as potential, if not actual, counter-revolutionaries, and hounded accordingly. Cossacks protested about this attempt to split Cossack from Cossack, to disrupt their sense of brotherhood, and at the way the lines were drawn. Some villages refused outright to accept the introduction of class struggle campaigns, claiming that they were all equal. Soviet authorities on the Don reported that 'Comrades from Ust-Medveditsa declared repeatedly that in their districts there were neither *kulaks* nor poor, and we have heard such declarations from other districts'.[7] But the ideologists were adamant. There must be differences, they insisted; and against considerable opposition they succeeded in forcing their opinions home. The exacerbation of class resentments, the call for 'decisive struggle with the *kulaks*' put out in the spring of 1921[8] produced more fear and turmoil. And yet Cossacks had plenty else to worry about.

By 1921 the broad steppes of the Don and Kuban were in a state of ruin. On the Don, less than half the area cultivated in 1916 was under seed in 1920; there were only half the number of horses and pigs there had been in 1917 and two-thirds the number of cattle. Factories were in a shambles, mines were flooded, and the metallurgical works at Rostov had ground to a halt for lack of raw materials. A typical Kuban *stanitsa* had lost the best of its cattle, tools and equipment. The land, worn out by repeated cereal growing over the years, was now seriously undercultivated, and the consequent famine reduced four households out of five almost to destitution by 1923.[9] Yet the government looked to the grain producing areas, of which the Cossack provinces were among the most important, to feed the starving towns. Any programme of industrial development, of a great leap forward, depended on it. But in July 1921 the Regional

Economic Council of south-east Russia announced that the Cossack areas of the northern Caucasus, expected to supply nearly thirty per cent of all the grain needed, had provided only four million out of a scheduled nineteen and a quarter million tons.[10] Seed corn was scarce and poor in quality, so were the stocks of animals. Huge areas of hay were left 'unmown because of a lack of [working] cattle and because of the extreme exhaustion' of the population. But lack of labour and the drought that summer were not the only reasons for continuing failure. Fields left fallow reflected general doubts about the future. With the state offering only promissory notes and worthless currency in return for their grain, many Cossacks were not prepared to grow a surplus.

This was the vicious circle which the government was trying to break by sending grain collection detachments to scour the countryside and empty Cossack barns. But besides confiscating hidden surplus grain, they often took a family's subsistence for the year and its seed for the next. 1921 had ended with chaos, poverty, and an atmosphere of hopelessness. Officials reported in December that the decline in agriculture on the Don had 'assumed catastrophic proportions'. The area under cultivation was still half that of 1917, the number of horses was down by nearly two-thirds now and of oxen by a quarter.[11]

By dint of an extraordinary effort, of exhortations, promises and the use of draconian methods of enforcement the seven lean years were brought to an end. The harvest of 1922 was better, the cattle began to multiply again. By the close of that year the Don Soviets could report good progress towards economic recovery and the 'final destruction of banditry',[12] though a few small groups of desperadoes still lingered on. A major factor in the recovery was the government's new economical policy (N.E.P.) announced in the spring of 1921. In allowing farmers greater freedom of action, and opening up limited opportunities for private trading, it encouraged many a reluctant Cossack to sow more land and to bring out hidden grain. The markets began to thrive again on the Don, the Kuban, and in the east, where mustachioed Cossacks were now to be seen 'coining' money by selling horses and cattle they had driven into the bazaars of the Syr Darya.[13]

The outlook was improving but conditions were still hard. The Don was full of wandering orphans searching for some sheltering roof, and resentment against the new revolutionary values was running strong. A report from a Don district towards the end of 1922 claimed that although the poor were sympathetic to the Soviet cause, they were refusing to support the campaign against the *kulaks*.[14] Friction between Cossacks and 'outsiders' persisted, and it was an uphill struggle to attract Cossacks who enjoyed the confidence of their fellow villagers to play a part in local affairs.

The Cossacks in exile heard with ineffectual despair of the changes in their homeland. 'The Bolsheviks are trying to destroy Cossackdom by every means', wrote Naumenko, the Kuban Ataman in exile. Peasant outsiders were now privileged above the Cossacks. 'They have settled millions of non-Cossack population in the Cossack region', he claimed, and 'scattered the more active element among the Cossacks to remote parts of the state.'[15] Thousands had indeed been deported; there was widespread resentment among the remaining Cossacks, and with 'the fight for bread' reaching a climax, the Soviet authorities realised that sullen acceptance of the new order was not enough.

By the beginning of 1925 it was clear that new ways could be forced on the Cossacks only at the cost of imperilling the economic programme. Concessions must be made. A five-year programme to provide adequate plots of land for poorer Cossacks, as well as for peasants, was embarked on, and more generous agricultural credit was extended to the Cossack areas. It was decided to review the position of *stanitsa* atamans and of other elected local leaders, who had been deprived of their rights although they were apparently loyal to the regime. Efforts to attract more Cossacks into the Party were redoubled, and in January 1925 a limited amnesty was proclaimed. These measures had a measure of success. A report on one Don district in 1925 noted that though there was 'a certain amount of dissatisfaction' among the richer Cossacks because of the weight of the agricultural taxes', the mood of the majority showed 'a considerable improvement by comparison with . . . the end of 1924'.[16]

'The final . . . destruction of the land privileges of the Cossacks as a special class'[17] was still the aim, but the government now appreciated that a high proportion even of the poorer Cossacks had been alienated quite unnecessarily by officials, who tended to treat all Cossacks as enemies of the people. In August 1925 the North Caucasus Executive Committee exhorted local functionaries to rid themselves of their 'negative' attitude to Cossacks, to distinguish between those who deserved 'support and encouragement' and those who did not. Cossacks, it maintained, should be treated no worse than peasants and tribesmen and must be persuaded that Soviet Russia did not seek their destruction as such. Cossacks should be allowed to wear traditional dress, sing their own songs, throw parties, and be encouraged to join the army.[18] In other words, the Cossacks were to enjoy no special privileges, but the bullying was to stop.

The point was rammed home by Mikoyan who freely admitted that the civil war had 'set the peasant on the Cossack's neck. Beforehand it was the other way round. But now . . . there ought to be equal rights'. If the Cossack was to take an active part in Soviet life and Party work, the Party and the authorities must go halfway to meet him. 'It is wrong that the Cossack way of life has been cramped', said Mikoyan. Some features of it, like the Cossacks' love for the horse and *djigitovka*, should be encouraged, and the idea that a Cossack hat 'defines a counter-revolutionary' be scotched once and for all. Landholdings must be reorganised, but ordinary Cossacks should be assured that their land would 'not be taken away from them'.[19]

As a special sign of favour, Stalin and other leaders were proclaimed 'honorary Cossacks'. But the more liberal policy directives evidenced by Mikoyan were not always heeded by local officials. A Western journalist visiting the Kuban in 1926 saw few signs of Cossack life.[20] Some wore the traditional fur hats, but the wearing of Cossack uniform was banned; only those who had served with the Reds in Civil War were allowed to join the army, and the older people appeared sullen, aggrieved at being reduced to the status of mere *muzhiks*. Yet there were streaks of light amid the gloom. The churches were open, the old holidays were observed, and there were nights when the strains of Cossack song, the sound of Cossack balalaikas and the roar of Cossack laughter would drift out on to the village streets. There was still a lingering sense of insecurity, still the fear of persecution but the life was better than it had been. Incomes were rising, even taxes felt more bearable, and as the memory of the famine years receded a normality returned, and people could be gay again.[21] But not for long.

The 15th Party Congress called for mass collectivisation. At the end of 1929 it was confirmed that collectivisation on the Don and Kuban would be carried out within a year.[22] Stalin called for the destruction of the *kulaks* 'as a class', and the crunch had really come.

In order to provide for the landless and the marginal farmer, collective farms had been introduced into Cossack regions as early as 1920, but hardly more than five per cent of the farmers had entered them by the summer of 1928, and most of them had entered voluntarily, having no agricultural equipment or draught cattle to work the land by themselves. Now, however, collectivisation was to be compulsory. In the Urals and Siberia it would cover only fifty per cent of farms but on the Don and Kuban it would be virtually complete, for everyone.[23]

Collectivisation on this scale was not only a way of solving the problems of the agrarian poor, of those who, if they did not lack land, lacked the wherewithal to use it. It was a means of applying the techniques of industry to agriculture, of rationalising the food-producing system, of introducing a large-field system, of allowing the economic use of farm machinery, especially of tractors and other heavy equipment now being turned out of the factories. And collectivisation was also a way of creating equality between members of the rural communities, of eliminating the *kulak*.

The *kulaks*, branded enemies of Bolshevism but temporarily reprieved by N.E.P., were already in decline. Between 1927 and 1929 as a result of a campaign mounted against them, the proportion of *kulaks* using hired labour for more than fifty days a year dropped from sixty to ten per cent.[24] But the state was now determined not only to eliminate the *kulak* but to destroy the would-be *kulak*, and the *kulak* mentality.

All-out collectivisation aroused furious resentment, and not only from the more prosperous Cossacks. The efficient farmer felt, and sometimes with reason, that he would be exploited to the benefit of the inefficient and the lazy. Men were reluctant to surrender the few comforts earned by their own hard labour at, as it seemed to them, the capricious, if not malicious, behest of a distant authority. As 25,000 Communist agitators recruited from the factories poured into the countryside fears grew that collectivisation would make women communal property, and turn Cossacks and peasants into serfs, not of the landowning aristocracy this time, but of the state, and of the towns from which the state drew its chief support.

The Cossacks suffered most from the new campaign and the *kulaks* among them most of all. These were evicted from their farms together with their families often at only a few hours notice and were searched before leaving to ensure they were taking nothing valuable away. Not infrequently even modest farmers, including Bolshevik Cossacks who had prospered, were categorised as *kulaks*, and anyone who resisted or refused to join a collective was arrested and sent to labour camps and mines as an 'enemy of the people'.

The rough and sudden implementation of the new policy produced such confusion that by the middle of February 1930, barely a month after the start of the campaign on the Don, the Party Central Committee was forced into rushed steps to restore some degree of order and public confidence. Early in March, Stalin's article 'Dizzy from Success' spelt out justified criticisms of the speed and methods with which collectivisation was being carried out, though blame was reserved solely for the local leadership.[25] Some Party members were expelled for forcing collectivisation at gun-point, or for treating middling peasants as *kulaks*. Others who did such things went off scot-free.

In effect, Stalin's article created even more confusion, subject as it was to various, often contradictory, interpretations. Rumours now spread about that the collective farms were to be broken up. As a result, there was a sudden spate of resignations from the collectives and quarrels ensued about what tools and livestock people could take away with them. Directive followed directive in an attempt to clarify the policy and at last collectivisation was pressed forward at full spate again. By August 1930 the Northern Caucasus collectives had swallowed nearly ninety per cent of all the farms in the area and ninety-four per cent of the arable land. But the cost was heavy.

Some Cossacks tried to run away as their peasant ancestors had flitted centuries before, and a more sinister form of resistance developed. Farmers began to slaughter their livestock rather than let it pass into collective ownership. In June, in central Russia alone, four million horses and three million cows were destroyed and the losses were greatest in the Cossack country. Meat, milk, and working animals collapsed under the knife, and Cossacks indulged themselves in one last and desperate orgy of meat-eating. All over the south lands, men, women and children crammed their stomachs full of flesh and took sick from the surfeit. It was a manifestation of fear, of ignorance, of greed; it was an act of passive resistance, a 'scorched earth' tactic used against an enemy. And it was the destruction of the future, bringing hunger to the Cossack lands again.

There were outbreaks of more active opposition, too, centring chiefly around the *kulaks*. Weapons were dug up from hiding places, and the White activists in exile took hope once more. The bands of brigands increased again. But there was more than another bout of anarchistic lawlessness; there was armed rebellion. Cossacks of several Don stanitsas, armed with axes and pitchforks, rose up in protest, and as many as 45,000 Cossacks and tribesmen in the Caucasus area alone made a fight of it. They took several important towns, attacked an armoured train, fought a pitched battle with security forces near Mineralnyye Vody, and tanks, artillery and even aircraft had to be brought up to cope with them.

The troubles were continuous. The huge turnover in chairmen of collectives[26] was only one index of the pains created by the agrarian revolution. Between 1931 to 1933 there were risings on the Don, on the Terek, in Siberia and the Ukraine as well as on the Kuban. They were mercilessly crushed. As many as 15,000 insurgents were shot, and thousands more were condemned to labour camps. Entire villages were removed from the maps and thousands of politically reliable immigrants were brought in as settlers to the Cossack lands. More rebels took to the hills in Georgia and the deserts of Central Asia, and some of them lurked in the mountains until the Germans came in 1941.[27]

For all the suffering, much of it unnecessary, this was no pointless massacre such as the Germans were to perpetrate against the Jews. The decision to eliminate the *kulaks* may have been doctrinaire, but they did form the back-bone of opposition to the new order. And, if collectivisation was introduced too suddenly and with an unwarranted degree of force, it was seen as a means of solving Russia's age-long agrarian problem, of obtaining greater productivity at much less cost, and of ensuring that a growing number of city workers should never starve again. If many Bolsheviks hated Cossacks for their role under Tsarism and their, albeit fitful, support for the Whites, the Cossacks themselves were parochial, ignorant, and uncaring for the problems of others. The programme was rough, its implementation unnecessarily clumsy, but the flesh of ideology concealed a skeleton of practical sense. The degree of violence used may have been unnecessary on one side and futile on the other, but it reflected a genuine conflict between local wants and general needs, between individual interests and those of the community at large.

This was no consolation to the average Cossack. Alarmed by the sudden fall in grain production, in the autumn of 1932 Stalin had sent Kaganovich south to institute a purge. Party officials, local functionaries and ordinary collective farmers fell under his axe. Trading by the collectives were curtailed, credits and loans were called in. The populations of several Kuban villages were exiled to the arctic north, and fifteen black-listed stanitsas were cut off from all outside supplies.

The 'saboteurs' and 'wreckers' Stalin talked of did exist, but the repression was on an unwarrantedly massive scale. Kaganovich has been condemned by recent Soviet historians; even at the time men of unimpeachable Bolshevik loyalties dared to protest. In April 1933, Mikhail Sholokhov, a friend of Stalin's, drew his attention to the 'criminal actions' and 'scandalous activities' committed by officials on the Don, and asked for an inquiry into 'the tortures, the beatings, the massacres and outrages'. Stalin replied nonchalantly from his distant Kremlin, that there was another side of the story: that enemies were trying to sabotage Soviet power and must be crushed.[28] And the mass purge, the executions of collective farmers, instituted following Stalin's assertion that they harboured *kulaks*, went on till 1935.

The purge was accompanied by famine. As many as 50,000

died of starvation in the Kuban alone. On the Don in the early thirties hundreds fell dead of hunger and exhaustion in the streets of towns and villages. Homeless *kulaks*, waifs and orphans crouched in holes in the ground and waited to die. But the famine of 1932–3 was not quite as severe as that of 1921–2, and recovery was comparatively quick. In 1934 the Don was once again exporting grain to earn imports essential to the Russian economy, even though a hungry child risked severe punishment by filching a handful of it at the docks. By 1937 tractors were doing more than four-fifths of all the ploughing and sowing; harvest yields increased again, the cattle multiplied, and the income of collective farm members rose three-fold. After a quarter of a century, the harvest on the Don was said at last to have exceeded the volume produced on the eve of the First World War.[29]

But Cossackdom was dying. True, one or two new quasi-Cossack communities had been formed. In 1928 Skripnichenko, a demobilised Red Cossack officer, organised a 'Cossack' collective at Khlopivka in the Ukraine, and in 1929 these 'Cossacks' founded two communes, one of them near Lake Khanka in the Far East.[30] But the old institutional forms and the old culture were passing into limbo, as a group of obedient Cossacks suggested in a letter they addressed to Stalin in 1936. 'The old Don, the old Kuban, the old Terek exist no more', they wrote. 'The old, thrice-damned life of Cossacks, when working Cossacks were under the thumb of atamans, officers, and *kulaks* . . . is no more.

'Now there are new, Soviet, collectivised, happy Cossacks . . . who will not spare their lives for the works of Lenin and Stalin.' In fact, few groups in the Soviet Union were less content with the new life. But in suggesting that Cossack collective farmers were ready 'to stand shoulder to shoulder in the defence of our great homeland',[31] their statement of loyalty concealed a plea for recognition—recognition of their special status, their strong territorial attachments, their cultural singularities—recognition of those special qualities that identified them as that unique caste of men, the Cossacks, and which were now being threatened or destroyed. And, in fact, the publication of the letter heralded a relaxation in the official line towards the Cossacks.

With Nazi Germany on the march and the country seemingly

in danger, Russia needed its Cossacks again. In April 1936, in recognition of the 'devotion of the Cossacks to Soviet power', most 'limitations' on Cossack service in the Red Army were removed. Marshal Voroshilov ordered five cavalry divisions to be given Cossack names, and proclaimed recruitment for them open to men of the Don, Terek and Kuban.[32] Cossacks' uniforms were restored, and although the new divisions were not wholly Cossack in composition, since anyone living in the old Cossack provinces, peasants, factory workers, Armenians or Jews, might also wear the *cherkesska* and swing the sabre, morale among the Cossacks did improve. The same year Kuban and Don Cossack choirs performed at the Bolshoi. The trappings if not the substance of Cossack distinctiveness were to be preserved.

It was the émigrés, huddling together for shelter now in a cold non-Russian world, who saw themselves as the guardians of Cossack traditions now. They founded societies and published journals in which their heritage was recalled in poems, stories and extracts from unpublished novels.[33] They discussed their history and speculated on the possibilities of a political future for Cossackdom based on the old traditions. But there was no agreement among them on what these traditions really were.

Constitutional democrats like Yefremov emphasised the egalitarian element in Cossackdom. Historians like Svatikov and Shcherbina recalled the democracy of the *krug*, and the attempts to create independent liberal Cossack states after the Revolution. Others, influenced by the theories of Ukrainian nationalists, tried to demonstrate 'the different natures of the Cossack and the Russian . . . peoples', to show that free Cossackdom, or 'Cossackia', had always been 'separate' from Russia, and that the Don Cossacks were 'the youngest nation in Europe'.[34] While some looked back in pride to times when Cossacks had fought for equality and independence; others were still caught up in the toils of Tsarist mystique, and felt bound to apologise for Razin, Bulavin and Pugachev, and to boast that for the last 150 years and more Cossacks had 'served Russia with faith and truth'.[35] And it was such right-wingers, chiefly ex-generals, who retained leadership of the exiles, paraded at the Arc de Triomphe and laid wreaths on the tomb of the Unknown Warrior.

Caught up in the widespread mood of disillusionment with

democratic forms of government that swept through Europe in the period between the two world wars many right-wingers still looked to a Tsar as the only safeguard for Cossack interests and privileges, and deemed all political parties hostile to their interests.[36] But some of the exiles came to be reinforced in their prejudices and extreme right-wing beliefs by the popularity of certain myths current in Europe, and especially in Germany, at that time. The rabid Ivan Rodionov spewed forth torrents of venom against the Jews as the cause of their distress, claimed that only the Cossacks had saved Tsarist Russia from 'Jewish subjugation', and that they had been the first to fight 'bloody Jewish Bolshevism', which wanted to conquer the world.[37] This gospeller of hate found shelter in a Cossack nest formed by General Krasnov in Berlin. Both of them contributed to a monthly, which also enjoyed the recognition of the Metropolitan Yevlogy. The publication painted the old idealised picture of Cossacks as loyal 'frontier knights', and disseminated the mischievous lies of the Old Black Hundreds.

Krasnov himself had turned novelist and professed himself free of party ties. But he had not lost his taste for authoritarian politics. Moving to France he became adviser on Cossack affairs to the Grand Duke Nicholas, and as Hitler's anti-communist crusade developed, Krasnov's views seemed increasingly compatible with those of the Nazi leaders. He looked to be the man to lead the Cossacks home again, and exact due vengeance from the Bolsheviks.

But though the heart of many an exile leapt when the German tanks rolled into Russia in 1941, the invasion was to rally most Cossacks in Russia to the Soviet banner. Whatever their views of Stalin and of Communism, they were patriots still and had the Russians' fear, loathing and contempt for Germans above other foreigners.

The 100,000 Cossacks in the Red Army at the outbreak of the war were joined by a host of volunteers and conscripts. Even the politically unreliable were drafted into pioneer battalions. As in 1812, when Napoleon had invaded Russia, the Cossacks were called upon to fight rearguard actions, to cover another miserable retreat, and, once more in the limelight, they rose valiantly to their task. As the German armour crashed its path of ruin

329

towards the gates of Leningrad and Moscow, Cossacks under General Lev Dovator counter-attacked. With flowing capes and glinting sabres they galloped in among the German tanks and, true to their Don and Zaporozhian inheritance, they made several dashing, heart-lifting raids behind the German lines. They provided one of the few bright propaganda stories to raise Soviet morale amid the gloom. Once more, like Ataman Mezhakov in the Times of Troubles, Cossacks were riding to the rescue of the Russian state; once again, like Platov's men 130 years before, Cossacks became a symbol of resistance to foreign intervention.

Russians read of Dovator's heroism, of how Don Cossacks cast their capes like a black carpet over the ice near Rostov and rode across with muffled step to sabotage the German rear. Military journals published articles on how to fight Germans Cossack style[38] with feigned retreats and ambushes, or how to disrupt the enemy's communications; how to use cold steel, and play cat and mouse with enemy tanks. But theirs were largely propaganda victories. The Cossacks' heroism was undeniable, but a man on horseback stood little chance against a tank. In the words of Marshal Malinovski, the Cossack cavalry was 'very beautiful and picturesque, but pretty ineffective in this kind of war'.[39] This was a war of movement, unlike that of 1914–17, but the techniques of the *Blitzkrieg* were even less suitable to the Cossacks' method of waging war. They suffered appalling losses, and Dovator himself was killed before the end of 1941. Like their traditional social forms and their old economic arrangements, the Cossacks' traditional military skills were also out of date.

But, though not always on horseback, other Cossack units fought on with the same verve and as much distinction as Dovator's men, and they were rewarded in the old style. Several units were to be accorded the designation 'Guards' for outstanding services, and the fourth Guards Kuban Cavalry Corps was but one Cossack unit which gathered in all the highest Soviet awards for gallantry in the war.[40]

By the autumn of 1942 German forces had occupied a substantial area of the Don and Kuban and *Pravda* appealed to the 'Cossacks of the quiet Don, the swift Kuban and the stormy Terek' to 'rise up for a life and death struggle against the

German invaders!' Though Soviet officials feared the Crimean Tatar and some Caucasian tribesmen might join the enemy, they were more confident about the Cossacks. 'They have their grievances', one Western observer was told early in the war, 'but they are Russian. . . . Maybe a few will rat on us, but certainly not many.'[41] And on the whole the Cossacks at home responded well to the call. But some did 'rat'. Cossacks of at least one stanitsa rose up against the local Soviet authorities, and marched to join the advancing Germans. Cossack fugitives and some mountain tribesmen of the Caucasus greeted the invaders with open arms. On the Don, a Cossack called Sergei Pavlov established himself in the Ataman's Palace at Novocherkassk where he formed local collaborators into a police force. Towards the end of 1942 he presided over a krug attended by some 200 villagers and asked the Germans to sanction the formation of a Cossack army to fight the Bolsheviks.

His plan gained no immediate approval, but meanwhile a Cossack major called Kononov, a graduate of the Frunze Military Academy and a veteran of the Finnish war, had deserted with his regiment of riflemen, and had been allowed by the Germans to form a squadron of Cossack deserters and prisoners of war. The men and boys who joined him saw themselves conducting a crusade and took passionate oaths to this effect, vowing to clear 'the most evil enemy of mankind—Communism'[42] off Russian and off Cossack soil. Kononov's battalion exchanged raids with Soviet cavalry units, killing commissars and capturing 'tongues'. Kononov also conducted a front-line campaign with pamphlet and loud-hailer to tempt Soviet soldiers to desert and join him. His was much superior in quality to the crude German propaganda which threatened, vaunted German superiority, and so merely bolstered the Russian soldier in his patriotic determination. Kononov made brave promises to abolish collective farms and bring freedom of work, of property, of speech.[43] But his promises brought over only a few deserters.

Nevertheless there were many in the old Cossack regions who resented the campaigns of recent years against Cossack distinctiveness and the loss of their special Cossack status under Soviet rule. Hopes ran high among them that when the Germans

331

arrived they would immediately abolish the collective farms, and allow Cossacks to elect their own atamans again. Some hoped the Germans would grant them complete autonomy as in the days of old, and treat the Cossack soldiers who joined them equally, as allies. They were to be disappointed. German policy was ambivalent from the start. In April 1942 Hitler had personally sanctioned the formation of volunteer Cossack units, and several were soon formed, one of them named, somewhat ironically, after Count Platov. Then, in October 1942, General Wagner approved the establishment, under close supervision, of a small, self-governing Cossack district in the Kuban, where collectivisation was to be abolished. But the Cossack renegades who joined the Germans were to operate under German command and were mostly to be attached to German security divisions operating against the partisans. The enthusiasm of the Cossack deserter-volunteers was only grudgingly accepted, and Hitler's portrait was constantly thrust before them for adoration as their liberator. The army was glad enough of Cossack help but the SS would not entertain the idea of Cossack autonomy, and Rosenberg's *Ostministerium* thought that, since the Cossacks were Russians, they should be classed as *Untermenschen*.

Here Krasnov's long association with Hitler and the Nazi cause bore fruit. He supported a Cossack Nationalist Party formed in Prague, whose members recognised the Führer as 'supreme dictator of the Cossack Nation',[44] and installed at the head of it a 'central Cossack office' in Berlin, he laboured to counter the impression that Cossacks were mere Russians. In the end he persuaded the racial theorists that 'according to the latest research' Cossacks were the 'descendants of a mixture of Nordic and Dinaric races' and had 'thus preserved strong blood ties with their original German homeland'.

On the whole, the Nazis gained more enthusiastic support among the old guard of exiled Cossacks than among those still in the homeland, most of whom, whatever their views of Stalin, were alienated by German arrogance and the swingeing mass reprisals for Soviet partisan activity. The Don Guardsmen in Paris also refused to be recruited, but Generals Andrei Shkuro and V. Naumenko, now 'Ataman' of the Kuban, and other prominent White Cossack leaders from Paris, Belgrade, and

Berlin all massed under the Nazi banners, donated icons to the new Cossack units, and wrote in flattering terms to their commanders. Krasnov himself saw 'the sons of the quiet Don, the free Kuban, the stormy Terek', as rising up again 'to rescue . . . Cossack liberty', and gave the new movement his unqualified support.[45]

Yet the plans for the creation of a 'Greater Cossackia', a puppet state stretching from the central Ukraine to the river Samara, hung fire. It was decided to expand the small, experimental independent Cossack district already established on the Kuban, to abolish collectives and to recruit local Cossack volunteers. But before even these limited plans could be carried fully into effect the Germans were in retreat. Soviet forces, including Cossacks had triumphed at Stalingrad. The *Wehrmacht* pulled back from the Caucasus and the Kuban, and Cossacks who had collaborated, went with them. The roads filled up with refugees. Rebel Cossacks still sang the old host hymns, but the anti-Stalinist revolution they had expected had failed to materialise and their mirage of re-creating Cossack life was fading fast. But they had burned their boats. They could do nothing now but follow.

In February 1943 the Germans abandoned Novocherkassk. 'Ataman' Pavlov of the Don went with them and set up office at Krivoi Rog. A few weeks later he received permission to organise his own Cossack units. But recruits were scarcer than expected and many of the refugees from the Don, Kuban and Terek who were assembled in the south-east Ukraine that spring were so old or unfit that the Germans packed them off to work on local collective farms. The retreat continued. At the end of 1943 Pavlov set up his Cossack refugee camp at Kamenets-Podolski, but they were soon on the move again, to Sandomir, and to Novogrudok in White Russia where his five ramshackle regiments were posted out among the villages to fight the Soviet partisans. Despite the protection of his 'Cossack Guards' Pavlov was killed, and as the Soviet army approached, his successor, Domanov, again retreated with the Germans. Like some of the pro-Nazi Ukrainian units, his men paid their farewells to Russian soil with a trail of looting, rape and murder.

Meanwhile the German High Command had ordered the

formation of a Cossack division under Colonel Helmut von Pannwitz, a Russian-speaking Balt, and Kononov's unit was moved into Poland to form part of it. The division consisted of seven regiments, two each of Don and Kuban, one each of Terek and Siberian Cossacks and one mixed reserve regiment. Sentries with drawn sabres stood at the gates of Mlava camp and Cossack pennants flew above it. But apart from Kononov who retained his command, most Cossack officers were replaced by Germans, the equipment and the uniforms were German, and only a badge distinguished a Cossack from a German soldier.

As hopes of victory receded and they saw the overwhelming majority of Soviet citizens, including Cossacks, turn ferociously against the Germans, the renegades began to change their tune. Hitler no longer seemed to be their saviour, but 'the cruel enemy of our homeland'. Some of them thought of deserting to the Soviet side but having been 'misled' into joining the Nazis, they could hardly hope for quarter from the Russian government.[46] They were trapped.

Krasnov, sometime prophet of a united, 'patriotic' Russia and self-styled champion of Tsars, came to address them on the subject of 'Cossack patriotism'. They seemed quite fond of him and called him 'grandad', but this elderly, somewhat musty figure clad in German uniform and leaning heavily upon a stick, roused their pity rather than their courage.[47] More of them began to look to the Soviet General Vlasov who had deserted to the Germans. With Rosenberg's encouragement, Vlasov was proclaiming the formation of an All-Russian Liberation army of 'a million men' and scouring the prisoner of war camps for recruits. But few more than 150,000 Soviet citizens and soldiers were to join the Germans, and many of them only because of the disgusting conditions of the prison camps.

The morale of the Cossack volunteers fell lower still. The men of Pannwitz's division felt insulted by their German officers and N.C.O.s and began to retaliate. They raided the N.C.O. mess, forced some of the more arrogant Germans to strip and then beat them up, and a German N.C.O. who struck a Cossack was quietly murdered. Then in September 1943 they were ordered to move to France, to help guard the Western Wall against the expected Allied landing. At this they became seriously disturbed. They only wanted to fight their private war with Stalin, not against the British or the Americans. Krasnov and Pannwitz campaigned to have the order set aside, and, though some dispirited Cossacks were to serve in the Omaha sector on D-Day, the 1st Cossack division was sent, instead, to Yugoslavia to fight the partisans.

The taste of defeat had persuaded the Germans of the need to do more to raise their Cossacks' morale. They agreed to provide new uniforms, incorporating Cossack fur caps and the traditional scarlet-striped trousers, and, irony of ironies, arranged to send some of the younger men to cavalry school in Germany, for many Cossacks of the new, Soviet generation had never learnt to ride. More important than these sops to pride was the belated promise made by Rosenberg and Keitel in November 1943 to restore the Cossacks to their traditional lands with all the rights their forefathers had once enjoyed. By then, of course, the Cossack lands were being left behind. But to strengthen the determination of their Cossack collaborators, the Germans now promised them that, though 'military conditions temporarily barred them from their ancestral country', everything necessary would be provided for them to build up a Cossack life again in eastern Europe, under the Führer's protection. In return, the Cossacks must engage 'faithfully and obediently' to build a 'new Europe', with the aid of Germany and the Almighty. It was a new form of Tsar's pay, an inducement to serve the Third Reich, as once they had served the Russian crown. And though the Germans were soon to be hustled out of eastern Europe they were to keep the substance of their promise. The grotesque plan envisaging the artificial creation of a 'Cossack' puppet state outside the traditional Cossack regions was welcomed joyfully by Naumenko, the Kuban Ataman in exile in Berlin, and given wide publicity in the Cossack press of Hitler's Europe.[48]

In March 1944 the commander of the eastern volunteer forces of the German army sanctioned the establishment of a directorate of Cossack forces to include Naumenko, Pavlov, who was soon to be succeeded by Domanov, and Colonel Kulakov of von Pannwitz's division. It was to be headed by Krasnov who would represent Cossack interests to the German command. The new authority, closely supervised by Rosenberg's representative Dr. Himpel, set to work creating institutions, including a bank and a tribunal court, to serve in the creation of a Cossack puppet state in exile.

Pannwitz's Cossack division, based at Mielau in East Prussia, was moved to Yugoslavia to fight Tito's partisans, while Domanov's force of Don Cossacks was moved near Warsaw and then, through Germany, into the foothills of the Italian Alps. But Hitler's Cossacks were morally as well as geographically divided. The younger men, a generation distant from the Civil War, looked to the non-Cossack General Vlasov and his all-Russian movement, while the older men, of the 1917 vintage, preferred Krasnov, the Cossack separatist. In the end, most of the Cossacks in German service were to accept Vlasov's leadership, rejecting that of the obsolete Krasnov. Even Naumenko and Domanov, who had taken personal oaths to Hitler, were persuaded by the SS Governor-General of Istria to acknowledge Vlasov and merge with his 'Liberation Army'. But for the moment, though his leadership was undermined by intrigue, Krasnov remained the political chief, and was totally absorbed in constructing his new 'Cossack state'.

In the summer of 1944 about 10,000 Cossacks from the Don, Kuban and Terek were moved into Italy together with some 8,000 anti-Soviet tribesmen, scions of Caucasian minority groups. Domanov was there and with him a number of other generals—old Whites like Shkuro, Salamakhin of the Kuban who had charge of the Cossack cadets, and Sultan Girei Klitch, Tatar chief of the aptly named 'Savage' Caucasian Division. Whole families arrived—recent Cossack refugees, and émigrés of 1917–20, the custodians of a fossilised, outmoded way of life. In February 1945, as Soviet Cossacks stormed their way towards Berlin, General Krasnov arrived in Tolmezzo in the Italian Alps. It seemed an unlikely corner of the world for a new Cossack state, but so it had been ordained. And an aged Tsarist general who had fought the Bolsheviks in the Civil War and since dreamed his romantic dream so long in exile, at last had his opportunity. Krasnov issued a newspaper called *The Land of the Cossacks*, and encouraged his people to think of Tolmezzo as home.

The squares of the neat little Alpine town which the powers in Berlin had designated as the new 'Cossackia', were already covered with tents. Men in strange uniforms filled the streets and women knelt before icons at the doors of caravans. The place took on the aspect of some oriental bazaar. These Cossacks looked more tatty than picturesque, but the villagers round about had no cause to pity them. The intruders grazed their horses and camels on their pasturelands, took their food, stole their property and shot them in reprisal for partisan activity.

They were not to suffer the Cossacks long however. Tolmezzo was already being bombed and British troops were soon advancing towards it. In fact the fate of the new 'Cossackia' had already been decided thousands of miles away at Yalta where the Allied leaders had agreed that the Cossacks should be handed over to the Soviet authorities when victory came. That decision was about to be implemented.[49] In March, with the Russians near the Oder and the British advancing towards Venice, Krasnov called a council of war and decided to withdraw across the border into Austria. The covered wagons moved on again, and for the last time. Harried by the partisans, the tinkers' cavalcade of ox-drawn carts, horses and swaying camels threaded its way across the snow drifts, over the Carnian Alps, and into Carinthia. They entered Lienz on the 4th May to be greeted by the burgomaster and the Chief of Police.

Meanwhile, the Cossack cavalry from Yugoslavia, fighting off Titoist and Bulgarian detachments, was converging on the Drava valley. Von Pannwitz, its commander, offered to surrender it to the British if they would preserve the corps intact for the 'coming fight' with the USSR.[50] The offer was refused. Then news came that Germany had capitulated, that Hitler was dead. The Cossack oaths to the Führer were valid no longer and, on 19th May 1945, von Pannwitz surrendered to the 2nd British Armoured Division.

As many as 40,000 Cossacks, tribesmen and their followers were now encamped in the area of Lienz, their numbers already shrinking as the more circumspect drifted off to merge with the crowds of refugees cluttering the roads of central Europe. Then the British arrived to disarm the Cossacks. To avoid bloodshed, they told the officers they were wanted at Spittal, to attend a

337

conference at which their future would be discussed. Krasnov went quietly telling his wife he would be back in time for dinner. But he was never to return.

At Spittal, thirty-five generals and some 2,000 officers found themselves behind barbed wire, where they were informed that, next day, they would all be handed over to the Soviet authorities. Krasnov was resigned. But as the Cossacks grasped what their true fate was to be, there was resistance. There were sit-down strikes under black flags bearing the slogan 'Hunger and death before return to the Soviet Union', and violence which required 'armed force, sometimes resulting in fatal casualties' to put down[51]—force which was to give rise to extravagant tales of British 'atrocities' and 'treachery' in the émigré press. While old men, women and children, remained in camps in Austria, others were returned to the Soviet Union. But some of the detainees escaped into the mountains and the forests, or jumped from the trains carrying them east; and a few committed suicide. A handful of Krasnov's chief collaborators, Generals Sala-makhin, Borodin and Naumenko, the irrepressible Kuban Ataman, among them, somehow found their way to safety in America or France, despite their doubtful pasts. And the Argyll and Sutherland Highlanders collected a fine string of Cossack horses.

A dozen of the Cossack leaders were taken to Moscow for trial; most of the rest to Soviet prison camps, some to be released years later and drift back to the west, grumbling about their 'betrayal'. In fact the Cossacks had not been handed over without question. On 20th May 1945 Churchill had asked for a report on them, asking: 'Did they fight against us?' The answer was plain and affirmative. They had 'fought with ferocity, not to say savagery, for the Germans',[52] against partisans in Yugo-slavia and Italy, against Soviet troops, and against their own people during the time of the occupation. Their fate was inevitable, and not unjust. Though only a third of the officers were Soviet citizens, they were most of them traitors in the eyes of any law, and some could be classified legally as war criminals. Years before, Krasnov had broken his parole to the Soviet authorities. These exiles, who, for a quarter of a century, had expressed a ruthless determination to overthrow the Soviet

338

regime, could hardly wonder that Stalin wanted them; men who had sworn loyalty to the Nazis and had accepted the protection of and fought for the SS ought not to have been surprised at the lack of Allied sympathy. And their friends who protested on the grounds of humanity, forgot the bestial reputation these men had earned in the Civil War, and how they would have treated Bolsheviks had the roles been reversed.

Some months later the curtain was rung down on the last Cossack rebellion, the last Cossack bid for independence. A Soviet military court found Krasnov and his colleagues guilty of 'armed struggle against the Soviet Union . . . espionage, diversionary and terrorist activities', and pronounced sentence of death. In January 1947, Krasnov, sometime Don Ataman, commander of White Guards and 'agent of the German intelligence', hobbled to the gallows, as Razin and Pugachev had gone before. With him went Shkuro, Domanov, and von Pannwitz.[53]

The last of the Cossack romantics was dead, but his legend was to take root among the exiles many of whom saw him as a martyr. And as the Cold War developed his spiritual successors were to find some support in the United States. A Cossack Association was set up there which sponsored the idea of creating a new 'Cossackia'. Representatives of a 'Cossack National Liberation Movement' were fêted by the American Committee for Liberation from Bolshevism, and a World Cossack Association was founded to unite the 120,000 Cossacks of both exiles 'ready for the fight against World Communism'.[54]

But by no means all the exiles shared this view, and emphasis came to be placed more on welfare and on perpetuating some communal identity. Several rural communities were formed in Argentina, Venezuela and Chile though a plan to settle 10,000 Cossacks in Paraguay came to nothing. The best organised Cossack centres were in America and in France, though Cossacks were now spread the world over from Persia to the Philippines, from Israel to Peru.

Orthodox services were held, Cossack dress was worn, Cossack banners flown at local ceremonies, and 'atamans' were still elected. But old generals like Naumenko and Popov, who had led the campaign from the Salsk steppe in 1918, had little

339

appeal to members of the rising generations, and inter-communal rivalries and parochial squabbles overcame the will for unity. The 'mistakes' of 1917 were still worried out, but the cries: 'God is with us and we shall win' gradually faded into the distance. Journals published nostalgic idealisations of the old Cossack way of life, reprinted the anthems of the hosts and lovingly re-told tales from the heroic past. But gradually it became clear that, as the exiles' children became absorbed into the life of the adoptive countries, Cossack identity would be lost.

A generation of fathers was dying, and the sons were forgetting they were Cossacks. Fewer Cossacks in exile dreamt of a corner of the world that would one day be theirs. When Stalin died hoary heads nodded at the news that his successor was Malenkov, son of an officer in the Orenburg Host. But the Cossack world they had known had gone forever.

As for the bulk of the Cossacks who still inhabited the old lands of the Hosts, the German invasion had brought another tide of destruction, and the high proportion of middle-aged widows on the Kuban still bears witness to this fact. There was another drought, another period of hunger. Then, gradually, life became easier, and even prosperous. And it was this prosperity that succeeded in eliminating Cossack identity more surely than oppression had ever done.

Factory-produced smocks have replaced the gay *cherkesskas*, and television is beginning to oust the Cossack dance and the Cossack choir as forms of entertainment. Just as the end of Russia's frontier period had put an end to the original form of Cossackdom, just as the Revolution had rendered the Cossacks obsolete as a military caste, and the social and agrarian revolutions which followed had ruptured Cossack solidarity, so, now, the technological revolution began to obliterate all but the vestiges of Cossack life.

The face of their country has changed beyond recognition. The Volga, once the hunting ground of Cossack pirates, is dammed, diverted, and prickling with hydro-electric stations. A great canal cuts through the land between the Volga and the Don where Stenka Razin and his stormy-headed brigands dragged their boats. The rivers Ob and Irtysh which Yermak once navigated are now contaminated by industrial effluents,

General Dovator

Soviet Cossacks pursuing German troops, 1944

A Cossack serving
with the German
army in Northern
Italy, 1945 (see
description on
page 337)

Soviet Cossacks
off duty, 1944

and the sturgeon are no longer what they were. The face of Zaporozhiye, outpost of Tatar-fighters and refuge of the oppressed, is obliterated by a vast industrial complex, the smell of oil hangs over the Terek, and the barren wastes of the trans-Don steppe, once the haunt of Cossack fugitives, have been transformed by afforestation programmes. The ash-blue wormwood, and the ancient burial mounds are no longer the only features of the southern prairie, and whole stanitsas have been moved to make way for electricity-generating schemes.

After half a century of travail and disasters, quiet has come to the Cossack lands again. The sons of the Cossacks now have the electricity that Lenin promised them and they will grow more prosperous yet. Collective farmers and factory hands are proud to trace their descent from Cossacks, but the conditions which made Tolstoi's Yeroshka or Sholokhov's Gregor Melekhov have disappeared, and only the legends live on.

Soviet citizens in the Urals hang portraits of Yermak on their walls, and revere him as their ancestor. Men still point to Razin's mountain where his treasure is said to be concealed, and there is a statue in Kiev to Khmelnitski, 'hero of the Soviet Ukraine'. Pugachev and Bulavin are lauded in the history books, and even the loyalist Count Platov is praised as a patriot of 1812. The old songs are sung, cultural officials stage Cossack dances, and troupes of *djigits* perform extraordinary feats of horsemanship. The Cossacks are no longer a vital force—but their legend has become the heritage of every Russian.

References

INTRODUCTION

1. See R. A. Billington, *The American Frontier*, American Historical Association 1958, p. 22; also his *The Frontier Heritage*, New York 1966.
2. On the escape or 'safety valve' theory see F. J. Turner, 'The Significance of the Frontier in American History', 1893.
3. John A. Hawgood, *The American West*, Eyre & Spottiswoode, 1967, plate 18, opp. p. 233 (published in the U.S.A. as *America's Western Frontiers*).
4. See J. Hernandez, *Martin Fierro* (a ballad), Buenos Aires 1937, and in general E. J. Hobsbawm, *Primitive Rebels*, London 1959.
5. Some comparisons along these lines have been made by M. Ya. Fenomenov, *Razinovshchina i Pugachevshchina*, Moscow 1923.

CHAPTER 1

1. Conflicting theories on Cossack origins abound, some based on confusions between Cossacks, and Kazakhs, Kasogs and Khazars who inhabited the steppe at various times. Constantine Prophyrogenitus's tenth century reference to the lower Tanais (the Don) as 'Kazachia', the land of the Khazars, and 11th Persian reference to the nomadic Kazakhs led to the predication of earlier and different origins to the Cossacks than was the case. So did the appellation *Cherkess* (Circassian) which was also used to denote people from Cherkassy, the Ukrainian town and early Cossack centre, and hence in sixteenth-century Russian writing to denote Cossacks of the Ukraine in general (see A. Rigelman, *Istoriya o Donskom Kazachetsve*, 1778). Apparent ethnological and functional similarities between Cossacks and the twelfth- and thirteenth-century Dnieper *brodniki* and the nomadic Pechenegs employed as Kievan frontier guards against the Mongols have led historians to suggest that the Ukrainian Cossacks derived from pre-Tatar Turkic peoples (see Günter Stökl, *Die Entstehung des Kosakentums*, Münich 1953, and note 4 below). M. Lesur (*Histoire des Kosaques*, Paris 1814) presents a curious thesis while demolishing some even stranger ones. He supposes Cossacks to be racially separate from the Russians, apparently seeing 'something Asiatic' in their 'blue eyes' and

reddish beards (Vol. II, pp. 307-8). As physiognomist Lesur had successors in the twentieth century among racial theorists in Nazi Germany (see Chapter 11). More seriously, the paucity and ambiguity of the primary evidence has encouraged bitter debate, fraught with political and nationalist implications, between historians of eastern Europe. Their work has often contrived to cast more obscurity than light upon the problem. In particular, theories have been built up with the purpose of providing historical foundations for the political movement for Ukrainian nationalism. Attempts have been made, for example, to demonstrate a continuity of Ukrainian nationhood from the Kievans. M. Stakhiv in *V 300 littya Khmelnichchini (1648–1948)* (ed. B. Krupnitski, München 1948, pp. 65ff.) asserts that Ukrainian (Ruthenian) tribes were a discernable people in the eleventh century and that they were conscious of a unity when the Lithuanians and Poles arrived. It has also been claimed that the remnants of the Kievan peasantry who escaped the Tatars were joined by 'adventurous nobles of Poland, Lithuania and Rumania' and by truant serfs and outcasts, with whom they created a (Cossack) movement in the fourteenth and fifteenth centuries which 'saved' and 'developed' the Ukrainian language and 'Ukrainian national feeling' (M. A. Czaplicka, 'The Evolution of Cossack Communities', reprinted from the *Central Asian Society Journal*, 1918). Ignoring the question as to whether a differentiated Ukrainian language presents an argument for nationalism as strong as Welsh, Scottish or Cornish claims, there is no evidence of any but Tatar or tribal *kazaki* inhabiting the steppe zone in the fourteenth century, and there *is* evidence that most Ukrainian Cossacks were immigrants from the north. An early Cossack register shows the men coming from seventy-four west Russian and Lithuanian towns and from seven towns in Poland. They included some who originated in Moscow and the Volga area and also some Moldavians, Scandinavians, a German, a Serb and a Crimean Tatar (see V. Klyuchevski, *Kurs Russkoi Istorii*, trans. C. J. Hogarth as *A History of Russia*, New York 1960, Vol. III, p. 114). Nationalist claims rest on the assumption that the Mongol invasions hardly disturbed a continuous occupation of the steppe by 'Cossack farmers', but the Kievans never seemed to have gone far in colonising the steppe and Plano Carpini (*Hakluyt's Voyages*) shows the area south and east of Kiev to have been such a wilderness in the thirteenth century that few settlers, if any, could have survived in it. Recent estimates of the mid-sixteenth-century population of the Ukraine vary from 34,000 (Baronovich, *Naseleniye Predstepnoi Ukrainy v XVI v*, 1950, pp. 198ff.), to a few hundred thousands (Stökl, *op. cit.*, p. 150). And the population influx during the preceding decades suggests an infinitesimal fifteenth-century population.

2. S. Purchas, *Hakluytus Posthumus, or Purchas his Pilgrimes*, 1625, Vol. III, p. 641.

3. Slaves might rise to positions of wealth and power in the Turkish empire and many were treated better than Russian peasants, but the horrific Tatar raids created lasting Russian fears.

4. Despite myriad and intriguing explanations according to which the term 'Cossack' originated from the 'Sclavonian' words for 'nimbleness', 'goat', 'scythe', etc., and from the names of various other steppe peoples (see note 1 above), the word *kazak* (Cossack) has no ethnic significance. A tenth-century Arabic word meaning freebooter or nomad soldier (H. H. Howorth, *History of the Mongols*, London 1876–8, Vol. III, part i, p. 5), it was adopted by the Turco-Tatar world (see M. Lyubavski, 'Nachalnaya Istoriya Malorusskogo Kazachestva', *Zhurnal Ministerstva Narodnogo Prosveshcheniya*, 1895, Book VII, pp. 234ff.), coming into use among Tatars, Kumans, Polovtsians and other Turkic peoples, and Genoese colonists on the Black Sea coast by the beginning of the fourteenth century (the *Coman Codex* and the *Synaxarion Sugdaya*, see Stökl, *op. cit.*, pp. 39ff.) and denoting 'guard' or 'guardpost' (*ghasal cosak*). The use in Tatar and Russian was similar, but broadened in Russian and Polish contexts to designate a wandering soldier, or adventurer, a man without a defined occupation or a permanent home, a steppe trader or hired labourer.

5. Nikon Chronicle, *Polnoye Sobraniye Russkikh Letopisei*, Vol. XII, pp. 61f. See also D. Ilovaiski, *Istoriya Ryazanskago Knyazhestva*, Moscow 1850, p. 301 and Stökl, *op. cit.*, pp. 53ff.

6. Josafa Barbaro and Ambrogio Contarini, *Travels to Tana and Persia*, Hakluyt Society, London 1873, p. 159.

7. *Sbornik Imperatorskogo Russkogo Istoricheskogo Obshchestva*, 41, 1884, p. 413; Stökl, *op. cit.*, pp. 106–11.

8. D. I. Bagalei, *Ocherki iz Kolonisataii Stepnoi Okrainy Moskovskago Gosudarstva*, Moscow 1887, p. 91. See pp. 95ff. on the old frontier watches. For a recent comparative survey of the process by which the steppe-lands of central and eastern Europe were tamed see W. H. McNeill, *Europe's Steppe Frontier 1500–1800*, Chicago 1964.

9. Cossacks had a number of functional equivalents in the west where men were employed as frontier guards in return for land and tax concessions. Such were the Szeklers of Transylvania, warrior-peasants of nomad stock settled in Hungary from the twelfth century, the *haiduks*, landless plunderers, fishermen and stock-raisers of the Hungarian plains recruited by Magyar noblemen against the

Hapsburgs, and the *Grenzers* employed by Austria to guard the Slovenian and Croatian borders.

10. Contarini, *op. cit.*, p. 155.

11. Vigna, *Codice Diplomatico*, Vol. II, part ii, p. 114, No. 112; Stökl, *op. cit.*, p. 50.

12. Maciej z Miechow, *Descriptio Sarmatiarum*, Cracow 1521, C iii r.

13. See A. V. Chernov, *Vooruzhennyye Sily Russkogo Gosudarstva v XV–XVII vv*, Moscow 1954, p. 89.

14. See Tsar to the Governor of Astrakhan, 26th Feb. 1587, quoted by A. B. Karpov, *Uraltsy: Istoricheski Ocherk*, Part 1 (1550–1725), Uralsk 1911, p. 859.

15. *Istoricheskoye Opisaniye Zemli Voiska Donskogo*, 1903, pp. 3 and 18; see I. I. Smirnov, *Vosstaniye Bolotnikova 1606–1607*, 1951, pp. 123–4.

16. Giles Fletcher, *Of the Russe Commonwealth*, London 1591, pp. 20–21. In general on the condition of the Muscovite peasant in the later sixteenth century, fleeced by the state, ravaged by the *oprichnina*, struck by plague, famine and Tatar raiders, and the flights to which these gave rise, see Jerome Blum, *Lord and Peasant in Russia from the Ninth to the Nineteenth Century*, Atheneum ed., New York 1967.

17. *Relacye nuncyzow apostolskikh i innysh osib v Polsce od roku 1548 do 1690*, Vol. I, Berlin Poznan 1864, p. 248, quoted by V. A. Golobutski, *Chernomorskiye Kazaki*, 1956, p. 17. The harsh development of serfdom in Lithuania after the union with Poland in 1569 stimulated many flights down the Dnieper and the Bug rivers.

18. The description is contained in an official report on a Cossack caught in Novgorod in the reign of Tsar Boris, quoted in Smirnov, *op. cit.*, p. 125.

19. The term *ataman* is thought (erroneously) to have derived from the Polish *hetman*, a corruption of the German *Hauptmann* (captain). The term was in use among Tatars in Lithuanian service (Stökl, *op. cit.*, pp. 111f. also p. 31 note). See also D. I. Evarnitski, *Istoriya Zaporozhskikh Kozakov*, St. Petersburg 1892–7, Vol. I, p. 9 on derivation of *ataman, esaul, kosh*, etc., from the Tatar.

20. The first Sech is thought to have been sited on the island of Khortitsa in the Dnieper. I. Kamanin ('K Voprosu o Kozachestve do Bogdana Khmelnitskogo', *Chteniya v Istoricheskom Obshchestve Nestora*, Kiev 1894, p. 73) ascribes the foundation of the Sech to the end of the fifteenth century. However, Lassota (*Tagebuch des Erich Lassota von Steblau*, Halle 1866, p. 224) refers to the Lithuanian border magnate Prince Vishnevetski building a castle there in the 1550s, and N. I.

Kostomarov (*Sobraniye Sochinenii*, Vol. IV, Book ix, p. 17) ascribes this to between 1533 and 1550. Golobutski (*Zaporozhskoye Kazachestvo*, Kiev 1957, pp. 71ff.) considers Vishnevetski's fort on Khortitsa to have been directed against the Zaporozhians rather than the Tatars, that the first Zaporozhian Sech was on Tomakovka island. The argument is based on a somewhat selective re-reading of the chronicler Bielski (*Kronika Marcina Bielskiego*, Vol. III, Sanok 1856, especially, p. 169), but one aspect of Golobutski's argument has credence, for it is difficult to picture a magnate like Vishnevetski as a Cossack himself, as has often been alleged, rather than an employer of Cossack mercenaries. Cossacks would have had good reason to fall in with him for pay or because his generalship and armaments gave them better prospects of obtaining booty. Vishnevetski's predecessor, Eustace Dashkovits, the semi-independent Lithuanian magnate and war lord who held Cherkassy and Kaniev, had had the idea of hiring 2,000 Cossacks for local defence against Tatars. If Golobutski is wrong, Vishnevetski's Cossacks probably took over the fort on Khortitsa as the first Sech once their master had gone, or else built a new camp on Tomakovka.

21. Ivan IV to the Nogai Prince Yusuf, quoted by Smirnov, *op. cit.*, pp. 123-4.

22. The Terek community probably dates from the sixteenth century (see Ye. Maksimov, *Terskoye Kazachye Voisko*, Vladikavkaz 1890, pp. 6ff. and I. D. Popko, *Terskiye Kazaki so starodaraykh vremen*, vyp. I, Grebenskoye Voisko, St. Petersburg 1880) and was founded by Cossacks from the Don-Volga area. Those settling upstream were known as Grebensk Cossacks, but to avoid complicating the text I have used the term Terek to cover both Terek and Grebensk Cossacks.

23. Petr Rychkov, *Topografiya Orenburgskaya*, St. Petersburg 1762, Vol. II, pp. 6off. For the origins and early history of the Yaik Cossacks see A. Levshin, *Istoricheskoye i Statisticheskoyo Obozreniye Uralskikh Kozakov*, St. Petersburg 1823, pp. 4-5, and A. B. Karpov, *Uraltsy: Istoricheski Ocherk*, Part I, Uralsk 1911, pp. 35ff.

24. Evarnitski, *op. cit.*, Vol. I, p. 194.

25. See A. Pronshtein in V. Kuznetsov (ch. ed.), *Istoriya Dona s Drevneishikh Vremen do Velikoi Oktyabrskoi Sotsialnoi Revolyutsii*, Rostov-on-Don 1965, pp. 99-100 for another estimate.

26. Based on M. Shcherbatov, *Statistika i Rassuzhdenii Rossii*, 1776, quoted by I. Rozner, *Yaik pered Burei*, Moscow 1966, p. 75.

27. See V. Ulanov, 'Razinovshchina' in V. Kalasha (ed.), *Tri Veka*, Moscow 1912, Vol. I, p. 216.

28. Rozner, *op. cit.*, p. 65.

29. Rozner, *op. cit.*, pp. 34ff., P. Pallas, *Reise durch Verschiedene Provinzen*, St. Petersburg 1771–6, Rychkov, *op. cit.*, Vol. I, pp. 306–7.

30. I. V. Stepanov, *Krestyanskaya Voina v Rossii v 1670–1 gg: Vosstaniye Stepana Razina*, Leningrad 1966, Vol. I, pp. 277–8; Pronshtein in Kuznetsov, *op. cit.*

31. *A Relation of Three Embassies by the Earl of Carlisle*, 1669, p. 8.

32. Rozner, *op. cit.*, p. 58.

33. Samuel Collins, *The Present State of Russia*, London 1671, p. 132.

34. Pierre Chevalier (trans. Ed. Browne), *A Discourse on the Original Country . . . of the Cossacks*, London 1672, p. 13.

35. J. von Hammer, *Geschichte des Osmanischen Reiches*, Vol. V, pp. 43–5.

36. Najima in *Collecteanea z dziejopisow tureckich rzeczy do historyi polskiey sluzaccych*, Warsaw 1885, Vol. I, p. 181.

37. Pallas, *op. cit.*, quoted by Rozner, *op. cit.*, p. 8.

38. Purchas, *op. cit.*, Vol. III, p. 642.

39. See A. Pronshtein in V. Kuznetsov (ed.), *Istoriya Dona*, Rostov-on-Don 1965, p. 105.

40. Quoted by L. R. Wynar, 'Ukrainian Kozaks and the Vatican in 1594', *The Ukrainian Quarterly*, No. 1, 1965. Alexander Comulovich, the Papal Legate, represented Pope Clement. The Emperor's Ambassador was Lassota, whose diary (*Tagebuch, op. cit.*) is one of the few sources on the early Sech.

41. Purchas, *op. cit.*, Vol. III, p. 756.

42. See I. Nazarko, 'Znamenne Pismo Kozakiv do Papi Rimskogo', *Ukrainski Istorik*, No. 1–2 (5–6), New York and Münich 1965, pp. 22–7.

43. See A. Skalkovski, *Istoriya Novoi Sechi*, Odessa 1885, pp. 266 *passim*.

44. [P. Rychkov], *O Nachale Kozakov*, 1760, p. 295.

45. Okolski quoted by Golobutski, Zap. Kaz., *op. cit.*, p. 125.

46. N. A. de Salvandy, *Jan Sobieski*, Vol. I, Paris 1829, p. 182, quoting a letter to his son. Cossack democracy has been thought to derive from Russian city states like Pskov and Novgorod conquered by Muscovy in the fifteenth century. Their peoples are said to have fled to the 'wild country' bringing their traditions with them (see I. Bydakorov, *Istoriya Kazachestva*, Prague 1930, p. 112, and Svatikov, *op. cit.*, p.7). Similarly, Hrushevski and other historians of the Ukrainian school suggest that the Cossack assembly derived from the democratic *Veche* of ancient Kiev. Were this so, one would expect similarities of terminology and these are lacking. Cossackdom's democratic forms, like its primitive socialism (see note 50 below), seem rather to have been a factor of primitive social relationships,

a spontaneous response to frontier conditions (Cp. Turner, 'The West and American Ideals', *Washington Historical Quarterly*, Vol. V, October 1914, p. 245).

47. Quoted by Pronshtein in Kuznetsov, *op. cit.*, p. 128.

48. Lassota (*op. cit.*, p. 211) observed two assemblies. The ataman's inner cabinet met first, after which the *esauls* went to the 'great assembly' to consult the 'common people' (*chern*) (p. 214).

49. *Dopolneniya k Aktam Istoricheskim*, Vol. XII, 271 and 280.

50. Communal forms in agriculture were not peculiar to the Cossacks. The communal division of fisheries, pasture and arable land to avoid disputes was common among Russian peasants in the post-Kievan era (see Blum, *op. cit.*, pp. 510—11).

51. Quoted by Svatikov, *op. cit.*, p. 24.

52. *Donskiye Dela*, Bk. I, St. Petersburg 1898, 660–1.

53. Chevalier, *op. cit.*, p. 11 (1672). Evarnitski (*op. cit.*, 1892, pp. 184–5) insists that successful candidates must be free, single, Ukrainian-speaking, Russian Orthodox and have served a military apprenticeship of seven years. Though entry was more difficult in the eighteenth century there seems to have been little fixity in the rules for admission, although the religious qualification, and in earlier years bachelor status seem to have been necessary.

54. Carlisle, *A Relation, op. cit.*, p. 51.

55. J. von Klaproth, *Travels in the Caucasus and Georgia*, London 1814, p. 86.

56. Karpov, *op. cit.*, p. 140, quoting Pallas.

57. Levasseur, Sieur de Beauplan, trans. Churchill, *A Collection of Voyages and Travels*, Vol. I, 1732, pp. 578–9, pp. 4–5.

58. Golobutski, *Zap. Kaz., op. cit.*, p. 115.

59. *Donskiye Dela*, Book I, 340.

60. See Stepanov, *op. cit.*, Vol. I, p. 14.

CHAPTER 2

1. Yermak's origins, the date and place of his birth are all uncertain. His story emerges from legends and from chronicles—the Stroganov, Yesipov and Remezov (incorporating the Kungur) Chronicles (*Sibirskiye Letopisi*, St. Petersburg 1907)—which were composed long after his death and diverge on many points of fact (see S. Bakhrushin, 'Vopros o prisoyedinenii Sibiri v istoricheskoi literature', *Nauchnyye Trudy*, Moscow 1955, Vol. III, Part i, pp. 17ff., and V. I. Sergeyev, 'K voprosu o pokhode v Sibir druzhiny Yermaka', *Voprosy Istorii* No. 1, 1959, pp. 117–29). On Yermak's family originating from Suzdal see A. Voronikhin, 'K biografi Yermaka', *Voprosy Istorii*, No. 10, 1946, pp. 98–100. Voronikhin

considers Yermak himself to have come from the Urals. He also has been claimed for the Don (see N. Melnikov, *Yermak Timofeyevich Knyaz Sibirski: yego spodvizhniki i prodolzhateli*, Paris 1961, pp. 11–12 and 59–63) and for the Yaik (A. Dmitriyev, *Permskaya Starina*, No. 5, 1894, p. 220, and A. Karpov, *Uraltsy: Istoricheski Ocherk*, Part I: *Yaitskoye Voisko ot obrazovaniya voiska do perepisi Polkovnika Zakharova 1550–1725gg*, Uralsk 1911, p. 854). On Yermak's supposed date of birth see A. G. Popov, *Istoriya Voiska Donskago*, Novocherkassk 1812.

2. See Sergeyev, *loc. cit.*

3. N. Polushin, *Ataman Yermak Timofeyevich*, 1894, pp. 10–11.

4. See Sergeyev, *loc. cit.*

5. V. Bronevski, *Istoriya Donskago Voiska*, 1834, Vol. I, p. 64.

6. See V. Miller, *Istoricheskiya Pesni Russkago Naroda XVI–XVII vv*, Petrograd 1915, p. 477.

7. See Bakhrushin, *loc. cit.*

8. Article on Yermak in *Bolshaya Sovetskaya Entsiklopediya* (1952), etc. Sergeyev (*loc. cit.*) reckons that Yermak was in Orel (Kergeda) in the winter of 1577–8 and returned from the expedition up the river Sylva in the spring of 1579, setting out on the main expedition in the same year and it is possible that Yermak's service with the Stroganovs was continuous, without the break described here. The chronological arguments seem likely to be interminable. The numbers involved are also in doubt. Majority opinion has it that 540 Cossacks and 300 Lithuanians, Russians, Tatars and Germans retained by the Stroganovs left with him. Sergeyev reckons over 1,600 men. Yet despite the doubts over dates and numbers there is rough agreement on the route and the sequence of the principal events. See also G. Krasinski, 'Pokoreniye Sibir i Ivan Grozny', *Voprosy Istorii*, No. 3, 1947, pp. 80–99, and on Yermak, the Stroganovs and generally on the exploration of Siberia Y. Semyonov, *Siberia, its Conquest and Development*, Hollis and Carter 1963.

9. The attack on Saraichik has been attributed to Yermak, and also to Barbosha together with Koltso, who have claims to the attack on a Nogai ambassador to Persia as well. Barbosha is reputed to have been associated with Yermak (see Karpov, *op. cit.*, p. 51 and Sergeyev, *loc. cit.*).

10. *Sibirskiye Letopisi*, *op. cit.*, p. 315 *passim*. There is no subsequent mention of cannon however.

11. The Stroganov Chronicle, *Sib. Let.*, *op. cit.*, pp. 10–11. The chroniclers were clerics with an interest in stressing their hero's piety.

12. Quoted by Bronevski, *op. cit.*, Vol. I, pp. 63ff.

13. See Bakhrushin, 'Puti v Sibir v XVI–XVII vv', *op. cit.*, Vol. III, Part i, pp. 72ff.

M*

14. *Ibidem;* Benzley, 'The Russian Expansion towards Asia and the Arctic in the Middle Ages (to 1500)', *American Historical Review*, Vol. XIII, 1907–8, pp. 731–41.

15. The Remezov Chronicle, *Sib. Let.*, *op. cit.*, quoted by Sergeyev, *loc. cit.*, Sibir is called Isker or Kashlyk in some sources.

16. H. Howorth, *History of the Mongols from the ninth to the nineteenth century*, London 1876–8, Vol. II, part ii, p. 987. Throughout this chapter tribal legends have been linked with historical narrative to add colour. There is no evidence to suggest that they originated with the particular events described, only with the Yermak story as a whole.

17. See Bakhrushin, *Istoricheskiye Izvestiya*, Moscow University 1916, quoted by Melnikov, *op. cit.*, p. 108; Howorth, *op. cit.*, Vol. II, part ii, p. 989.

18. Sergeyev, *loc. cit.*

19. Quoted by Sergeyev, *loc. cit.*

20. Opinions differ as to whether the 300 Stroganov men (see note 8 above) left with Yermak or whether they followed on by the autumn of 1582. The article on Yermak in *Bol. Sov. Ent.*, *op. cit.*, has it that the 500 streltsy sent after Koltso's mission arrived in Siberia in the autumn of 1583, Bakhrushin (*op. cit.*, Vol. III, part i) and others that they came in 1584.

21. Sergeyev, *loc. cit.*

22. *Sibirskaya Letopis.* The casualties are probably exaggerated (Semyonov, *op. cit.*, p. 70).

23. Polushin, *op. cit.*, pp. 84ff. The story is also told by Howorth.

24. Howorth, *op. cit.*, Vol. II, part ii, p. 1001.

25. See R. H. Fisher, *The Russian Fur Trade*, Berkeley 1943.

26. Krasinski, *loc. cit.*

27. S. Collins, *The Present State of Russia*, 1671, pp. 76–7.

28. Bakhrushin, *op. cit.*, Vol. IV, 1959, p. 62.

29. Bakhrushin, 'Voyevody Tobolskogo Razryada v XVII v', *op. cit.*, Vol. III, part i, p. 279.

30. See T. Armstrong, *Russian Settlement in the North*, C.U.P. 1965, pp. 36–8. On portages between rivers as a factor in Russian expansion see R. Kerner, *The Urge to the Sea*, Un. of Calif. Press 1942.

31. J. Fisher, *Sibirische Geschichte*, Vol. I, 1768, quoted by Semyonov, *op. cit.*

32. S. V. Bakhrushin, 'Russkoye Prodvizheniye za Ural', *op. cit.*, Vol. III, part i, p. 152.

33. Quoted by P. Lyashchenko, *Istoriya Narodnogo Khozyaistva SSSR*, Leningrad 1952, Vol. I, p. 327.

34. N. S. Orlov, *Otkrytiye Russkikh Zemleprokhodtsev: Polyarnykh*

Morekhodov XVII na Severo-Vostoke Azii, Moscow 1951, pp. 93–5, quoted by Armstrong, *op. cit.*, pp. 32–3.

35. F. A. Golder, *Russian Expansion on the Pacific 1641–50*, Cleveland 1914, p. 45; *Dop. k Akt. Ist.*, *op. cit.*, Vol. III, 361.

36. See G. Krashennikov, *The History of Kamchatka and the Kurilski Islands with the Countries Adjacent*, trans. J. Grieve, Gloucester 1764, pp. 258–63. Individual Cossacks terrorised the natives but official state policy was relatively humane, at least by comparison with western colonialists in Asia and Africa. It was content to leave them in peace provided they paid reasonable tribute. Russian leniency, in contrast to the Americans' treatment of the Red Indians, may have been due to the fact that, lacking population of their own in Siberia, they were dependent on the indigenous native in order to exploit the country in any way at all, whereas the north American Indians soon got in the way of numerous immigrant farmers, miners and cattlemen. This argument would not hold good for Africa however.

37. Golder, *op. cit.*, p. 287.

38. Dezhnev's petition in Orlova, *op. cit.*, pp. 279–80. There is a translation of this and of extracts from several interesting sources on the Russians and Siberia in G. Lensen (Ed.), *Russia's eastward Expansion*, Prentice-Hall 1964, pp. 29–30.

CHAPTER 3

1 See A B. Karpov, *Uraltsy*, Part I, Uralsk 1911, p. 89.

2. For an account of the relief and subsequent siege of Kromy based on descriptions by Isaac Massa and others, see Ye. Razin, *Istoriya Voyennogo Iskusstva*, Vol. III, Moscow 1961, pp. 76ff.

3. See I. I. Smirnov, *Vosstaniye Bolotnikova 1606–1607*, 1951.

4. Tsar to Don Cossacks, 22nd Oct. 1625, *Donskiye Dela*, Bk. I, St. Petersburg 1898, 248.

5. See Karpov, *op. cit.*, pp. 109–110.

6. Quoted by Chernov, *Vooruzhenniye Sily Russkogo Gosudarstva*, p. 205.

7. Ataman Isai Martemyanov to the Tsar, 23.6.1623, quoted by Pronshtein, in Kuznetsov, *Istoriya Dona*, p. 128.

8. *Donskiye Dela*, Bk. I, pp. 387–9.

9. See A. A. Novoselski, *Borba Moskovskogo Gosudarstva s Tatarami v Pervoi Polovine XVII Veka*, Moscow-Leningrad 1948, pp. 237–9.

10. Don Cossack song quoted by Pronshtein, *op. cit.*, pp. 94–141.

11. N. A. Smirnov, *Rossiya i Turtsiya v XVI–XVII vv* (Uchenyye Zapiski Moskovskogo Universiteta, vyp. 94), Moscow 1945, Vol. I, pp. 21–2 *passim* on the struggle for Azov.

12. N. A. Smirnov, *op. cit.*, Vol. I, p. 18. It is possible that Muscovy had provided the engineer who laid the charge, as well as the gunpowder used to breach the walls.

13. Quoted by N. A. Smirnov, *op. cit.*, Vol. II, pp. 62–3.

14. For a full account of the siege of Azov see N. A. Smirnov, *op. cit.*, Vol. II, chapter vi. Exaggerated Turkish casualties quoted from Cornelius Kruis (*ibid.*, p. 75). See also Ye. I. Razin, *Istoriya Voyennogo Iskusstva*, Vol. III, Moscow 1961, pp. 68ff. and Pronshtein, *loc. cit.* Note that like the Swedes and unlike the English soldier of the time Cossacks had not been afraid to dig for victory (Cp. C. H. Firth, *Cromwell's Army*, Methuen 1962, pp. 175–8).

15. *Don. Del.*, *op. cit.*, Bk. 2, 260–1.

16. Quoted by Pronshtein, *loc. cit.*

17. See A. A. Lishin, *Akty Otnosyashchiyesya k Istorii Voiska Donskogo*, Novocherkassk 1891, docs. 21, 24, 25, quoted by I. V. Stepanov, *Krestyanskaya Voina v Rossii v 1670–1671gg*, Leningrad 1966, Vol. I, p. 288; Pronshtein, *loc. cit.*

18. Stepanov, *op. cit.*, Vol. I, pp. 297–9; S. G. Svatikov in *Donskaya Letopis*, Vienna 1923–4.

19. *Donskiye Dela*, *op. cit.*, Bk. II, 762.

20. *Donskiye Dela*, *op. cit.*, Bk. IV, 45.

21. Karpov, *op. cit.*, p. 248.

22. See Ye. Maksimov, *Terskoye Kazachye Voisko*, 1890, p. 23.

23. The force of registered Cossacks was known as the 'Zaporo zhian Army', but since this appellation has led writers to confuse them with true Zaporozhians of the Sech, I have avoided the term. There were ties between the two groups and the sons of registered Cossacks often spent a season or two on the Sech before being registered themselves, but they were fundamentally distinct in that the Zaporozhian Cossacks formed an independent community, while the registered Cossacks, mostly Ukrainian Cossack farmers, constituted a hired force of crown servicemen.

24. *Zherela do Istorii Ukraini-Rusi*, Vol. XV, p. 53; V. Golobutski, *Zaporozhskoye Kazachestvo*, Kiev 1957, p. 96.

25. See M. Korduba, *Cambridge History of Poland*, pp. 502ff.

26. For account of Ukrainian Cossackdom at the turn of the sixteenth and seventeenth centuries, and especially of the rebel leaders Loboda and Nalivaiko, see V. M. Domanitski, 'Kozachchina na Perelomi XVI–XVII v 1591–1603'; Lwow 1904–5, *Zapiski Naukovogo Tovaristva imeni Shevchenka*, Vols. LX–LXIV. Peasant self-identification with Cossacks was nothing new. Galician peasant rebels in 1490–1 had called themselves Cossacks. And the manifestation was often to be repeated, both in the Ukraine and in Russia

proper. For recent analysis of economic conditions in the Ukraine in the sixteenth and seventeenth centuries, see Y. Boiko, *Selyanskvo Ukrainy*, Kiev 1963.

27. *Volumina Legum*, Vol. I, p. 122; Golobutski, *op. cit.*, p. 156.

28. Sobieski, quoted by N. Kostomarov, *Sobraniye Sochinenii*, Book IV, Vol. IX, p. 52.

29. On Ostryanitsa and Guna see D. Bagalei, *Ocherki iz Istorii Kolonizatsii stepnoi Ukrainy Moskovskogo Gosudarstva*, Moscow 1887, pp. 177–8.

30. *Letopis Samovidtsa*, Kiev 1878; Kostomarov, *op. cit.*, Book IV, Vol. IX, pp. 142–3.

CHAPTER 4

1. See G. Vernadsky, *Bohdan, Hetman of the Ukraine*, New Haven 1941, p. 31.

2. Kostomarov, Sob. Soch., Book IV, Vol. IX, pp. 141–2.

3. *Istoriya Ukrainy v Dokumentakh i Materialakh*, Vol. III, pp. 122–3; Golobutski, *Zap. Kaz.*, *op. cit.*, p. 261.

4. For fuller description and analysis of Bogdan's battles see Ye. Razin, *Istoriya Voyennogo Iskusstva*, Vol. III, Moscow 1961, pp. 305–31. Razin, however, tends to minimise the Tatar contribution and skirt over the defeats. He compares Bogdan's military skills (p. 333) to those of Gustav Adolph of Sweden and of Marshal Turenne. Yu. Tis-Khromalyuk in another military study (*Boi Khmelnitskogo : Viiskovo-istorichna Studiya*, Münich 1954) prefers comparisons (pp. 173–4) with Alexander and Napoleon.

5. The informal alliance with the Don Cossacks soon proved embarrassing, since Bogdan was afraid their raids on Tatary would affect his good relations with the Khan. In November 1649 he wrote to the Tsar explaining that he had asked the Tatars not to attack Russian border towns and asking him to restrain the Don Cossacks from raiding the Tatars who were 'all on our side' (see I. Kripkayevich and I. Butich, *Dokumenty Bogdana Khmelnitskogo*, Kiev 1961, p. 150). In 1654 he made another appeal to the Tsar to dissuade the Don Cossacks from mounting raids on the Black Sea which would imperil his arrangements with the Crimea and Turkey (*Ibidem*, pp. 332–4).

6. Quoted by Kostomarov, *op. cit.*, Book IV, Vol. IX, p. 186. Despite attempts to shift the blame for the worst massacres onto peasant 'partisans' (see Osipov, *Bogdan Khmelnitski*, 1948, p. 159), this was the work of Colonel Ganzha and his men. Krivonos was among other Cossack leaders with a similar record. For a contemporary account by a Jew who escaped see Nathan Hannover,

Bogdan Khmelnitski, Leipzig 1883 (translated by S. Mandelkern from the Hebrew title 'The Abyss of Despair', which first appeared in Venice in 1653). An annotated Polish text is to be found in F. Rawita-Gawronska's *Sprawy i Rzeczy Ukrainskiye: Materialy do Dziejow Kozaczynny i Hajdamaczyzny*, Lwów 1914.

7. See Vernadsky, *op. cit.*, p. 51.

8. For account of two month's politicking between the battle of Pilyavka and the election of the Polish King see S. Tomashivski, *Pershi Pokhid Bogdana Khmelnitskogo v Galichinu*, Lviv 1914.

9. Quoted by Osipov, *op. cit.*, pp. 220ff.

10. *Relation des Cosaques, avec la vie de Kmielniski*, 1663, p. 4.

11. P. Chevalier, *Histoire de la guerre des Cosaques contre la Pologne...*, 2 pts., Paris 1663, trans. by E. Browne as *History of the wars of the Cossacks against Poland*, London 1672, p. 80.

12. See A. Chernov, *Vooruzhennyye Sily Russkogo Gosudarstva v XV–XVII vv*, Moscow 1954, p. 212 and note.

13. On municipal courts in the Ukraine after 1648 see Y. Padokh in E. Krupnitski (Ed.), *V 300-Littya Khmelnichchini (1648–1948)*, Münich 1948, pp. 93–127.

14. A government survey counted 62,949 rank and file Cossacks, 1,898 Cossack elders or officers and gentry, and 62,454 peasants in the Ukraine in 1654 (*Akty Yuzhno-Zapadnoi Rossii*, Vol. IX, No. 5). Assuming these to represent heads of households and the average household unit to consist of six persons one arrives at a total of 300–400,000 Ukrainian males. Osipov estimates 300,000 (*op. cit.*, p. 244) but there is insufficient demographic data to hazard any firm estimate. What is certain is that the number of claimants always exceeded the number provided for in any registration.

15. See M. Korduba, *Venetske Posolstvo do Khmelnitskogo (1650)r*, [1910]. On the treaty with the Turks see O. Pritsak in Krupnitski, *op. cit.*, pp. 143–64.

16. S. Grondski, *Historia Belli Cossaco-Polonici*, Pest 1789, p. 148.

17. Chevalier, *Second War of the Cossacks against Poland*, trans. Browne, London 1672, pp. 163–4.

18. Chevalier, *Second War, op. cit.*, p. 189.

19. The possibility of a Swedish alliance had been canvassed as early as 1630 (see I. Kripkayevich, *Kozachchina v politichnikh kombinatsiakh 1620–1630gg*, Lviv 1914.)

20. Kostomarov, *op. cit.*, Book IV, Vol. XI, p. 552. The act of union has been the subject of bitter debate, Russian historians on the whole celebrating it as the culminating objective of the wars, while some Ukrainian historians characterise it as a false and fatal step. The issue of Ukrainian nationalism ensured that the significance of

the union and the personality of Bogdan should continue to be gnawed at by historical polemicists. Ukrainians responded to the Tsarist yoke in the nineteenth century by founding an intellectual nationalist movement, based largely, like the German movement earlier in the century, on a view of history. A group of scholars, notably Hrushevski, re-discovered, as it were, a Ukrainian nationhood and looked to the Bogdan era in particular as an ideal age and on the order he founded as a nation state. More recently the struggles against the Poles have been termed a 'national-liberation' movement. In all, a nationality was predicated retrospectively to seventeenth-century Ukrainian Cossacks, though there is no evidence to suppose they themselves were conscious of it. The categories were not the same in the seventeenth as in the nineteenth century. The mass movement under Bogdan aimed at preserving and extending Cossack status, and Bogdan himself clearly appreciated the strategic factors which rendered any idea of a viable independent Ukraine impossible. The Tsarist government found these nationalist claims quite unacceptable, and the Soviet government has found it hardly less distasteful. A tryst with the nationalists after the revolution was soon ended, Pokrovski laying down a hard ideological line describing Bogdan as a tool of feudal lords who tried to exploit the war to the advantage of his own class of richer Cossacks (N. Popov (Ed.) *Ob Ukraine: Sbornik Statei i Materialov*, Kiev 1935, p. 135). There was a purge of the nationalist historians in the thirties and Hrushevski, returned from exile, was dismissed his post. But later the line on Bogdan has eased, and since the Second World War he has been restored to his former status as an historical hero (see A. Moskalenko, *Khmelnytski and the Treaty of Pereyaslav in Soviet Historiography*, New York 1955). The friendship between the Russian and Ukrainian peoples has been the dominant theme of late. Even though it was fear of the Poles, considerations of security for the Orthodox church, and, simply, the idea of obtaining a permanent guarantor of their freedoms, which motivated the Union with Muscovy (just as it was the desire for social status rather than national integrity which had led to the rising), the theme stresses the brotherly love that always existed between Ukrainian and Russian. The 300th anniversary of Pereyaslav was the occasion for a hundred-page panegyric on these lines in Kripkayevich's *Bogdan Khmelnitski* (Kiev 1954) and for Golobutski (*Osvoboditelnaya Voina Ukrainskogo Naroda pod Rukovodstvom Khmelnitskogo*, Moscow 1954, p. 3) to characterise the struggle as one by 'the Ukrainian people, forcibly torn from its elder brother, the Great Russian people' for reunion with it, and for 'its social and national freedom'.

355

21. For details see Kripkayevich and Butich, *op. cit.*

22. For a recent Polish view of the Ukrainian situation up to 1654, including a discussion of Sienkiewicz's best-selling historical novel on the period, *Ogniem i Mieczem* ('With Fire and Sword') see Z. Wøjcik, *Dzikie Pola w Ogniu*, Warsaw 1960. For a Polish politico-historical sketch of the whole field of Polish-Cossack relations see F. Rawita-Gawroński, *Kozaczyzna Ukraina w Rzeczypospolitej Polskiej do Konca XVIII wieku*, Warsaw [1922?].

23. For account of events following Bogdan's death, see V. Herasimchuk, 'Vygovski i Yuri Khmelnitski', *Zherela do Istorii Ukrainy Rusi*, Vol. LIX, pp. 1–40 and Vol. LX, pp. 1–70; also Kostomarov, *Getmanovane Ivana Vygovskogo* (Istorichny Monografii Mikoly Kostomarov, Vol. VI), Ternopol 1891.

CHAPTER 5

1. *The Voiages and Travels of John Struys* (trans. from the Dutch), London 1684, p. 174.

2. *A Relation concerning the Rebellion by S. Razin*, F. Newcome, London 1672, p. 4.

3. *A Relation, op. cit.*, p. 5.

4. There had been cases of landlords illegally restraining peasant flight since at least the 1550s, but the *Sobornoye Ulozheniye* of 1649, which codified the laws on lord and peasant abolishing most of the latter's rights and legal status, was the culminating point in the process of enserfing the Russian farmer. See Jerome Blum, *Lord and Peasant in Russia*, Atheneum, New York 1967, pp. 249 and 262ff.

5. *Akty Istoricheskiye*, Vol. IV, 374.

6. Quoted by A. Pronshtein in V. Kuznetsov (Ed.), *Istoriya Dona*, Rostov-on-Don 1965, p. 117. See also E. V. Chistyakov, *Vasili Us—Spodvizhnik Stepana Razina*, Moscow 1963.

7. *Sobraniye Pesen AN/SSSR*, p. 42, quoted by I. V. Stepanov, *Krestyanskaya Voina pod Predvoditelstvom S. T. Razin*, Moscow 1957, p. 28.

8. *Sbornik Dokumentov AN/SSSR*, Vol. I, No. 47, quoted by Stepanov, *Krestyanskaya Voina v Rossii v 1670–1671*, Vol. I, Leningrad 1966, p. 311.

9. Governor Unkovski's report, 14th March 1667, Ye. A. Shvetsova, *Krestyanskaya Voina pod Predvoditelstvom Stepana Razina*, Moscow 1954–62, Vol. I, p. 73; messages, and instructions to Ataman Yakovlev 18th June, 21st July and [23rd—] July 1667, pp. 89–94; report on Don Cossack *krug* 21st December 1667, pp. 97–8.

10. *A Relation, op. cit.*, p. 5.

11. See N. I. Kostomarov, *Bunt Stenki Razina*, 1859, p. 431.

12. For the fullest account of Razin's Caspian adventures see Stepanov, *Krest. Voi. v Ross.*, *op. cit.*, Vol. I, pp. 310–370. On the participation of Yaik Cossacks in the expedition see A. B. Karpov, *Uraltsy: Istoricheski Ocherk*, Part I, Uralsk 1911, pp. 251ff.

13. *The Travels of Sir John Chardin and the Coronation of Solyman III, King of Persia*, London 1686, pp. 143–4.

14. Chardin, *op. cit.*, p. 145; Shvetsova, *op. cit.*, Vol. I, p. 147.

15. Tsar to the Shah, 3rd May 1668, Shvetsova, *op. cit.*, Vol. I, pp. 105–6.

16. Chardin, Solyman, *op. cit.*, pp. 153–4.

17. Report on Razin's activities on the Volga and Caspian, Shvetsova, *op. cit.*, Vol. I, pp. 134–156.

18. Stepanov, among other Soviet historians, describes the expedition as an episode in a class war, and as a 'form of elemental protest of the oppressed masses who could not see ways of struggling against the ruling orders' (*Krest. Voi. v Ross*, *op. cit.*, Vol. I, p. 368). The Don Cossack *golytba* had no class quarrel with the Persians. The expedition was rather a flight from class war, and it was singularly misdirected as a protest, taking the form, as it did, of hitting an innocent third party on the nose.

19. Struys, *op. cit.*, p. 186.

20. See S. Konovalov, 'Ludwig Fabritius's Account of the Razin Rebellion', *Oxford Slavonic Papers*, No. 6, 1955, esp. p. 79.

21. *Dopolneniya k Aktam Istoricheskim*, Vol. VI, p. 18.

22. Struys, *op. cit.*, p. 187.

23. Struys, *op. cit.*, p. 187.

24. Quoted by Stepanov, *Krest. Voi v Ross.*, *op. cit.*, p. 365.

25. Struys, *op. cit.*, p. 190.

26. Quoted by Pronshtein in Kuznetsov, *op. cit.*, p. 121.

27. Stepanov, *Krest. Voi. Razina*, *op. cit.*, p. 39.

28. See P. I. Lyashchenko, *Istoriya Narodnogo Khozyaistva SSSR*, 1952, Vol. I, pp. 294 *passim*.

29. Razryadny Prikaz to Prince Urusov in Kazan, July 1670, Shvetsova, *op. cit.*, Vol. I, pp. 196–200.

30. *A Relation*, *op. cit.*, pp. 6–7.

31. Struys, *op. cit.*, p. 196.

32. Captain Butler's letter, 6th March 1671, Struys, *op. cit.*, p. 368.

33. *Ibidem*.

34. Butler's letter, Struys, *op. cit.*, p. 372.

35. Struys, *op. cit.*, p. 192.

36. Stepanov, *Krest. Voi. Razina*, *op. cit.*, pp. 72–3.

37. *Prelestnaya gramota*, September 1670, Shvetsova, *op. cit.*, Vol. II, part i, p. 65, and others *passim*.

38. *A Relation, op. cit.,* p. 11. Stepanov (*Krest. Voi. Razina, op. cit.,* pp. 45–6) doubts if Razin was responsible for the rumours.

39. 'O Bunte Stenki Razina', Akdd. 1763 Nov., p. 420, quoted by Kostomarov, *op. cit.,* p. 481.

40. *A Relation, op. cit.,* p. 10.

41. Newsletters dated 8th February and 27th May from English agents in Europe, *Calendar of State Papers Domestic 1671,* pp. 81 and 279.

42. Prince Urusov's Report, October 1670 in Shvetsova, *op. cit.,* Vol. II, part i, pp. 137–40.

43. See *A Relation, op. cit.,* p. 13. In its treatment of the 'amnestied' insurgents of Astrakhan, etc. the Muscovite government was not far in advance of other European countries of the time. Samuel Pepys, for instance, in his diary, records many executions of and reprisals against Commonwealth men after the supposedly bloodless Restoration of Charles II and a general promise of the King's grace (e.g. entries for 15th, 19th–21st Oct. 1660, 19th, 22nd and 27th Jan., 19th April and 14th June 1661).

44. *A Relation, op. cit.,* p. 16.

45. For the indictment, see Shvetsova, *op. cit.,* Vol. III, pp. 83–7.

46. I. Telyashev to Razryadny Prikaz, October 1707, Shvetsova, *op. cit.,* Vol. III, p. 394.

47. For evidence of the spread of Razin's legend in folk song see V. F. Miller, *Istoricheskiya Pesni Russkago Naroda XVI–XVII vv,* Petrograd 1915, pp. 685–777.

48. Letter dated 3rd August, *Calendar of State Papers Domestic 1671,* p. 412.

49. Kostomarov, *op. cit.,* p. 504 and note; also his interview in the 1850s with a 110-year-old peasant near present-day Volgograd (Tsaritsyn), p. 505.

CHAPTER 6

1. S. Solovev, *Istoriya Rossiei s Drevneishikh Vremen,* XII (3rd. ed.), quoted by S. G. Svatikov, 'Donskoi Voiskovoi Krug', *Dunskaya Letopis,* Vol. I, pp. 169–265.

2. G. Kotoshchikin, *O Rossii v Tsarstvovaniye Alekseya Mikhailovicha,* St. Petersburg 1884, p. 107, quoted by A. Popov, *Istoriya Vozmushcheniya Stenki Razina,* p. 24.

3. See Yu. A. Toporkov, 'K trekhstoletiyu uchrezhdeniya slobodskikh kazachikh polkov', *Russki Voyenno-istoricheski Vestnik,* Paris, No. 9, 1951, pp. 2–34. On the emigration from the Ukraine to the Slobodskaya Ukraine and the latter's early development see V. Yurkevich, *Yemigratsiya na Skhid i Zalyudnennya Slobozhanshchiki za B. Khmelnitskogo,* Kiev 1932.

4. The Zaporozhians' letter to the Sultan and another to the Khan are reproduced in W. P. Cresson, *The Cossacks: Their History and Country*, New York 1919, pp. 42–3, and C. Field, *The Great Cossack*, 1947, p. 112, based on the Annals of Kiev (Vol. II, 1891, p. 382). Also *Russkaya Starina*, St. Petersburg 1872, Vol. VI, pp. 450–1 and D. I. Evarnitski, *Ivan Dmitriyevich Sirko*, St. Petersburg 1894, pp. 97–8. On its dating see V. Golobutski, *Zaporozhskoye Kazachestvo*, Kiev 1957, p. 124.

5. Quoted by Pronshtein in Kuznetsov, *Istoriya Dona*, p. 143; Svatikov, *Rossiya i Don*, p. 185. See also evidence of Cornelius Kreis in 1699 quoted in N. A. Smirnov, *Rossiya i Turtsiya*, Vol. I, p. 20.

6. Quoted by Pronshtein in Kuznetsov, *op. cit.*, p. 175.

7. *Bulavinskoye Vosstaniye: Sbornik Dokumentov*, Moscow 1935, p. 365.

8. S. Solovev, 'Bulavinski Bunt', *Russki Vestnik*, 1897.

9. Generally on the Bulavin revolt see also Ye. P. Podyapolskaya, *Vosstaniye Bulavina 1707–9*, Moscow 1962, V. I. Lebedev, *Bulavinsk-oye Vosstaniye*, Moscow 1934, and A. Pronshtein, *Zemlya Donskaya v XVIII Veke*, Rostov-on-Don 1961.

10. Quoted by Ian Grey, *Peter the Great*, Macmillan 1962, p. 299. Generally on Mazepa, his revolt and its aftermath see N. Kostomarov, *Mazepa i Mazepintzy*, St. Petersburg 1905, Borys Krupnitski, *Hetman Mazepa und seine Zeit (1687–1709)*, Leipzig 1942, and R. Smal-Stocki (Ed.), *Mazepa: Zbirnik*, 2 vols., Warsaw 1938–9. Some contributions to the latter work and such works as Ye. Malanyuk's *Illustrissimus Dominus Mazepa*, New York 1960 are underlaid by a violent anti-Russian bias. On the fate of the western Ukraine from the Treaty of Andryusovo to the time of Peter the Great see V. Antonovich, *Ostanni Chasi Kozachchini na Pravoberezh Pislya Aktiv 1679–1716rr* (Ruska Istorichna Biblioteka), Lvov 1896, pp. 129–274. For sources on the Zaporozhians in the period, see D. Evarnitski, *Istochniki dlya Istorii Zaporobhskikh Kozakov*, 2 vols., Vladimir 1903; on relations between Mazepa and Gordiyenko see his *Istoriya Zaporozhskikh Kozakov 1688—1734*, Vol. III. On Mazepa's treaty with the Swedes see 'The Swedish-Ukrainian Treaties of Alliance 1708–9', *The Ukrainian Quarterly*, Vol. XII, No. 1, 1956, pp. 47–57.

11. On Gordiyenko and the Zaporozhians' return see P. A. Ivanov, 'Materialy po Istorii Zaporozhya v XVIII veke', *Zapiski Imperatorskago Odesskago Obshchestva Istorii i Drevnostei*, Vol. XX, Odessa 1897, pp. 60–100. Orlik, a largely inconsequential figure, has had an unjustifiably large amount of attention. Borshchak, W. Stepankowski, J. Tokarzhevski and Krupnitski have all devoted monographs to him. See Karashevich, *Diyarii Getmana Pilip Orlika*, Warsaw 1936 (Pratsy Ukr. Nauk. Inst., Vol. XVII).

12. Quoted by Karpov, *op. cit.*, p. 742.

13. See Ivanov, *loc. cit.*

14. Diary of the Zaporozhian delegation, Ivanov, *loc. cit.*

15. C. H. von Manstein, *Memoirs of Russia (1727–1744)*, London 1770, p. 16.

16. A. A. Andriyevski, 'Materialy po Istorii Zaporozhya i Pogranichnykh Otnoshenii', *Zapiski Imp. Odesskago Obshchestva, op. cit.*, Vol. XVI, 1893, pp. 117–266, and Vol. XVII, 1894, pp. 85ff and 218ff.

17. Manstein, *op. cit.*, p. 17; Prince S. Myshetski, *Istoriya o Kazakakh Zaporozhskikh*, Moscow 1847, appendix, pp. 81–2, cited by V. A. Golobuski, *Chernomorskoye Kazachestvo*, Kiev 1956, p. 55, see also pp. 63–4.

18. V. Krebs, *Umanskaya Reznya*, Kiev 1879, p. 32, quoted by S. Ya. Borovoi, 'Yevrei v Zaporozhskoi Sechi', *Istoricheski Sbornik Akad. Nauk/SSSR*, Leningrad, No. 1, 1934, pp. 141–90.

19. See Golobutski, *op. cit.*, p. 62 and his *Zaporozhskoye Kazachestvo*, Kiev 1957, pp. 347–8.

20. See Natalya Polonska-Vasilenkova, 'Maino Zaporizkoi Starshini', *Narisi z sotsialno-yekonomichnoi Istorii Ukraini* (Pratsi Komissii Sotsialno-Yekonomichnoi Istorii Ukrainy, ed. Bagalei), Kiev 1932, pp. 43–206, for inventory of ex-Ataman Kalnishevski's property, taken upon the destruction of the Sech (pp. 127–49).

21. In contrast to Golobutski (*Zap. Kaz., op. cit.*, pp. 369–70), who paints a dark picture of *kuren* life, D. I. Evarnitski (*Istoriya Zaporozhskihk Kozakov*, St. Petersburg 1892–7) describes it, rather idealistically, as full of brightness and jollity.

22. Cossacks working in the *palanki*, the up-country districts, were often paid a pittance as little as a kopek a day (see Golobutski, *Zap. Kaz., op. cit.*, pp. 370 and 374, *Chern. Kaz., op. cit.*, p. 88). Golobutski's views contrast with those of such historians as Evarnitski and A. A. Skalkovski (*Istoriya Novoi-Sechi* and other works), who adopt a romantically ideal view of Zaporozhians as a sort of religious order of chivalry. Their views in turn stem from eighteenth-century writings appealing to popular romantic attitudes. Some contemporaries (G. F. Miller, *Rassuzhdeniya*, p. 58) assert that the Zaporozhians did not cultivate the land and had 'a contempt for commerce' at least beyond satisfying their immediate needs though this is patently untrue, at least for the eighteenth century. True, S. I. Myshetski (*op. cit.*) who was actually stationed on the Sech for a time describes the Cossacks comparing themselves to the Knights of Malta but this was an excellent line with which to feed their Russian overseers. The view is still fashionable (see B. E. Nolde, *La Formation*

de l'Empire Russo, Paris 1952–3), but in fact, any such similarities are few and superficial. Golobutski also berates the idealists including M. Slabchenko ('Sotsialno-pravova Organisatsiya Sichi Zaporizkoi' *Pratsi Komini dlya Viuchuvannya Zakhidno-Ruskogo ta Ukraisnkogo Prava*, vip. III, Kiev 1927, p. 234) for suggesting that strict formulae governed the acceptance of new Cossacks. The elaborate conditions, tests and apprenticeships the recruits allegedly had to undergo do not pass critical examination. A most valuable source on the Zaporozhians at the time of the new Sech is the account of a member of the Host during that period, N. Korzh (*Ustnoye Povestovaniye Byvshego Zaporozhtsa L. Korzha*, Odessa 1842).

23. See *Kievskaya Starina*, Dec. 1889, p. 630. In 1734 the total force, excluding colonists and married men, was reckoned at 10,000 (Skalkovski, *Opyt Staticheskogo Opisaniya Novorossiiskogo Kraya*, Part II, Odessa, pp. 220–1). In October 1755 the Ataman reported to Hetman Razumovski of the Ukraine that the Zaporozhians numbered 27,000. Of these some 12,000 probably owned property (*zimovyye*) and were married, the rest bachelors (*seroma*) and probably poor. In 1759 11,769 Zaporozhians were on the serving list, of whom only 5,000 were cavalrymen. Golobutski (*Chern. Kaz., op. cit.*, p. 54) reckons the total population at this time as exceeding 100,000. But even assuming that most *zimovnyye* Cossacks were married and the presence of a substantial non-Cossack population, 70,000 would seem to be a more realistic figure.

24. Golobutski (*Chern. Kaz., op. cit.*, pp. 28–9) stresses that elections on the Sech were undemocratic in that poor Cossacks could not attend. Indeed, A. Rigelman (*Letopisnaya Novestovaniye o Maloi Rossii*, 1847, p. 73) comments: 'They could not all attend the assembly . . . because most of them were absent [working on the farms and fisheries] downstream, where they lived two years or more without going home'. Nevertheless if poorer Cossacks working in the outback could not always attend, there was a considerable body of poorer Cossacks always stationed on the Sech and it seems highly improbable that these elements could not command a majority in the open assembly whenever they wished. Moreover even when the *seroma* did unite to elect their own rival candidate as Ataman they always seem to have chosen a prosperous elder. This fact also operates against Golobutski's suggestion (*Zap. Kaz., op. cit.*, p. 117) that most 'working' Cossacks in trade, labouring on the *zimovniki*, and small farmers in their own right, were divided from the elders by overridingly conscious class differences.

25. See Andriyevski, *loc. cit.*, Part II, pp. 152–3. This sum was paid in 1763 and 1768.

26. Remark of Russian officer in 1749, *Kievskaya Starina*, May 1883, p. 131.

27. Manstein, *op. cit.*, p. 20.

28. See Borovoi, *loc. cit.*

29. Quotation cited by Golobutski, *Zap. Kaz.*, *op. cit.*, p. 398. The views of Soviet historians diverge somewhat with regard to the *gaidamaks*. V. Grekov (*Bunt siromi na Zaporizhzhi 1768r*, Kiev 1927) sees them as conservative nationalists clinging to tradition; to Golobutski (*Zap. Kaz.*, *op. cit.*, p. 406 and 382 note) they are anti-feudalist avengers, fighting tyranny. They themselves seem to have been conscious chiefly of the need to make a living, when necessary by brigandage, to entertain themselves and to succour the Ukrainian peasantry with whom they still had close affinities, by killing and tormenting their traditional enemies, the *pans* and the Jews. On measures taken against the *gaidamaks* see Col. Cherny's report of 2.6.1768, cited by Golobutski, *Chern. Kaz.*, *op. cit.*, p. 99. On the *gaidamak* movement in general and the troubles of 1768 in particular see also Yakiv Shulgin, *Nacherk Koliivshchini*, Lviv 1898, Skalkovski, *Nayezdy Gaidamak na zapadnuyu Ukrainu v XVIII stol. 1735–1768*, Odessa 1845, A. B. Antonovich, *Rozvidki pro Narodni Rukhi na Ukraini-Rusi v XVIII v*, Lviv 1897, Andriyevski, *loc. cit.*, pp. 134ff., Golobutski, *Zap. Kaz.*, pp. 382ff., and S. M. Dubnow, *History of the Jews in Russia and Poland*, Jewish Publication Society of America 1916–20, Vol. I, pp. 182ff.

30. Kalnishevski quoted by Golobutski, *Chern. Kaz.*, *op. cit.*, p. 101.

31. See Evarnitski's *Po Sledam Zaporozhtsev*, St. Petersburg 1898, pp. 163ff. on his searches in the archives of the Solovetsk monastery on the White Sea.

32. Pronshtein in Kuznetsov, *op. cit.*, pp. 142–52.

33. I. G. Rozner (*Yaik pered Burei*, Moscow 1966, p. 48) suggests that ordinary Cossacks wanted friendly relations with the neighbouring Bashkirs, Kazakhs, Kalmyks and Tatars, but that the elders organised raids against them in the interests of the government. However it seems unlikely that Cossacks would have been reluctant to carry out such raids from which poor men, as well as elders and the richer men, were able to profit by stealing the nomads' horses and herds.

34. Quoted by Rozner, *op. cit.*, p. 92. His theme of exploitation of poor Cossacks on the Yaik by the rich is the same as Golobutski's. No one is motivated by anything other than economic self-interest. Conscience, religion, tradition, and social pressures count for nothing.

35. See Rozner, *op. cit.*, p. 23.

36. Rozner, *op. cit.*, pp. 102–3.

37. Report of Internal Affairs Ministry, quoted by Rozner, *op. cit.*, p. 41.

CHAPTER 7

1. On Pugachev's date of birth see note by V. V. Mavrodin (Ed.), *Krestyanskaya Voina v Rossii v 1773–1775 godakh: Vosstaniye Pugacheva.* Vol. II, Leningrad 1966, pp. 69–70.

2. S. Piontkovski (Ed.), 'Dopros Ye. Pugacheva v Moskve v 1774–1775g', *Krasny Arkhiv*, Vol. 69–70 1935, pp. 159–237.

3. R. V. Ovchinnikov (Ed.), 'Sledstviye i Sud nad Ye. I. Pugachevym', *Voprosy Istorii*, No. 3 1966, pp. 124–38. This transcript of the interrogations and subsequent trial of Pugachev and his associates is continued in No. 5 1966, pp. 107–21, and No. 7 1966, pp. 92–109. See also Piontkovski, *loc. cit.*

4. Piontkovski, *loc. cit.*

5. Mavrodin, *op. cit.*, Vol. II, pp. 73–4.

6. For Pugachev's career on the Terek see *Russkaya Starina*, 1883, Books 1–3, pp. 167–70; *Russkiya Chteniya*, No. 1 1848, pp. 118–32; also note in Piontkovski, *loc. cit.*

7. See S. G. Svatikov in *Donskaya Letopis*, Vienna 1923–4, Vol. I, pp. 201ff.

8. Piontkovski, *loc. cit.* (note 12), which includes the description in Pugachev's passport. For Pugachev's wife's, Sofia's, description, see A. S. Pushkin, *Istoriya Pugachevskago Bunta*, 1834, Vol. I, note 14, pp. 12ff.

9. Ovchinnikov, *Vop. Ist.*, No. 5 1966, *loc. cit.*

10. Ovchinnikov, *Vop. Ist.*, No. 3 1966, *loc. cit.*

11. *Ibidem.* For events culminating in the Yaik Cossack revolt see Chapter 6, and I. G. Rozner, *Yaik pered Burei*, Moscow 1966.

12. Piontkovski, *loc. cit.*; N. M. Firsov, *Pugachevshchina: Opyt Sotsialno-Psikhologicheskoi Kharakteristiki*, St. Petersburg 1907, p. 165; Ovchinnikov, *Vop. Ist.*, No. 7 1966, *loc. cit.*

13. Quoted by A. Pronshtein in V. Kuznetsov (ed.), *Istoriya Dona*, Rostov-on-Don 1965, p. 187.

14. See Rozner, *op. cit.*, p. 185.

15. Rebel faith in a 'good Tsar' was not confined to Russia, it was international. Robert Ket, who headed a rebellion in England in 1549, issued orders in the King's name, believing, as Razin's followers were to do, that, since they were just, he must approve of them. Similarly the English peasants who rioted in 1830, believed their demands to be lawful as well as just and, consequently, that the King must grant them (see E. J. Hobsbawm and George Rudé,

Captain Swing, Lawrence and Wishart 1969). The rebels' sense of natural justice, combined with their persistent monarchic faith, led them to call for change in the name of King or Tsar, or, if the incumbent took steps against them, to dispute his legitimacy and proclaim an alternative Tsar.

16. Golubstov (ed.), *Pugachershchina*, Vol. II, p. 131. For Shigayev's description of Pugachev, see Piontkovski, *loc. cit.*

17. Golubstov, *op. cit.*, Vol. I, p. 25. This volume contains 271 manifestos, orders, decrees, etc. issued by Pugachev and the rebels. Most of the latter ones tend to be repetitive. They are characterised by grammatical lapses and by a general ponderousness in style (though the language of this first one was admired by Pushkin). However, much official correspondence of the time was characterised by even greater heaviness.

18. See Ovchinnikov in Mavrodin, *op. cit.*, Vol. II, pp. 421–2.

19. Piontkovski, *loc. cit.*

20. Karavayev's evidence, quoted in Piontkovski, *loc. cit.*

21. See A. Chuloshnikov, 'Kazak-Kirgizskiye Kochevyye Ordy i Pugachevshchina 1773–4', *Novy Vostok*, No. 25 1926, pp. 201ff.; see also Pushkin, *op. cit.*, Vol. I, pp. 22f.

22. M. J. (M. Zhizhka), the Examination of Pugachev ataman A Khlopusha, *Krasny Arkhiv*, Vol. 68 1935, pp. 162–72.

23. N. Dubrovin, *Pugachev i yego Soobshchinniki*, 3 vols., St. Petersburg 1884, Vol. II, p. 18 for *ukaz* issued to the people of Rassypnaya.

24. Pushkin, *op. cit.*, Vol. I, p. 26.

25. It was from this event that Pushkin probably derived the plot of his novel, *The Captain's Daughter*.

26. The peasant Alexei Kirpilov's description of Pugachev at Sakmara (6th October 1773); see Pushkin, *op. cit.*, Vol. I, pp. 30ff.

27. See Spirkov on Pugachev's 'State War College' in Mavrodin, *op. cit.*, Vol. II, pp. 444–64.

28. See Mavrodin on the organisation and tactics of Pugachev's forces, *op. cit.*, p. 466.

29. General Ker to General Chernyshev, 11th November 1773, Pushkin, *op. cit.*, Vol. I, p. 49.

30. M.J., Khlopusha's examination, *Krasny Arkhiv*, *loc. cit.*; for conditions of the Ural factory peasants see R. Portal, *L'Oural au XVIIIᵉ siècle*, Paris 1950.

31. See report by I. S. Myasnikov, official in the Ufa and Isetsk district, in Golubstov, *op. cit.*, Vol. II, pp. 268–70; *Doprosy Yemelyanu Pugachevu i Pismo o nem Gosudarini Imperatritsy Yekateriny II k Grafu Paninu*, Moscow 1858, p. 25; on the use of artillery in Pugachev's army see N. Ye. Grebenyuk in *Sbornik Issledovanii i*

Materialov Artilleriiskogo-Istoricheski Muzei, vyp. III, Leningrad 1958.

32. Shranovich's interrogation, Golubtsov, *op. cit.*, Vol. III, p. 210.

33. Piontkovski, *loc. cit.*

34. On the risings in Bashkiria, see Parei in Mavrodin, *op. cit.*, Vol. II, pp. 206–36.

35. On the rising in western Siberia, see Andrushenko in Mavrodin *op. cit.*, Vol. II, pp. 355–78.

36. Remark by Salavat Yulayev, the Bashkir chieftain and father of Yulai, quoted in article on peasant war in *Bolshaya Sovetskaya Entsiklopediya*, 2nd edition.

37. See Perfilev's account in 'Glavnye Posobniki Pugacheva', *Russkaya Starina*, Vol. XVI 1876, pp. 479–88.

38. Quoted by Ovchinnikov in Mavrodin, *op. cit.*, Vol. II, p. 429.

39. Statement by T. I. Podurov, 10.5.1774; Golubtsov, *op. cit.*, Vol. II, pp. 187–9; see also Zarubin-Chika's statement pp. 128–36.

40. Pushkin, *op. cit.*, Vol. I, p. 19.

41. See Ovchinnikov in Mavrodin, *op. cit.*, Vol. II, p. 442.

42. Zarubin-Chiki's statement, September 1774, Golubtsov, *op. cit.*, Vol. II, pp. 128–36.

43. Golubtsov, *op. cit.*, Vol. III, p. 7.

44. Interrogation of the serf K. S. Kolesnikov, 18th December 1773, Golubtsov, *op. cit.*, Vol. III, pp. 8–9.

45. See Mavrodin, *op. cit.*, Vol. II, p. 14. The appeals fell on extremely fertile ground. Between 1762 and 1772 there had been at least forty large peasant outbreaks in Russia proper.

46. Firsov, *op. cit.*, p. 153; see Piontkovski, *loc. cit.*, Spirkov in Mavrodin, *op. cit.*, Vol. II, p. 451. The best available selection of these documents is in Golubtsov, *op. cit.*, especially Vol. I. A few of the later documents do bear the roughly scrawled signature 'Peter'.

47. Podurov's statement, Golubtsov, *op. cit.*, Vol. II, pp. 187–9.

48. Golubtsov, *op. cit.*, Vol. II, pp. 111–12.

49. K. Usayev's story, in *Russkaya Starina*, *loc. cit.*

50. See statement by Maxim Shigayev and Gorshkov, Golubtsov, *op. cit.*, Vol. II, pp. 104–7 and 112–15; Pushkin, *op. cit.*, Vol. I, p. 45.

51. Spirkov in Mavrodin, *op. cit.*, Vol. II, pp. 452–4.

52. Spirkov on the 'College of War' in Mavrodin, *op. cit.*, Vol. II, pp. 458–60.

53. Pushkin, *op. cit.*, Vol. I, p. 85, and Firsov, *op. cit.*, p. 152.

54. Firsov, *op. cit.*, pp. 120–1.

55. See Andrushenko on the rising in western Siberia in Mavrodin, *op. cit.*, Vol. II, p. 363.

56. Pushkin, *op. cit.*, Vol. I, pp. 91–3.

57. Pushkin, *op. cit.*, Vol. I, p. 98.

58. The testimony of Tvorogov and Chumakov is also in *Russkaya Starina, loc. cit.*

59. Report of Lieutenant S. Kabanov, August 1774, Golubtsov, *op. cit.*, Vol. II, p. 307.

60. Piontkovski, *loc. cit.*

61. Tvorogov's and Chumakov's evidence, *Russkaya Starina*, 1876, pp. 489–94 *loc. cit.*

62. Sofia's interrogation, *Russkaya Starina*, 1876.

63. *Russ. Star.*, 1876, *loc. cit.*

64. Quoted in article on Pugachev revolt in *Bol. Sov. Ent., op. cit.*

65. See Golubtsov, *op. cit.*, Vol. I, pp. 40–1.

66. Piontkovski, *loc. cit.*, and Pugachev's interrogation of 8th November 1774; see also V. A. Golobutski, *Chernomorskoye Kazachestvo*, Kiev 1956, p. 105, and Chapter 7 on the *gaidamaks*.

67. Manifesto to Don Cossacks quoted by S. G. Svatikov, *Donskaya Letopis*, Vienna 1923–4, Vol. I, p. 203.

68. Major General Potapov to the College of War, December 1773, quoted by Andrushenko in his article on the Don during the rising in Mavrodin, *op. cit.*, Vol. II, p. 411.

69. Andrushenko, *loc. cit.*, p. 410; see also A. P. Pronshtein (Ed.), *Don i Nizhneye Povolozhye v Period Krestyanskoi Voiny 1773–1775*, Rostov 1961, and *Zemlya Donskaya v XVIII veke*, Rostov-on-Don 1961, also in Kuznetsov, *op. cit.*, pp. 189–90.

70. Golubtsov, *op. cit.*, Vol. II, pp. 152–3 and note; Piontkovski, *loc. cit.*

71. Pushkin, *op. cit.*, Vol. I, p. 155.

72. Piontkovski, *loc. cit.*; Golubtsov, *op. cit.*, Vol. II, p. 155; Ovchinnikov, *Voprosy Istorii*, No. 5 1966, *loc. cit.* See Chapter VI on Nekrasov.

73. Chumakov and Tvorogov, see *Russkaya Starina, loc. cit.*

74. Ovchinnikov, *Vop. Ist.*, No. 3 1966, *loc. cit.*; see especially the second report of Pugachev's interrogation at Yaitsk of 16th September 1774. For documents relating to the last period of the revolt and the capture of Pugachev, including reports by officers concerned in its suppression between August and December 1774, especially those of Col. Mikhelson, see Ya. K. Grot, 'Materialy dlya istorii Pugachevskogo Bunta', *Sbornik Otdeleniya Russkago Yazyka i Slovestnosti Imperatorskoi Akademii Nauk*, Vol. XV No. 4, St. Petersburg 1876, pp. 1–144.

75. Pushkin, *op. cit.*, Vol. I, pp. 162–3.

76. Ovchinnikov, *Vop. Ist.*, No. 3 1966, *loc. cit.* For some extraordinary tales retailed abroad see *Le Faux Pierre III, ou la Vie et les Avantures de Rebelle Yemeljan Pugatschew* by R.S.G.W.D.B., London 1775; also *Leben und Abentheuer des Rebellen J. Pugatschew*, 1776. Concoctions hardly less imaginative are contained in H. Krasinski's *The Cossacks of the Ukraine*, 1848, which describes Polish exiles organising and drilling Pugachev's followers, and banners inscribed with the motto 'Redivivus et ultor'—'Risen and avenged' (p. 149 *passim*). There is no evidence to support these assertions.

77. Ovchinnikov, *Vop. Ist.*, No. 3 1966, *loc. cit.*

78. Catherine to Voltaire, dated 29th December 1774, Pushkin, *op. cit.*, Vol. I, p. 164 (other correspondence p. 74).

79. Ovchinnikov, *loc. cit.*

80. For an eye-witness account of Pugachev's execution—a letter from Moscow published in French—see the *Gazette d'Utrecht*, No. XVIII, 3rd March 1775, translated in *Doprosy Yemelyanu Pugachevu* 1858, pp. 73–4.

81. S. I. Tkhorzhevski, *Pugachevshchina v Pomeshchechiei Rossii*, Moscow 1930, pp. 109–114, According to one account nearly 800 men, 474 women and 304 children of noble rank were killed in the revolt (Blum, *Lord and Peasant in Russia*, Atheneum New York 1967, p. 557).

82. Report by General Reinsdorp dated 25th June 1775, Golubtsov, *op. cit.*, Vol. II, pp. 288–9; order signed by the official Peter Chuchalov, January 1775, *op. cit.*, Vol. II, pp. 275–6.

83. Catherine's manifesto dated 17th March 1775 quoted in Ovchinnikov, *loc. cit.* Her successors shared the feeling. Tsar Nicholas, who personally censored Pushkin's history (*op. cit.*), refused to allow him to call it a 'History of Pugachev' and substituted the title 'History of the Pugachev Revolt', saying 'a criminal like Pugachev doesn't have a history (V. G. Belinski, *Estetika i Literaturnaya Kritika*, Moscow 1959, Vol. II, note 22, p. 744).

84. See, for instance, the pamphlet *1773–1873 v Pamyat Stoletiya Pugachevshchina*, 2nd ed., London 1874, recalling (p. 24) Pugachev's 'charter' to the Yaik Cossacks and his promises of 'eternal freedom' for Russia. Also *Yemelyan Pugachev chestnomu Kazachestvu i vsemu lyndu Russkomu shlet nizki poklon*, 1854.

85. Quoted by Firsov, *op. cit.*, p. 173. For comparisons of Pugachev's and Razin's revolts with those of Watt Tyler, the *jacquerie* in France, the *gusitski* wars in Czechoslovakia and especially the sixteenth century peasant wars in Germany, see M. Ya. Fenomenov, *Razinovshchina i Pugachevshchina*, Moscow 1923.

CHAPTER 8

1. Rumyanteev to Catherine 4.6.1775, A. N. Pirovanov, *Donskiye Kazaki*, St. Petersburg 1909, p. 65.

2. *The London Chronicle*, IV, 305, 9–12th December 1758; report from a Prussian source, *The Gentleman's Magazine*, Vol. XXVIII 1758, pp. 449–51.

3. Letter from the Prussian army under Marshal Lehwald and published in Berlin, *The Gentleman's Magazine*, Vol. XXVIII, p. 432.

4. Philip Longworth, *The Art of Victory: the Life and Achievements of Generalissimo Suvorov 1729–1800*, Constable 1965, pp. 209 and 56.

5. Longworth, *op. cit.*, p. 193.

6. According to Golobutski ('O sotsialnykh otnosheniyakh v Zadunaiskoi Sechi', *Istoricheskiye Zapiski Akad. Nauk/SSSR*, No. 30, 1949) the trans-Danube Sech attracted the poorest Ukrainian Cossacks. Some went first to Turkish-occupied Ochakov which they used as a base from which to mount some desultory raids on Russian positions, until the Turks decided it politic to remove them to the Danube. Catherine tried to tempt them back to Russia, but with little success, and at the start of the 1806–12 Russo-Turkish war, General I. I. Mikhelson made another appeal to them, promising them amnesty. A thousand men responded immediately and in 1807 the Budzhak Cossack Host was formed in the Danube estuary. Its 39 *kurens* contained descendants of the Nekrasovites already in Turkish territory and some Zaporozhians who had lived in Moldavia until after 1791. The leaders of the new community were appointed, not elected. But Mikhelson's experimental creation of a new Cossack community was a failure. Despite the incorporation of Greeks, Serbs, Bulgarians and Albanians who served against Napoleon and the Turks in 1806–12, and of some gypsies (see M. P. Khoroshchin, *Kazachi Voiska*, St. Petersburg 1881), the number of ex-Zaporozhians gradually declined; many of the remainder drifted to the Kuban and some returned to Turkish protection. Continued Russian agitation to tempt these out of the Turkish orbit had scant results though some returned ten years later rather than fight against Russian troops who were advancing along the Danube. These had helped to suppress a Greek rising against Turkish rule, but the strain on their loyalty to the Turks reached breaking point when they heard they were to be sent to Egypt (K. K. Abaza, *Kazaki: Dontsy, Uraltsy, Kubantsy, Tertsy*, St. Petersburg 1890, p. 243). The Danube Cossack community was composed predominantly of bachelors and made up for a steady flow of desertions by accepting runaways from Russia. In 1828–9 the majority of ex-Zaporozhians who returned from

Turkey were formed into a new Cossack community, re-named the Azov Host in 1831.

7. V. A. Bednov, *Materialy k Istorii Kolonizatsii Byvshykh Zaporozhskikh Vladenii*, Yekaterinoslav 1914, p. 38, cited by Golobutski, *Chern. Kaz.*, *op. cit.*, p. 124; see *Kievskaya Starina*, April 1885, pp. 783–90 and Golobutski, *Chern. Kaz.*, *op. cit.*, p. 112.

8. Quoted in *Otechestvennyye Zapiski*, Vol. VI 1839, section ii, p. 9.

9. Alexander I's *ukaz* to the military governor of Nikolayev, quoted by Golobutski, *Chern. Kaz.*, *op. cit.*, pp. 176–7. The community continued to be known as the Black Sea Cossack Host until well into the nineteenth century, when the name was changed to the Kuban Cossack Host. I have used the latter term throughout, however, to avoid confusion.

10. F. Shcherbina (*Ocherki Yushno-Russki Artel*, pp. 181–2) stresses the communistic character of the Zaporozhian fishing industry ('fishing equipment was probably held in common, the division of income equal, the rights of members equal'). This judgement is disputed by Golobutski (*Chern. Kaz.*, *op. cit.*, pp. 280–2) who shows that the cost of equipment even for small-scale fishing was considerable, that a seine could cost 230 rubles, a boat between 50 and 100, and that the man who provided the capital often took as much as a half-share in the proceeds of the cooperative. However this does not exclude the possibility of the existence of equal-share cooperatives, nor that Shcherbina's view may hold good for the earlier period of Cossackdom, though Golobutski's must prevail from the late eighteenth century.

11. See inventories in Golobutski, *Chern. Kaz.*, *op. cit.*, pp. 253–5.

12. Ataman Kotlyarevski's order of December 1798, I. I. Dmitrenko, *Sbornik Materialov po Istoriei Kubanskogo Kazachego Voiska*, Vol. IV, doc. 360, quoted by Golobutski, *Chern. Kaz.*, *op. cit.*, p. 321.

13. N. M. Firsov, *Pugachevshchina*, 1907.

14. Pronshtein in Kusnetsov, *op. cit.*, p. 171.

15. See V. Mamyshev, *General-ot-Kavalerii Graf M. I. Platov*. This work is in itself an example of the indoctrination literature on the Cossacks which became considerable in the nineteenth century (see Chapter 9). Mamyshev quotes speeches by Platov to illustrate the man's remarkable courage, his contempt for 'the damned Tatars', his religious sense, his patriotism and his loyalty to the throne.

16. *The Oracle or Daily Advertiser*, 29.3.1799; *St. James's Chronicle*, 8.4.1799; *Morning Herald*, 16.8.1799; E. Walsh, *A Narrative of the Expedition to Holland in the Autumn of the Year 1799*, London 1800, p. 47.

17. P. N. Krasnov, *Kazaki v Nachale XIX Veka*, St. Petersburg 1896, p. 42.

18. Sir R. T. Wilson, *Brief Remarks on the Character and Composition of the Russian Army*, London 1810, p. 27.

19. Wilson, *op. cit.*, pp. 27 *passim*.

20. K. K. Benkendorff, *The Cossacks: A Memoir*, London 1849, pp. 25–8.

21. Sir R. Wilson, quoted by M. S. Anderson, *Britain's Discovery of Russia*, Macmillan 1958, p. 220 note.

22. Eugene Tarlé, *Napoleon's Invasion of Russia 1812*, London 1942 (trans. from the original: *Nashestviye Napoleona Rossiyu-1812 god*), p. 67, quoting Barclai de Tolly to the Tsar 17th June 1812.

23. Wilson, *op. cit.*, p. 28; Tarlé, *op. cit.*, p. 219. See Wilson's case (*op. cit.*, p. 32) for keeping the Cossack Corps united as a separate arm.

24. *Characteristic Portraits of the various Tribes of Cossacks*, 1840, pp. 8ff., Benkendorff, *op. cit.*, p. 25.

25. *Char. Por.*, *op. cit.*, p. iii; Benkendorff, *op. cit.*, p. 20 note.

26. *The Gentleman's Magazine*, lxxxiv, Part I, p. 688.

27. Platov's order: quoted by Mamyshev, *op. cit.*, pp. 117, 118.

CHAPTER 9

1. Edward Clarke, *Travels in Various Countries of Europe, Asia and Africa*, London 1810–23, Vol. I, p. 396.

2. See Moritz Wagner, *Der Kaukasus und das Land des Kosaken in den Jahren 1843 bis 1846*, Dresden and Leipzig 1848, Vol. II, p. 93; Julius H. Klaproth, *Travels in the Caucasus and Georgia*, London 1814, p. 85, and also Clarke, *op. cit.*, Vol. I, p. 384.

3. A. A. Skalkovski on the Rostov fair, quoted by Zolotov in V. Kuznetsov, *Istoriya Dona*, Rostov-on-Don 1965, p. 222; see also Clarke, *op. cit.*

4. Kalproth, *op. cit.*; p. 85, Clarke, *op. cit.*, Vol. I, pp. 380–1; *Characteristic Portraits of the Various Tribes of Cossacks*, 1840, p. 16, and Zolotov in Kuznetsov, *op. cit.*, p. 211.

5. Antoine Louis de Romanò, *Coup d'Oeil Philosophique sur le Pays Occupe par les Cosaques du Don*, Milan 1807, Vol. II, p. 164; Zolotov in Kuznetsov, *op. cit.*, pp. 195–6.

6. See Zolotov on the economic development of the Don 1800–1850 in Kuznetsov, *op. cit.*, especially p. 197.

7. Gen. Chernyshev's report quoted by Zolotov in Kuznetsov, *op. cit.*, p. 195.

8. Quoted by V. Mamyshev, *General-et-Kavalerii Graf. M. I. Platov*, p. 204.

9. Quoted by K. K. Abaza, *Kazaki: Dontsy, Uraltsy, Kubantsy, Tertysy*, St. Petersburg 1890, pp. 124–5.

10. On the incident in Uralsk see L. L. Masyanov in *Kazachi Soyuz*, Paris, No. 2 1950, p. 5; on Turchaninov see Albert J. Parry, 'John B. Turchin: Russian General in the American Civil War', *The Russian Review*, Hanover N.H., U.S.A., Vol. I, No. 2 1942.

11. N. I. Masterov on education on the Don, in Kusnetsov, *op. cit.*, p. 482.

12. Lermontov to A. A. Lopukhin, 17.6.1840 on his visit to Novocherkassk, I. L. Andronikov and others (eds.), *M. Yu. Lermontov: Sobraniye Sochinenii*, Vol. IV, Moscow 1958, pp. 464–5.

13. Wagner's conversation with Major V. Igurov, Wagner, *op. cit.*, Vol. I, pp. 53–4, 79, 80–2.

14. Clarke, *op. cit.*, Vol. I, pp. 441–2.

15. F. A. Shcherbina ('Zemelnaya Obshchina Kubanskogo Kazachestva', *Kubanski Sbornik*, Vol. II) diagnoses the land troubles on the Kuban as being due to the elders' use of 'foreign' labour on their farms, and blames the presence of these peasant outsiders (*inogorodnyye*) for the land shortage and consequent troubles. He is criticised by Golobutski for reflecting class interest and for confusing the *obshchina* (common-holding of land by Cossack villagers) with competing private ownership. Golobutski places emphasis on practical, as opposed to legal, reasons why Cossacks were often unable to work their plots on their own account. I. Popka (*Chernomorskiye Kazaki*, 1858, pp. 76–7) describes a free land grab continuing right up to 1850; see also V. Golobutski, *Chernomorskoye Kazachestvo*, Kiev 1956, pp. 224–6.

16. Golobutski, *op. cit.*, p. 263.

17. On Bursak see Golobutski, *op. cit.*, pp. 260–2, 266 *passim*.

18. The memoirs of A. S. Fomenko (Yekaterinodar 1903, p. 9), quoted by Golobutski, *op. cit.*, p. 326.

19. Golobutski (*op. cit.*, pp. 290–3) again takes issue with Shcherbina (*Istoriya Kubanskago Kazachyago Voiska*, Yekaterinodar 1910, Vol. II, chapter xxviii) for denying the use of hired labour apart from the *zabrodchiki*, a particular kind of fishermen.

20. Golobutski, *op. cit.*, p. 173; General Paskevich quoted by I. Bentkovski, *Materialy dlya Istorii Kolonisatsii Sevornogo Kavkaza*, Yekaterinodar 1881, p. 111; 'Kratki Istori i mediko-topograficheski Ocherk Kubanskogo Kordona', *Zhurnal Ministerstva Vnutrennykh Del*, No. 4, 1836, quoted by Golobutski, *op. cit.*, pp. 217–8.

21. Ye. D. Felitsyn (ed.) and F. A. Shcherbina, *Kubanskoye Kazachye Voisko 1696–1888*, Voronezh 1888, etc.

22. J. A. Longworth, *A Year Among the Circassians*, London 1840, Vol. II, pp. 122–6.

23. Bentkovski, *loc. cit.*

24. Yermolov quoted by Bentkovski, *op. cit.*, p. 92.

25. See Shcherbina, *op. cit.*, Vol. II, p. 666; *Statisticheskiye Trudy Shtukenberga*, Vol. III, St. Petersburg 1857, pp. 37–8. The comparative tables of numbers of horses, cattle and sheep 1840 and 1841 is reproduced by Golobutski, *op. cit.*, p. 270; see also *ibid.* pp. 250–1.

26. Alexandre Dumas, *Adventures in the Caucasus* (trans. E. Murch), Owen 1962, p. 36.

27. Ye. Maksimov, *Terskoye Kazachye Voisko*, 1890, pp. 29–30, 80 and 90, 39, 158, 143 and 50.

28. *Zhurnal M-va Vnutrennykh Del, loc. cit.*

29. Roman K. Bogdanov, 'Vospominaniya Amurskogo Kazaka o Proshlom s 1849 na 1880 god', *Priamurskiye Vedomesti* 1900, Nos. 341, pp. 17–19, and 342, pp. 14–17, trans. in G. A. Lensen's *Russia's Eastward Expansion*, Spectrum 1964, pp. 96–103.

30. J. S. Curtiss, *The Russian Army under Nicholas I 1825–1855*, Duke Un. Press 1965, p. 107; F. von Stein, *Russische Kosakenheere* (Petermanns Mitt. erg 16) 1884, p. 24.

31. Stein, *op. cit.*, p. 38; G. Simoleit, *Die Donkosaken und Ihr Land*, Königsberg 1930, pp. 74–5. See also table of Cossack war establishment in 1892 in *The Cossack Armies*, Simla 1895, pp. 61 and 68ff., A. H. Springer, *Die Kosaken 1877*, p. 118. For Cossack war establishment 1853 and 1880 see Khoroshchin, *Kazachiye Voiska*, 1881, p. 271. For the 1895 Cossack war establishment and in general on their dress, equipment, recruitment, training, tactics, horses, roles in war, etc., see A. Niessel, *Les Cosaques*, 1899, pp. 213–466.

32. Penchenko (in Kuznetsov, *op. cit.*, p. 286) on 'Ustav o Voinskoi Povinnosti Donskogo Voiska' 17th April 1875; *Kubanski Sbornik*, Vol. XIII, Yekaterinodar 1894, p. 8, quoted by Golobutski, *op. cit.*, p. 168; *The Cossack Armies*, *op. cit.*, pp. 65 and 66 note.

33. Stein, *op. cit.*, p. 34; Springer, *op. cit.*, pp. 76–7; *The Cossack Armies*, *op. cit.*, pp. 33–4; Masyanov, *loc. cit.*

34. K. K. Benkendorff, *The Cossacks: A Memoir*, London 1849, pp. 14–16.

35. *The Cossack Armies*, *op. cit.*, p. 83.

36. Benkendorff, *op. cit.*, p. 19.

37. *Russki Arkhiv*, Vol. VII 1869, No. 7, p. 2133, quoted by Curtiss, *op. cit.*, p. 144.

38. Curtiss, *op. cit.*, pp. 143–4.

39. A. L. Zisserman, *Dvatsat Pyat Let na Kavkaze (1842–1867)*, St. Petersburg 1879, Vol. I, p. 185, quoted by Curtiss, *op. cit.*, p. 141.

40. *Voyenny Sbornik*, quoted in *The Cossack Armies*, *op. cit.*, p. 83.

41. M–v, 'Otryvki is pokhodnykh zapisok', *Voyenny Sbornik*, Vol. III, 1860, p. 49, quoted by Curtiss, *op. cit.*, p. 142.

42. Porovski, quoted by I. G. Rozner, *Yaik pered Burei*, Moscow 1966, pp. 8–9.

43. Robert R. McCormick, *With the Russian Army*, N.Y. 1915, pp. 179–81.

44. *The Cossack Armies*, *op. cit.*, pp. 47–8.

45. See Zolotov in Kuznetsov, *op. cit.*, pp. 254ff. for the provisions of the 1835 *Polozheniye*.

46. *Svod Voyennykh Postanovlenii*, 1838, Part I, Book 2, supplement: 'Polk. Inst. dlya Voiska Donskago', cited by Curtiss, *op. cit.*, p. 144.

47. See Springer, *op. cit.*, p. 23; Svatikov in *Donskaya Letopis*, Vol. I, pp. 246ff., and Demeshin and Zader in Kuznetsov, *op. cit.*. p. 347. See also Stein, *op. cit.*, p. 24, population tables in Niessel, *op. cit.*, p. 129, and N. I. Krasnov, *Materialy dlya Geografii i Statistiki Zemli Voiska Donskogo*, 1863, a major source on the Don in the mid-nineteenth century.

48. The Kuban Cossacks also held three-quarters of the land in their province, the Terek Cossacks rather more, while the Ural and Seven Rivers Cossacks were the exclusive owners. Overall, Cossacks held two-thirds of the land in all Cossack provinces. For proportions of land in private ownership, host reserve and stanitsa commonlands see article on 'Kazachestvo' in *Bolshaya Sovetskaya Entsiklopediya*.

49. Svatikov in *Donskaya Letopis*, Vol. I, p. 224; Zolotov in Kuznetsov, *op. cit.*, p. 199.

50. *Priazov Krai*, 24th August 1899, quoted by Demeshin and Zader in Kuznetsov, *op. cit.*, pp. 347–9.

51. For Cossack budgets see Stein, *op. cit.*, p. 29; *The Cossack Armies*, *op. cit.*, pp. 27–9.

52. Svatikov in *Donskaya Letopis*, Vol. I, pp. 224ff.

53. *The Cossack Armies*, *op. cit.*, p. 9.

54. See Khlystov on the development of industry on the Don in Kuznetsov, *op. cit.*, p. 304.

55. For settlement sizes in the Cossack regions see Stein, *op. cit.*, p. 32.

56. *Voyenny Sbornik* 1888, quoted in *The Cossack Armies*, *op. cit.*, pp. 13–14.

57. Khlystov in Kuznetsov, *op. cit.*, pp. 290–2; Ye. I. Demeshin and A. G. Zader on agriculture on the Don at the end of the nineteenth and the beginning of the twentieth century, in Kuznetsov, *op. cit.*, pp. 347ff; Simoleit, *op. cit.*, p. 95.

N

58. For numbers of horses, cattle and sheep in proportion to population 1870 and 1879 see Stein, *op. cit.*, p. 27. For value of fish industry income in 1879 see Stein, *op. cit.*, p. 28.

59. A. Herzen, *Collected Works*, Lemke, Vol. IX 1919, p. 159; Bakunin quoted by Svatikov, *Donskaya Letopis*, Vol. I, p. 229.

60. See Masterov in Kuznetsov, *op. cit.*, pp. 482–6.

61. See Svatikov in *Donskaya Letopis*, Vol. I, p. 234.

62. M. A. Czaplicka, 'The Evolution of Cossack Communities', *Journal of the Central Asian Society* 1918, p. 2.

63. See 'Tikhoretski Pogrom', *Iz Sovremenny Zhizni*, pp. 1–41, Geneva 1902. This socialist pamphlet describes the alleged rape and death in detention on a stanitsa near Grozny (Vladikavkaz) of a girl, probably a prostitute. Her case roused local railway workers and gave rise to an orgy of machine-breaking on Cossack farms in the district.

64. Maurice Baring, *What I Saw in Russia*, Nelson [1913], pp. 177–81, *passim*. On Don Cossacks in the Russo-Japanese War see D. S. Babichev in Kuznetsov, *op. cit.*, pp. 366ff. Also T. Rostovtsev, *Chervertaya Donskaya Kazachya Diviziya v Russkoi-Yaponskoi Voine*, Kiev 1910.

CHAPTER 10

1. Lenin, *Sochineniya*, Vol. XXIX, p. 257.

2. Quoted by Yu. I. Scry in his article on the 1905 revolution on the Don in V. I. Kuznetsov, *Istoriya Dona*, Rostov-on-Don 1965, pp. 369–400.

3. Sery, *loc. cit.*

4. I. Borisenko, *The Soviet Republic in the Northern Caucasus in 1918*, Vol. I, p. 23, and G. Pokrovski, *The Denikin System*, pp. 11 and 13, cited by W. H. Chamberlain, *The Russian Revolution*, Vol. I, p. 388 note 9.

5. See F. A. Shcherbina in *Kazachestvo: Mysli Sovremennikov o Proshlom i Budushchem Kazachestva* (a symposium), Paris 1928, pp. 347–77.

6. J. Efremov (Yefremov), *Cossacks of the Don*, Paris 1919, pp. 10–11. See V. A. Zolotov on agrarian relations on the Don in the early twentieth century, Kuznetsov, *op. cit.*, pp. 400–12.

7. Zolotov, *loc. cit.*

8. See S. G. Svatikov in *Donskaya Letopis*, Vol. I, Vienna 1923–4, pp. 250ff. on the 3rd and 4th Dumas and Cossack affairs.

9. See Wilhelm Köhler (Ed.), *Die Kosaken des Zaren (1914–15)*, Minden and Leipzig [1915?] for examples of anti-Cossack war propaganda stories.

10. N. N. Golovin, *On Russia's Military Effort during the World War of 1914–17; The Cossack Struggle for Freedom;* Babichev, Kuznetsov, *op. cit.*, p. 473.

11. M. Philips Price, *War and Revolution in Asiatic Russia,* London 1918, pp. 169, 202, 227, 161. See also Marina Yurlova, *Cossack Girl* (1915–19), Cassell 1934.

12. Quoted by V. S. Panchenko in article on the workers' movement on the Don during the First World War, in Kuznetsov, *op. cit.*, p. 465.

13. Zolotov, *loc. cit.*

14. N. N. Sukhanov, *The Russian Revolution* (trans. Carmichael), C.U.P. 1955, pp. 6, 15 and 19 on attitudes of Cossacks in Petrograd in February 1917.

15. Quoted in article on 'Kazachestvo' in *Bolshaya Sovetskaya Entsiklopediya.*

16. Sukhanov, *op. cit.*, pp. 93–4. See also P. N. Krasnov, *Kazachya 'Samostiinost'*, Berlin 1922.

17. Philips Price, *op. cit.*, p. 287.

18. (P. N. Vrangel), *The Memoirs of General Wrangel* (trans.), London 1929, p. 20.

19. Philips Price, *op. cit.*, pp. 294–5.

20. Shcherbina, *loc. cit.*

21. A. I. Denikin, *Ocherki iz Russkoi Smuty,* Paris 1922, Berlin 1924, Vol. II, p. 119.

22. *Bol. Sov. Ent.*, *loc. cit.*

23. See section on 'The South-East Union' 1917 in *Donskaya Letopis, op. cit.* and *passim* for attempts to organise Cossack self-government after the Revolution.

24. *Kratki Istoricheski Ocherk i Otchet Kazachyego Otdela VTsIK po Oktyabr 1919g,* March 1917–April 1919 (*KOVTsIK*), pp. 5–6.

25. *Obshchekazachi Zhurnal* (Farmingdale 1946–), No. 17, October 1952, p. 53. See also John Reed, *Ten Days that Shook the World,* Lawrence and Wishart 1961, p. 20.

26. *Armiya i Flot* (a Bolshevik paper), 23.12.1917/5.1.1918.

27. Sukhanov, *op. cit.*, pp. 618–9; Chamberlin, *op. cit.*, Vol. I, pp. 313–30. See also P. N. Sobelev *et al.*, *History of the October Revolution* (English edition), Moscow 1966, p. 141.

28. I. Deutscher, *The Prophet Armed, Trotsky: 1879–1921,* O.U.P. 1954, p. 330.

29. *KOVTsIK*, pp. 11–14.

30. Sukhanov, *op. cit.*, p. 660; Reed, *op. cit.*, pp. 241 and 243.

31. *KOVTsIK*, pp. 20–1.

32. Sobelev, *op. cit.*, pp. 201–2.

33. *Bol. Sov. Ent.*, *loc. cit.*; 'South-East Union', *loc. cit.*

34. The words of the Cossack officer Izvarin in M. A. Sholokhov's *Tikhi Don*, translated by Stephen Garry under the title *And Quiet Flows the Don*, Putnam 1934/1960, p. 554.

35. Lenin, *op. cit.*, Vol. XXVI, p. 15.

36. See David Footman, *Civil War in Russia*, Faber 1961, p. 46.

37. Ivan Ulyanov, *Sovetskaya Respublika i Kazaki*, Moscow 1920, p. 7; *KOVTsIK*, pp. 27–8; see also E. H. Carr, *The Bolshevik Revolution*, 1917–1923, Vol. I, pp. 294–5 note.

38. Appeal by Council of Peoples Commissars, *KOVTsIK*, pp. 22–4, trans. by Reed, *op. cit.*, note 66.

39. *KOVTsIK*, p. 32.

40. General A. S. Lukomski, *Reminiscences*, Vol. I, pp. 295–6, quoted by Chamberlin, *op. cit.*, Vol. I, pp. 377–8.

41. Quoted by Footman, *op. cit.*, pp. 44–5.

42. Denikin, *op. cit.*, Vol. II, p. 318; Chamberlin, *op. cit.*, Vol. I, pp. 381–2 and 386.

43. See P. I. Pavlovski, *Annenkovshchina*, Moscow and Leningrad 1928.

44. Denikine (Denikin), *The White Army* (abridged translation), Cape 1930, pp. 47–9.

45. L. Trotski, *How the Revolution Armed Itself*, Vol. II, Book I, p. 174, quoted by Chamberlin, *op. cit.*, Vol. II, p. 211; Sholokhov, *The Don Flows Home to the Sea*, 1940/1966.

46. I. Lunchenkov, *Za Chuzhiye Grekhi*, Moscow 1925.

47. P. N. Krasnov, 'Vsevelikoye Voisko Donskoye' in I. V. Gessen (Ed.), *Arkhiv Russkoi Revolyutsii*, Berlin 1921–7, Vol. V, p. 251.

48. See section on the Don revolt in *Donskaya Letopis*, *op. cit.*

49. Sholokhov, *The Don Flows Home*, *op. cit.*, p. 168.

50. Sholokhov, *The Don Flows Home*, *op. cit.*, p. 564.

51. See, for example, 'A Mortal Enemy' (in *Tales from the Don*, Four Square 1964), 'The Way and the Road', and other of Sholokhov's stories written 1924–6.

52. Quoted by Chamberlin, *op. cit.*, Vol. II, p. 80.

53. Krasnov, 'Vsev. Voi. Don.', *loc. cit.*, p. 226.

54. Krasnov, 'Vsev. Voi. Don.', *loc. cit.*, p. 304.

55. *KOVTsIK*, pp. 32–4.

56. *Klich Trudovykh Kazakov*, 1.9.1918.

57. Ivan Ulyanov, *Sovetskaya Respublika i Kazaki*, Moscow 1920, pp. 16–18.

58. *Klich Trudovykh Kazakov*, 15.12.1918.

59. Denikin, *The White Army*, *op. cit.*, p. 298; *Kubanski Krai*, 1954, yr. 4, No. 1, p. 20, and No. 2, 1959, pp. 7ff, and No. 2, 1957, pp.

2ff. on Ryabovol. Also Filimonov, 'Razgrom Kubanskoi Rady' in *Arkhiv Russkoi Revolyutsii, op. cit.*, Vol. V, pp. 322–9.

60. Denikin, *The White Army, op. cit.*, p. 298.

61. *K Kazakam* (Proclamation by VTsIK), Moscow 1919.

62. Report of Ivan Ulyanov of the Cossack Department to the 7th All-Russian Congress of Soviets, November 1919, see *KOVTsIK*, pp. 43–4. Ulyanov, leading member of the 21-strong Cossack Department at this time, was a peasant, not a Cossack, as was at least one other member. Six out of the twenty-one were Communist Party members. They included one *esaul*, two lawyers and a doctor. A third of them were from the Don.

63. *K Kazakam, op. cit.*

64. *KOVTsIK*, pp. 45ff.

65. Chamberlin, *op. cit.*, Vol. II, p. 285.

66. S. M. Budenny, *Proidenny Put*, Moscow 1958, p. 245, quoted by John Erickson, *The Soviet High Command*, Macmillan 1961, p. 51.

67. On these Red Ukrainian Cossacks and their later history see I. Dubinski and G. Shevchuk, *Chervone Kozatstvo*, Kiev 1961.

68. RSFSR proclamation issued by Cossack Department of VTsIK, 1920.

69. Galin in 'Evening' by Isaac Babel, *Red Cavalry*, Knopf 1929, pp. 171–2.

70. Ulyanov, *Sov. Rep., op. cit.*, pp. 27–8.

71. Resolution of 1st Congress of Working Cossacks quoted in *Bol. Sov. Ent., loc. cit.*

72. V. I. Lenin, *Rech na pervom vseressiiskom Syezde Trudovykh Kazakov*, Moscow 1920 (Report of 1.3.1920 and published in *Pravda*).

73. Simolcit, *Die Donkosaken und Ihr Land*, 1930, p. 151.

74. Gregor Melekhov to Koshevoi in Sholokhov's *The Don Flows Home, op. cit.*, p. 731.

75. Fugitive Cossack to Aksinia in Sholokhov's *The Don Flows Home, op. cit.*, p. 655.

CHAPTER 11

1. See P. I. Kryukov, *Kazaki v Chataldzhe in na Lemnose v 1920–1921gg*, Belgrade 1924 and I. Lunchenkov, *Za chuzhiye Grekhi: Kazaki v Emigratsii*, Moscow 1925.

2. See *Donskaya Letopis*, Vienna 1923–4, Vol. II, pp. 297–371.

3. Lunchenkov, *op. cit.; Sovetski Yug*, No. 35, 15.2.1923, quoted by P. U. Barchugov (Ed.), *Vosstanovitelny Period na Donu (1921–5gg): Sbornik Dokumentov*, Rostov-on-Don 1962, p. 224.

4. P. Korolevich, *Istoriya Pereseleniya Kazakov v Respubliku Peru*, Novy Sad 1930.

5. See E. J. Lindgren, 'An example of culture contact without conflict: Reindeer Tungus and Cossacks of Northwestern Manchuria', *American Anthropologist*, Vol. XL, No. 4, Oct.–Dec. 1938, pp. 605–21.

6. Boris Ryabykh, *Obshchekazachi Zhurnal*, No. 7, Sep. 1948, p. 21.

7. Don Region Executive Committee to all district excoms, 20.1.1921, Barchugov, *op. cit.*, p. 49.

8. Barchugov, *op. cit.*, pp. 60–2.

9. Barchugov, *op. cit.*, pp. 7–9; J. Maynard, *The Russian Peasant*, Collier 1962, p. 188.

10. Regional Economic Council for South-East Russia to peasants and Cossacks, 21.7.1921, quoted by Barchugov, *op. cit.*, pp. 101–3.

11. Barchugov, *op. cit.*, pp. 166–8.

12. Barchugov, *op. cit.*, p. 204.

13. Ralph Fox, *Peoples of the Steppes*, 1925, p. 78.

14. Barchugov, *op. cit.*, p. 196.

15. Naumenko in *Kazachestvo*, Paris 1928, pp. 11ff.

16. Barchugov, *op. cit.*, pp. 404–6.

17. Resolution of the augmented plenum of the Don Committee of the RKP(b) on land distribution, April 1925, Barchugov, *op. cit.*, pp. 408–9.

18. Circular of North Caucasus Region Excom, 26th Aug. 1925, Barchugov, *op. cit.*, pp. 420–3.

19. Mikoyan's address to the Regional Committee of the North Caucasus RKP(b), 13th November 1925, quoted by Barchugov, *op. cit.*, pp. 440–1.

20. M. Hindus, *The Cossacks*, 1946, pp. 114 *passim*.

21. See letter from a recent emigrant from the Kuban in *Obshchekazachi Zhurnal*, No. 14, April 1952, pp. 32–4.

22. B. A. Abramov in V. P. Danilov (Ed.), *Ocherki Istorii Kollektiviztsii Selskogo Khozyaistva v Soyuznykh Respublikakh*, Moscow 1963, p. 93; also Danilov and Ivnitski, *op. cit.*, p. 35. The volume concerning the Don in this series of published documents on collectivisation has not been issued at the time of writing.

23. See Abramov in Danilov, *op. cit.*, pp. 69–150.

24. Abramov in Danilov, *op. cit.*, p. 88.

25. This has been explicitly stated in recent Soviet analysis. Danilov and Ivnitski in Danilov, *op. cit.*, p. 46.

26. Abramov in Danilov, *op. cit.*, pp. 134–5.

27. See *Obshchekazachi Zhurnal*, No. 5, Jan. 1948, pp. 11ff. and No. 7, Sep. 1948, p. 23. Konstantin Cherkassov, *General Kononov*, Melbourne 1963, Vol. I, pp. 11ff, Hindus, *op. cit.*, p. 118.

References

28. Sholokhov to Stalin 16.4.1933 and Stalin's reply quoted by Danilov, *op. cit.*, pp. 55–6.

29. Danilov and Ivnitski, Danilov, *op. cit.*, p. 60; V. Kotelnikov, *Don, Kuban, Terek*, 1950, p. 36.

30. See I. Dubinski and G. Shevchuk, *Chervone Kozatstvo*, Kiev 1961, p. 159.

31. *Pravda* 18.3.1936.

32. Quoted in article on 'Kazachestvo', *Bolshaya Sovetskaya Entsiklopediya* 1937.

33. See for example, *Kazachi Byt: Literaturny Sbornik*, Paris 1925, A. I. Kuprin and others *Kazachi Literaturno-Obshchestvenny Almanakh*, Paris *c.* 1930.

34. I. F. Bydakorov, *Istoriya Kazachestva*, Prague 1930, p. 172. See pp. 116ff. on his Cossack nationalist thesis.

35. See A. P. Bogayevski in *Kazachestvo*, Paris 1928, pp. 7ff.

36. See I. N. Kurochka, *Gryadushchiye Sudby Kazachestva*, Paris 1927.

37. Ivan Rodionov in *Kazachi Sbornik*, No. 1, Berlin 1922, pp. 23–4. Also his article on pp. 11ff.

38. See for example *Krasnaya Zvezda* 22.2.1942.

39. Alexander Werth, *Russia at War 1941–1945*, Pan 1965, p. 702 note.

40. *Dokumenty Otvagi i Geroizma Kubantsev v Velikoi Otechestvennoi Voine 1941–1945: Sbornik Dokumentov in Materialov*, Krasnodar 1965, p. 273.

41. Werth, *op. cit.*, p. 522, quoting conversation with Konstantin Umanski, July 1942.

42. Cherkassov, *op. cit.*, pp. 132–3.

43. Konov's leaflet to Belov's corps quoted by Cherkassov, *op. cit.*, pp. 151–3.

44. Alexander Dallin, *German Rule in Russia 1941–1945*, Macmillan 1957, p. 301; Werth; *op. cit.*, p. 528.

45. Krasnov's letter of 20.12.1941 quoted in Cherkassov, *op. cit.*, pp. 146–7.

46. Cherkassov, *op. cit.*, pp. 83–4.

47. Cherkassov, *op. cit.*, pp. 181–2.

48. See Cherkassov, *op. cit.*, *Kazachya Lava*, No. 16, 1.8.1944 and *Kazachi Vestnik*, No. 73, 1.8.1944 (Prague).

49. See Pier Arrigo Carnier, *L'Armata Cosacca in Italia (1944–1945)*, Milano, 1965, p. 34.

50. *Kubanski Krai*, No. 1, 1960, pp. 7ff.

51. *'The Kensingtons': Princess Louise's Kensington Regiment. Second World War*, [1952], p. 223; F. S. V. Donnison, *Civil Affairs and Military Government North-West Europe 1944–1946*, HMSO 1961

379

(Official History of the Second World War), p. 289. See also C. R. B. Knight, *Historical Records of the Buffs 1919–1948*, London 1951; G. I. Malcolm in A. D. Malcolm, *History of the Argyll and Sutherland Highlanders 8th Battalion 1939–47*, London 1949; Cyril Ray, *Algiers to Austria: a History of 78 Division in the Second World War*, London 1952.

52. W. S. Churchill, *The Second World War*, Vol. VI, p. 647; Donnison, *op. cit.*, p. 289.

53. *Pravda* 17.1.1947.

54. See notice in *Obshchekazachi Zhurnal*, No. 16, Aug. 1952. Also *Kubanski Krai*, No. 1, 1955, p. 21.

Select Bibliography

ABAZA, K. K.: *Kazaki: Dontsy, Uraltsy, Kubantsy, Tertsy*, St. Petersburg 1890.

Akty Yuzhno-Zapadnoi Rossii.

ALEKSASHENKO, A. P.: *Krakh Denikinshchiny*, Moscow 1966.

ANDERSON, M. S.: *Britain's Discovery of Russia*, Macmillan 1958.

ANDRIYEVSKI, A. A.: *Materialy po Istorii Zaporozhya i Pogranichnykh Otnoshenii*, (Zapiski Imperatorskago Oddeskago Obshchestva Istorii i Drevnostei, Vols. XVI and XVII), Odessa 1893 and 1894.

ANDREYEVSKI, I. Ye. and others (eds.): *Entsiklopedicheski Slovar*, St. Petersburg 1890–1906.

ANDRUSYAK, M.: *Mazepa i Pravoberezhzha*, Lvov 1938.

ANTONOVICH, V. B.: *Korotka Istoriya Kozachchini*, Kolony 1913.
'Ostanni Chasi Kozachchini na Pravoberezh Pislya Aktiv 1679–1716rr', *Ruska Istorichna Biblioteka*, Lvov 1896, pp. 129–274.

[Akheograficheskaya Kommissiya], *Akty Istoricheskiye*, 5 vols., St. Petersburg 1841–2.

[Arkheograficheskaya Kommissiya], *Donskiye Dela*, 5 vols., St. Petersburg 1898–1917 (Russkaya Istoricheskaya Biblioteka, Vols. 18, 24, 26, 29 and 34).

[Arkheograficheskaya Kommissiya], *Dopolneniya k Aktam Istoricheskim*, 12 vols., St. Petersburg 1846–72.

[Arkheograficheskaya Kommissiya], *Polnoye Sobraniye Russkikh Letopisei*, St. Petersburg.

[Arkheograficheskaya Kommissiya], *Sibirskiye Letopisi*, St. Petersburg 1907.

ARMSTRONG, T. E.: *Russian Settlement in the North*, C.U.P. 1965.

A v B: *Die Kosaken in Ihrer Geshchichtliche Entwicklung*, 1860.

BABEL, Isaac: *Konarmiya*, 1st ed. 1924, 3rd. revised ed. 1928, stories trans. by J. J. Harland under title *Red Cavalry*, Knopf, London 1929.

BÄCHTOLD, R.: *Südwestrussland im Spätmittelalter (1240–1500)*, 1951.

BAGALEI, D. I.: *Ocherki iz Istorii Kolonizatsii Stepnoi Ukrainy Moskovskogo Gosudarstva*, Moscow 1887.

BAKHRUSHIN, S. V.: *Nauchnyye Trudy*, Vol. III (parts 1 and 2) and IV, Moscow 1955–9.

BARCHUGOV, P. U. (ed.): *Vosstanovitelny Period na Donu (1921–5gg):
Sbornik Dokumentov*, Rostov-on-Don, 1962.

BARONOVICH: *Naseleniye Predstepnoi Ukrainy v XVI V*, 1950.

BEDNOV, V. A.: *Materialy k Istorii Kolonizatsii Byvshykh Zaporozhskikh
Vladenii*, Yekaterinoslav 1914.

BENKENDORFF, K. K.: *Des Cosaques et leur Utilité à la Guerre*, 1831;
The Cossacks: A Memoir, London 1849.

BENTKOVSKI, I.: *Materialy dlya Istorii Kolonizatsii Severnogo Kavkaza:
Pamyatnaya Kniga Kubanskoi Oblasti*, Yekaterinodar 1881.

BERZ, L. I. and KHMELEVSKI, K. A.: *Geroicheskiye Gody Oktyabrskaya
Revolyutsiya i Grazhdanskaya Voina na Donu*, Rostov 1964.

BIELSKI, Marcin and Joachim: *Kronika Polska M. Bielskiego*, Cracow
1597; Sanok 1856.

BILLINGTON, J. H.: *The Icon and the Axe*, Weidenfeld and Nicolson
1966.

BLUM, Jerome: *Lord and Peasant in Russia from the Ninth to the Nineteenth
Century* (4th print), Athenaeum, New York 1967.

BOIKO, Ye. D.: *Selyanstvo Ukrainy V Drehy Polovyni XVI—Pershy
Polovyni XVII Stolittya*, Kiev 1963.

BOLDYREV, N. D.: 'Neizvestnoye o St. Razin i Ye. Pugacheve: Razin
na eshafote', *Sovetskiye Arkhivy*, No. 3, 1966, pp. 74–7.

Bolshaya Sovetskaya Entisklopediya.

BOROVOI, S. Ya.: 'Yevrei v Zaporozhskoi Sechi', *Istoricheski Sbornik*,
Akad. Nauk/SSSR, Leningrad, No. 1, 1934, pp. 141–90.

BORSHCHAK, I. and MARTEL, R.: *Vie de Mazeppa*, 1931.

BOTIN, Ye. G. and others: *Dokumenty Otvagi i Geroizma: Kuban v
Velikoi Otechestvennoi Voine 1941–1943*, Krasnodar 1965.

BRONEVSKI, V.: *Istoriya Donskago Voiska* (4 parts), St. Petersburg
1834.

(BULAVIN): *Bulavinskoye Vosstaniye: Sbornik Dokumentov*, Moscow 1935.

BYDAKOROV, I. F.: *Istoriya Kazachestva*, Prague 1930.

Cambridge History of Poland, C.U.P. 1950.

CAMPENHAUSEN, P. B. von: *Travels through Several Provinces of the
Russian Empire with an Account of the Zaporog Cossacks*, London
1808.

CARNIER, Pier Arrigo: *L'Armata Cosacca in Italia (1944–1945)*, de
Vecchi Milan 1965.

CARR, E. H.: *The Bolshevik Revolution 1917–1923*, Macmillan 1950.

CHAMBERLIN, W. H.: *The Russian Revolution*, Macmillan 1935.
Characteristic Portraits of the Various Tribes of Cossacks, Ackermann
1840.

CHARDIN, J.: *The Travels of Sir John Chardin, etc.*, London 1686.

CHERKASSOV, K.: *General Kononov*, Vol. I, Melbourne 1963.

CHERNOV, A.: *Vooruzhennyye Sily Russkogo Gosudarstva V XV–XVII VV*, Moscow 1954.

Chervonoye Kazachestvo 1918–23, Kharkov 1924.

CHEVALIER, Pierre: *Histoire de la Guerre des Cosaques contre la Pologne*, Paris 1663; (trans. E. Browne), *A Discourse of the Original Country, etc. of the Cossacks*, 1672.

CHISTYAKOV, E. V.: *Vasili Us: Spodvizhnik Stepana Razina*, Moscow 1963.

CHULOSHNIKOV, A.: 'Kazak-Kirgizskiye Kochevyye Ordy i Pugachevshchina 1773–4, *Novyy Vostok*, No. 25 1926.

CHURCHILL: *A Collection of Voyages and Travels*, 1732.

CLARKE, Edward: *Travels in Various Countries of Europe, Asia and Africa*, London 1810–23.

COLLINS, Samuel: *The Present State of Russia*, London 1671.

CRESSON, W. P.: *The Cossacks: Their History and Country*, New York 1919.

CURTISS, J. S.: *The Russian Army under Nicholas I 1825–1855*, Duke University Press 1965.

CZAPLICKA, M. A.: *Evolution of the Cossack Communities*, reprinted from Central Asian Society Journal, London 1918.

DALLIN, A.: *German Rule in Russia 1941–1945*, London 1957.

DANILOV, V. P. (ed.): *Ocherki Istorii Kollektivizatsii Selskogo Khozyaistva v Soyuznykh Respublikakh*, Moscow 1963.

DENIKIN, A. I.: *The White Army*, London 1930, a summary of *Ocherki Russkoi Smuty*, 5 vols., Paris 1921–6.

DENISOV, S. V.: *Zapiski. Grazhdanskaya Voina na Yuge Rosii 1918–20gg*, Constantinople 1921.

DMITRENKO, I. I.: *Opis Kazachikh Del Moskovskogo Otdeleniya Obshchago Arkhiva Glavnogo Shtaba*, St. Petersburg 1899.

Sbornik Materialov po Istoriei Kubanskogo Kazachyego Voiska.

DMITRIEV-MAMONOV, A. I.: *Pugachevshchina v Sibiri*, Moscow 1898. *Pugachevski Bunt v Zaurale i Sibiri*, St. Petersburg 1907.

DOBRYNEN, V.: *Borba s Bolshevizmom na Yuge Rossii: Uchastiye v Borbe Donskogo Kazachestva*, Prague 1921.

Dokumenty ob Osvoboditelnoi Voine Ukrainskogo Naroda 1648–1654, Kiev 1965.

DOMANITSKI, V.: 'Kozachchina na Perelomi XVI–XVII v (1591–1603)', *Zapiski Naukovogo Tovaristva imeni Shevchenka*, Vol. LXII 1904, Bk. vi, pp. 41–113, Vol. LX, pp. 1–32, Vol. LXI, pp. 33–64, Vol. LXIII, pp. 115–36, Vol. LXIV, pp. 137–71.

Donskaya Letopis: Sbornik Materialov po Noveishei Istorii Donskogo Kazachestva Sovremeni Russkoi Revolyutsii 1917 Goda, Vienna 1923–4.

Donskaya Pchela.

Donskaya Rech.

Donskiye Oblastnyye Vedomosti.

Donskiye Voiskovyye Vedomosti.

DUBINSKI, I. V. and SHEVCHUK, G. M.: *Chervone Kozatsvo*, Kiev 1961.

DUBNOW, S. M.: *History of the Jews in Russia and Poland*, Jewish Publication Society of America 1916–20, 3 vols.

DUBROVIN, N. T.: *Pugachev i yego Soobshchniki*, St. Petersburg 1884, 3 vols.

ERCKERT, R. von: *Der Ursprung des Kosaken*, Berlin 1882.

EVARNITSKI-YAVORNITSKI, D. I.: *Istochniki dlya Istorii Zaporozhskikh Kozakov*, Vladimir 1903, 2 vols.

Istoriya Zaporozhskikh Kozakov 1686–1734, St. Petersburg 1892–7, 3 vols.

Ivan Dmitriyevich Sirko, St. Petersburg 1894.

Ocherki po Istorii Zaporozhskikh Kozakov, St. Petersburg 1889.

Sbornik Materialov dlya istorii Zaporozhskikh Kozakov, St. Petersburg 1888.

Po Sledam Zaporozhtsev, St. Petersburg 1898.

Zaporozhye v Ostatkakh Stariny i Predaniyakh Naroda, 1888.

FELITSYN, E. D. (and Shcherbina): *Kubanskoye Kazachye Voisko 1696–1888*, Voronezh 1888.

FENOMENOV, M. Ya.: *Razinovshchina i Pugachevshchina*, Moscow 1923.

FIELD, C.: *The Great Cossack. The Rebellion of Sten'ka Razin*, London 1947.

FIRSOV, N. N.: *Pugachevshchina: opyt sotsiologo-psikhologicheskoi Kharakteristiki*, St. Petersburg and Moscow 1907.

FISHER, R. H.: *The Russian Fur Trade*, Berkeley 1943.

FLETCHER, Giles: *Of the Russe Commonwealth*, London 1591.

FRANKO, D. I.: 'Khmelnishchina 1648–1649 rokiv u suchasnikh virshakh', *Zapiski Naukovogo Tovaristva Imeni Shevchenka*, Yr. 7 1898, Bks. III and IV, Vols. XXIII and XXIV.

GAISINOVICH, A. E.: *La Revolte de Pougatchev*, Paris 1938 (trans. from *Pugachev*, Moscow 1937).

GERASIMOV: *Esquisse de l'Histoire des Cossacques du Don*, 1919.

La Lutte des Cossacques du Don contre les Bolcheviks, 1919.

GESSEN, I. V.: *Arkhiv Russkoi Revolyutsii*, Berlin 1921–7.

'Glavnyye Posobniki Pugacheva', *Russkaya Starina*, Vol. XVI, 1876.

GOGOL, N.: *Taras Bulba*, 1834.

GOLDER, F. A.: *Russian Expansion on the Pacific 1641–50*, Cleveland 1914.

GOLOBUTSKI, V. A.: *Chernomorskoye Kazachestvo*, Kiev 1956.
Diplomaticheskaya Istoriya Osvoboditelnoi Voiny Ukrainskogo Naroda 1648–1654gg, Kiev 1962.
'O Sotsialnykh Otnosheniyakh v Zadunaiski Sechi', *Istoricheskiye Zapiski AN/SSSR*, Vol. 30, Moscow 1949.
Osvoboditelnaya Voina Ukrainskogo Naroda pod Rukovodtvom Khmelnitskogo (1648–1654), Moscow 1954.
Zaporizka Sich v ostanni chasi svogo isnuvannya 1734–1775, Kiev 1961.
Zaporozhskoye Kazachestvo, Kiev 1957.
GOLUBTSOV (Ed.), *Pugachevshchina*, Moscow and Leningrad, 3 vols., 1926–31.
GOTE, Yu.: *Smutnoye Vremya*, Moscow 1921.
GOZULOV, A. I.: *Narodnoye Khozyaistvo Dona do i posle Oktyabrya*, Rostov-on-Don 1947.
GREENBERG, L.: *The Jews of Russia*, Yale U.P. 1944–51, 2 vols.
GREKOV, V.: *Bunt Siromi na Zaporizhzhi 1768 r*, Kiev 1927.
GREKOV, V. D., BAKHRUSHIN, S. V. and LEBEDEV, V. L.: *Istoriya SSSR*, Moscow 1939, 2nd ed. 1947–.
GREKOV, V. D.: *Novyye Materialy o Dvizhenii Stepana Razina*, 1927.
GREY, Ian: *Peter the Great*, London 1962.
GRONDSKI, S.: *Historia Belli Cossaco-Polonici*, Pest 1789.
GROT, Ya. K.: 'Materialy dlya Istorii Pugachevskago Bunta', *Sbornik Otdeleniya Russkago Yazyka i Slovestnost Imperatorskoi Akad. Nauk*, Vol. XV, No. 4, St. Petersburg 1876, pp. 1–144.
HAMMER, J. von: *Geschichte des Osmanischen Reiches*, 4 vols., Pest 1834–6.
HANNOVER, Nathan ben M.: *Bogdan Khmelnitski: Letopis . . . o Sobytiakh 1648–53*, Leipzig 1883 (trans. of *Yeven metzulah*, 1st Hebrew ed., Venice 1653; trans. into English by A. Mesch as *Abyss of Despair*, N. Y. 1950).
HARRIS, J.: *Navigantium atque Itineratium . . .*, 1744; *Collection of Voyages and Travels*, London 1748.
HERASIMCHUK, V.: 'Vygovski i Yuri Khmelnitski', *Zherela do Istorii Ukrainy Rusi*, Vol. LIX, pp. 1–40 and Vol. LX, pp. 1–70.
HINDUS, M.: *The Cossacks*, London 1946.
HOWARD, Charles (1st Earl of Carlisle): *A Relation of Three Embassies from his Sacred Majestie Charles II to the Great Duke of Muscovie, the King of Sweden, and the King of Denmark, Performed by the Earle of Carlisle in the Years 1663 and 1664*, London 1669.
HOWORTH, Sir H. H.: *History of the Mongols from the Ninth to the Nineteenth Century*, London 1876–8, 3 vols.
HRUSHEVSKI, M.: *Istoriya Ukrainy-Rusy*.
Istoriya Ukrainskogo Kazachestva, St. Petersburg 1913–14, 2 vols.

Khmelnitski i Khmelnishchina, Lvov 1901.
(ed.): *Materialy do Istorii Ukrainskoi Kozachchini*, Lvov 1908.
IGNATOVICH, I. I.: *Krestyanskoye Dvizheniye na Donu v 1820 g*, Moscow 1937.
ILOVAISKI, D. I.: *Istoriya Ryazanskago Knyazhestva*, 1858.
IVANOV, A. N. and others: *Trudyashchiyesya Dona—Frontu*, Rostov 1965.
IVANOV, P. A.: 'Materialy po istorii Zaporozhya v XVIII v', *Zapiski Imperatorskago Odesskago Obshchestva Istorii i Drevnostei*, Vol. XX, 1897, pp. 60–100.
KAMYSHANSKI, B.: *I am a Cossack*, London 1934.
KARAMZIN, N. M.: *Istoriya Gosudarstva Rossiiskago*, 5th ed., 3 vols., St. Petersburg 1843.
KARPOV, A. B.: *Uraltsy: Istoricheski Ocherk, Part I: Yaktskoye Voisko ot Obrazovaniya Voiska do Perepisi Polkovnika Zakharova 1550–1725 gg*, Uralsk 1911.
KATANAYEV, G.: *Zapadno-Sibirskoye Sluzhiloye Kazachestvo i yego Rol v Obsledovanii i Zanyatii Russkimi Sibiri i Srednei Azii*, St. Petersburg 1908.
Kazachestvo: Mysli Sovremennikov o Proshlom, Nastoyashchem i Budushchem Kazachestva, Paris 1928.
Kazachi Byt (Obshchestvo Vzaimopomoshch Studentov Donskikh Kozakov vo Frantsii), Paris 1925.
Kazachi Golos (Argentina).
Kazachi Literaturno-Obshchestvenny Almanakh, Paris.
Kazachi Otdel (Cossack Department), Proclamations of 1919–20.
Kazachi Sbornik (Lichtenhorst Cossack Settlement), Berlin 1922.
Kazachi Soyuz, Paris 1950–3.
Kazak (issued by Gen. V. G. Naumenko), U.S.A.
KERNATSENSKI, V. D.: 'O Nekotorykh Voprosakh Istoriografii Orenburgskogo Kazachestva (Sovetski Period)', *Trudy Moskovskogo Istoricheskogo-Arkhivnogo Instituta*, Vol. 21, 1965, pp. 104–117.
KERNER, R. J.: *The Urge to the Sea*, University of California Press 1942.
KHOROSHCHIN, M. P.: *Kazachi Voiska: Opyt Voyenno-Statisticheskago Opisaniya*, St. Petersburg 1881, see also (Choroschin and) von Stein, von Tettau.
KLAPROTH, Julius H.: *Travels in the Caucasus and Georgia performed in the Years 1807 and 1808*, trans. from German by F. Shobert, London 1814.
Klich Trudovykh Kazakov (Organ of the Cossack Committee at VTsIK).
KLYUCHEVSKI, V.: *Kurs Russkoi Istorii*, trans. C. J. Hogarth, *A History of Russia*, N.Y. 1960, 5 vols.; Vol. IV trans. by L. Archibald, *Peter the Great*, Macmillan 1965.

KORDUBA, M.: 'Die Anfänge des Ukrainischen Kozakentums', *Zeitschrift für Osteuropäische Geschichte*, Vol. II, 1912, pp. 367–81.

Venetske Posolstvo do Khmelnitskogo (*1650r*), [1910].

KORF, S. A.: *The Constitution of the Cossacks*, Paris 1919.

KOROLENKO, P.: *Chernomortsy*, St. Petersburg 1874.

KOROLEVICH, P. T.: *Istoriya Pereseleniya Kazakov v Respubliku Peru*, N vy Sad 1930.

KORZH, N.: *Ustnoye Povestovaniye Byvshego Zaporozhtsa N. L. Korzha*, Odessa 1842.

KOSTOMAROV, N. I.: *Sobraniye Sochineniya*, 8 vols., St. Petersburg 1903–6.

KOTELNIKOV, V.: *Don, Kuban Terek*, Moscow 1950.

KOTOSHIKHIN, G. K.: *O Rossii v tsarstvovaniye Alekseya Mikhailovicha*, St. Petersburg 1840 (4th ed., St. Petersburg 1906).

KRASINSKI, G.: 'Pokoreniye Sibiri i Ivan Grozny', *Voprosy Istorii*, No. 3, 1947.

KRASINSKI, H.: *The Cossacks of the Ukraine*, London 1848.

KRASNOV, N. I.: *Materialy dlya Geografii i Statistiki Zemli Voiska Donskogo*, 1863.

KRASNOV, P. N.: *Kazachya 'Samostiinost'*, Berlin 1922.

Kratki Istoricheski Ocherk i Otchet Kazachego Otdela VTsIK po Oktyabr 1919.

KRIKUNOV, V. P.: *Krestyanskoye Dvizheniye na Donu i Severnom Kavkaze v 60–70gg XIX Veka*, Grozny 1965.

KRIPYAKEVICH, I. P.: *Bogdan Khmelnitski*, Kiev 1954.

and BUTICH, I.: *Dokumenty Bogdana Khmelnitskogo 1648–1657*, Kiev 1961.

Istoriya Kozachchini, Lvov 1934.

Kozachchina v politichnikh kombinatsiyakh 1620–3orr, Lvov 1914.

KRUPNITSKI, B.: *Getman Pilip Orlik* (*1672–1742*): *oglyad yogo politichnoi diyalnosti*, Warsaw 1938 (Pratsi Ukrainskogo Naukovogo Institutu, Vol. 42).

Hetman Mazepa und seine Zeit (*1687–1709*), Leipzig 1942.

(ed.): *V 300 Littya Khmelnichchini* (*1648–1948*), Münich 1948.

KRYUKOV, P. I.: *Kazaki v Chataldzhe i na Lemnose v 1920–1921 gg*, Belgrade 1924.

Kubanski Kalendar, Belgrade 1931.

Kubanski Krai: Kuban Cossack Magazine (U.S.A).

KUROCHKA, I. N.: *Gryadushchiya Sudby Kazachestva*, Paris 1927.

KUZNETSOV, V. I. (Ch. ed.): *Istoriya Dona s Drevneishikh Vremen do Velikoi Oktyabrskoi Sotsialnoi Revoluyutsii*, Rostov-on-Don 1965.

LASSOTA, E.: *Tagebuch des Erich Lassota von Steblau*, Halle 1866.

LENIN, V. I.: *Rech na Pervom Vserossiiskom Syezde Trudovykh Kazakov*, Moscow 1920.

LENSEN, G. A.: *Russia's Eastward Expansion*, Prentice-Hall 1964.

LEONTOVICH, V.: *Pervyye Boi na Kubani*, Münich 1923.

LESUR, C. L.: *Histoire des Kosaques*, 2 vols., Paris 1814.

LEVASSEUR, G.: Sieur de Beauplan, *Description d'Ukranie, etc.*, 1660 (1st ed., Rouen 1650).
Descriptio Borysthenis Fluvii, etc., J. Blaeu, *Le Grand Atlas Geographiae*, Amsterdam 1662, Vol. II, Part ii, *Description du Fleuve Borysthene*..., J. Blaeu, *Le Grand Atlas 1667*, Vol. II, part ii.

LEVSHIN, A. I.: *Istoricheskoye i Statisticheskoye Obozreniye Uralskikh Kazakov*, St. Petersburg 1823.

LINDGREN, E. J.: 'An Example of Culture Contact without Conflict: Reindeer Tungus and Cossacks of Northwestern Manchuria', *American Anthropologist*, Vol. 40, No. 4, 1938, pp. 605–21.

LIPINSKI, W.: *Z Dziejow Ukrainy*, Kiev 1912.

LISHIN, A. A.: *Akty otnosyashchiyesya k istorii Voiska Donskogo*, Novo-cherkassk 1891.

LISTOPADOV, A. M.: *Donskiye Byliny*, Rostov-on-Don 1945.
Pesni Donskikh Kazakov, [Moscow] 1950.

LONGWORTH, J. A.: *A Year Among the Circassians*, 2 vols., London 1840.

LONGWORTH, Philip: *The Art of Victory: the Life and Achievements of Generalissimo Suvorov (1729–1800)*, Constable 1965, Holt, Rinehart and Winston 1966.

LUNCHENKOV, I.: *Za Chuzhiye Grekh: Kazaki v Emigratsii*, Moscow 1925.

LYASHCHENKO, P. I.: *Istoriya Narodnogo Khozyaistva SSSR*, 2 vols., Moscow 1952.

LYUBAVSKI, M.: 'Nachalnaya Istoriya Malorusskogo Kazachestva', *Zhurnal Ministerstva Narodnogo Prosveshcheniya*, 1895, Book VII.

McNEILL, W. H.: *Europe's Steppe Frontier (1500–1800)*, Un. of Chicago Press 1964.

MAKSIMOV, Ye.: *Terskoye Kazachye Voisko: Istorichesko-Statistichny Ocherk*, 1890.

MAMYSHEV, V.: *General-ot-kavalerii Graf M. I. Platov*, St. Petersburg 1904.

MANSTEIN, G. H. von: *Memoirs of Russia* ... *(1727–1744)*, London 1770.

MARTYNOV, M. N.: *Vosstaniye Yemelyana Pugacheva: Sbornik Dokumentov*..., Moscow 1935.

MASSA, I. A.: *Histoire des Guerres de la Moscovie (1601–1610)*, 2 vols., Brussels 1866.

388

Materialy po Istorii Zaporozhya v XVIII v, Odessa 1897.

MAVRODIN, V. V. (ed.): *Krestyanskaya Voina v Rossii v 1773–1775 Godakh: Vosstaniye Pugacheva*, Leningrad 1961, Vol. I; Vol. II 1966; Vol. III not issued at the time of writing.

MAYNARD, Sir J.: *Russia in Flux*, Collier 1962.
The Russian Peasant, Collier 1962.

MELNIKOV, N. M.: *Yermak Timofeyevich Knyaz Sibirski: yego spodvizhniki i prodolzhateli*, Paris 1961.

MILLER, V. F.: *Istoricheskiya Pyesni Russkago Naroda XVI–XVII VV*, Petrograd 1915.

MIRONENKO, M. F.: *Pod gvardeiskim znamenom*, Stavropol 1965.

MYSHETSKI, Prince S. I.: *Istoriya o Kazakakh Zaporozhskikh*, Odessa 1897.

NAUMENKO, V.: *Velikoye Predatelstvo*, N.Y. 1962.

NIESSEL, H. A.: *Les Cosaques*, Paris 1899.

NOLDE, Boris E.: *La Formation de l'Empire Russe*, 2 vols., Paris 1952–3.

NOVIKOV, N. I.: 'Opisaniye Obishaemoi Zemli Voiskom Donskim', *Drevnyaya Rossiska Vivliofika*, Vol. XIX 1791, pp. 251–84.

NOVOSELSKI, A. A.: *Borba Moskovskogo Gosudarstva s Tatarami v Pervoi Polovine XVII Veke*, Moscow-Leningrad, 1948.

O'BRIEN, Carl B.: *Muscovy and the Ukraine 1654–67*, Berkeley 1963.

Obshchekazachi Zhurnal (All Cossacks Journal), Farmingdale U.S.A. 1946–54.

OHLOBIN, O.: *Getman Ivan Mazepa ta yogo Doba*, N.Y. 1960.

OSIPOV, K.: *Bogdan Khmelnitski*, Moscow 1948.

OVCHINNIKOV, Ya. V. (ed.): 'Sledstviye i Sud nad Ye. I. Pugachevym' *Voprosy Istorii*, 1966, Nos. 3, pp. 124–38, 5, pp. 107–21, and 7, pp. 92 109.

PALLAS, P. S.: *Reise durch Verschiedene Provinzen des Russischen Reiches*, St. Petersburg 1771–6; *Travels through the Southern Provinces of the Russian Empire in the Years 1793–94*, 2 vols., 2nd ed., London. J. Stockdale 1812 (1st ed., London 1802–3).

(PANIN, P. I.): Bumagi . . . o Pugachevskom Bunte, *Sbornik Russkago Istoricheskago Obshchestva*, 1871.

PAVLOVSKI, P. I.: *Annenkovshchina*, Moscow and Leningrad 1928.

PETROV, S.: *Pugachev v Penzenskom Kraye*, Pensa 1950.

PETROVSKI, N. N.: *Bogdan Khmelnitski*, Moscow 1944.

PIONTKOVSKI, S. (ed.): 'Dopros Ye. Pugacheve v Moskve v 1774–1775g', *Krasny Arkhiv*, Vol. 69, p. 70, 1935/2–3, pp. 159–237.

PIROVANOV, A. N.: *Donskiye Kazaki*, St. Petersburg 1909.

PLATONOV, S. F.: *Ocherki po Istoriyii Smuty v Moskovskom Gosudarstve XVI–XVIIvv*, St. Petersburg 1899.

PODHORODECKI, L.: *Sicz Zaporoska*, Warsaw 1960.

PODYAPOLSKAYA, Ye. P.: *Vosstaniye Bulavina 1707–1709*, Moscow 1962.
POELLMANN, H.: *Beitrag zur 'A'ltesten Geschichte des Kosakentums*, Münich 1888.
POLONSKA-VASILENKOVA, N.: *Maino Zaporozkoi Starshini yak Dzherelo dlya Sotsialno-yekonomichnogo Doslidzhennya Istorii Zaporizhzhya*, (Pratsy Komissii Sotsialno-Yekonomichnoi Istorii Ukrainy, Vol. I—ed. Bagalei), Kiev 1932.
Zaporizhiya XVIII Stolittya ta yogo Spadshchyna, Münich 1965.
POLUSHIN, N.: *Ataman Yermak Timofeyevich*, Moscow 1894.
POPKA, I.: *Chernomorskiye Kozaki v ikh Grazhdanskom i Voyennom Bytu*, St. Petersburg 1858 (1st ed., 1852).
Terskiye Kazaki so starodavaykh vremen, St. Petersburg 1880.
POPOV, A. G.: *Istoriya Voiska Donskago*, Novocherkassk 1812.
POPOV, A. N.: *Istoriya Vozmushcheniya Stenki Razina*, Moscow 1857.
POPOV, I. A.: *Otkuda Povelos Nashe Razoreniye i kak nam ot nego Izbavitsya*, Moscow 1920.
PRICE, Philips M.: *War and Revolution in Asiatic Russia*, London 1918.
PRONSHTEIN, A. P. (ed.): *Don i Nizhneye Povolozhe v Period Krestyanskoi Voiny 1773–1775*, Rostov-on-Don 1961.
'Usileniye Krepostnogo Gneta na Donu v XVIII V', *Voprosy Istorii*, No. 6, 1955, pp. 56–66.
(ed.): *Zemlya Donskaya v XVIII Veke*, Rostov-on-Don 1961.
PRYANISHNIKOV, I. P.: *Materialy dlya Istorii Voiska Donskago*, Novocherkassk 1864.
(PUGACHEV): *Doprosy Ye. P. i Pismo o nem Gosudaryni Imperatritsy Yekateri ny II k Grafu P. I. Paninu*, Moscow 1858.
PURCHAS, S.: *Hakluytus Posthumus, or Purchas His Pilgrimes*, 4 parts, London 1625.
PUSHKIN, A. S.: Istoricheskaya i Statisticheskaya Obozreniye Uralskikh Kazakov, *Polnoye Sobraniye Sochinenii*, Vol. VI, Moscow 1950.
Istoriya Pugachevskago Bunta, 1834, 3 vols.
Kapitanskaya Doch, 1836, trans. R. Edmonds, *The Captain's Daughter*, Spearman 1958.
RAWITA, GAWRÓNSKI, F.: *Kozaczyzna Ukrainna w Rzeczypospolitej Polskiej do Konca XVIII Wieku*, Warsaw [1922?].
Sprawy i Rzeczy Ukraińskie: Materialy do Dziejów Kozaczyzny i Hajdamaczyzny, Lvov 1914.
(RAZIN, S.): *A Relation Concerning the particulars of the Rebellion by S. Razin*, 1672.
RAZIN, Ye. A.: *Istoriya Voyennogo Iskusstva*, Vol. III, Moscow 1961.
'Relation des Cosaques (avec la vie de Kmielniski . . .), *Relations de Divers Voyages*, 1663 Part I.

RIGELMAN, A.: *Istoriya o Donskom Kazachestve*, 1778 and 1847.
ROMAN`, A. L. de: *Coup d'Oeil Philosophique sur le Pays Occupé par les Cosaques du Don*, 2 vols., Milan 1807.
ROZNER, I. G.: *Kazachestvo v Krestyanskoi Voine 1773–5*, Lvov 1966.
Voprosy Istorii No. 10, 1958, on Yaik Cossack rising of 1772.
Yaik pered Burei, Moscow 1966.
The Russian Commonwealth, 1.xi.1918.
[RYCHKOV?]: *O Nachale . . . Kozakov*, 1760.
RYCHKOV, P.: *Topografiya Orenburgskaya*, 2 parts, St. Petersburg 1762.
SAVANT, J. and TOUROVEROV, N.: *Les Cosaques*, Paris 1951.
SAVELEV, A.: *Voisko Donskoye (1570–1870)*, 1870.
Sbornik Materialov dlya Opisaniya Kavkaza, 1881–1908.
SCHERER, J. B.: *Annales de la Petite-Russie: ou Histoire des Cosaques-Saporogues et des Cosaques de l'Ukraine*, 2 vols., Paris 1788.
SEMYONOV, Yuri: *Siberia: Its Conquest and Development*, Hollis and Carter, London 1963.
SERGEYEV, V. I.: 'K Voprosu o Pokhode v Sibir Druzhiny Yermaka', *Voprosy Istorii*, 1959, No. 1.
SHCHERBINA, F. A.: *Istoriya Kubanskago Kazachyago Voiska*, Yekaterinodar 1910.
SHCHETNEV, V.: 'Iz Istorii Klassovoi Borby v Kubanskoi Stanitse (1920–7), *Nauchnyye Trudy Krasnodarskogo Pedagogicheskogo Instituta*, No. 67 1966, pp. 5–36.
SHOLOKHOV, M.: *Nauka Nenavisti*, Moscow 1942 (trans. in *One Man's Destiny* by H. C. Stevens, Putnam 1967).
Oni Srazhalis za Rodinu, 1959 (trans. by H. C. Stevens, *Tales from the Don*, Putnam 1961).
Tikhi Don, 1928– (trans. by Steven Garry, [H. C. Stevens], *Quiet Flows the Don* 1929 and *The Don Flows Home to the Sea*, 1940, *Virgin Soil Upturned* (trans. as *Seeds of Tomorrow* in U.S.A.) and *Harvest on the Don*).
SHVETSOVA, Ye. A. (compiler): *Krestyanskaya Voina pod Predvoditelstvom Stepana Razina*, Vol. I 1954, Vol. II Part i 1957, Vol. II, Part ii 1959, Vol. III, Moscow 1962.
SIENKIEWICZ, Henryk: *With Fire and Sword* (trans. J. Curtin), Dent 1898, also *The Deluge, Pan Michael*.
SIMOLEIT, Gustav: *Die Donkosaken und Ihr Land*, Königsberg 1930.
SKALKOVSKI, A. A.: *Istoriya Novoi Sechi*, Odessa 1885.
Nayezdy Gaidamak na Zapadnuyu Ukrainu v XVIII Stoletiya, 1773–1768 Odessa 1845.
SKOBTSOV, D. Ye.: *Tri Goda Revolyutsii i Grazhdanskoi Voiny na Kubane.*
SLABCHENKO, M.: *Sotsialno-Pravogo Organizatsiya Sichi Zaporizkoi,*

391

(Pratsy Komini dlya Vyuchuvannya Zakhidno-Ruskogo ta Ukrainskogo Prava, vip III), Kiev 1927.

SMAL-STOCKI, R. (ed.): *Mazepa: Zbirnik* (Pratsi Ukrainskogo Naukovogo Institutu, Vols. XLVI and XLVII in historical series), Warsaw 1938-9.

SMIRNOV, I. I.: *Vosstaniye Bolotnikova 1606-1607*, Leningrad 1951.

SMIRNOV, N. A.: *Rossiya i Turtsiya v XVI-XVII VV*, Vols. 1-2 (Uchennyye Zapiski vyp. 94), Moscow 1946.

SOLOVEV, S.: 'Bulavinski Bunt', *Russki Vestnik*, 1897.

Istoriya Rossiyei s Drevneishikh Vremen (3rd ed.), 29 vols., St. Petersburg 1857-79.

SPRINGER, A. H.: *Die Kosaken*, Leitmeritz 1877.

STEIN, F. von: *Die Russische Kosakenheere*, (Petermanns Mitteilungen, erg. 16), Gotha 1883-4. See Khoroshchin.

STEPANOV, I. V.: *Krestyanskaya Voina pod Predvoditelstvom S. T. Razina*, Moscow 1957.

Krestyanskaya Voina v Rossii v 1670-1gg: Vosstaniye Stepana Razina, Leningrad 1966, Vol. I (further volumes not yet issued at time of writing).

STÖKL, Günter: *Die Entstehung des Kosakentums*, Münich 1953.

(STRUYS, J.): *The Voiages and Travels of John Struys*, trans. from the Dutch, London 1684.

SUKHANOV, N. N.: *The Russian Revolution 1917* (abridged and edited trans. by J. Carmichael from *Zapiski O Revolyutsii*, 1922-3), C.U.P. 1955.

SUMNER, B. H.: *Survey of Russian History*, Duckworth 1947.

SVATIKOV, S. G.: *Rossiya i Don (1549-1917)*, Vienna 1924.

TARLÉ, Ye.: *Nashestviye Napoleona na Rossiyu—1812 God*, trans. 'G. M.' as *Napoleon's Invasion of Russia 1812*, London 1942.

TETTAU, von: *Die Kasakenheere*, Berlin 1892. (See Khoroshchin, N. Krasnov, Abaza, etc. on which this work is based); see also *The Cossack Armies . . . compiled from Russian Sources by Freiherr von Tettau*, trans. (and abridged) by the Hon. H. D. Napier, Simla 1895.

TKATSCHEV, B.: 'There never was a Cossackia', *Novoye Russkoye Slovo*, N.Y., 15.5.1960.

TKHORZHEVSKI, S. T.: *Pugachevshchina v Pomeshchichei Rossii*, Moscow 1930.

'Donskoye Voisko v Pervoi Polovine 17ogo Stoletiya', *Russkoye Proshloye*, No. 3, 1923, pp. 9-28.

TOLSTOI, L.: *The Cossacks* (many translations into English), 1862.

TOMASHIVSKI, S.: *Pershi Pokhid Bogdana Khmelnitskogo v Galichinu*, Lvov 1914.

TOPORKOV, Yu. A.: 'K Trekhsotiletiya Uchrezhdeniya Slobodskikh Kazachikh Polkov 1651–1951', *Russki Voyenno-Istoricheski Vestnik*, No. 9, Paris 1951, pp. 2–24.

TSCHEBOTAREFF, G. P.: *Russia—My Native Land*, N.Y., London, Toronto 1964.

TUMILEVICH, F. V. (ed.): *Narodnaya Ustnaya Poesiya Dona*, Rostov-on-Don 1963.

ULYANOV, I.: *Dumy Volnogo Kazaka: Kto Budet Upravlyat Kazakami Posle Tsarskikh Generalov*, Moscow 1920.

Sovetskaya Respublika i Kazaki, Moscow 1920.

VERNADSKY, G.: *Bohdan, Hetman of the Ukraine*, New Haven 1941.

Vestnik Kazachyego Soyuza, Paris 1948–.

Volne Kozatstvo, Prague, 1925–.

VORONIKHIN, A.: 'K Biografii Yermaka', *Voprosy Istorii* No. 10, 1946.

VRANGEL, P. N.: *Memoirs of General Wrangel*, London 1929.

WAGNER, M.: *Der Kaukasus und das Land der Kosaken in den Jahren 1843 bis 1846*, 2 vols., Dresden and Leipzig 1848.

WERTH, A.: *Russia at War 1941–1945*, Pan 1965.

WILSON, Sir R. T.: *Brief Remarks on the Character and Composition of the Russian Army*, London 1810.

WÒJCIK, Z.: *Dzikie Pola w Ogniu: o Kozaczyznie w Dawnej Rzeczypospolitej*, Warsaw 1960.

WYNAR, L. R.: 'Ukrainian Kozaks and the Vatican in 1594', *The Ukrainian Quarterly*, No. 1, Spring 1965, N.Y., pp. 65–78.

(Y)EFREMOV: *Cossacks of the Don*, Paris 1919.

YURKEVICH, V.: *Emigratsiya na Skhid i Zalyudnennya Slobozhanshchini za B. Khmelnitskogo*, Kiev 1932.

ZHIZHKA, M. V. (ed.): 'Dopros Pugachevskogo Atamana A. Khlopushi', *Krasny Arkhiv*, Vol. 68, No. 1, 1935, pp. 162–71.

Index